Table of Contents

Designed and Produced by Home Planners, Inc.

Editorial and Corporate Offices:
3275 West Ina Road, Suite 110
Tucson, Arizona 85741

Distribution Center:
29333 Lorie Lane
Wixom, Michigan 48393

Rickard Bailey, President
Cindy J. C. Lewis, Publications Manager
Paulette Mulvin, Editor

First Printing, January 1992

10   9   8   7   6

Library of Congress Catalog Card Number: 91-076716
ISBN: 0-918894-93-X

Photo Credits
Tim Becker, Creative Images: p.4 (Design N2520, Steve & Heidi Rebelowski, owners); Andrew D. Lautman: Cover (Design N2826, Jerry & Rebecca Mattern, owners); Laszlo Regos: Cover & p. 6 (Design N2921, Charles & Catherine Talcott, owners), p. 3 (Design N2683, Kellet & Saylor, Builders), p. 5 (Design N2563, Perry & Heidi Pentiuk, owners); Carl Socolow: Cover & p. 2 (Design N2774, John & Jane Deardorff, owners); Roger Whitacre: p. 7 (Design N2894, Gretchen Kay Carlson & Kent Richard Hulet, owners/builders). On the Cover: For more information and floor plans for designs on the cover, see Page 2 (N2774), Page 92 (N2826) and Page 6 (N2921).

Design N2774

First Floor: 1,366 square feet
Second Floor: 969 square feet
Total: 2,335 square feet

L **D**

● This design has something for the whole family. There is the quiet corner living room, an efficient U-shaped kitchen with pass-through to the beamed-ceiling breakfast room, sliding glass doors to the rear terrace, and a service entrance with laundry and pantry. The basement can be finished at a later time for expanded space. Upstairs are four bedrooms including a master suite with private bath.

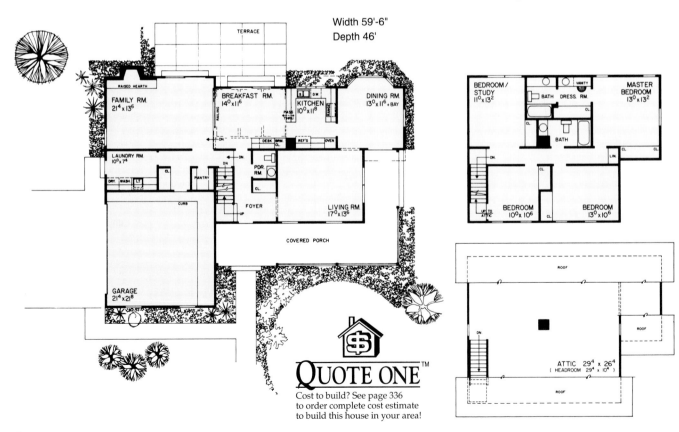

Width 59'-6"
Depth 46'

QUOTE ONE™

Cost to build? See page 336
to order complete cost estimate
to build this house in your area!

Design N2683 First Floor: 2,126 square feet; Second Floor: 1,882 square feet; Total: 4,008 square feet

L **D**

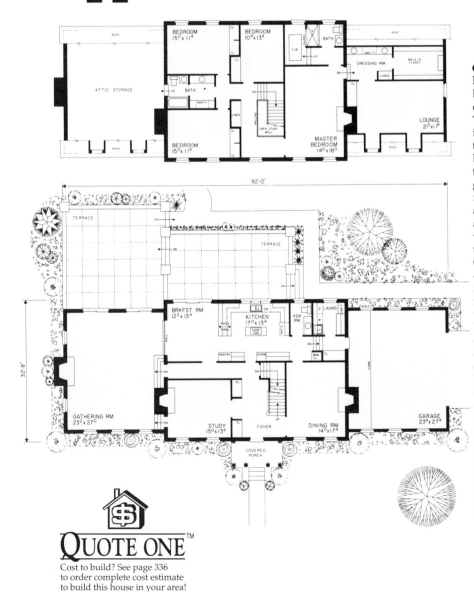

● This historical Georgian home has its roots in the 18th-Century. Dignified symmetry is a hallmark of both front and rear elevations. The full two-story center section is delightfully complimented by the 1½-story wings. Interior livability has been planned to serve today's active family. The elegant gathering room, three steps down from the rest of the house, has ample space for entertaining on a grand scale. It fills an entire wing and is dead-ended so that traffic does not pass through it. Guests and family alike will enjoy the two rooms flanking the foyer, the study and formal dining room. Each of these rooms will have a fireplace as its highlight. The breakfast room, kitchen, powder room and laundry are arranged for maximum efficiency. This area will always have that desired light and airy atmosphere with the sliding glass door and the triple window over the kitchen sink. The second floor houses the family bedrooms. Take special note of the spacious master bedroom suite. It has a deluxe bath, fireplace and sunken lounge with dressing room and walk-in closet. Surely an area to be appreciated.

QUOTE ONE™

Cost to build? See page 336 to order complete cost estimate to build this house in your area!

Design N2520 First Floor: 1,419 square feet
Second Floor: 1,040 square feet; Total: 2,459 square feet

L **D**

● From Tidewater Virginia comes this historic
adaptation, a positive reminder of the charm of
Early American architecture. Note how the
center entrance opens to a fine floor plan.

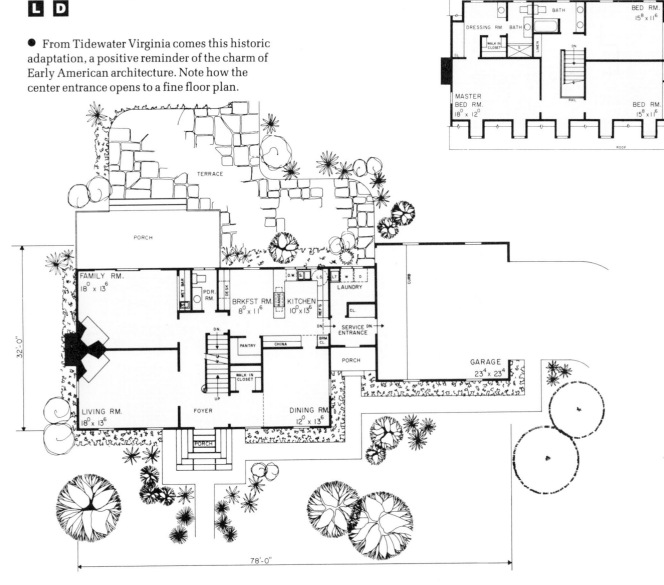

Design N2563

First Floor: 1,500 square feet
Second Floor: 690 square feet
Total: 2,190 square feet

L **D**

● You'll have all kinds of fun deciding just how your family will function in this dramatically expanded half-house. There is lots of attic storage, too. Observe three car garage.

QUOTE ONE™

Cost to build? See page 336 to order complete cost estimate to build this house in your area!

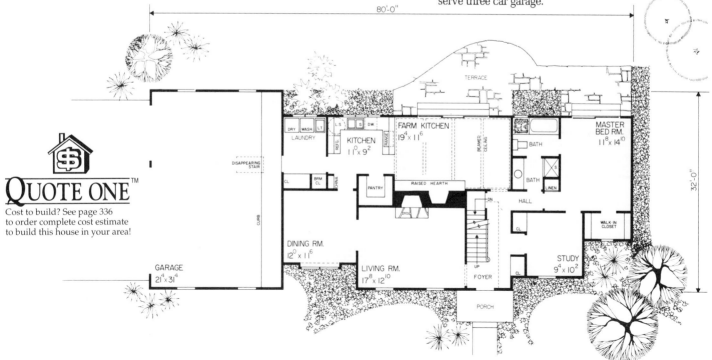

5

● This contemporary design also has a great deal to offer. Study the living areas. A fireplace opens up to both the living room and country kitchen. Privacy is the key word when describing the sleeping areas. the first floor master bedroom is away from the traffic of the house and features a dressing/exercise room, whirlpool tub and shower and a spacious walk-in closet. Two more bedrooms and a full bath are on the second floor. The three car garage is arranged so that the owners have use of a double-garage with an attached single on reserve for guests. The cheerful sun room adds 296 sq. ft. to the total.

Width 97'
Depth 102'-8"

Design N2920

First Floor: 3,067 square feet
Second Floor: 648 square feet
Total: 3,715 square feet

L **D**

● Something new? Something new, indeed!! Here is the introduction of two rooms which will make a wonderful contribution to family living. The clutter room is strategically placed between the kitchen and garage. It is the nerve center of the work area. It houses the laundry, provides space for sewing, has a large sorting table, and even plenty of space for the family's tool bench. A handy potting area is next to the laundry tray. Adjacent to the clutter room, and a significant part of the planning of this whole zone, are the pantry and freezer with their nearby counter space. These facilities surely will expedite the unloading of groceries from the car and their convenient storing. Wardrobe and broom closets, plus washroom complete the outstanding utility of this area. The location of the clutter room with all its fine cabinet and counter space means that the often numerous family projects can be on-going. This room is ideally isolated from the family's daily living patterns. The media room may be thought of as the family's entertainment center. While this is the room for the large or small TV, the home movies, the stereo and VCR equipment, it will serve as the library or study. It would be ideal as the family's home office with its computer equipment. Your family will decide just how it will utilize this outstanding area.

Design N2915
Square Footage: 2,758

L **D**

QUOTE ONE™

Cost to build? See page 336 to order complete cost estimate to build this house in your area!

Design N3355

Square Footage: 1,387

L **D**

● Though it's only just under 1,400 total square feet, this plan offers three bedrooms (or two with study) and a sizable gathering room with fireplace and sloped ceiling. The galley kitchen provides a pass-through snack bar and has a planning desk and attached breakfast room. Besides two smaller bedrooms with a full bath, there's an extravagant master suite with large dressing area, double vanity and raised whirlpool tub.

QUOTE ONE™

Cost to build? See page 336 to order complete cost estimate to build this house in your area!

Width 55'-8"
Depth 52'

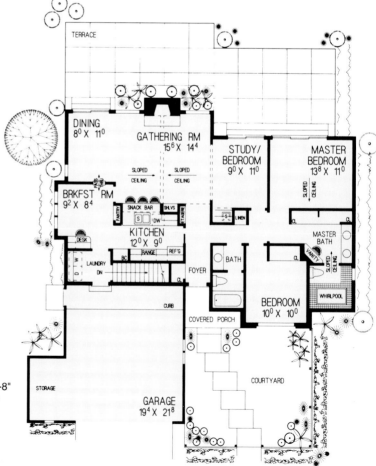

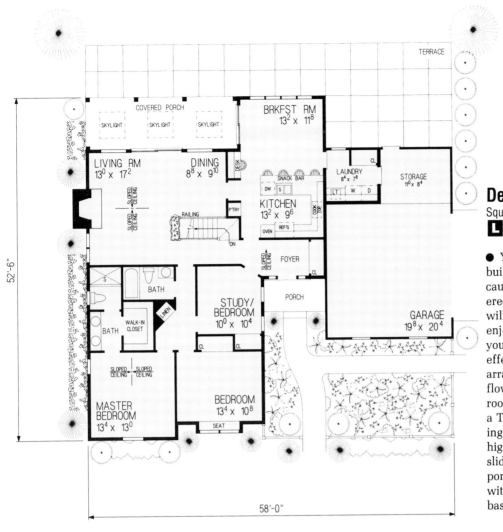

TERRACE

COVERED PORCH

SKYLIGHT   SKYLIGHT   SKYLIGHT

BRKFST RM
13² x 11⁸

LIVING RM
13⁰ x 17²

DINING
8⁸ x 9¹⁰

SLOPED CEILING   SLOPED CEILING

DESK

LAUNDRY
8⁴ x 7⁸

CL

STORAGE
11⁰ x 8⁴

RAILING

DW   S

SNACK BAR

LT   W   D

P'TRY

KITCHEN
13² x 9⁶

COOK TOP

OVEN   REF'G

DN

SLOPED CEILING

FOYER

CL

52'-6"

BATH

WALK-IN CLOSET

LINEN

STUDY/
BEDROOM
10⁰ x 10⁴

PORCH

GARAGE
19⁸ x 20⁴

BATH

CL   CL

SLOPED CEILING   SLOPED CEILING

MASTER
BEDROOM
13⁴ x 13⁰

BEDROOM
13⁴ x 10⁸

SEAT

58'-0"

Design N3340

Square Footage: 1,611

L

● You may not decide to build this design simply because of its delightful covered porch. But it certainly will provide its share of enjoyment if this plan is your choice. Notice also how effectively the bedrooms are arranged out of the traffic flow of the house. One bedroom could double nicely as a TV room or study. The living room/dining area is highlighted by a fireplace, sliding glass doors to the porch, and an open staircase with built-in planter to the basement.

QUOTE ONE™

Cost to build? See page 336 to order complete cost estimate to build this house in your area!

Design N3314

Square Footage: 1,951

L

● Formal living areas in this plan are joined by a three-bedroom sleeping wing. One bedroom, with foyer access, could function as a study. Two verandas and a screened porch enlarge the plan and enhance indoor/outdoor livability. Notice the abundant storage space.

QUOTE ONE™

Cost to build? See page 336 to order complete cost estimate to build this house in your area!

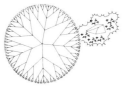

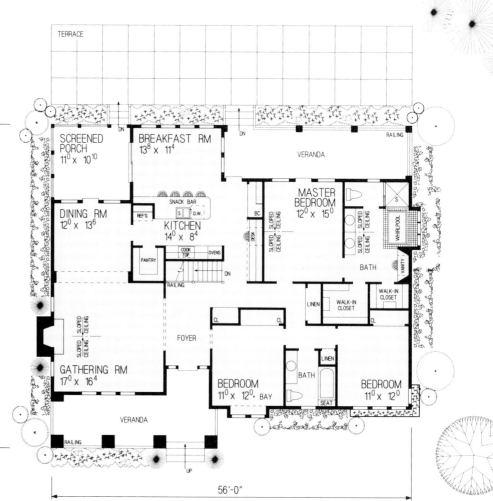

TERRACE

SCREENED PORCH
11⁰ x 10¹⁰

BREAKFAST RM
13⁸ x 11⁴

VERANDA

RAILING

DINING RM
12⁰ x 13⁶

SNACK BAR

REF'G   S   D.W.

KITCHEN
14⁰ x 8⁴

BC

MASTER BEDROOM
12⁰ x 15⁰

SLOPED CEILING

SLOPED CEILING

WHIRLPOOL

S

PANTRY

COOK TOP   OVENS

DN

DESK

BATH

VANITY

RAILING

48'-8"

SLOPED CEILING

SLOPED CEILING

FOYER

CL   CL

LINEN

WALK-IN CLOSET

WALK-IN CLOSET

GATHERING RM
17⁰ x 16⁴

LINEN

BATH

BEDROOM
11⁰ x 12⁰ BAY

SEAT

BEDROOM
11⁰ x 12⁰

VERANDA

RAILING

UP

56'-0"

12

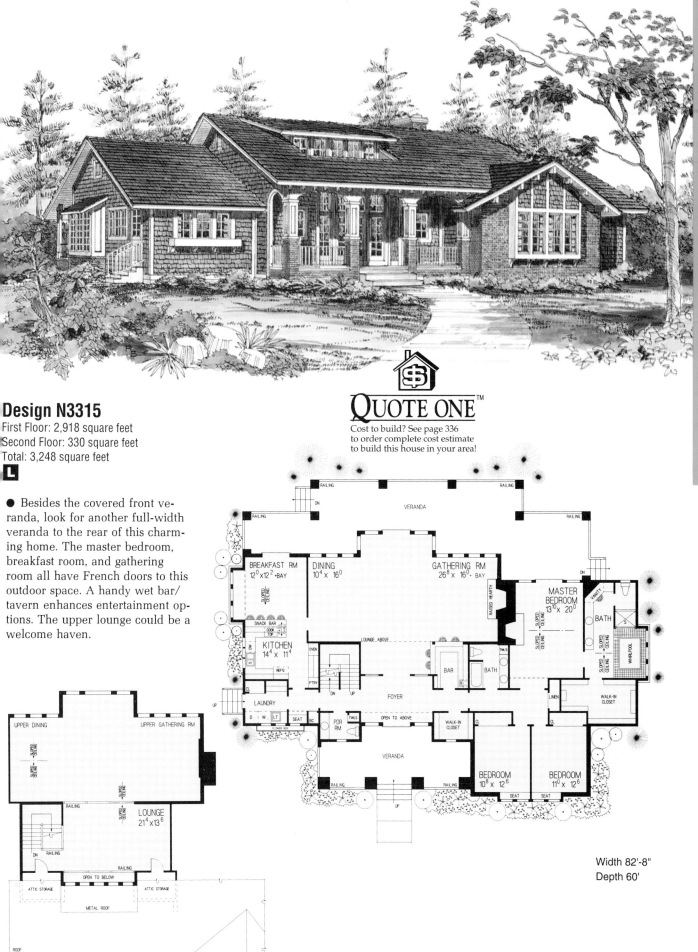

Design N3315

First Floor: 2,918 square feet
Second Floor: 330 square feet
Total: 3,248 square feet

L

● Besides the covered front veranda, look for another full-width
veranda to the rear of this charming home. The master bedroom,
breakfast room, and gathering
room all have French doors to this
outdoor space. A handy wet bar/
tavern enhances entertainment options. The upper lounge could be a
welcome haven.

QUOTE ONE™

Cost to build? See page 336
to order complete cost estimate
to build this house in your area!

Width 82'-8"
Depth 60'

13

Design N2947
Square Footage: 1,830

L **D**

● This charming one-
story Traditional home
greets visitors with a
covered porch. A galley-
style kitchen shares a
snack bar with the spa-
cious gathering room
where a fireplace is the
focal point. An ample
master suite includes a
luxury bath with whirl-
pool tub and separate
dressing room. Two addi-
tional bedrooms, one that
could double as a study,
are located at the front of
the home.

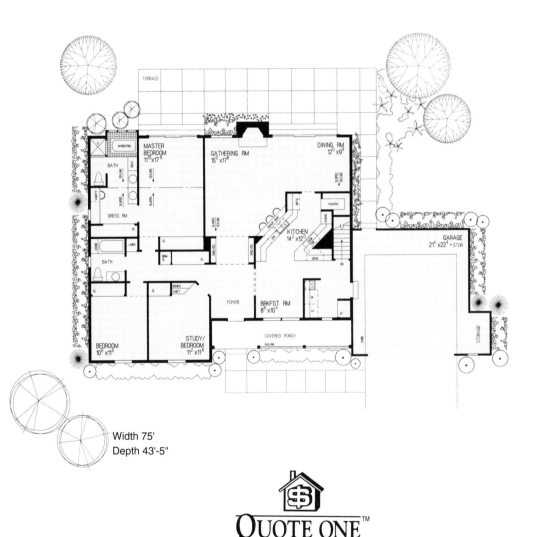

Width 75'
Depth 43'-5"

QUOTE ONE™

Cost to build? See page 336
to order complete cost estimate
to build this house in your area!

Photo by Andrew D. Lautman

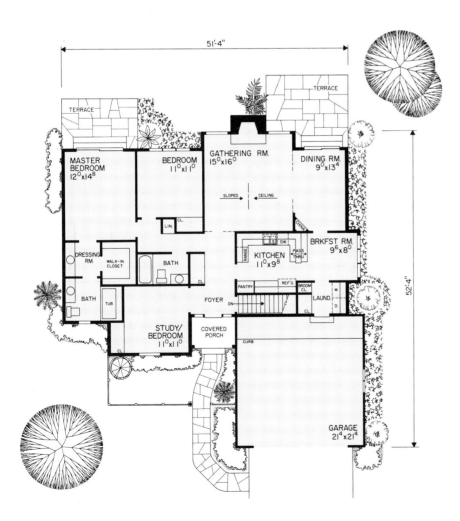

Design N2878
Square Footage: 1,521

L **D**

● There is a great deal of livability
in this one-story design. The efficient floor plan makes optimum use
of limited floor space. Ideally located, the gathering room is warmed
by a fireplace. Its sloped-ceiling
gives it a spacious appeal. Adjacent
is the dining room which opens up
to the rear terrace via sliding glass
doors for dining alfresco. Ready to
serve the breakfast room and dining
room, there is the interior kitchen.
The laundry, basement stairs and
garage door are nearby. Two with
an optional third bedroom are tucked away from the more active areas
of the house. The master bedroom
has sliding glass doors to the terrace
for outdoor enjoyment. Study this
cozy, clapboard cottage and imagine
it as your next home.

QUOTE ONE™

Cost to build? See page 336
to order complete cost estimate
to build this house in your area!

15

Design N2946

First Floor: 1,581 square feet
Second Floor: 1,344 square feet
Total: 2,925 square feet

L **D**

Quote One™

Cost to build? See page 336
to order complete cost estimate
to build this house in your area!

● Here's a traditional design that's made for down-home hospitality, the pleasures of casual conversation, and the good grace of pleasant company. The star attractions are the large covered porch and terrace, perfectly relaxing gathering points for family and friends. Inside, though, the design is truly a hard worker; separate living room and family room, each with its own fireplace; formal dining room; large kitchen and breakfast area with bay windows; separate study; workshop with plenty of room to maneuver; mud room; and four bedrooms up, including a master suite. Not to be overlooked are the curio niches, the powder room, the built-in bookshelves, the kitchen pass-through, the pantry, the planning desk, the workbench, and the stairs to the basement.

Design N2889

First Floor: 2,349 square feet
Second Floor: 1,918 square feet
Total: 4,267 square feet

L **D**

Quote One™

Cost to build? See page 336 to order complete cost estimate to build this house in your area!

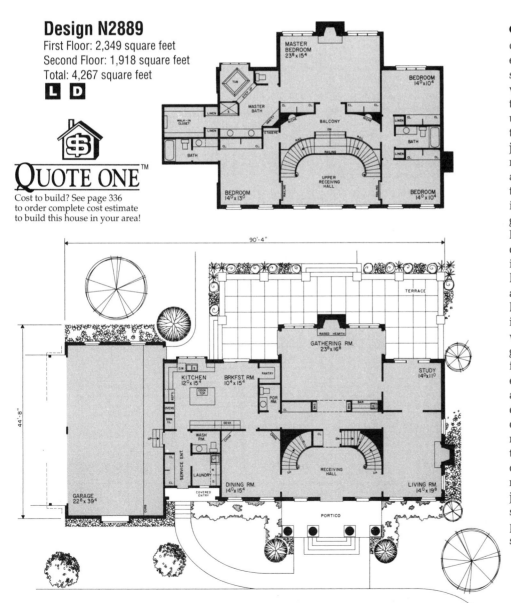

● This is truly classical Georgian design at its best. Some of the exterior highlights of this two-story include the pediment gable with cornice work and dentils, the beautifully proportioned columns, the front door detailing and the window treatment. These are just some of the features which make this design so unique and appealing. Behind the facade of this design is an equally elegant interior. Imagine greeting your guests in the large receiving hall. It is graced by two curving staircases and opens to the formal living and dining rooms. Beyond the living room is the study. It has access to the rear terrace. Those large, informal occasions for family get-togethers or entertaining will be enjoyed in the spacious gathering room. It has a centered fireplace flanked by windows on each side, access to the terrace and a wet bar. The work center is efficient: the kitchen with island cook top, breakfast room, washroom, laundry and service entrance. The second floor also is outstanding. Three family bedrooms and two full baths are joined by the feature filled master suite. If you like this basic floor plan but prefer a French exterior, see Design N2543.

Design N2984

First Floor: 3,116 square feet
Second Floor: 1,997 square feet
Total: 5,113 square feet

L

● An echo of Whitehall, built in 1765 in Anne Arundel County, Maryland, resounds in this home. Its classic symmetry and columned facade herald a grand interior. There's no lack of space whether entertaining formally or just enjoying a family get-together, and all are kept cozy with fireplaces in the gathering room, study, and family room. An island kitchen with attached breakfast room handily serves the nearby dining room. Four second floor bedrooms include a large master suite with another fireplace, a whirlpool, and His and Hers closets in the bath. Three more full baths are found on this floor.

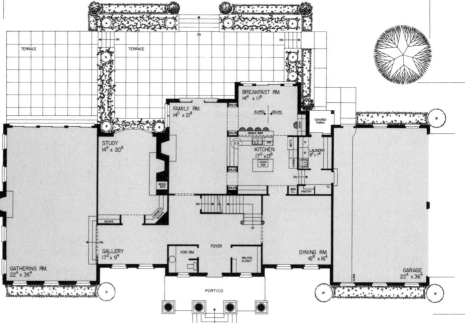

Design N3303

First Floor: 2,563 square feet; Second Floor: 1,496 square feet
Total: 4,059 square feet

L

● With its stately columns and one-story wings, this design is a fine representation of 18th Century adaptations. Formal living and dining areas flank the entry foyer at the front of the home. Look for a fireplace in the living room, china cabinet built-ins in the dining room. More casual living dominates the back section in a family room and kitchen/breakfast room combination that features access to the rear terrace and plenty of space for cooking and informal dining. The left wing garage is connected to the main structure by a service entrance adjacent to the laundry. The right wing contains the private master suite. Four second floor bedrooms share two full baths and each has its own walk-in closet.

QUOTE ONE™

Cost to build? See page 336
to order complete cost estimate
to build this house in your area!

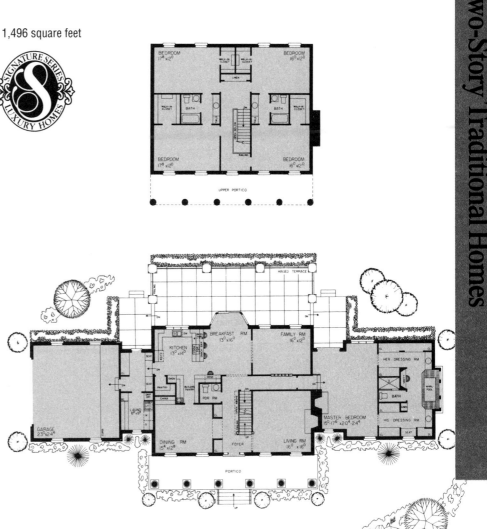

Width 111'-8"
Depth 46'-2"

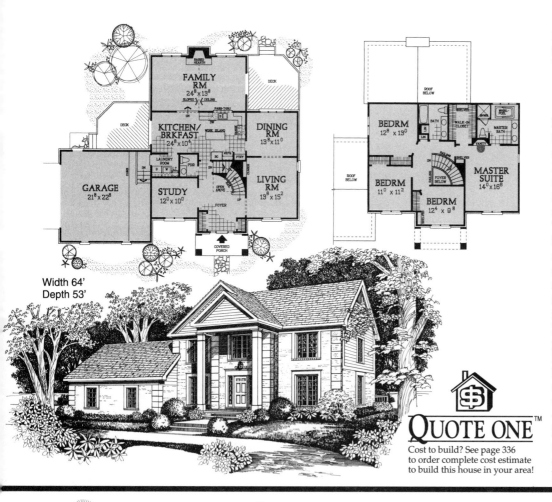

Width 64'
Depth 53'

Design N3472

First Floor: 1,532 square feet
Second Floor: 1,168 square feet
Total: 2,700 square feet

L

● This stately two-story home makes a grand first impression with its columned front entry. Inside, the gracious foyer opens to a study on the left and a living room and dining room on the right. The spacious kitchen includes a work island and an open breakfast area. An expansive family room is just a step down from the kitchen and features a raised hearth. From here, a rear deck provides superb outdoor livability. Upstairs, four bedrooms include a master bedroom suite with a walk-in closet and a private whirlpool bath. A full hall bath with dual lavatories is conveniently located to three secondary bedrooms.

QUOTE ONE™
Cost to build? See page 336
to order complete cost estimate
to build this house in your area!

Design N3341 First Floor: 2,337 square feet
Second Floor: 1,232 square feet; Total: 3,569 square feet

L

● What a grand impression this home makes! A spacious two-story foyer with circular staircase greets visitors and leads to the dining room, media room and two-story gathering room with fireplace. The well-equipped kitchen includes a snack bar for informal meals. A luxurious master suite downstairs and four bedrooms upstairs complete this impressive plan.

QUOTE ONE™
Cost to build? See page 336
to order complete cost estimate
to build this house in your area!

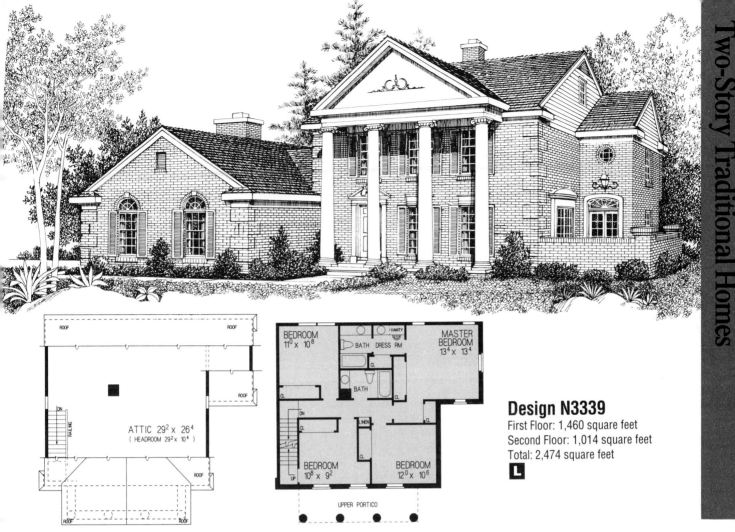

Design N3339

First Floor: 1,460 square feet
Second Floor: 1,014 square feet
Total: 2,474 square feet

L

● This Colonial four-bedroom features the livable kind of plan you're looking for. A formal living room extends from the front foyer and leads to the formal dining area and nearby kitchen. A sunken family room has a raised-hearth fireplace. Three family bedrooms share a bath and are joined by the master bedroom with its own full bath.

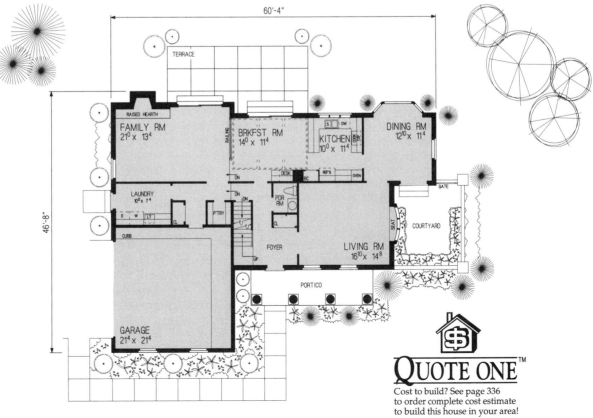

Quote One™

Cost to build? See page 336
to order complete cost estimate
to build this house in your area!

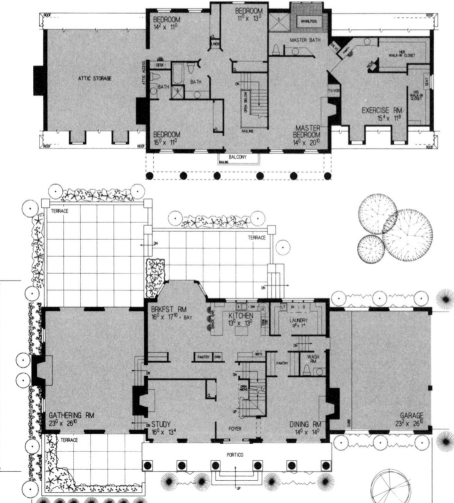

Design N3337

First Floor: 2,167 square feet
Second Floor: 1,992 square feet
Total: 4,159 square feet

L

● The elegant facade of this design with its columned portico, fanlights, and dormers houses an amenity-filled interior. The gathering room, study and dining room, each with fireplace, provide plenty of room for relaxing and entertaining. A large work area contains a kitchen with breakfast room and snack bar, laundry room and pantry. The four-bedroom upstairs includes a master suite with a sumptuous bath and an exercise room.

QUOTE ONE™

Cost to build? See page 336 to order complete cost estimate to build this house in your area!

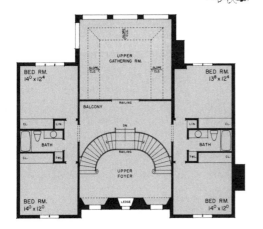

Design N3380

First Floor: 3,350 square feet
Second Floor: 1,203 square feet
Total: 4,553 square feet

● Reminiscent of a Mediterranean villa, this grand manor is a showstopper on the outside and a comfortable residence on the inside. An elegant receiving hall boasts a double staircase and is flanked by the formal dining room and the library. A huge gathering room is found to the back. The master bedroom is found on the first floor for privacy. Upstairs are four additional bedrooms and two full baths.

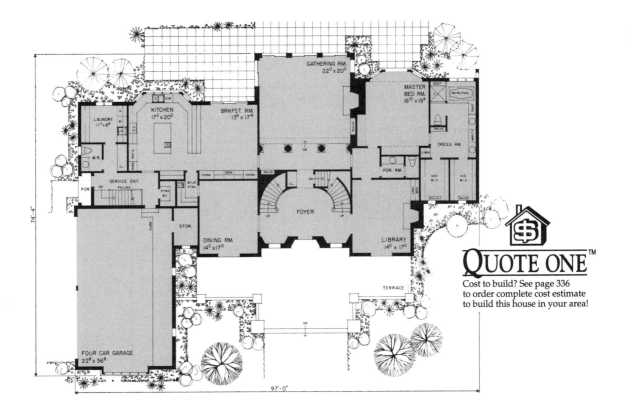

QUOTE ONE™

Cost to build? See page 336
to order complete cost estimate
to build this house in your area!

Design N2133 First Floor: 3,024 square feet; Second Floor: 826 square feet; Total: 3,850 square feet

D

● A country-estate home which will command all the attention it truly deserves. The projecting pediment gable supported by the finely proportioned columns lends an aura of elegance. The window treatment, the front door detailing, the massive, capped chimney, the cupola, the brick veneer exterior and the varying roof planes complete the characterization of an impressive home. Inside, there are 3,024 square feet on the first floor. In addition, there is a two bedroom second floor should its development be necessary. However, whether called upon to function as one, or 1-1/2 story home it will provide a lifetime of gracious living. Don't overlook the compartment baths, the big library, the coat room, the beamed ceiling family room, the two fireplaces, the breakfast room and the efficient kitchen. Note pass-thru to breakfast room.

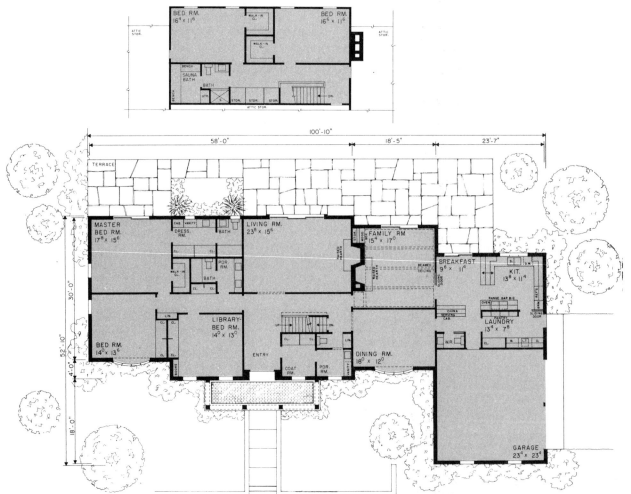

Design N2977 First Floor: 4,104 square feet; Second Floor: 979 square feet; Total: 5,083 square feet

L

QUOTE ONE™

Cost to build? See page 336
to order complete cost estimate
to build this house in your area!

Width 132'
Depth 53'-6"

● Both front and rear facades
of this elegant brick manor de-
pict classic Georgian symmetry.
A columned, Greek entry opens
to an impressive two-story
foyer. Fireplaces, built-in
shelves, and cabinets highlight
each of the four main gathering
areas: living room, dining room,
family room, and library.

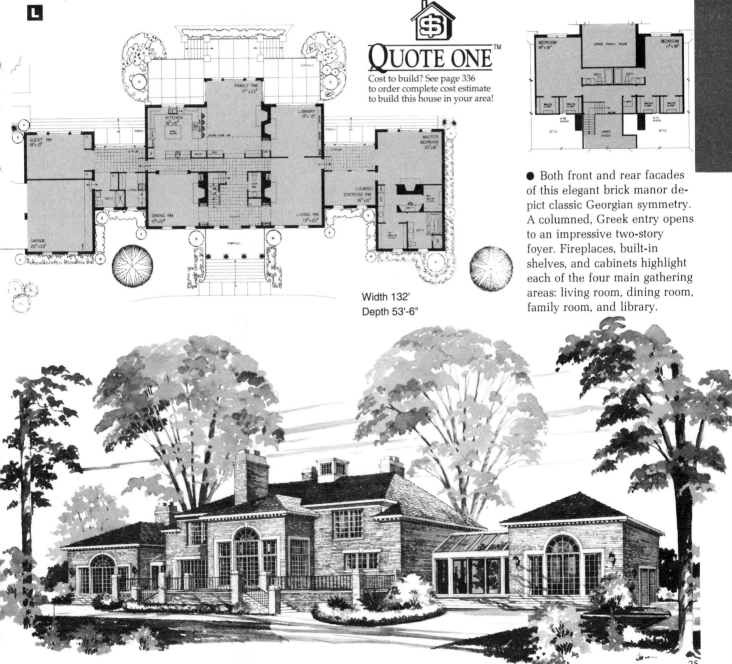

Design N3349

First Floor: 2,807 square feet
Second Floor: 1,363 square feet
Total: 4,170 square feet

● Grand traditional design comes to the forefront in this elegant two-story. From the dramatic front entry with curving double stairs to the less formal gathering room with fireplace and terrace access, this plan accommodates family lifestyles. Notice the split-bedroom plan with the master suite on the first floor and family bedrooms upstairs. A four-car garage handles the

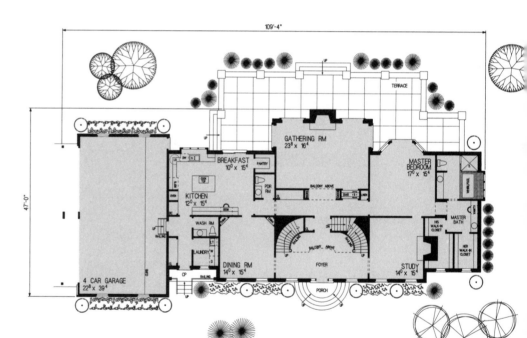

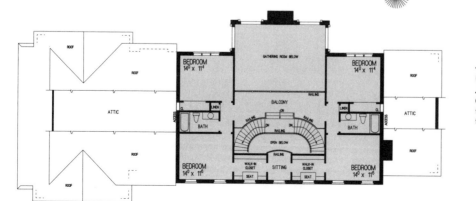

QUOTE ONE™

Cost to build? See page 336
to order complete cost estimate
to build this house in your area!

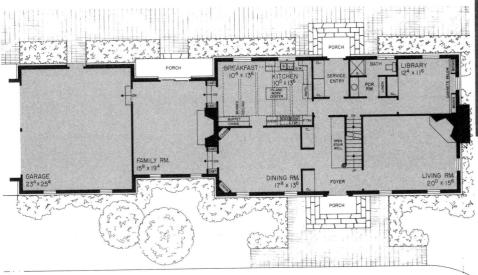

Design N2192

First Floor: 1,884 square feet
Second Floor: 1,521 square feet
Total: 3,405 square feet

L **D**

● This is surely a fine adaptation from the 18th-Century when formality and elegance were by-words. The authentic detailing of this design centers around the fine proportions, the dentils, the window symmetry, the front door and entranceway, the massive chimneys and the masonry work. The rear elevation retains all the grandeur exemplary of exquisite architecture. The appeal of this outstanding home does not end with its exterior elevations. Consider the formal living room with its corner fireplace. Also, the library with its wall of bookshelves and cabinets. Further, the dining room highlights corner china cabinets. Continue to study this elegant plan.

Width 99'
Depth 29'-6"

GARAGE 23⁴ x 25⁴

PORCH

FAMILY RM. 15⁸ x 19⁴

BREAKFAST 10⁴ x 13⁶

KITCHEN 10⁰ x 13⁶

PORCH

SERVICE ENTRY

PDR. RM.

BATH

LIBRARY 12⁴ x 11⁶

DINING RM. 17⁸ x 13⁶

FOYER

LIVING RM. 20⁰ x 15⁶

PORCH

BEDROOM 12⁰ x 11⁶

BATH

SEAT VANITY SEAT LIN.

PDR. RM.

DRESSING RM.

WALK-IN CL.

BEDROOM 17⁰ x 13²

OPEN STAIRWELL

UP TO ATTIC

MASTER BEDROOM 17⁸ x 15⁶

STUDY/ SEWING 11⁰ x 17⁰

BATH

ROOF

CEILING CLG.

PLAYROOM STUDIO/GUEST RM. 21⁰ x 17⁰

ROOF

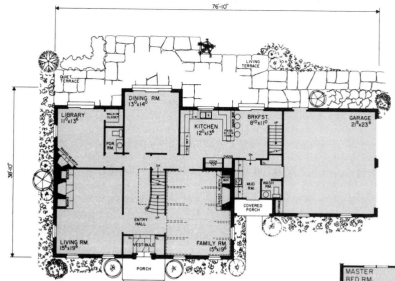

Design N1858

First Floor: 1,794 square feet
Second Floor: 1,474 square feet
Studio: 424 square feet
Total: 3,692 square feet

● From the delightful spacious front entry hall, to the studio or maid's room over the garage, this home is unique: four fireplaces, three full baths, two extra washrooms, a family room plus a quiet library. Note the separate set of stairs to the studio or maid's room. The kitchen is well-planned and strategically located between dining room and breakfast room.

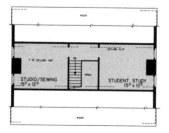

Design N2633

First Floor: 1,338 square feet
Second Floor: 1,200 square feet
Third Floor: 506 square feet
Total: 3,044 square feet

● This pleasing Georgian features a front porch with a roof supported by 12″ diameter wooden columns. Sliding glass doors link the terrace and family room, providing an indoor/outdoor area for entertaining. The floor plan has been designed to serve the family efficiently. The stairway in the foyer leads to four second-floor bedrooms. The third floor is windowed and can be used as a studio and study.

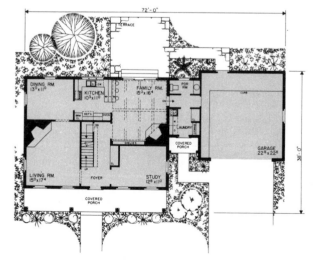

Design N2283
First Floor: 1,559 square feet
Second Floor: 1,404 square feet
Total: 2,963 square feet

L D

● Reminiscent of the stately character of Federal architecture during an earlier period in our history, this two-story is replete with exquisite detailing. The cornice work, pediment gable, dentils, brick quoins at the corners, beautifully proportioned columns, front door detailing, window treatment and massive twin chimneys are among the features which make this design so unique and appealing.

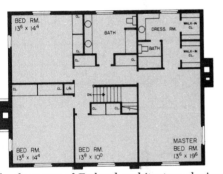

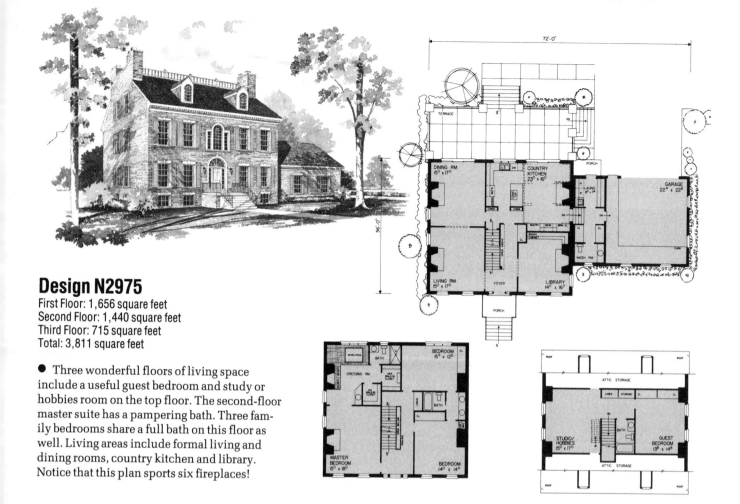

Design N2975

First Floor: 1,656 square feet
Second Floor: 1,440 square feet
Third Floor: 715 square feet
Total: 3,811 square feet

● Three wonderful floors of living space include a useful guest bedroom and study or hobbies room on the top floor. The second-floor master suite has a pampering bath. Three family bedrooms share a full bath on this floor as well. Living areas include formal living and dining rooms, country kitchen and library. Notice that this plan sports six fireplaces!

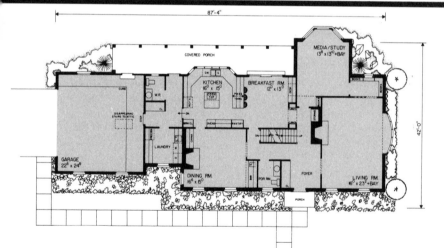

Design N2963

First Floor: 2,046 square feet
Second Floor: 1,644 square feet
Total: 3,690 square feet

● The rambling proportions of this house reflect Colonial precedents. Both the dining and living rooms boast large fireplaces. Family meals are likely to be served in the cozy breakfast room attached to the kitchen. The study is tucked away behind the living room. Upstairs, four bedrooms provide a comfortable retreat for each family member.

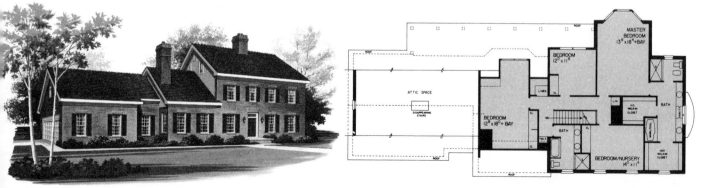

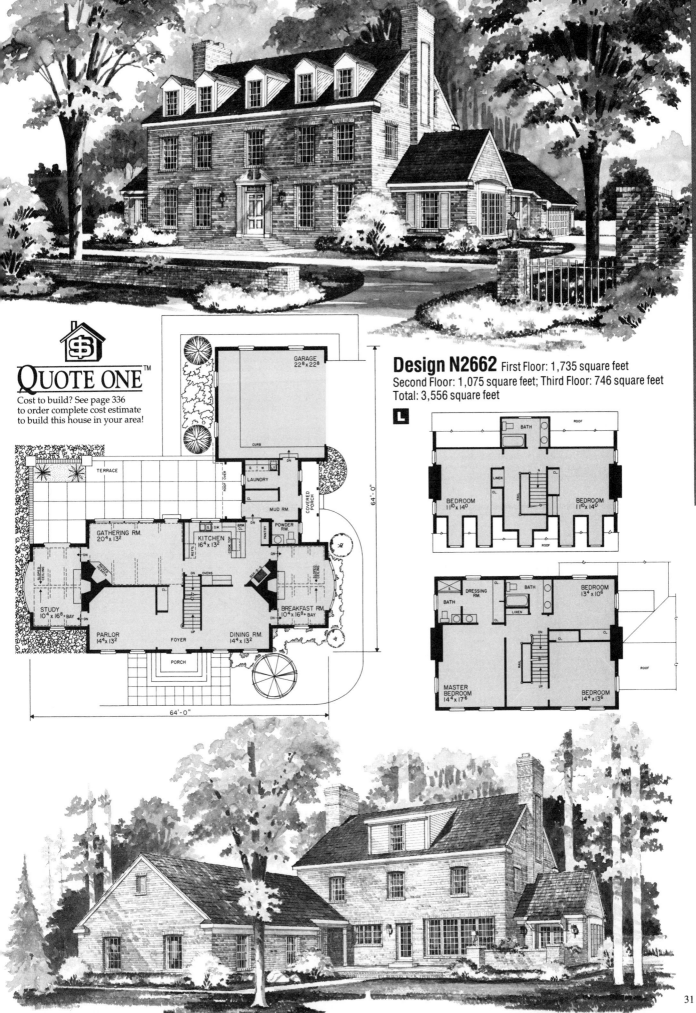

Quote One™

Cost to build? See page 336 to order complete cost estimate to build this house in your area!

Design N2662

First Floor: 1,735 square feet
Second Floor: 1,075 square feet; Third Floor: 746 square feet
Total: 3,556 square feet

L

GARAGE 22⁸ x 22⁸

TERRACE

LAUNDRY

MUD RM.

COVERED PORCH

POWDER RM.

GATHERING RM. 20⁴ x 13²

KITCHEN 16⁴ x 13²

PANTRY

STUDY 10⁴ x 16⁸ BAY

SLOPED CEILING

OVENS

BREAKFAST RM. 10⁴ x 16⁸ BAY

SLOPED CEILING

PARLOR 14⁴ x 13²

FOYER

DINING RM. 14⁴ x 13²

PORCH

64'-0"

64'-0"

BATH

ROOF

BEDROOM 11¹⁰ x 14⁰

LINEN

BEDROOM 11¹⁰ x 14⁰

ROOF

DRESSING RM.

BATH

BATH

LINEN

BEDROOM 13⁴ x 10⁶

MASTER BEDROOM 14⁴ x 17⁶

BEDROOM 14⁴ x 13⁶

ROOF

Design N2176

First Floor: 1,485 square feet
Second Floor: 1,175 square feet
Total: 2,660 square feet

L **D**

● A big, end living room featuring a fireplace and sliding glass doors is the focal point of this Georgian design. Adjacent is the formal dining room strategically located but a couple of steps from the efficient kitchen. Functioning closely with the kitchen is the family room.

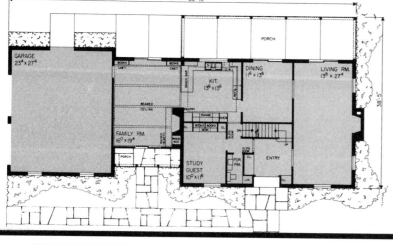

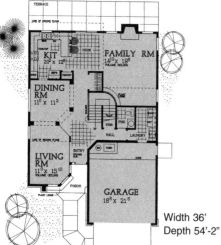

Width 36'
Depth 54'-2"

Design N3477 First Floor: 1,246 square feet
Second Floor: 906 square feet; Total: 2,152 square feet

L

● Brick, wood siding and varied rooflines create a comfortable exterior for this three-bedroom plan. The spacious family room rises into a volume ceiling while featuring a fireplace and both side and rear views—truly an attention-getting room. Open to the family room, the breakfast area contains a convenient snack bar in common with the U-shaped kitchen. Upstairs, the master bedroom pleases with its walk-in closet and private bath with double-bowl vanity. Two accommodating bedrooms make use of an additional full bath.

QUOTE ONE™

Cost to build? See page 336 to order complete cost estimate to build this house in your area!

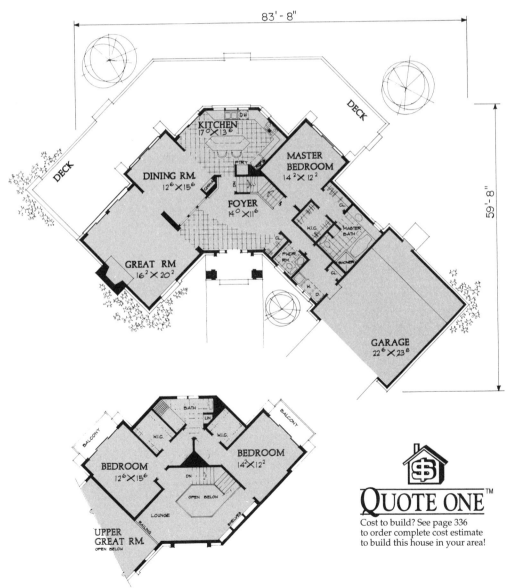

83' - 8"

DECK

DECK

DECK

KITCHEN
17⁰ X 13⁶

DINING RM.
12⁶ X 15⁶

MASTER
BEDROOM
14² X 12²

FOYER
14⁰ X 11⁶

GREAT RM
16² X 20²

W.I.C.

MASTER
BATH

SHOWER

GARAGE
22⁶ X 23⁸

59' - 8"

BEDROOM
12⁶ X 15⁶

BEDROOM
14² X 12²

BATH

LIN

W.I.C.

W.I.C.

BALCONY

BALCONY

DN

OPEN BELOW

LOUNGE

SHELVES

UPPER
GREAT RM.
OPEN BELOW

RAILING

Design N3310

First Floor: 1,668 square feet
Second Floor: 905 square feet
Total: 2,573 square feet

L **D**

● If you're looking for a different angle on a new home, try this enchanting transitional house. The open foyer creates a rich atmosphere. To the left you'll find a great room with raised-brick hearth and sliding glass doors that lead out onto a wraparound deck. The kitchen enhances the first floor with a snack bar and deck access. The master bedroom, with balcony and bath with whirlpool, is located on the first floor for privacy. Upstairs, two family bedrooms, both with balconies and walk-in closets, share a full bath. Don't overlook the lounge and elliptical window that give the second floor added charisma.

QUOTE ONE™

Cost to build? See page 336 to order complete cost estimate to build this house in your area!

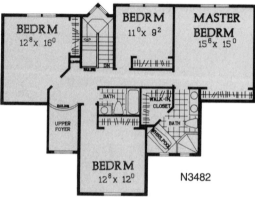

N3470

N3482

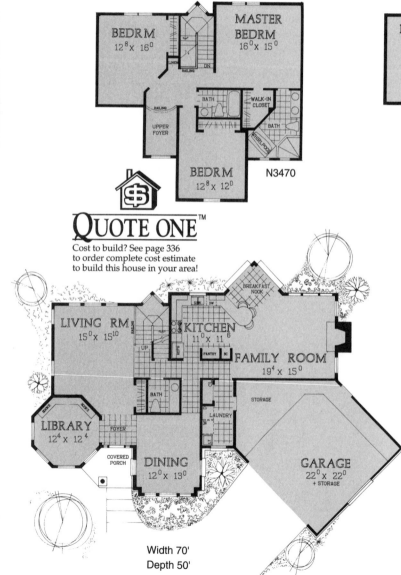

QUOTE ONE™

Cost to build? See page 336
to order complete cost estimate
to build this house in your area!

Width 70'
Depth 50'

Design N3470/N3482

First Floor: 1,460 square feet
Second Floor: 955/1,150 square feet
Total: 2,415/2,610 square feet

L **D**

● The first floor of both of these plans is the same. Whichever plan you choose, the focal point will definitely be the gazebo-styled library with its dramatic ceiling and cathedral windows. This artistic window treatment continues to the formal dining room. Nearby is the spacious corner living room and the open kitchen with its unique circular snack-bar pass-through to the angled breakfast nook. The comfortable family room contains a charming fireplace. The difference in the two plans lies in the construction of the second floor. Design N3470 features two bedrooms with a shared bath and a large master bedroom with a walk-in closet and a corner whirlpool and shower. Design N3482 includes an additional fourth bedroom.

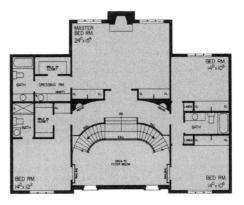

Design N2543 First Floor: 2,345 square feet
Second Floor: 1,687 square feet; Total: 4,032 square feet

L **D**

● Though quite different on the outside, the homes on these two pages have floor plans that are nearly identical. This best selling French adaptation is highlighted by effective window treatment, delicate cornice detailing, appealing brick quoins and excellent proportion. Inside are a gathering room, formal living and dining rooms, study, gourmet kitchen and four upstairs bedrooms.

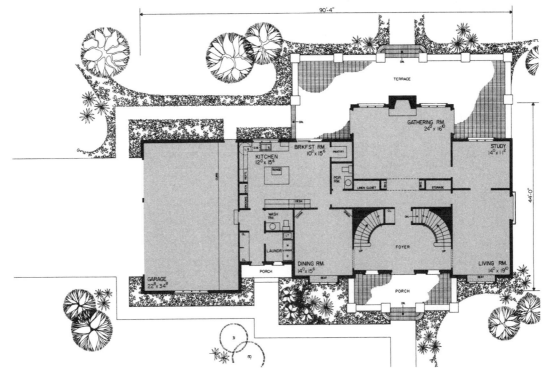

Design N1228

First Floor: 2,583 square feet
Second Floor: 697 square feet
Total: 3,280 square feet

L **D**

Width 93'-10"
Depth 67'-10"

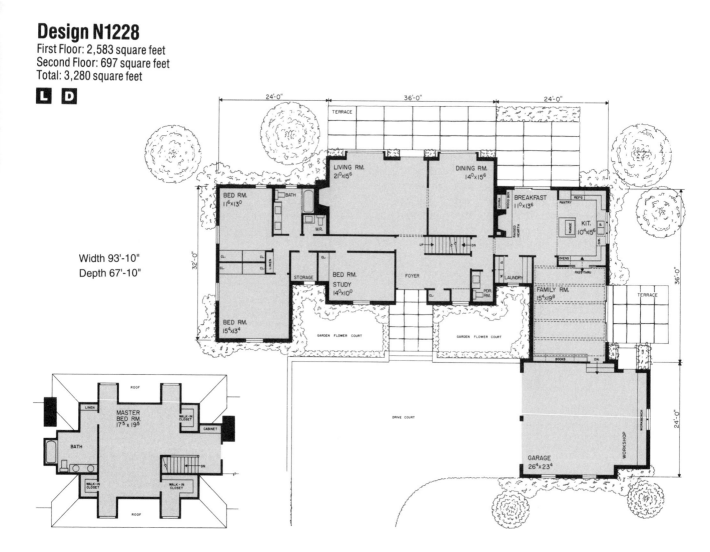

● This beautiful house has a wealth of detail taken from the rich traditions of French Regency design. The roof itself is a study in pleasant dormers and the hips and valleys of a big flowing area. A close examination of the plan shows the careful arrangement of space for privacy as well as good circulation of traffic. The spacious formal entrance hall sets the stage for good zoning. The informal living area is highlighted by the updated version of the old country kitchen. Observe the fireplace, built-in wood box, and china cabinet. While there is a half-story devoted to the master bedroom suite, this home functons more as a one-story country estate design than as a 1½ story.

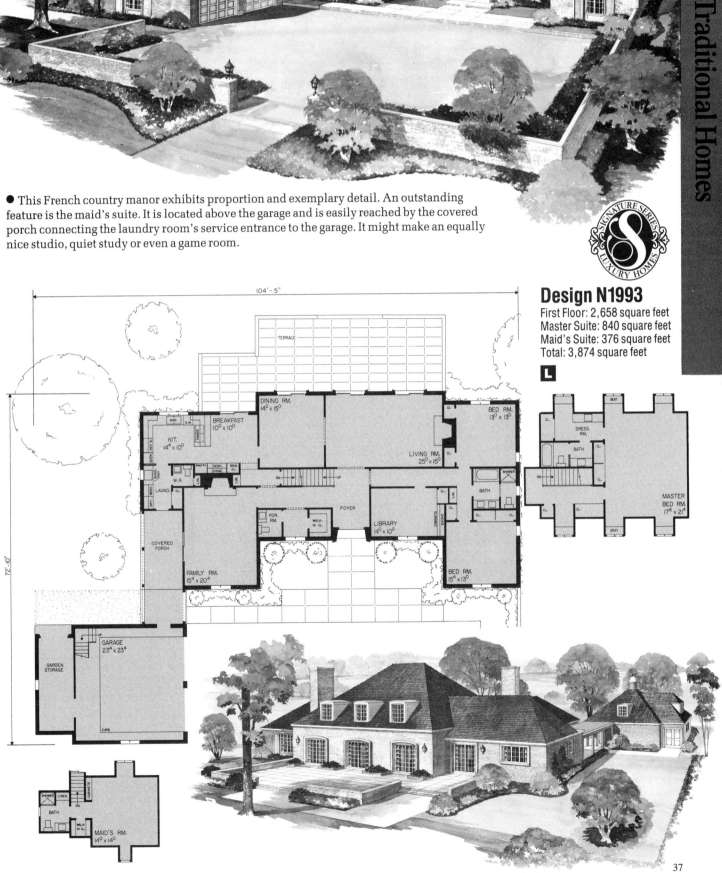

● This French country manor exhibits proportion and exemplary detail. An outstanding feature is the maid's suite. It is located above the garage and is easily reached by the covered porch connecting the laundry room's service entrance to the garage. It might make an equally nice studio, quiet study or even a game room.

Design N1993

First Floor: 2,658 square feet
Master Suite: 840 square feet
Maid's Suite: 376 square feet
Total: 3,874 square feet

Design N2610

First Floor: 1,505 square feet
Second Floor: 1,344 square feet
Total: 2,849 square feet

L **D**

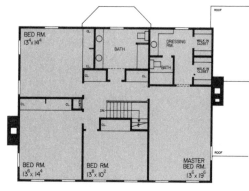

● This full two-story traditional will be worthy of note wherever built. It strongly recalls images of a New England of yesteryear. And well it might; for the window treatment is delightful. The front entrance detail is inviting. The narrow horizontal siding and the corner boards are appealing as are the two massive chimneys. The center entrance hall is large with a handy powder room nearby. The study has built-in bookshelves and offers a full measure of privacy. The interior kitchen has a pass-through to the family room and enjoys all that natural light from the bay window of the nook. A beamed ceiling, fireplace and sliding glass doors are features of the family room. The mud room highlights a closet, laundry equipment and an extra wash room. Study the upstairs with those four bedrooms, two baths and plenty of closets. An excellent arrangement for all.

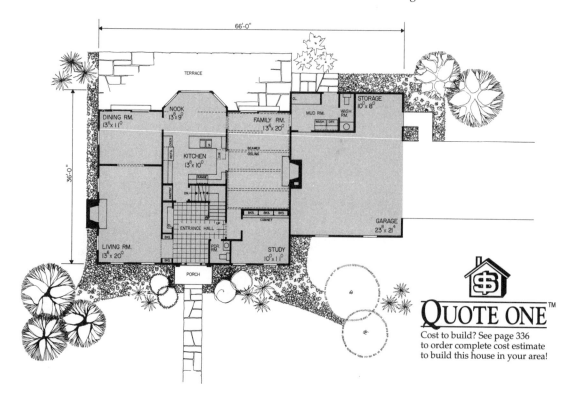

Quote One™
Cost to build? See page 336
to order complete cost estimate
to build this house in your area!

Design N2640

First Floor: 1,386 square feet
Second Floor: 1,232 square feet
Total: 2,618 square feet

L **D**

● Here is a gracious exterior which adopts many features common to New England-style Federal homes. The symmetry and proportions are outstanding. Inside, a fine, functioning plan. Note stairs to attic for additional storage and livability.

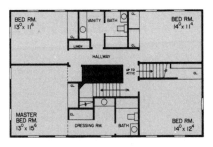

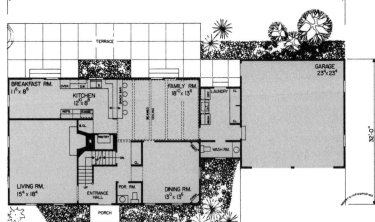

WIDTH 48'
DEPTH 32'

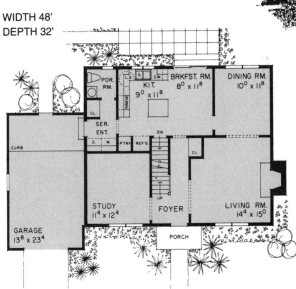

Design N3571

First Floor: 964 square feet
Second Floor: 783 square feet
Total: 1,747 square feet

L **D**

QUOTE ONE™

Cost to build? See page 336 to order complete cost estimate to build this house in your area!

● For those interested in both traditional charm and modern convenience, this Cape Cod fits the bill. Enter the foyer and find a quiet study to the left, a living room with a fireplace to the right. Straight ahead: the kitchen and breakfast room. The island countertop affords lots of room for meal preparation. The service entry introduces a laundry and powder room. Look for three bedrooms upstairs and a pampering master bath: whirlpool, shower, double vanity and walk-in closet.

Design N3503

First Floor: 1,748 square feet
Second Floor: 1,748 square feet
Third Floor: 1,100 square feet
Total: 4,596 square feet

L **D**

● A brick exterior serves as a nice introduction to a charming home. Enter the eleven-foot-high foyer and take a seat in the warm living room and its focal-point fireplace. Built-in shelves grace the hallway as well as the living and dining rooms. The handy kitchen with island and snack bar opens up into a conversation room with bay and fireplace. The service entrance leads to both laundry and garage. This house features four bedrooms: the master with fireplace, walk-in closet and whirl-pool; two family bed-rooms that share a full bath with double-bowl vanity; and a guest bed-room that shares the third floor with the library. This design would work well on a narrow lot.

QUOTE ONE™

Cost to build? See page 336 to order complete cost estimate to build this house in your area!

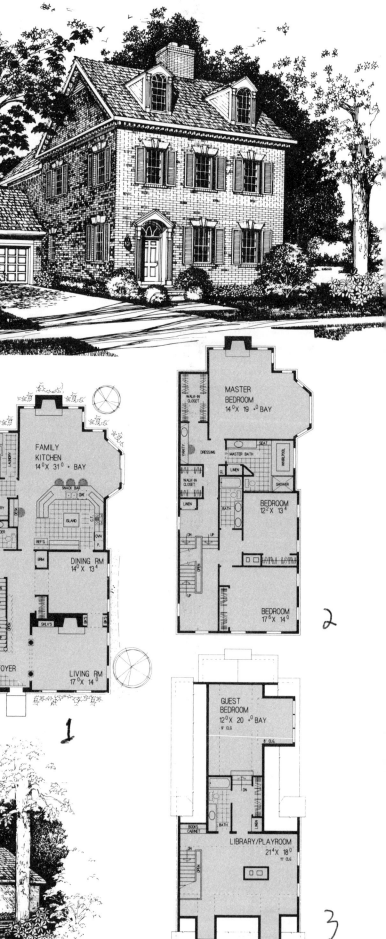

Width 50'
Depth 63'

Design N2659
First Floor: 1,023 square feet
Second Floor: 1,008 square feet; Third Floor: 476 square feet
Total: 2,507 square feet

L **D**

● The facade of this three-storied, pitch-roofed house has a symmetrical placement of windows and a restrained but elegant central entrance. The central hall, or foyer, expands midway through the house to a family kitchen. Off the foyer are two rooms, a living room with fireplace and a study. The windowed third floor attic can be used as a study and studio. Three bedrooms are housed on the second floor.

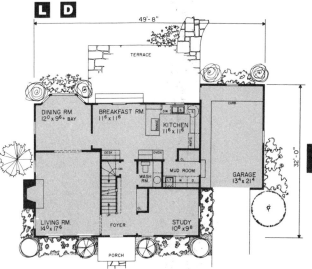

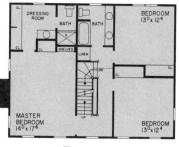

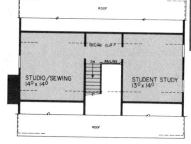

QUOTE ONE™

Cost to build? See page 336
to order complete cost estimate
to build this house in your area!

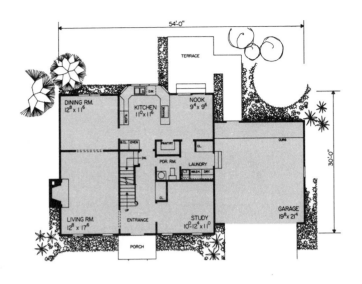

Design N2731 First Floor: 1,039 square feet
Second Floor: 973 square feet; Total: 2,012 square feet

L **D**

● The multi-paned windows with shutters of this two-story highlight the exterior delightfully. Inside the livability is ideal. Formal and informal areas are sure to serve your family with ease. Note efficient U-shaped kitchen with handy first-floor laundry. Sleeping facilities on second floor.

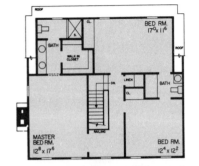

● The appeal of this Colonial home will be virtually everlasting. It will improve with age and service the growing family well. Imagine your family living here. There are four bedrooms, 2½ baths, plus plenty of first floor living space.

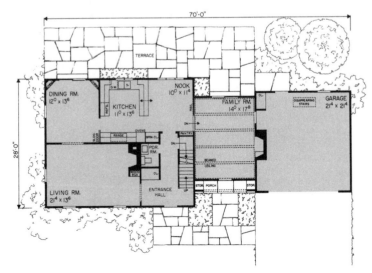

Design N2211 First Floor: 1,214 square feet
Second Floor: 1,146 square feet; Total: 2,360 square feet

L **D**

42

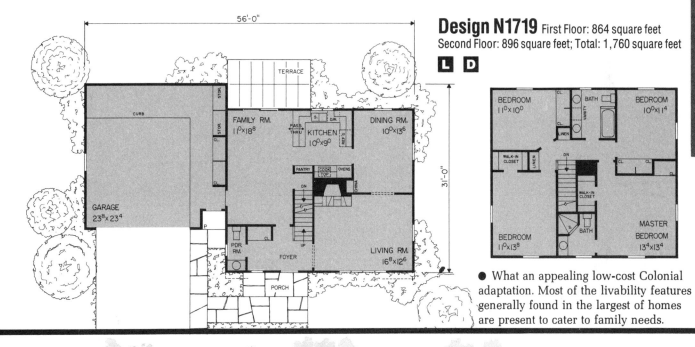

56'-0"

TERRACE

FAMILY RM.
11⁰x18⁸

PASS THRU

KITCHEN
10⁰x9⁰

DINING RM.
10⁰x13⁶

CURB

PANTRY COOK TOP OVENS

CHINA

GARAGE
23⁸x23⁴

DN

UP

LIVING RM.
16⁸x12⁶

PDR RM.

FOYER

PORCH

31'-0"

Design N1719 First Floor: 864 square feet
Second Floor: 896 square feet; Total: 1,760 square feet

L **D**

BEDROOM
11⁰x10⁰

BATH

VANITY

BEDROOM
10⁰x11⁴

CL

LINEN

WALK-IN CLOSET

LINEN

DN

CL CL

CL

WALK-IN CLOSET

BEDROOM
11⁰x13⁸

BATH

MASTER BEDROOM
13⁴x13⁴

● What an appealing low-cost Colonial adaptation. Most of the livability features generally found in the largest of homes are present to cater to family needs.

Design N2733 First Floor: 1,177 square feet; Second Floor: 1,003 square feet; Total: 2,180 square feet

L D

Width 54'
Depth 33'

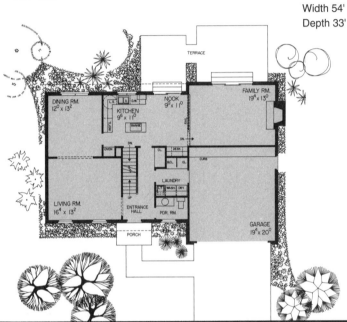

Cost to build? See page 336
to order complete cost estimate
to build this house in your area!

● This is definitely a four bedroom Colonial with
charm galore. The kitchen features an island range
and other built-ins. All will enjoy the sunken family room with fireplace, which has sliding glass
doors leading to the terrace.

Design N2538

First Floor: 1,503 square feet
Second Floor: 1,095 square feet
Total: 2,598 square feet

L **D**

● This Salt Box is charming, indeed. The livability it has to offer to the large and growing family is great. The entry is spacious and is open to the second floor balcony. For living areas, there is the study in addition to the living and family rooms.

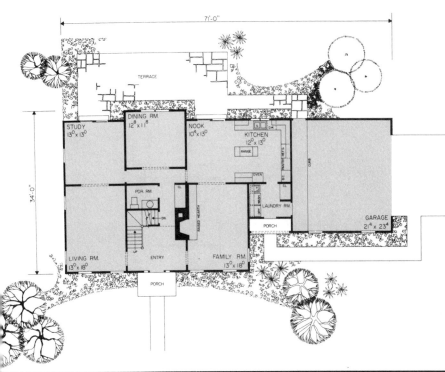

Design N2622

First Floor: 624 square feet
Second Floor: 624 square feet
Total: 1,248 square feet

L **D**

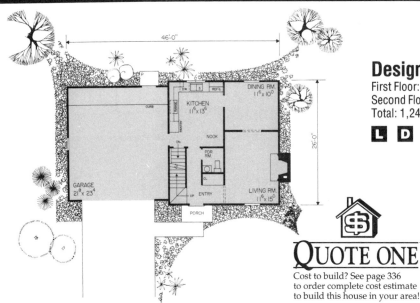

QUOTE ONE™

Cost to build? See page 336 to order complete cost estimate to build this house in your area!

45

Design N3485

First Floor: 1,586 square feet
Second Floor: 1,057 square feet
Total: 2,643 square feet

L

● A covered porch introduces the foyer of this delightful two-story plan. From here, formal areas open up with the living room on the right and the dining room on the left. Note the pot-shelf that extends around the dining room. A den backs up the formal areas of the house and shares a two-way fireplace with the family room. In the kitchen, an island cooktop facilitates food preparation. A double oven is built-in nearby. Upstairs, three bedrooms include a master suite with its own bath. The secondary bedrooms each partake in a hall bath with dual lavatories.

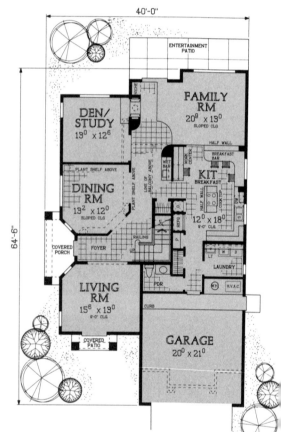

QUOTE ONE™

Cost to build? See page 336
to order complete cost estimate
to build this house in your area!

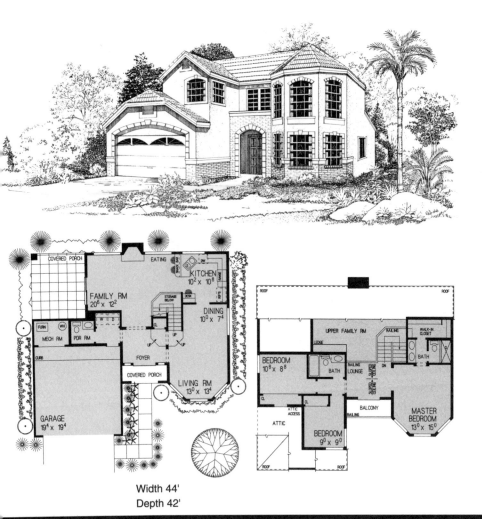

Design N3417

First Floor: 875 square feet
Second Floor: 731 square feet
Total: 1,606 square feet

L

● Perfect for a starter home, this design is compact yet features great livability. The plan provides both formal and informal living areas. There's a living room with a bay window and an adjacent dining area. Open to the kitchen, the spacious family room is large enough to accommodate an informal eating area. The second floor boasts a balcony lounge overlooking the family room, the master bedroom with bay window and two smaller family bedrooms.

QUOTE ONE™

Cost to build? See page 336 to order complete cost estimate to build this house in your area!

Width 44'
Depth 42'

Design N3492

First Floor: 1,361 square feet
Second Floor: 1,327 square feet
Total: 2,688 square feet

L

● In this Southwestern adaptation, verandas provide ample opportunity for enjoying lazy summer afternoons—outdoor living at its best. Guests will take delight in sitting in the parlor or strolling out the dining room's French doors and onto the back veranda. The U-shaped kitchen features a snack bar and opens up into a nook and family room. Here you'll find a built-in wood box and a wood stove. The octagon-shaped media room adds spice to the design. Four family bedrooms make up the second floor. Highlights of the master bath include a double-bowl vanity and a stunning whirlpool.

QUOTE ONE™

Cost to build? See page 336 to order complete cost estimate to build this house in your area!

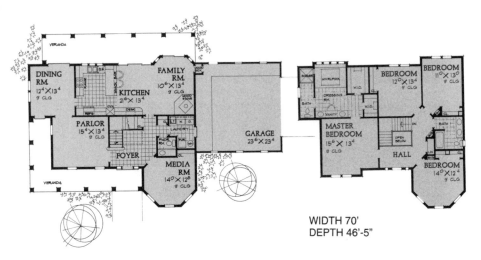

WIDTH 70'
DEPTH 46'-5"

Design N2668 First Floor: 1,206 square feet
Second Floor: 1,254 square feet; Total: 2,460 square feet

L

● This elegant exterior houses a very livable plan. Every bit
of space has been put to good use. The front country kitchen
is a good place to begin. It is efficiently planned with its island cook top, built-ins and pass-thru to the dining room.
The large great room will be the center of all family activities. Quiet times can be enjoyed in the front library. Study
the second floor sleeping areas.

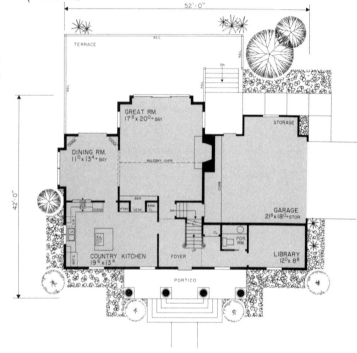

QUOTE ONE™

Cost to build? See page 336
to order complete cost estimate
to build this house in your area!

48

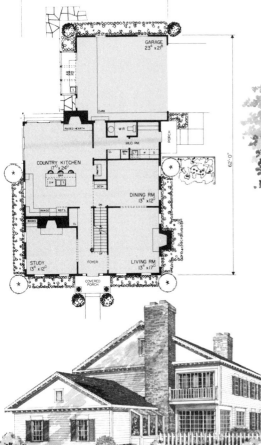

Design N2979

First Floor: 1,440 square feet
Second Floor: 1,394 square feet
Total: 2,834 square feet

● The memory of Noah Webster's house, built in 1823, in New Hampshire is recalled by this Greek Revival adaptation. In addition to the formal living and dining rooms, there is a huge country kitchen and handy mud room. There is also a study. Upstairs there are four bedrooms and three full baths. Don't miss the four fireplaces or the outdoor balcony of the master bedroom. A basement provides additional space for recreation and the pursuit of hobbies.

Design N2667

First Floor: 1,827 square feet
Second Floor: 697 square feet
Total: 2,524 square feet

L

● Two one-story wings flank the two-story center section of this design which echoes the architectural forms of 18th-Century Tidewater Virginia. The left wing is a huge living room; the right the master bedroom suite, service areas and garage. The kitchen, dining room and family room are centrally located with the three bedrooms above.

A Mount Vernon Reminiscence

● This magnificent manor's streetview illustrates a centralized mansion connected by curving galleries to matching wings. What a grand presentation this home will make! The origin of this house dates back to 1787 and George Washington's stately Mount Vernon. The underlying aesthetics for this de-sign come from the rational balancing of porticoes, fenestration and chimneys. The rear elevation of this home also deserves mention. Six two-story columns, along with four sets of French doors, highlight this view. Study all of the intricate detailing that is featured all around these exteriors.

The flanking wings create a large formal courtyard where guests of today can park their cars. This home, designed from architecture of the past, is efficient and compact enough to fit many suburban lots. Its interior has been well planned and is ready to serve a family of any size.

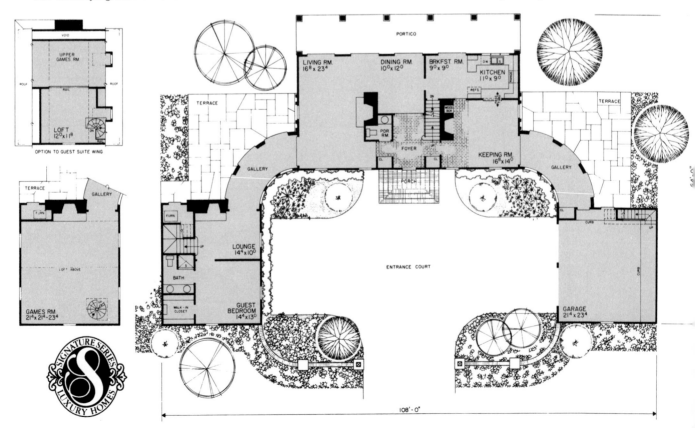

Design N2665 First Floor: 1,152 square feet; Second Floor: 1,152 square feet
Total: 2,304 square feet (Excludes Guest Suite and Galleries)

● The main, two-story section of this home houses the living areas. First - there is the large, tiled foyer with two closets and powder room. Then there is the living room which is the entire width of the house. This room has a fireplace and leads into the formal dining room. Three sets of double

French doors lead to the rear portico from this formal area. The kitchen and breakfast room will function together. There is a pass-thru from the kitchen to the keeping room. All of the sleeping facilities, four bedrooms, are on the second floor. The gallery on the right leads to the garage; the one on the left,

to a lounge and guest suite with studio above. The square footages quoted above do not include the guest suite or gallery areas. The first floor of the guest suite contains 688 sq. ft.; the second floor studio, 306 sq. ft. The optional plan shows a game room with a loft above having 162 sq. ft.

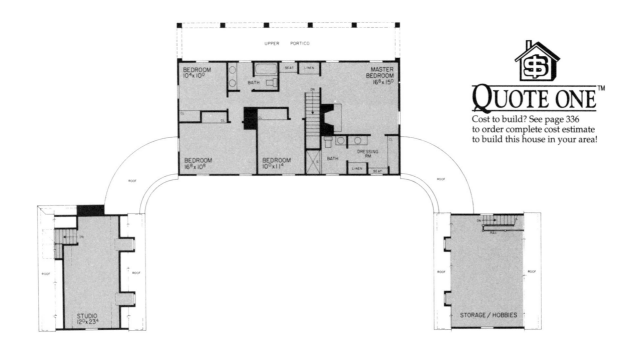

QUOTE ONE™

Cost to build? See page 336 to order complete cost estimate to build this house in your area!

Design N3457

First Floor: 1,252 square feet
Second Floor: 972 square feet
Total: 2,224 square feet

L

QUOTE ONE™

Cost to build? See page 336
to order complete cost estimate
to build this house in your area!

● For family living, this delightful three-bedroom plan scores big. Stretching across the back of the plan, casual living areas take precedence. The family room focuses on a fireplace and enjoys direct access to a covered porch. The breakfast room allows plenty of space for friendly meals—the island kitchen remains open to this room thus providing ease in serving meals and, of course, conversations with the

cook. From the two-car garage, a utility area opens to the main-floor living areas. Upstairs, the master suite affords a quiet retreat with its private bath; here you'll find a whirlpool tub set in a sunny nook. A balcony further enhances this bedroom. The two secondary bedrooms share a full hall bath with a double-bowl vanity.

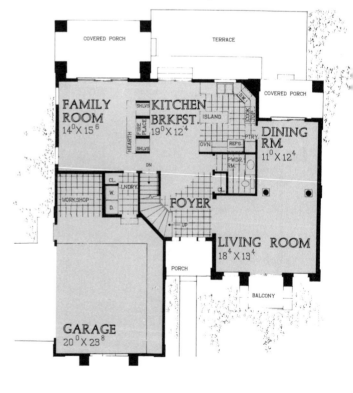

WIDTH 48'
DEPTH 58'

Design N3459

First Floor: 1,392 square feet
Second Floor: 1,178 square feet
Total: 2,570 square feet

L

● This innovative, compact plan affords over 2,500 square feet in living space! A central, angled staircase provides an interesting pivot with which to admire the floor plan. To begin with, the living room rises to two stories and even sports a front porch. The dining room, with its bumped-out nook, enjoys the use of a china alcove. The island kitchen finds easy access to the dining room and blends nicely into the airy breakfast room. A large pantry and a built-in desk also grace the kitchen and the breakfast room, respectively. In the family room, relaxed living comes through with the introduction of a fireplace and access to a covered patio and a terrace. The second floor will please all your family members with its four bedrooms, including a master suite with a private bath.

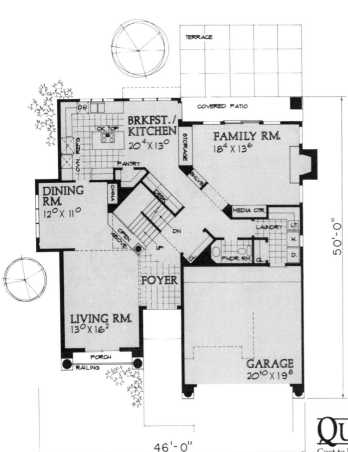

QUOTE ONE™
Cost to build? See page 336
to order complete cost estimate
to build this house in your area!

Design N3463

First Floor: 1,163 square feet
Second Floor: 1,077 square feet
Total: 2,240 square feet

L

● Fine family living takes off in this grand two-story plan. The tiled foyer leads to a stately living room with sliding glass doors to the back terrace. Columns separate it from the dining room. For casual living, the family room/breakfast room combination works well. On the second floor, the master bedroom draws attention with a fireplace, access to a deck and a spoiling bath. The study niche in the hallway shares the outside deck. Two family bedrooms are also on the second floor.

Width 36'
Depth 63'

QUOTE ONE™
Cost to build? See page 336
to order complete cost estimate
to build this house in your area!

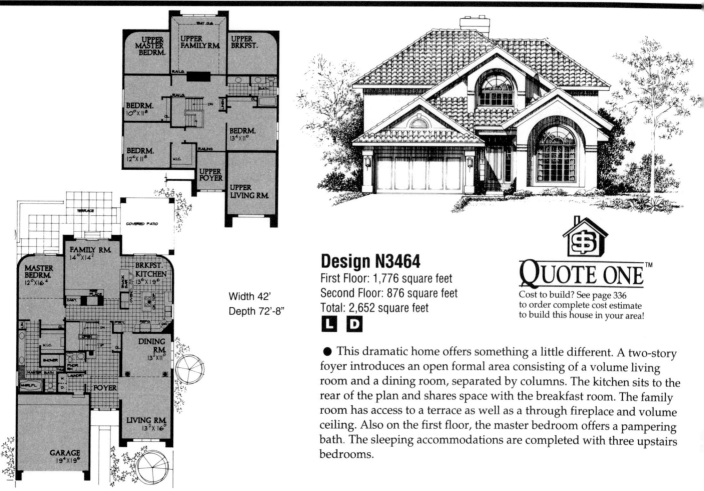

Width 42'
Depth 72'-8"

Design N3464

First Floor: 1,776 square feet
Second Floor: 876 square feet
Total: 2,652 square feet

L D

QUOTE ONE™
Cost to build? See page 336
to order complete cost estimate
to build this house in your area!

● This dramatic home offers something a little different. A two-story foyer introduces an open formal area consisting of a volume living room and a dining room, separated by columns. The kitchen sits to the rear of the plan and shares space with the breakfast room. The family room has access to a terrace as well as a through fireplace and volume ceiling. Also on the first floor, the master bedroom offers a pampering bath. The sleeping accommodations are completed with three upstairs bedrooms.

Design N3455

First Floor: 1,408 square feet
Second Floor: 667 square feet
Total: 2,075 square feet

L **D**

● Whether you're just starting out or looking
to retire, this 1½-story, sun-country design will
make an excellent home. The focal point of the
first floor, the two-story living room utilizes a
central fireplace and columns for comfort and
elegance. Open to the living room, the dining
room complements this space with its influx of
natural light. The kitchen services this room
easily and also enjoys a cozy breakfast nook.
An island work counter in the kitchen guaran-
tees ease in food preparation. Note the service
entry to the garage; a full washer/dryer set-up
adds convenience to laundry chores. On the
second floor you'll find a skylit balcony—a
dramatic yet purposeful design feature—leading to two bedrooms.

QUOTE ONE™

Cost to build? See page 336
to order complete cost estimate
to build this house in your area!

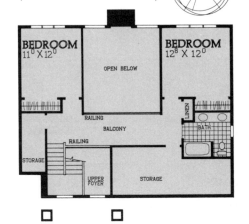

Design N2680

First Floor: 1,707 square feet
Second Floor: 1,439 square feet
Total: 3,146 square feet

L D

● This Early American, Dutch Colonial offers many fine features. The foyer allows easy access to all rooms on the first floor. Note the large country kitchen with beamed ceiling and fireplace. A large, formal dining room and powder room are only a few steps away. The study and the living room also have fireplaces. Two bedrooms, a full bath and the master bedroom suite are on the second floor. A fourth bedroom and bath are accessible through the master bedroom or by stairs in the service entrance.

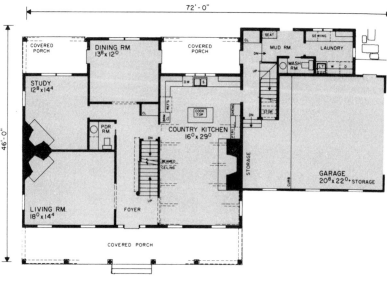

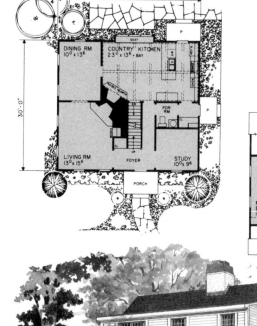

Design N2661

First Floor: 1,020 square feet
Second Floor: 777 square feet
Total: 1,797 square feet

L D

QUOTE ONE™
Cost to build? See page 336 to order complete cost estimate to build this house in your area!

● Any other starter house or retirement home couldn't have more charm than this design. Its compact frame houses a very livable plan. An outstanding feature of the first floor is the large country kitchen. Its fine attractions include a beamed ceiling, raised-hearth fireplace, built-in window seat and a door leading to the outdoors. A living room in the front of the plan has another fireplace which shares the single chimney. The rear dormered second floor houses the sleeping and bath facilities.

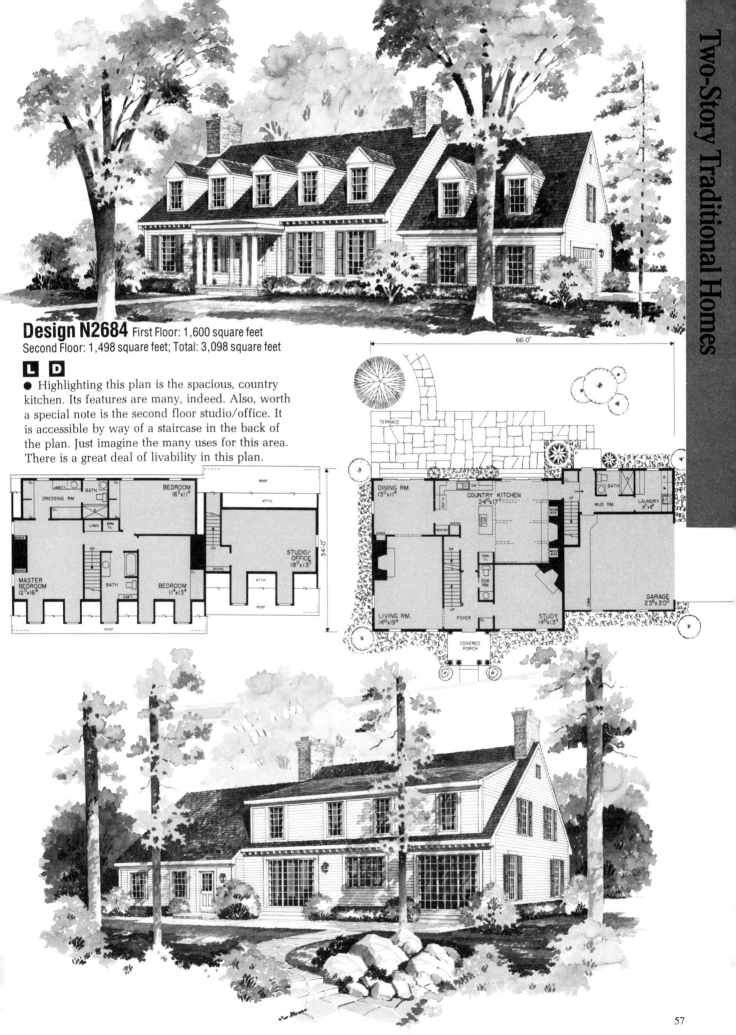

Design N2684 First Floor: 1,600 square feet
Second Floor: 1,498 square feet; Total: 3,098 square feet

L **D**

● Highlighting this plan is the spacious, country kitchen. Its features are many, indeed. Also, worth a special note is the second floor studio/office. It is accessible by way of a staircase in the back of the plan. Just imagine the many uses for this area. There is a great deal of livability in this plan.

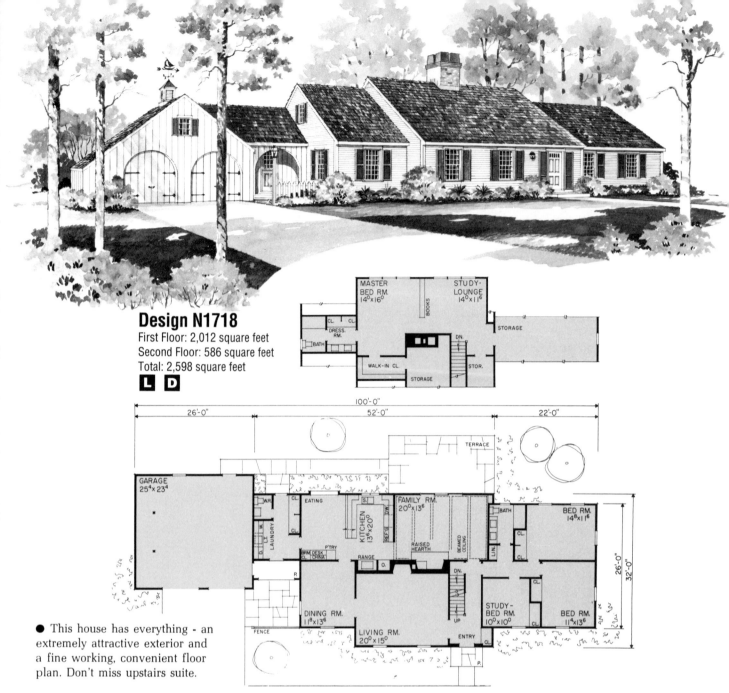

Design N1718

First Floor: 2,012 square feet
Second Floor: 586 square feet
Total: 2,598 square feet

L D

MASTER BED RM. 14⁰x16⁰
STUDY-LOUNGE 14⁰x11⁶
BOOKS
CL. CL.
DRESS. RM.
BATH
STORAGE
DN.
WALK-IN CL.
STORAGE
STOR.

100'-0"
26'-0"
52'-0"
22'-0"

GARAGE 25⁴x23⁴
TERRACE
W.R.
CL.
EATING
S.
FAMILY RM. 20⁰x13⁶
BATH
BED RM. 14⁸x11⁶
LAUNDRY
CL.
KITCHEN 13⁶x20⁰
REFG.
DW
LIN.
CL.
CL.
BRM DESK
CL. CHINA
P'TRY
RAISED HEARTH
BEAMED CEILING
O.
RANGE
Q.
DN.
DINING RM. 11⁸x13⁶
STUDY-BED RM. 10⁰x10⁰
CL.
BED RM. 11⁴x13⁶
26'-0"
32'-0"
FENCE
LIVING RM. 20⁰x15⁰
UP
ENTRY
CL.
P.

● This house has everything - an extremely attractive exterior and a fine working, convenient floor plan. Don't miss upstairs suite.

Design N1987 First Floor: 1,632 square feet
Second Floor: 980 square feet; Total: 2,612 square feet

L D

● The comforts of home will be endless and enduring when experienced and enjoyed in this Colonial adaptation. What's your favorite feature?

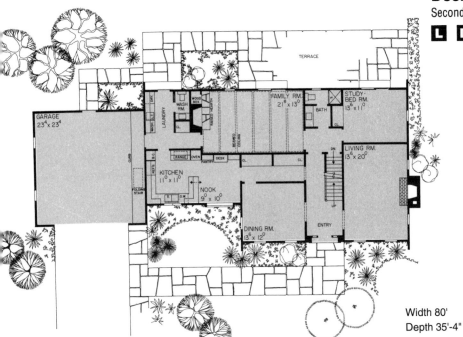

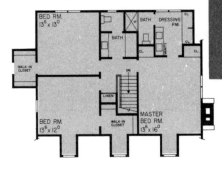

Width 80'
Depth 35'-4"

Design N2131
First Floor: 1,214 square feet
Second Floor: 1,097 square feet
Total: 2,311 square feet

L D

● The Gambrel-roof home is often the very embodiment of charm from the Early Colonial Period in American architechtural history. Fine proportion and excellent detailing were the hallmarks of the era.

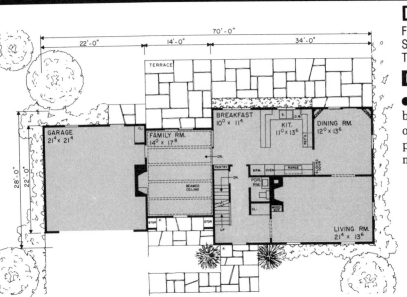

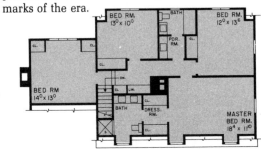

Design N1791 First Floor: 1,157 square feet
Second Floor: 875 square feet; Total: 2,032 square feet

L **D**

QUOTE ONE™

Cost to build? See page 336
to order complete cost estimate
to build this house in your area!

● Wherever you build this moderately sized house
an aura of Cape Cod is sure to unfold. The symmetry is pleasing, indeed. The authentic center entrance seems to project a beckoning call.

Design N1870 First Floor: 1,136 square feet
Second Floor: 936 square feet; Total: 2,072 square feet

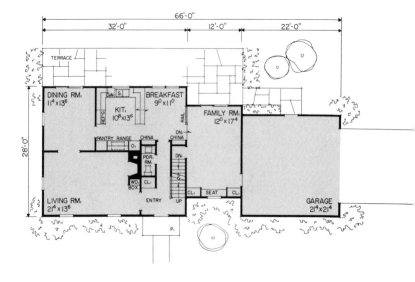

● Besides an enchanting exterior, this home has
formal dining and living rooms, plus informal family and breakfast rooms. Built-ins are located in
both of these informal rooms. U-shaped, the kitch-
en will efficiently service both of the dining areas.
Study the sleeping facilities of the second floor.

Design N2396 First Floor: 1,616 square feet
Second Floor: 993 square feet; Total: 2,609 square feet

D

● Another picturesque facade right
from the pages of our Colonial heritage.
The authentic features are many. Don't
miss the stairs to area over the garage.

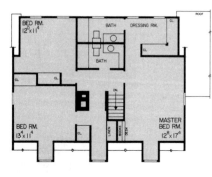

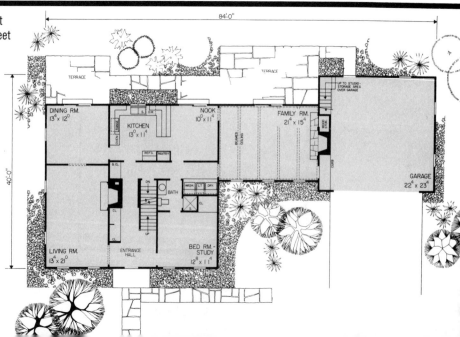

Design N3372

First Floor: 1,259 square feet
Second Floor: 942 square feet
Total: 2,201 square feet

L D

● Charm is the key word for this delightful plan's exterior, but don't miss the great floor plan inside. Formal living and dining rooms flank the entry foyer to the front; a family room and breakfast room with beamed ceilings are to the rear. The kitchen and service areas function well together and are near the garage and service entrance for convenience. Upstairs are the sleeping accommodations: two family bedrooms and a master suite of nice proportion.

Design N3493

First Floor: 2,024 square feet
Second Floor: 717 square feet
Total: 2,741 square feet

L

● As you enter this traditional plan, you are greeted with warmth and livability. The dining room includes a comfortable window seat and connects conveniently to the efficient kitchen with its snack bar to the breakfast area and to the large family room. Beyond the formal living room are two family bedrooms with access to the terrace and a covered patio, a shared full bath and a conveniently located laundry room. The luxurious master suite is located on the second floor for privacy and features a separate study and sitting area, a private deck and an amenity-filled bath.

Width 55'-4"
Depth 57'-8"

Design N3343 First Floor: 1,953 square feet
Second Floor: 895 square feet; Total: 2,848 square feet

L

● Beyond the simple traditional styling of this home's exterior are many of the amenities required by today's lifestyles. Among them: a huge country kitchen with fireplace, an attached greenhouse/dining area, a media room off the two-story foyer, split-bedroom planning, and a second-floor lounge. There are three bedrooms upstairs, which share a full bath.

Quote One™
Cost to build? See page 336 to order complete cost estimate to build this house in your area!

DINING RM
15⁸ X 13⁰
9'-9" CEILING

FAMILY RM
15⁸ X 29²
VOLUME CEILING

KIT
11² X 25⁴

GARAGE
19⁰ X 21⁶

TERRACE

PORCH

MASTER BEDROOM
14¹⁰ X 15⁴

OPEN TO FAMILY ROOM BELOW

BEDRM
12¹⁰ X 8¹⁰

BEDRM
14⁰ X 13⁶

Width 38'-10"
Depth 57'

QUOTE ONE™

Cost to build? See page 336
to order complete cost estimate
to build this house in your area!

Design N3494 First Floor: 1,226 square feet
Second Floor: 1,000 square feet; Total: 2,226 square feet

L

● A bayed breakfast nook adds interest to the interior and exterior of this engaging design—note that the major first-floor living areas occupy the rear of the house. The family room has a number of fine assets including a fireplace, a plant shelf and a volume ceiling. An angled colonnade leads to the dining room with a window bay and passage to the kitchen where a corner sink and a wealth of counter space lend character. All of the upstairs bedrooms find privacy in their staggered locations. The master suite takes advantage of a sloped ceiling, a walk-in closet and an exclusive bath. One of the two family bedrooms features a sloped ceiling; both share a full hall bath with dual lavatories.

Design N3334 First Floor: 2,193 square feet
Second Floor: 831 square feet; Total: 3,024 square feet

L

● A traditional favorite, this home combines classic style with progressive floor planning. Four bedrooms are split — master suite and one bedroom on the first floor, two more bedrooms upstairs. The second-floor lounge overlooks a large, sunken gathering room near the formal dining area. A handy butler's pantry connects the dining room and kitchen.

UPPER GATHERING RM

ATTIC

BEDROOM
10⁰ X 13⁰

BATH

LOUNGE
20⁰ X 11⁶

WHIRLPOOL

UPPER FOYER

ATTIC ACCESS

BEDROOM
12⁴ X 15⁴

ATTIC

UPPER BEDROOM

QUOTE ONE™

Cost to build? See page 336
to order complete cost estimate
to build this house in your area!

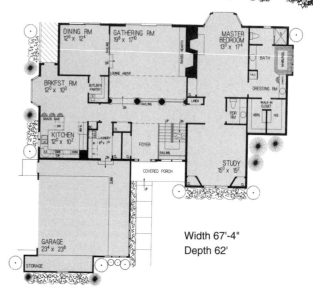

DINING RM
12⁶ X 12⁴

GATHERING RM
19⁸ X 17¹⁰

MASTER BEDROOM
13⁴ X 17⁴

BATH

BRKFST RM
12⁰ X 10⁰

BUTLER'S PANTRY

LOUNGE ABOVE

DRESSING RM

WALK-IN CLOSET

HERS   HIS

PDR RM

SNACK BAR

KITCHEN
12⁰ X 10²

LAUNDRY

FOYER

STUDY
15⁰ X 15²

COVERED PORCH

GARAGE
23⁴ X 23⁸

STORAGE

Width 67'-4"
Depth 62'

Design N3450

First Floor: 1,801 square feet
Second Floor: 1,086 square feet
Total: 2,887 square feet

L D

● A striking facade includes a covered front porch with four columns. To the left of the foyer is a large gathering room with a fireplace and bay window. The adjoining dining room leads to a covered side porch. The kitchen includes a snack bar, pantry, desk, and eating area. The first-floor master suite provides a spacious bath with walk-in closet, whirlpool and shower. Also on the first floor: a study and a garage workshop. Two bedrooms and a lavish guest suite share the second floor.

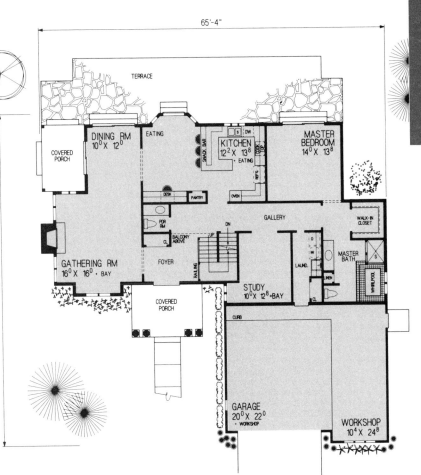

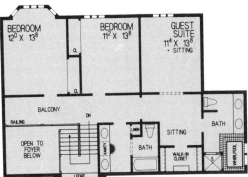

Cost to build? See page 336
to order complete cost estimate
to build this house in your area!

Design N2967

First Floor: 1,877 square feet
Second Floor: 467 square feet
Total: 2,344 square feet

L

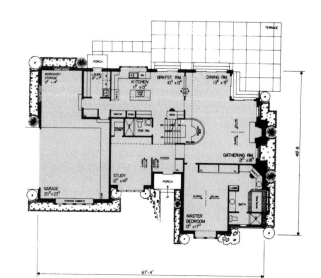

● Special interior amenities abound in this
unique 1½-story Tudor. Living areas include
an open gathering room/dining room area with
fireplace and pass-through to the breakfast
room. Quiet time can be spent in a sloped-ceiling
study. Look for plenty of workspace in the
island kitchen and workshop/storage area.
Sleeping areas are separated for utmost privacy:
an elegant master suite on the first floor, two
bedrooms and a full bath on the second.

Design N3342

First Floor: 1,467 square feet
Second Floor: 715 square feet
Total: 2,182 square feet

L

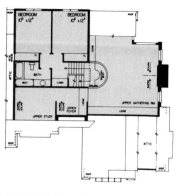

Width 55'-8"
Depth 55'

● Just the right amount of living space is con-
tained in this charming traditional house and
it's arranged in a great floor plan. The split-
bedroom configuration, with two bedrooms (or
optional study) on the first floor and the master
suite on the second floor with its own studio,
assures complete privacy. The living room has
a second-floor balcony overlook and a warming
fireplace. The full-width terrace in back is
counterbalanced nicely by the entry garden
court.

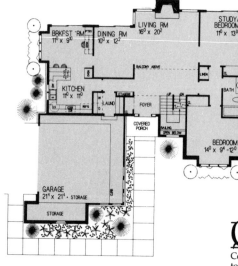

Cost to build? See page 336
to order complete cost estimate
to build this house in your area!

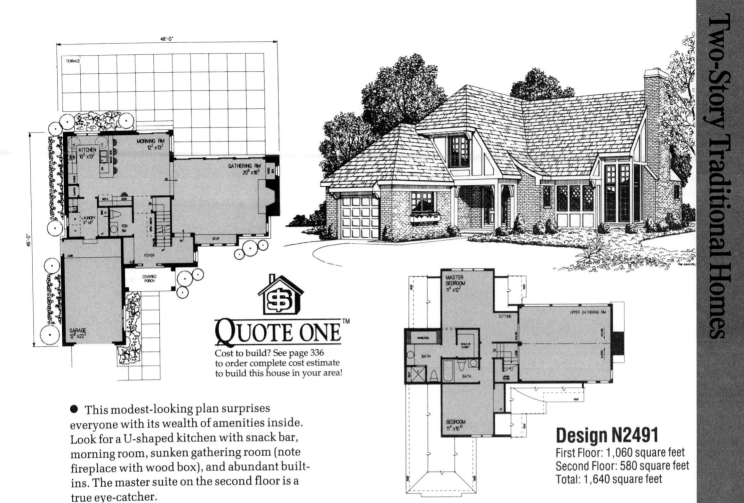

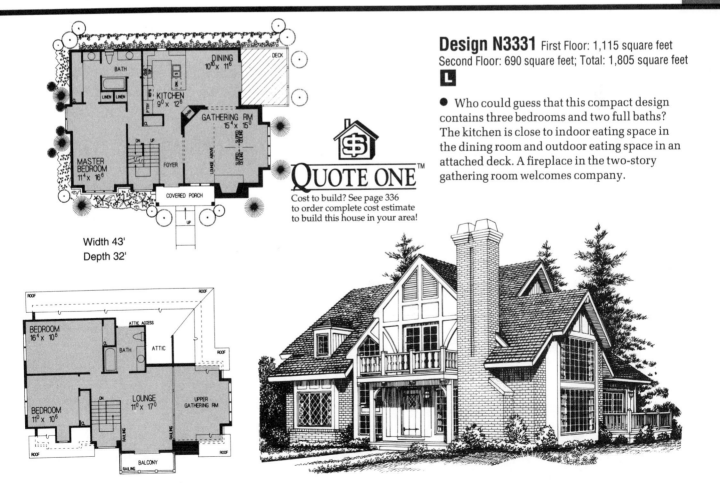

QUOTE ONE™

Cost to build? See page 336
to order complete cost estimate
to build this house in your area!

● This modest-looking plan surprises
everyone with its wealth of amenities inside.
Look for a U-shaped kitchen with snack bar,
morning room, sunken gathering room (note
fireplace with wood box), and abundant built-
ins. The master suite on the second floor is a
true eye-catcher.

Design N2491
First Floor: 1,060 square feet
Second Floor: 580 square feet
Total: 1,640 square feet

Design N3331 First Floor: 1,115 square feet
Second Floor: 690 square feet; Total: 1,805 square feet
L

● Who could guess that this compact design
contains three bedrooms and two full baths?
The kitchen is close to indoor eating space in
the dining room and outdoor eating space in an
attached deck. A fireplace in the two-story
gathering room welcomes company.

Width 43'
Depth 32'

QUOTE ONE™

Cost to build? See page 336
to order complete cost estimate
to build this house in your area!

Design N3302

First Floor: 1,326 square feet
Second Floor: 542 square feet
Total: 1,868 square feet

L

● A cottage fit for a king! Appreciate the highlights: a two-story foyer, a rear living zone (gathering room, terrace, and dining room), pass-through snack bar in kitchen, a two-story master bedroom. Two upstairs bedrooms share a full bath.

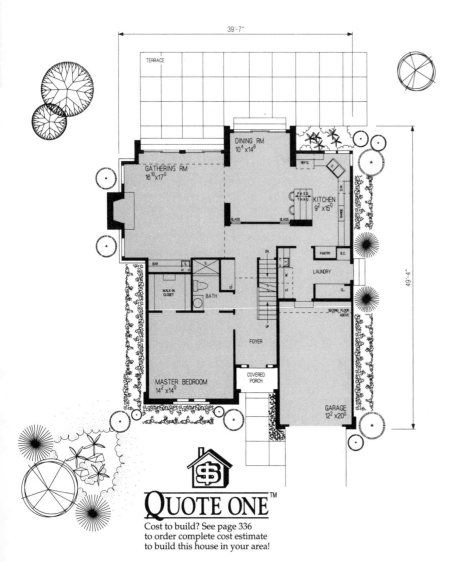

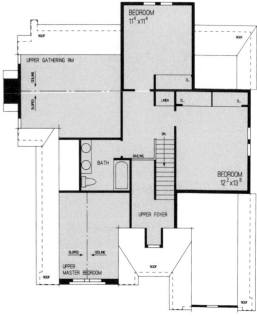

QUOTE ONE™

Cost to build? See page 336 to order complete cost estimate to build this house in your area!

● This Tudor design has many fine features. The exterior is enhanced by front and side bay windows in the family and dining rooms. Along with an outstanding exterior, it also contains a modern and efficient floor plan within its modest proportions. Flanking the entrance foyer is a comfortable living room. The U-shaped kitchen is conveniently located between the dining and breakfast rooms.

Design N2800 First Floor: 999 square feet
Second Floor: 997 square feet; Total: 1,996 square feet

L D

QUOTE ONE™
Cost to build? See page 336 to order complete cost estimate to build this house in your area!

Width 60'
Depth 28'-10"

● The charm of old England has been captured in this outstanding two-story design. Interior livability will efficiently serve the various needs of all family members. The first floor offers both formal and informal areas along with the work centers. Features include: a wet bar in the dining room, the kitchen's snack bar, first-floor laundry and a rear covered porch.

QUOTE ONE™
Cost to build? See page 336 to order complete cost estimate to build this house in your area!

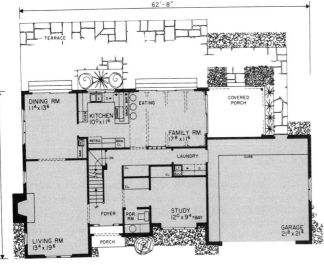

Design N2854 First Floor: 1,261 square feet
Second Floor: 950 square feet; Total: 2,211 square feet

L D

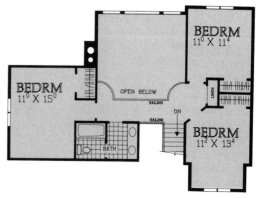

Design N3458

First Floor: 1,617 square feet
Second Floor: 725 square feet
Total: 2,342 square feet

L **D**

● Palladian windows adorn the facade of this excellent, fully functional plan. The foyer introduces the formal zones of the house with a volume living room to the left and a dining room to the right. The kitchen easily services this area and also enjoys a large breakfast room on the other side. A step away, the service entry presents a washer and dryer as well as passage to the two-car, side-load garage. A curb in the garage expands to storage space or becomes a perfect spot for a workbench. For sleeping, four bedrooms each exhibit uniqueness. The master suite—on the ground level—has terrace access, a generous, private bath and a walk-in closet. Upstairs, a balcony overlooking the two-story family room leads to the secondary bedrooms. A compartmented bath with dual lavs adds to convenience.

Width 62'
Depth 41'

OPEN BELOW
RAILING

BEDRM
11⁸ X 10⁰

BEDRM
11⁸ X 11²

LINEN

DN

TUB

BATH

WHIRLPOOL

SHOWER

DN

RAILING

BALCONY RAILING

MASTER BATH

MASTER BEDROOM
16⁴ X 15⁰

OPEN BELOW

QUOTE ONE™

Cost to build? See page 336
to order complete cost estimate
to build this house in your area!

Design N3452

First Floor: 1,545 square feet
Second Floor: 805 square feet
Total: 2,350 square feet

L

● Clean lines and tasteful window treatment
create a pleasing facade. The formal living
room (with vaulted ceiling) and dining room
are open to each other. To the right of the foyer
is a parlor that may serve as a guest bedroom,
with a full bath nearby. The island kitchen easily serves the octagonal breakfast room and the
family room with a vaulted ceiling and a fireplace. A rear patio can be accessed from the
family room or breakfast room. Two stairways
lead to the second floor. Balconies overlook the
living and family rooms. The master bedroom
features a luxurious bath and a walk-in closet,
while two family bedrooms share a full bath.

FAMILY ROOM
20¹⁰ X 13⁴

BRKFST
10⁰ X 10⁰

SNACK BAR

KITCHEN
11⁸ X 15²

SINK

PANTRY

DN

DINING ROOM
11² X 13⁰

UP

DN

UP

REF'G

OVEN

CL.

CL.

D.

W.

L.T.

LAUNDRY

RAILING

PWDR. RM.

SHOWER

LIVING ROOM
15⁰ X 15²
OPEN ABOVE

UP

PARLOR
10⁸ X 9²

GARAGE
19⁰ X 21²

FOYER

PORCH

49'-0"

55'-8"

Width 66'
Depth 68'-4"

Design N3502

First Floor: 2,086 square feet
Second Floor: 2,040 square feet
Total: 4,126 square feet

L D

● This lovely stone farmhouse is reminiscent of
the solid, comfortable homes once so prevalent on
homesteads throughout America. Inside, the formal dining room connects directly to the living
room and indirectly to the island kitchen through
a butler's pantry. The family room and breakfast
room have beam ceilings and are both open to the
kitchen. On the second floor are three bedrooms
and a guest room with a private bath. The master
bedroom has a fireplace and a fine bath with a
separate shower and a whirlpool tub. Two walk-in
closets grace the dressing area. The two secondary
bedrooms share a full bath with double vanity.

Width 43'
Depth 52'-8"

Design N2959

First Floor: 1,003 square feet
Second Floor: 1,056 square feet
Total: 2,059 square feet

● Here the stateliness of Tudor styling is captured in a design suited for a narrow building
site. This two-story has all the livability found
in many much larger homes. The 29-foot living/
dining area stretches across the entire rear of
the house and opens to a large terrace. The efficient U-shaped kitchen is found near the mud
room with adjacent wash room. Enhancing
first-floor livability is the study with huge
walk-in closet. Upstairs are three bedrooms,
two baths and an outdoor balcony.

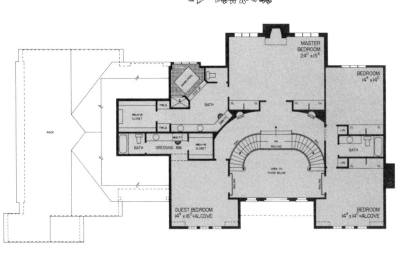

Design N2957

First Floor: 2,557 square feet
Second Floor: 1,939 square feet
Total: 4,496 square feet

L D

● The decorative half timbers and stone wall-cladding on this manor are stately examples of Tudor architecture. A grand double staircase is the highlight of the elegant, two-story foyer that opens to each of the main living areas. The living and gathering rooms are anchored by impressive central fireplaces. Handy built-ins, including a lazy susan and desk, and an island workstation with sink and cooktop, are convenient amenities in the kitchen. The adjacent breakfast room opens to the terrace for a sunny start to the day. Functioning with both the kitchen and the formal dining room is the butler's pantry. It has an abundance of cabinet and cupboard space and even a sink for a wet bar. Accessible from both the gathering and living rooms is the quiet study. If desired this could become a media center, sewing room or home office. The outstanding master suite features a cozy bedroom fireplace, picturesque whirlpool bath, and a convenient walk-in closet. Three additional second-floor bedrooms include a guest suite with dressing room and walk-in closet. Every part of this house speaks elegance, formality and the time-honored values for which Tudor is renowned.

Width 97'-4"
Depth 53'

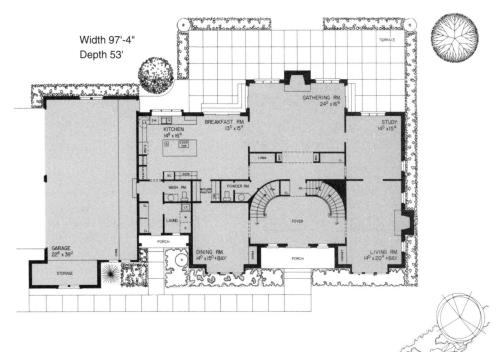

Design N3369

First Floor: 2,740 square feet
Second Floor: 2,257 square feet
Total: 4,997 square feet

L **D**

● Tudor styling at its best graces this home's facade and the floor plan is laid out in a complementary grand manner. There's living space for any activity: a quiet library, a great hall with fireplace for entertaining, cozy family room with adjacent breakfast room, and a laundry room large enough to double as a hobbies center. The second floor holds three family bedrooms each with its own bath and a private master suite with garden whirlpool.

QUOTE ONE™
Cost to build? See page 336
to order complete cost estimate
to build this house in your area!

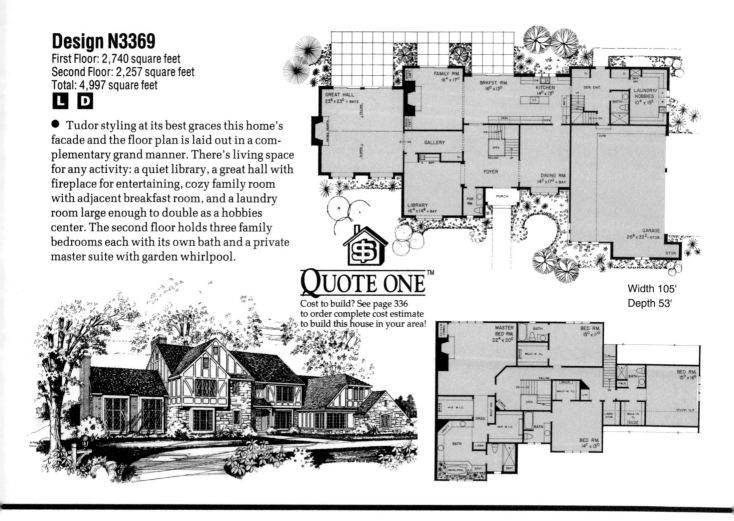

Width 105'
Depth 53'

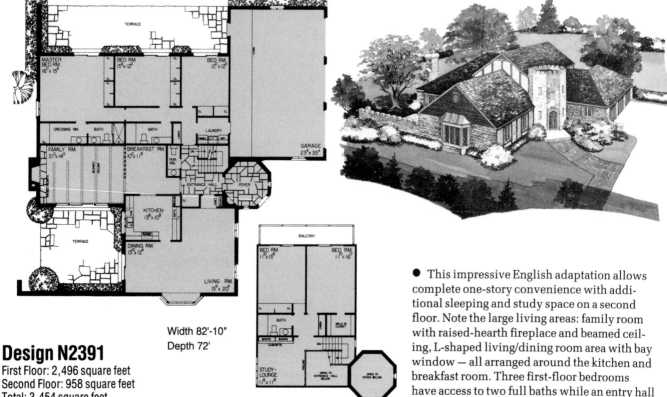

Width 82'-10"
Depth 72'

Design N2391

First Floor: 2,496 square feet
Second Floor: 958 square feet
Total: 3,454 square feet

● This impressive English adaptation allows complete one-story convenience with additional sleeping and study space on a second floor. Note the large living areas: family room with raised-hearth fireplace and beamed ceiling, L-shaped living/dining room area with bay window — all arranged around the kitchen and breakfast room. Three first-floor bedrooms have access to two full baths while an entry hall powder room serves guests nicely. The large three-car garage provides a service entrance to the laundry.

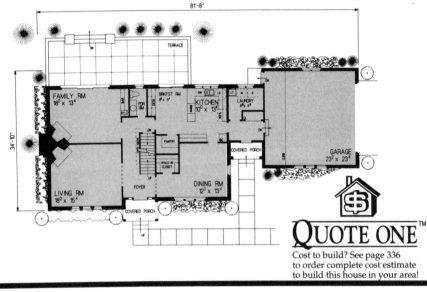

Design N3335

First Floor: 1,504 square feet
Second Floor: 1,348 square feet
Total: 2,852 square feet

L

● This is a first-rate Tudor with three bedrooms upstairs and casual and formal living downstairs. Corner fireplaces in the family room and living room will be favorite gathering spots. From the efficient U-shaped kitchen move to a convenient service area and two-car garage.

QUOTE ONE™

Cost to build? See page 336
to order complete cost estimate
to build this house in your area!

Design N3354

First Floor: 3,556 square feet
Second Floor: 684 square feet
Total: 4,240 square feet

L **D**

● This 1½-story Tudor design makes the most of living spaces on its first floor. There are formal living and dining rooms, a media room with built-ins, and a large country kitchen for informal gatherings. The master suite is enhanced with its own exercise room. Upstairs are two family bedrooms which will serve nicely as guest rooms if needed.

Width 97'-8"
Depth 101'-4"

QUOTE ONE™

Cost to build? See page 336
to order complete cost estimate
to build this house in your area!

75

Design N3381

First Floor: 2,485 square feet
Second Floor: 1,864 square feet
Total: 4,349 square feet

L **D**

● A place for everything and everything in its place. If that's your motto, this is your house. A central foyer allows access to every part of the home. To the left sits the spacious gathering room with fireplace and music alcove. Straight ahead, the open living and dining rooms offer sweeping views of the back yard. The modern kitchen and conversation area are situated to the right of the home. Near the entrance, a library with bay window and built-in bookcase is found. Look for extra amenities throughout the home: curio cabinets in the foyer, stairwell, conversation area and hall; built-in desk; walk-in closet and a second fireplace. Upstairs, the master suite features an enormous walk-in closet and a pampering bath. Another bedroom has a private bath, while the remaining two bedrooms share a bath with dual lavs.

QUOTE ONE™

Cost to build? See page 336 to order complete cost estimate to build this house in your area!

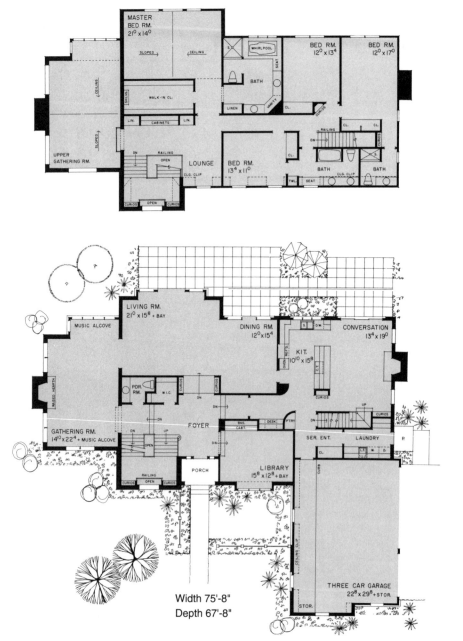

Width 75'-8"
Depth 67'-8"

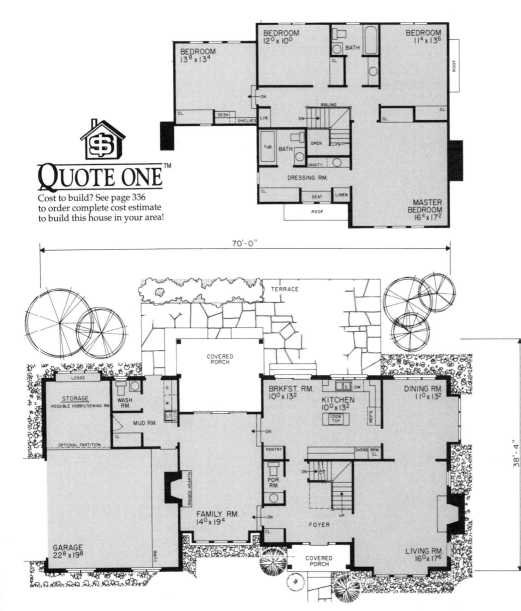

BEDROOM
13⁸ x 13⁴

BEDROOM
12⁰ x 10⁰

BATH

BEDROOM
11⁴ x 13⁶

ROOF

CL.

DN

CL.

DESK

SHELVES

LIN.

DN

RAILING

OPEN

CL.

TUB

BATH

VANITY

DRESSING RM.

CL.

SEAT

LINEN

ROOF

MASTER
BEDROOM
16⁴ x 17²

Quote One

Cost to build? See page 336
to order complete cost estimate
to build this house in your area!

70'-0"

TERRACE

COVERED
PORCH

LEDGE

STORAGE
POSSIBLE HOBBY/SEWING RM.

WASH
RM.

MUD RM.

OPTIONAL PARTITION

CL.

BRKFST. RM.
10⁰ x 13²

KITCHEN
10⁰ x 13²

COOK
TOP

DINING RM.
11⁰ x 13²

REFG.

DN

PANTRY

OVENS

BRM
CL.

PDR.
RM.

DN

RAISED HEARTH

FAMILY RM.
14⁰ x 19⁴

UP

FOYER

CL.

GARAGE
22⁸ x 19⁸

CURB

COVERED
PORCH

LIVING RM.
16⁰ x 17⁶

38'-4"

Design N2855
First Floor: 1,372 square feet
Second Floor: 1,245 square feet
Total: 2,617 square feet

L **D**

● This elegant Tudor
house is perfect for the
family who wants to move-
up in living area, style and
luxury. As you enter this
home you will find a large
living room with a fire-
place on your right. Adjacent, the formal dining
room has easy access to
both the living room and
the kitchen. The kitchen/
breakfast room has an open
plan and access to the rear
terrace. Sunken a few
steps, the spacious family
room is highlighted with a
fireplace and access to the
rear, covered porch. Note
the optional planning of
the garage storage area.
Plan this area according to
the needs of your family.
Upstairs, your family will
enjoy three bedrooms and
a full bath, along with a
spacious master bedroom
suite. Truly a house that
will bring many years of
pleasure to your family.

Design N3558

First Floor: 2,328 square feet
Second Floor: 603 square feet
Total: 2,931 square feet

L **D**

● This home will keep even the most active family from feeling cramped. A broad foyer opens to a living room that measures 24 feet across and features sliding glass doors to a rear terrace and a covered porch. Adjacent to the kitchen is a conversation area with additional access to the covered porch, a snack bar, fireplace and a window bay. A butler's pantry leads to the formal dining room. Placed conveniently on the first floor, the master suite features a roomy bath with a huge walk-in closet and dual vanities. Two large bedrooms are found on the second floor.

QUOTE ONE™

Cost to build? See page 336
to order complete cost estimate
to build this house in your area!

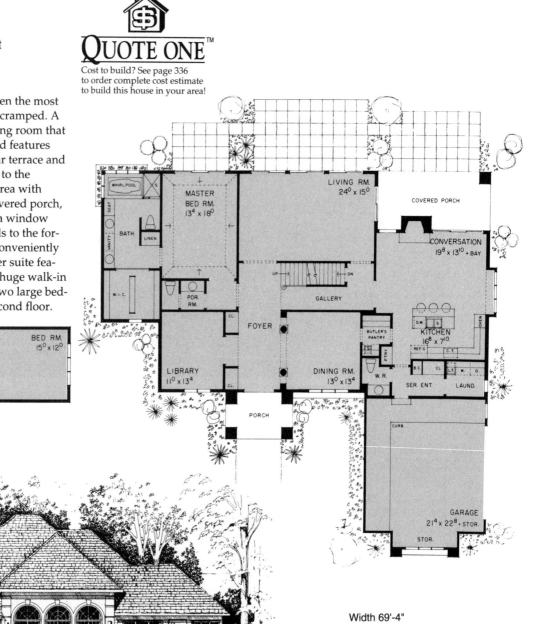

Width 69'-4"
Depth 66'

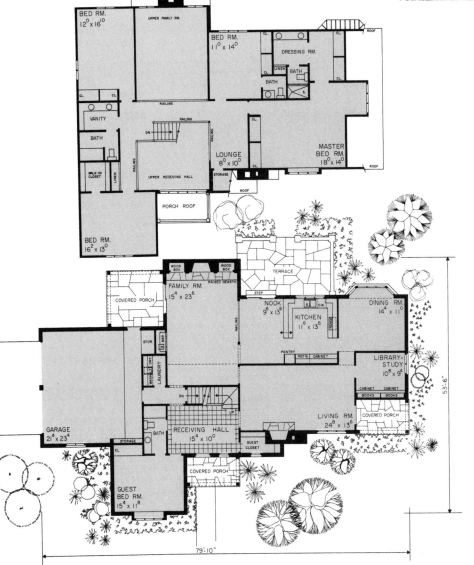

Design N2356

First Floor: 1,969 square feet
Second Floor: 1,702 square feet
Total: 3,671 square feet

L **D**

● Here is truly an exquisite Tudor adaptation. The exterior, with its interesting roof lines, window treatment, stately chimney and its appealing use of brick and stucco, could hardly be more dramatic. Inside, the drama really begins to unfold as one envisions his family's living patterns. The delightfully large receiving hall has a two story ceiling and controls the flexible traffic patterns. The living and dining rooms, with the library nearby, will cater to the formal living pursuits. The guest room offers another haven for the enjoyment of peace and quiet. Observe the adjacent full bath. Just inside the entrance from the garage is the laundry room. For the family's informal activities there are the interactions of the family room - covered porch - nook - kitchen zone. Notice the raised hearth fireplace, the wood boxes, the sliding glass doors, built-in bar and the kitchen pass-thru. Adding to the charm of the family room is its high ceiling. From the second floor hall one can look down and observe the activities below.

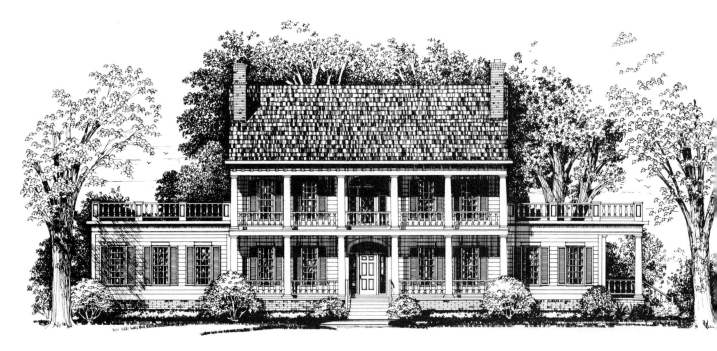

Design N3508

First Floor: 2,098 square feet
Second Floor: 1,735 square feet
Total: 3,833 square feet

L

● Make history with this modern version of Louisiana's "Rosedown House." Like its predecessor—built in the 1800s—the modern adaptation exhibits splendid Southern styling, but with today's most sought-after amenities. The formal zone of the house is introduced by a foyer with a graceful, curving staircase. The dining and living rooms flank the foyer—each is highlighted by a fireplace. Off the living room, a library or music room offers comfort with a corner fireplace and a covered porch. This room also accesses the family room where more informal living takes off with a nearby breakfast room, expansive kitchen and rear covered porch. Upstairs, three bedrooms (one with its own bath) and a study (which may convert to an additional bedroom, if desired) include a gracious master suite. It opens with double doors and furthers this romantic feeling with a fireplace. A large dressing room with walk-in closets leads to the luxury bath. Two covered balconies complete the superb livability found in this plan.

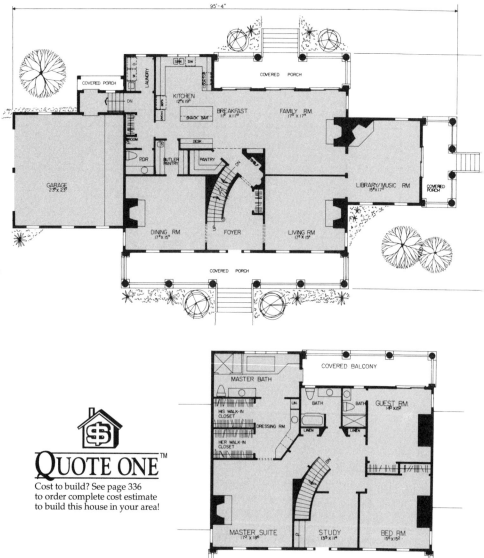

QUOTE ONE™

Cost to build? See page 336
to order complete cost estimate
to build this house in your area!

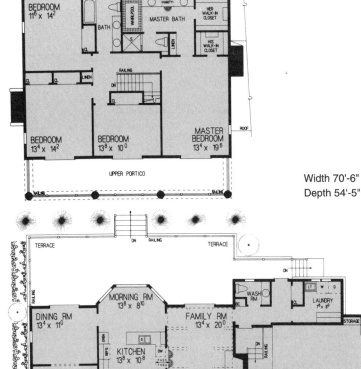

Width 70'-6"
Depth 54'-5"

BEDROOM
11⁶ x 14⁴

BATH

MASTER BATH

HER WALK-IN CLOSET

WHIRL POOL

VANITY

METAL ROOF

ROOF

HIS WALK-IN CLOSET

LINEN

S

RAILING

DN

LINEN

CL

CL

CL

BEDROOM
13⁴ x 14²

BEDROOM
13⁸ x 10⁰

MASTER BEDROOM
13⁴ x 19⁶

ROOF

UPPER PORTICO

RAILING

TERRACE

DN

RAILING

TERRACE

DN

RAILING

DINING RM
13⁴ x 11⁰

MORNING RM
13⁸ x 8¹⁰

FAMILY RM
13⁴ x 20⁰

WASH RM

LT   W   D

LAUNDRY
7⁴ x 8²

CL

OVEN

REF'G

DW

S

COOK TOP

P'TRY

DN

STORAGE

DN

KITCHEN
13⁸ x 10⁸

THRU

BOOKS   BOOKS   BOOKS

CLOS

GARAGE
25⁸ x 21⁸

CURVES

FOYER

LIVING RM
13⁴ x 19⁸

CURIO

PDR RM

STUDY
10⁰ x 10⁸

PORTICO

RAILING

RAILING

UP

Design N3333

First Floor: 1,584 square feet
Second Floor: 1,344 square feet
Total: 2,928 square feet

L

● This Southern Colonial adaptation boasts an up-to-date floor plan which caters to the needs of today's families. The entrance hall is flanked by formal and informal living areas: to the left a spacious living room and connecting dining room, to the right a cozy study and family room. A large kitchen with bay-windowed morning room is convenient to both the dining and family rooms. The upstairs sleeping area includes four bedrooms.

QUOTE ONE™
Cost to build? See page 336
to order complete cost estimate
to build this house in your area!

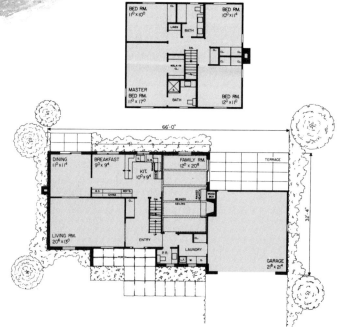

Design N1285

First Floor: 1,202 square feet
Second Floor: 896 square feet
Total: 2,098 square feet

L **D**

● Such a pretty traditional farmhouse
design — and with so much to offer in the way
of floor planning. From the front entry, turn left
into a good-sized living room with attached
dining room. A right turn leads to a well-placed
powder room and laundry or farther back to the
beamed-ceiling family room (note the fireplace
with wood box here). The kitchen and adjacent
breakfast room will make mealtimes a pleasure.
Upstairs, four bedrooms share space with two
baths.

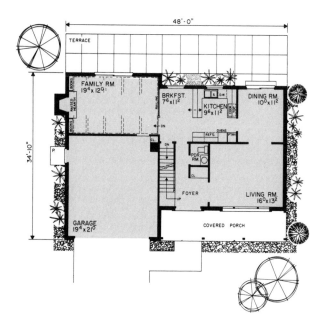

OPTIONAL 3-BEDROOM PLAN

Design N1956

First Floor: 990 square feet
Second Floor: 728 square feet
Total: 1,718 square feet

D

● The blueprints for this home
include details for both the three-
bedroom and the four-bedroom
options. The first-floor livability
does not change.

QUOTE ONE™

Cost to build? See page 336
to order complete cost estimate
to build this house in your area!

Design N2540
First Floor: 1,306 square feet
Second Floor: 1,360 square feet; Total: 2,666 square feet

L **D**

● This efficient Colonial abounds in features. A spacious entry flanked by living areas. A kitchen flanked by eating areas. Upstairs, four bedrooms including a sitting room in the master suite.

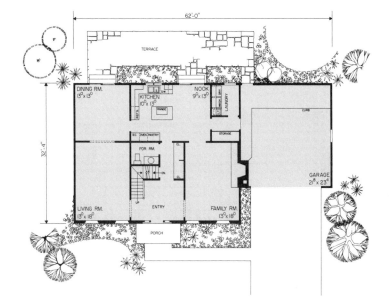

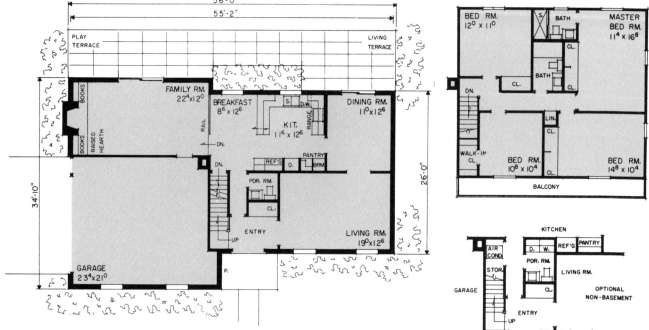

Design N1371 First Floor: 1,172 square feet; Second Floor: 896 square feet; Total: 2,068 square feet

L **D**

● If you like traditional charm and the tried and true living patterns of the conventional two-story idea, you'll not go wrong in selecting this design as your next home. In fact, when you order blueprints for N1371 you'll receive details for building all three optional elevations. So, you needn't decide which front exterior is your favorite right now. Any one of these will surely add a touch of class to your new neighborhood.

QUOTE ONE™

Cost to build? See page 336
to order complete cost estimate
to build this house in your area!

Floor plan labels (first floor): PLAY TERRACE, DINING TERRACE, FAMILY RM. 19⁴ x 12⁰, BEAMED CEILING, BOOKS, RAILING, BREAKFAST 8⁰ x 11, SINK, D.W., DINING RM. 11⁰ x 11⁰, KIT. 10⁰ x 11⁰, RANGE, GARAGE 19⁴ x 21⁰, DN., CL., PANTRY, REF'G, OVEN, PDR. RM., CL., ENTRY up, LIVING RM. 18⁰ x 13⁰, PORCH

Dimensions: 50'-0", 20'-8", 29'-4", 26'-0", 34'-10"

Floor plan labels (second floor): BED RM. 10⁴ x 9⁴, SHOWER, BATH, MASTER BED RM. 11⁰ x 15⁰, CL., CL., BATH, CL., DN., CL., LIN., CL., BED RM. 9⁴ x 10⁰, CL., BED RM. 14⁴ x 10⁰

Design N1957 First Floor: 1,042 square feet; Second Floor: 780 square feet; Total: 1,822 square feet

L **D**

● When you order your blueprints for this design you will receive details for the construction of each of the three charming exteriors pictured above. Whichever the exterior you finally decide to build, the floor plan will be essentially the same except the location of the windows. This will be a fine home for the growing family. It will serve well for many years. There are four bedrooms and two full baths (one with a stall shower) upstairs.

Design N3444

First Floor: 1,453 square feet
Second Floor: 520 square feet
Total: 1,973 square feet

L **D**

QUOTE ONE™

Cost to build? See page 336
to order complete cost estimate
to build this house in your area!

● This compact plan offers full-scale livability on two floors. The first floor begins with an elegant living room—a bay window here allows for an infiltration of natural light. The dining room remains open to this room and will delight with its spaciousness. The kitchen is just beyond and extends room enough for a dinette set. Comfortable gatherings are the name of the game in the family room which enjoys shared space with the kitchen area. A warming fireplace gains attention here as do a pair of graceful windows that flank it. Also on the first floor, the master bedroom expands into a spacious and luxurious bathroom. A garden tub set below a window is sure to satisfy as is a large walk-in closet. For family and guests, two upstairs bedrooms are situated around a Hollywood bath.

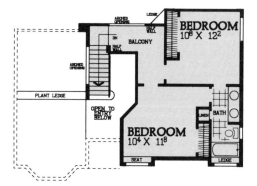

Design N3484

First Floor: 1,139 square feet
Second Floor: 948 square feet
Total: 2,087 square feet

L **D**

QUOTE ONE™

Cost to build? See page 336
to order complete cost estimate
to build this house in your area!

● An angled entry offers a new perspective on the formal areas of this house: living room on the left; dining room on the right. Both rooms exchange views through a columned hallway; a potshelf and a niche add custom touches to this already attention-getting arrangement. At the back of the first floor, a family room with built-in bookshelves and an entertainment-center niche opens to the kitchen and nook where both cooking and dining become a delight. The second floor provides interest with its balcony open to the living and family rooms. Three bedrooms include a master suite with a sloped ceiling, separate closets and a private bath. The two-car garage has direct access to the house.

Design N3479

First Floor: 914 square feet
Second Floor: 1,050 square feet
Total: 1,964 square feet

● This four-bedroom family home has a distinctive interior design. The gathering room features two bay windows, a sloped ceiling, a fireplace and a built-in entertainment center. A low wall separates the gathering room from the formal dining area. A rear terrace can be accessed from sliding glass doors here. Informal meals may take place in the bay-windowed breakfast nook. The kitchen includes a snack bar, a built-in planning desk and a walk-in pantry. The sleeping area is located quietly on the second floor. The master bedroom is highlighted by a sloped ceiling and includes two closets and a deluxe master bath with dual vanities and a whirlpool tub.

Cost to build? See page 336
to order complete cost estimate
to build this house in your area!

Design N3445

First Floor: 1,147 square feet
Second Floor: 1,116 square feet
Total: 2,263 square feet

L **D**

QUOTE ONE™

Cost to build? See page 336
to order complete cost estimate
to build this house in your area!

Width 42'-10"
Depth 55'-2"

● A two-story foyer opens to a formal living room with a front-facing bay window. Traffic flows easily to the adjacent dining room. The U-shaped kitchen opens to a sunny breakfast nook. It also enjoys the convenience of two Lazy Susans. Informal activities take place in the spacious family room with fireplace. A powder room and utility area are conveniently located on the first floor. On the second floor, the master bedroom features a sloped ceiling and a bath with tub and shower. Three family bedrooms share a full bath with dual vanities.

Design N3495

First Floor: 1,457 square feet
Second Floor: 1,288 square feet
Total: 2,745 square feet

L **D**

● The very best in modern design comes into play with this extraordinary two-story home. Columns and half walls define the formal living and dining rooms—a curved niche adds appeal to the latter. The family room contains a sloped ceiling and angled corner fireplace. In the kitchen is an abundance of counter and storage space. Two full bathrooms grace the upstairs: one in the master suite and one that serves three secondary bedrooms.

QUOTE ONE™

Cost to build? See page 336
to order complete cost estimate
to build this house in your area!

Width 42'
Depth 63'-4"

Design N3568

First Floor: 1,882 square feet
Second Floor: 1,763 square feet
Total: 3,645 square feet

L **D**

● Traditional styling takes on added dimension in this
stately two-story home. An angled wing encloses the
sunken living room and a roomy study. The dining
room introduces the other half of the house. Here, the
resident gourmet will enjoy the kitchen with its ample
counter space and island cooktop. The breakfast room
remains open to the kitchen and, through a pair of
columns, the family room. The second floor offers excellent sleeping quarters with four bedrooms. The master
suite features a balcony and a fireplace. A huge walk-in
closet and a lavish bath finish off the room. Three additional bedrooms include one with a private bath.

QUOTE ONE™

Cost to build? See page 336
to order complete cost estimate
to build this house in your area!

Width 94'-2"
Depth 57'

QUOTE ONE™

Cost to build? See page 336
to order complete cost estimate
to build this house in your area!

Design N2927

First Floor: 1,425 square feet
Second Floor: 704 square feet
Total: 2,129 square feet

D

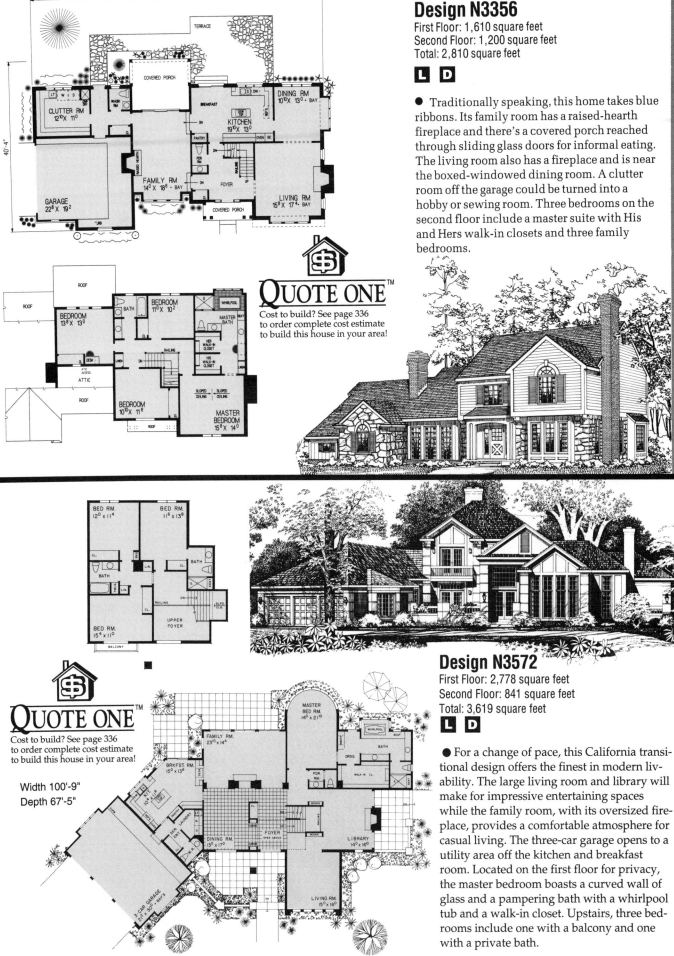

Design N3356
First Floor: 1,610 square feet
Second Floor: 1,200 square feet
Total: 2,810 square feet

L **D**

● Traditionally speaking, this home takes blue ribbons. Its family room has a raised-hearth fireplace and there's a covered porch reached through sliding glass doors for informal eating. The living room also has a fireplace and is near the boxed-windowed dining room. A clutter room off the garage could be turned into a hobby or sewing room. Three bedrooms on the second floor include a master suite with His and Hers walk-in closets and three family bedrooms.

QUOTE ONE™
Cost to build? See page 336 to order complete cost estimate to build this house in your area!

Width 100'-9"
Depth 67'-5"

Design N3572
First Floor: 2,778 square feet
Second Floor: 841 square feet
Total: 3,619 square feet

L **D**

● For a change of pace, this California transitional design offers the finest in modern livability. The large living room and library will make for impressive entertaining spaces while the family room, with its oversized fireplace, provides a comfortable atmosphere for casual living. The three-car garage opens to a utility area off the kitchen and breakfast room. Located on the first floor for privacy, the master bedroom boasts a curved wall of glass and a pampering bath with a whirlpool tub and a walk-in closet. Upstairs, three bedrooms include one with a balcony and one with a private bath.

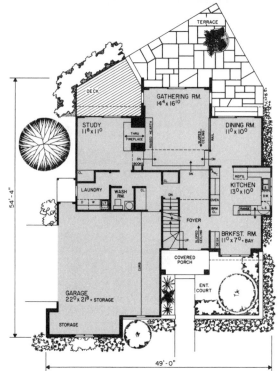

Design N2826 First Floor: 1,112 square feet
Second Floor: 881 square feet; Total: 1,993 square feet

D

ALTERNATE KITCHEN / DINING RM. /
BREAKFAST RM. FLOOR PLAN

● This is an outstanding example of the type of informal, traditional-style architecture that has captured the modern imagination. The interior plan houses all of the features that people want most - a spacious gathering room, formal and informal dining areas, efficient, U-shaped kitchen, master bedroom, two children's bedrooms, second floor lounge, entrance court and rear terrace and deck. Study all areas of this plan carefully.

QUOTE ONE™
Cost to build? See page 336 to order complete cost estimate to build this house in your area!

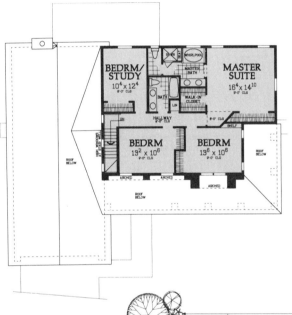

Design N3326

First Floor: 1,595 square feet
Second Floor: 1,112 square feet
Total: 2,707 square feet

● This four-bedroom family plan makes the grade with defining exterior details that create a Southwestern charmer. The floor plan opens with a foyer that introduces a grand living room. In the U-shaped kitchen, a central island facilitates cooking ease. A pass-through snack bar connects the kitchen and breakfast room. Nearby, the family room delights with its warming hearth and access to an entertainment patio. A large utility area sits near the garage. Upstairs, the master bedroom suite includes two closets and a private bath with a garden tub and dual lavatories.

QUOTE ONE™

Cost to build? See page 336 to order complete cost estimate to build this house in your area!

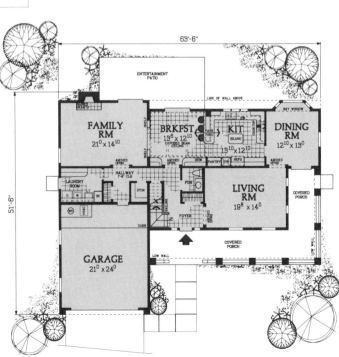

Design N3476

First Floor: 1,170 square feet
Second Floor: 838 square feet
Total: 2,008 square feet

L

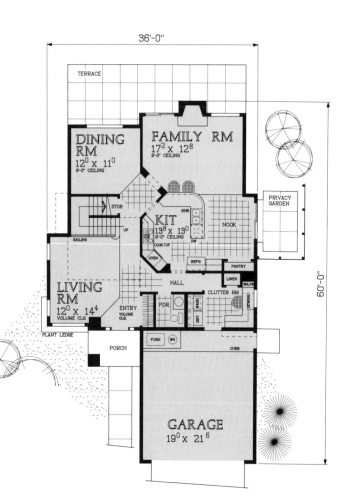

Quote One™

Cost to build? See page 336
to order complete cost estimate
to build this house in your area!

● A vaulted ceiling in the living room and a centered fire-place in the family room set the stage for the formal and casual areas of this home. A hub kitchen boasts a round counter for serving both the family room and the breakfast area; a pantry in this area offers plenty of storage space. The utility room, separating the main-floor living areas from the garage, acquires both light and views from a side window. Three bedrooms—all with ample closet space, including a walk-in closet in the master suite—define the second-floor sleeping quarters. A full hall bath with a double-bowl vanity services two of the bedrooms—the master bedroom utilizes its own bath.

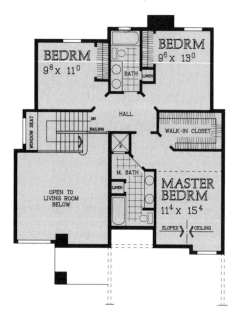

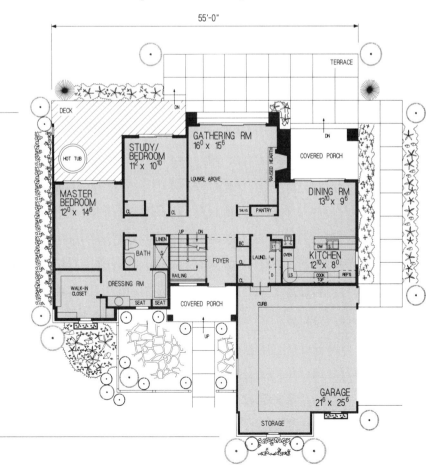

QUOTE ONE™

Cost to build? See page 336
to order complete cost estimate
to build this house in your area!

Design N3330

First Floor: 1,394 square feet
Second Floor: 320 square feet
Total: 1,714 square feet

● Outdoor living and open floor planning
are highlights of this moderately sized plan.
Amenities include a private hot tub on a
wooden deck that is accessible via sliding
glass doors in both bedrooms, and a two-
story gathering room. An optional second-
floor plan allows for a full 503 square feet
of space with a balcony.

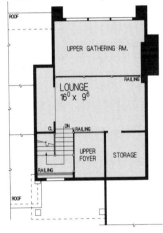

UPPER GATHERING RM.

LOUNGE
16⁰ x 9⁶

UPPER FOYER

STORAGE

RAILING   BALCONY

MASTER BEDROOM
16⁰ x 19⁰

UPPER FOYER

BATH

OPTIONAL FLOOR PLAN

Design N3471

First Floor: 3,166 square feet
Second Floor: 950 square feet
Guest Living Area: 680 square feet
Total: 4,796 square feet

L

● Western farmhouse-style living is captured in this handsome design. The central entrance leads into a cozy parlor—half walls provide a view of the grand dining room. Entertaining's a cinch with the dining room's built-in china alcove, service counter and fireplace. The country kitchen, with a large island cooktop, overlooks the gathering room with its full wall of glass. The master bedroom will satisfy even the most discerning tastes. It boasts a raised hearth, porch access and a bath with a walk-in closet, separate vanities and a whirlpool. You may want to use one of the additional first-floor bedrooms as a study, the other as a guest room. To round out the first floor, you'll also find a clutter room with a pantry, freezer space and access to storage space. Two family bedrooms and attic storage make up the second floor. Note, too, the separate garage and guest house which make this such a winning design.

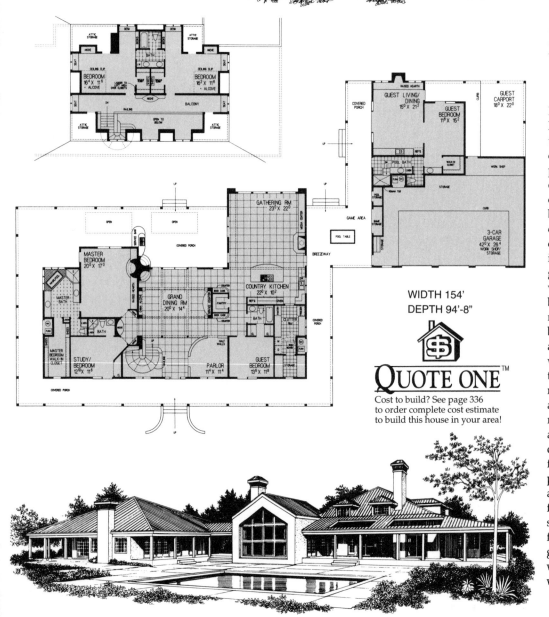

WIDTH 154'
DEPTH 94'-8"

Quote One™

Cost to build? See page 336 to order complete cost estimate to build this house in your area!

Design N3404

First Floor: 3,358 square feet
Second Floor: 868 square feet
Total: 4,226 square feet

L

● Farmhouse design does a double take in this unusual and elegant rendition. Notice that most of the living takes place on the first floor: formal living room and dining room, gigantic family room with enormous firepit and porch access, guest bedroom or den and master bedroom suite. Upstairs there are two smaller bedrooms and a dramatic balcony overlook to the family room below.

QUOTE ONE™

Cost to build? See page 336 to order complete cost estimate to build this house in your area!

Width 112'
Depth 74'

Design N3352

First Floor: 1,148 square feet
Second Floor: 1,010 square feet
Total: 2,158 square feet

L **D**

UPPER GATHERING RM

MASTER BEDROOM
14⁰ x 18⁰

BEDROOM
11⁰ x 10⁸

RAILING

LOUNGE

CL

ROOF

LINEN

HIS WALK-IN CLOSET

DN

BATH

CL

M. BATH

WHIRLPOOL

S

HER WALK-IN CLOSET

UPPER FOYER

VANITY

BEDROOM
11⁰ x 10⁸

UPPER GARAGE

ROOF

TERRACE

DECK

GATHERING RM
14⁰ x 17⁰

STUDY
11⁸ x 11⁰

DINING RM
11⁴ x 10⁰

LOUNGE ABOVE

CL

P.

LAUNDRY

D W

WASH RM

CL

DN

PANTRY

REF'G

KITCHEN
13⁰ x 10⁰

OVENS

BC

COOK TOP

DW

LS

GARAGE
22⁰ x 21⁸

FOYER

UP

BRKFST
11⁰ x 9⁰

PORCH

CURB

STORAGE

54'- 8"

47'- 0"

$ QUOTE ONE™

Cost to build? See page 336
to order complete cost estimate
to build this house in your area!

● Rustic looking with a contemporary feel —
that's the beauty of this design. Interior rooms
include an open gathering room with through-
fireplace to cozy study, formal dining room
near the kitchen/breakfast room combination,
and three bedrooms on the upper level. Note
the balcony lounge overlooking the gathering
room and well-appointed master bath.

Design N3563

First Floor: 1,023 square feet
Second Floor: 866 square feet
Total: 1,889 square feet

● Practical to build, this wonderful transitional plan combines the best of contemporary and traditional styling. Its stucco exterior is enhanced by arched windows and a recessed arched entry plus a lovely balcony off the second-floor master bedroom. A walled entry court extends the living room to the outside. The double front doors open to a foyer with a hall closet and a powder room. The service entrance is just to the right and accesses the two-car garage. The large living room adjoins directly to the dining room. The family room is set off behind the garage and features a sloped ceiling and a fireplace. Sleeping quarters consist of two secondary bedrooms with a shared bath and a generous master suite with a well-appointed bath.

QUOTE ONE™

Cost to build? See page 336 to order complete cost estimate to build this house in your area!

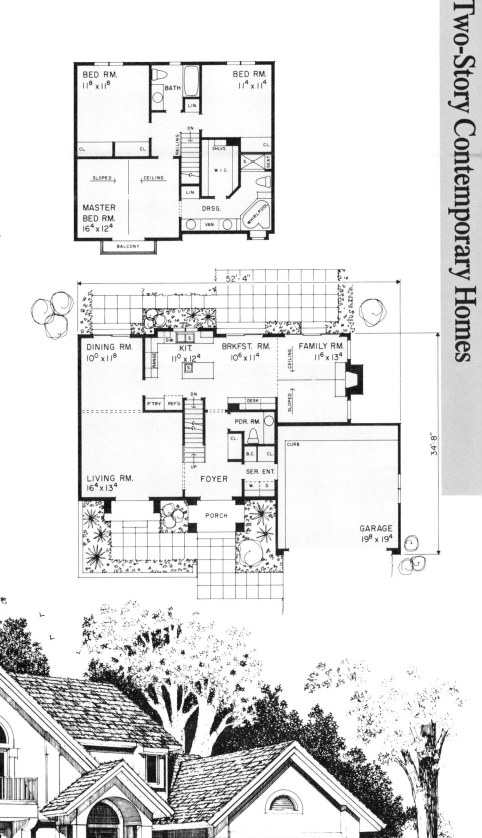

Design N2905

First Floor: 1,342 square feet
Second Floor: 619 square feet
Total: 1,961 square feet

L **D**

QUOTE ONE™

Cost to build? See page 336
to order complete cost estimate
to build this house in your area!

● All of the livability in this plan is in the back! Each first-floor room, except the kitchen, has access to the rear terrace via sliding glass doors — a great way to capture an excellent view. This plan is also ideal for a narrow lot because its width is less than 50 feet. Two bedrooms and a lounge, overlooking the gathering room, are on the second floor.

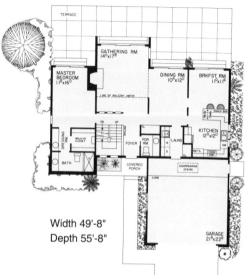

Width 49'-8"
Depth 55'-8"

Design N2562

First Floor: 2,459 square feet
Second Floor: 1,107 square feet
Lower Level: 851 square feet
Total: 4,417 square feet

D

● Here is an exciting contemporary design for the large, active family. It can function as either a four- or five-bedroom home. As a four-bedroom home the parents will enjoy a wonderful suite with study and exceptional bath facilities. Note stall shower, plus sunken tub. The upstairs features the children's bedrooms and a spacious balcony lounge which looks down to the floor below. The sunken gathering room has a sloped, beamed ceiling, dramatic raised-hearth fireplace and direct access to the rear terrace.

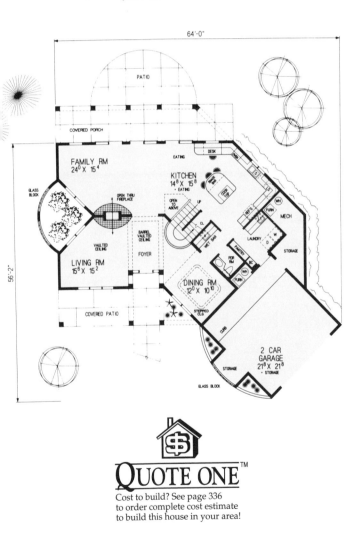

Design N3409

First Floor: 1,481 square feet
Second Floor: 1,287 square feet
Total: 2,768 square feet

L

● Glass block walls and a foyer with barrel vaulted ceiling create an interesting exterior. Covered porches to the front and rear provide for excellent indoor/outdoor living relationships. Inside, a large planter and through-fireplace enhance the living room and family room. The dining room has a stepped ceiling. A desk, eating area and snack bar are special features in the kitchen. The master suite features a large walk-in closet, bath with double bowl vanity and separate tub and shower, and a private deck. Three additional bedrooms share a full bath.

QUOTE ONE™

Cost to build? See page 336
to order complete cost estimate
to build this house in your area!

Design N3338

First Floor: 1,314 square feet
Second Floor: 970 square feet
Total: 2,284 square feet

L

QUOTE ONE™

Cost to build? See page 336
to order complete cost estimate
to build this house in your area!

● For new parents or empty-nesters, this plan's master suite has an attached nursery or sitting room. Downstairs there's a formal living room and dining room and the more casual family room with snack-bar eating area. A front study is near the powder room.

Design N3347 First Floor: 1,915 square feet
Second Floor: 759 square feet; Total: 2,674 square feet

L

● Open living is the key to the abundant livability of this design. The gigantic gathering room/dining room area shares a through-fireplace with a unique sunken conversation area. An L-shaped kitchen has a pass-through snack bar to the breakfast room. On the second floor, two bedrooms are separated by a lounge with a balcony overlook.

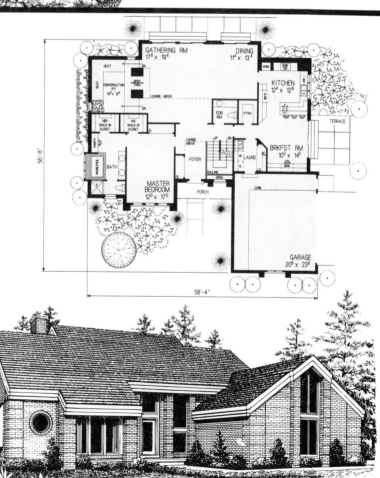

QUOTE ONE™

Cost to build? See page 336
to order complete cost estimate
to build this house in your area!

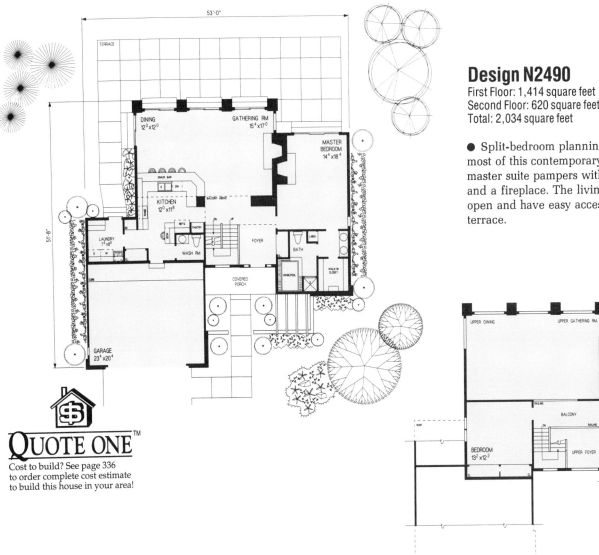

Design N2490

First Floor: 1,414 square feet
Second Floor: 620 square feet
Total: 2,034 square feet

● Split-bedroom planning makes the most of this contemporary plan. The master suite pampers with a lavish bath and a fireplace. The living areas are open and have easy access to the rear terrace.

QUOTE ONE™

Cost to build? See page 336 to order complete cost estimate to build this house in your area!

TERRACE

DECK
SKYLITE
HOT TUB

STUDY/
BED RM.
11⁰ x 11⁰

GREAT RM.
16⁰ x 14²

LOUNGE ABOVE

COVERED
PORCH

MASTER
BED RM.
12⁰ x 14⁶

CL.

LINEN

RAISED HEARTH

GL. SHLVS.
PANTRY

DINING
14⁰ x 9⁴

BATH

LINEN
CL.

UP DN

FOYER

BRM.
CL.

LAUND.

BATH

OVENS

DW

KITCHEN
13⁰ x 8⁰

RANGE

REF'G

DRESSING RM.

SHLVS.

WALK-IN
CLOSET

VANITY

SEAT

TUB

PORCH
OPEN ABOVE

CL.

ROOF LINE

CURB

GARAGE
21⁴ x 21⁸

54'-8"

52'-0"

UPPER GREAT RM.

CL.

LOUNGE / HOBBIES
16⁰ x 9²

CL.

SKYLITE

DN

RAILING

UPPER
FOYER

STOR./
BATH

RAILING

Design N2822

First Floor: 1,363 square feet
Second Floor: 351 square feet
Total: 1,714 square feet

● Here is a truly unique house whose interior was designed with the current decade's economies, lifestyles and demographics in mind. While functioning as a one-story home, the second floor provides an extra measure of livability when required. In addition, this two-story section adds to the dramatic appeal of both the exterior and the interior. Within only 1,363 square feet, this contemporary delivers refreshing and outstanding living patterns for those who are buying their first home, those who have raised their family and are looking for a smaller home and those in search of a retirement home.

QUOTE ONE™

Cost to build? See page 336 to order complete cost estimate to build this house in your area!

BALCONY

LOUNGE / GUEST RM. /
GRANDCHILDREN'S RM.
16⁰ x 19²

CL.

CL.

DN

RAILING

UPPER
FOYER

BATH

RAILING

ALTERNATE SECOND FLOOR

Design N3562

First Floor: 1,182 square feet
Second Floor: 927 square feet
Total: 2,109 square feet

L **D**

● Interesting detailing marks the exterior of this home as a beauty. Its interior makes it a livable option for any family. Entry occurs through double doors to the left side of the plan. A powder room with curved wall is handy to the entry. Living areas of the home are open and well-planned. The formal living room shares a through fireplace with the large family room. The dining room is adjoining and has a pass-through counter to the L-shaped kitchen. Special details on this floor include a wealth of sliding glass doors to the rear terrace and built-ins throughout. Upstairs are three bedrooms with two full baths.

QUOTE ONE™

Cost to build? See page 336
to order complete cost estimate
to build this house in your area!

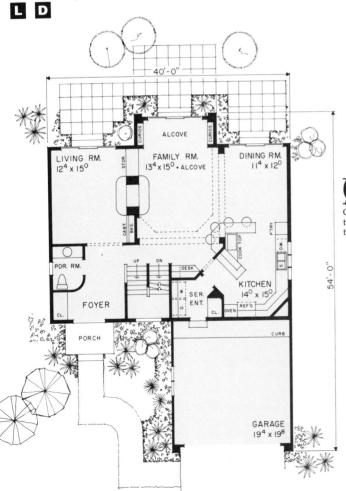

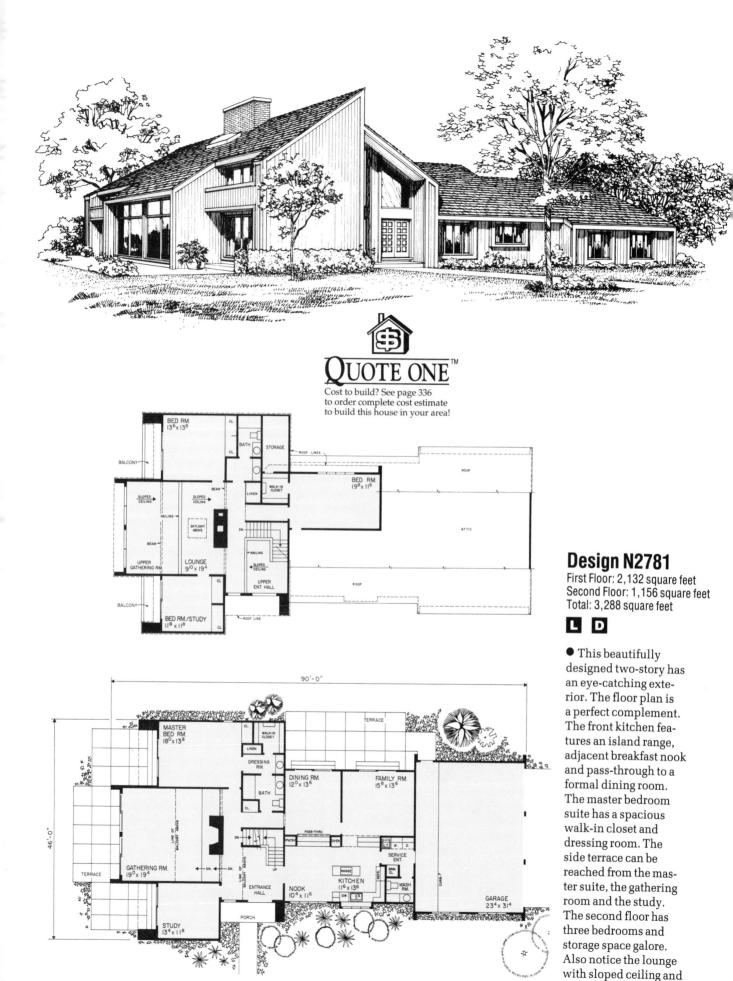

QUOTE ONE™

Cost to build? See page 336
to order complete cost estimate
to build this house in your area!

BED RM.
13⁶ x 13⁸

CL.

BATH

STORAGE

ROOF LINES

CL.

ROOF

BALCONY

SLOPED CEILING

SLOPED CEILING

BEAM

RAILING

SKYLIGHT ABOVE

WALK-IN CLOSET

LINEN

BED RM.
19⁸ x 11⁶

ATTIC

BEAM

LOUNGE
9¹⁰ x 19⁴

DN.

RAILING

UPPER GATHERING RM.

SLOPED CEILING

UP

BALCONY

CL.

UPPER ENT. HALL

ROOF

BED RM./STUDY
11⁸ x 11⁸

CL.

ROOF LINE

Design N2781

First Floor: 2,132 square feet
Second Floor: 1,156 square feet
Total: 3,288 square feet

L **D**

● This beautifully
designed two-story has
an eye-catching exte-
rior. The floor plan is
a perfect complement.
The front kitchen fea-
tures an island range,
adjacent breakfast nook
and pass-through to a
formal dining room.
The master bedroom
suite has a spacious
walk-in closet and
dressing room. The
side terrace can be
reached from the mas-
ter suite, the gathering
room and the study.
The second floor has
three bedrooms and
storage space galore.
Also notice the lounge
with sloped ceiling and
skylight.

90'-0"

MASTER BED RM.
18⁰ x 13⁸

CL.

WALK-IN CLOSET

LINEN

TERRACE

DRESSING RM.

DINING RM.
12⁰ x 13⁶

FAMILY RM.
15⁸ x 13⁶

BATH

46'-0"

CL.

LINE OF BALCONY ABOVE

DN.

PASS-THRU

PNTRY.

OVEN

W. D.

SERVICE ENT.

TERRACE

GATHERING RM.
19⁰ x 19⁴

DN.

DN.

UP

LINE OF BALCONY ABOVE

RANGE

BRM. CL.

KITCHEN
11⁶ x 13⁶

WASH RM.

ENTRANCE HALL

NOOK
10⁴ x 11⁶

DW

REF.

GARAGE
23⁴ x 31⁴

STUDY
13⁴ x 11⁸

PORCH

Width 66'-7"
Depth 54'-10"

Design N3439

First Floor: 1,424 square feet
Second Floor: 995 square feet
Total: 2,419 square feet

L

QUOTE ONE™

Cost to build? See page 336
to order complete cost estimate
to build this house in your area!

● Featuring a facade of wood and window glass, this home presents a striking first impression. Its floor plan is equally as splendid. Formal living and dining areas flank the entry foyer—both are sunken two steps. Also sunken from the foyer is the family room with its attached breakfast nook. A fireplace in this area sits next to a built-in audiovisual center. A nearby study with an adjacent full bath doubles as a guest room. Upstairs are three bedrooms including a master suite with a whirlpool spa and a walk-in closet. Plant shelves adorn the entire floor plan.

Design N3473

First Floor: 1,675 square feet
Second Floor: 1,058 square feet
Total: 2,733 square feet

QUOTE ONE™

Cost to build? See page 336
to order complete cost estimate
to build this house in your area!

Width 74'-1"
Depth 57'-4"

● The heart of this house is in the uniquely shaped family area that combines with a delightful home theatre. A fireplace in the middle of the family room commands attention and provides a great centerpiece for entertaining. The adjacent eating area accesses the rear deck and connects to the large kitchen with its two pantries and a convenient laundry. A formal dining room and a formal living room round out the first floor. The second floor contains two family bedrooms with a shared bathroom, a balcony overlooking the dining room and a master suite with a luxurious bath that features a whirlpool and a large walk-in closet.

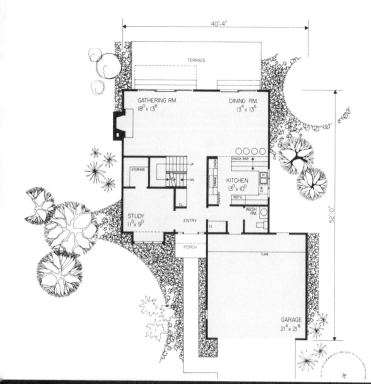

Design N2711 First Floor: 975 square feet
Second Floor: 1,024 square feet; Total: 1,999 square feet

L **D**

● Special features! A complete master suite with a private balcony plus two more bedrooms and a bath upstairs. The first floor has a study with a storage closet. A convenient snack bar between kitchen and dining room. The kitchen offers many built-in appliances. Plus a gathering room and dining room that measures 31 feet wide. Note the curb area in the garage and fireplace in gathering room.

Design N2925 First Floor: 1,128 square feet; Second Floor: 844 square feet; Total: 1,972 square feet

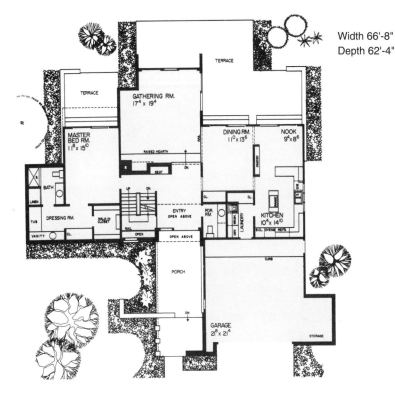

Width 66'-8"
Depth 62'-4"

Design N2729 First Floor: 1,590 square feet
Second Floor: 756 square feet; Total: 2,346 square feet

L

● Entering this home will be a pleasure through the sheltered walk-way to the double front doors. And the pleasure and beauty does not stop there. The entry hall and sunken gathering room are open to the upstairs for added dimension. There is fine indoor-outdoor living relationships in this design. Note the private terrace, a living terrace plus the balcony.

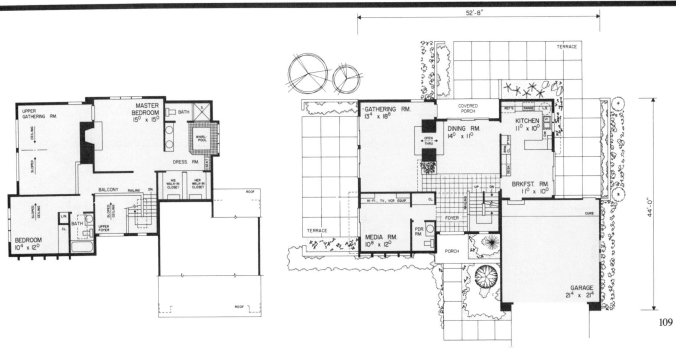

Design N3446

First Floor: 1,532 square feet
Second Floor: 1,200 square feet
Total: 2,732 square feet

L **D**

● A unique facade harbors a spacious, two-story foyer with an angled stairway. To the left is the formal living room with fireplace, and the formal dining room. To the right is a quiet den. The kitchen and breakfast room take advantage of a sunny bay. The family room features a second fireplace and a vaulted ceiling with three skylights. Another fireplace is found in the master bedroom. Secondary bedrooms share a full bath.

QUOTE ONE™

Cost to build? See page 336
to order complete cost estimate
to build this house in your area!

Width 60'-4"
Depth 48'-8"

QUOTE ONE™

Cost to build? See page 336
to order complete cost estimate
to build this house in your area!

Width 40'-7"
Depth 57'-8"

Design N3456

First Floor: 1,130 square feet
Second Floor: 1,189 square feet
Total: 2,319 square feet

L

● This volume home opens to a wealth of living potential with a media room to the right and formal living and dining rooms to the left. A covered porch, accessed from both the dining and breakfast rooms, adds outdoor dining potential. The kitchen contains a built-in desk and a snack bar pass-through to the breakfast area. Upstairs, four bedrooms include a master suite with balcony and three family bedrooms.

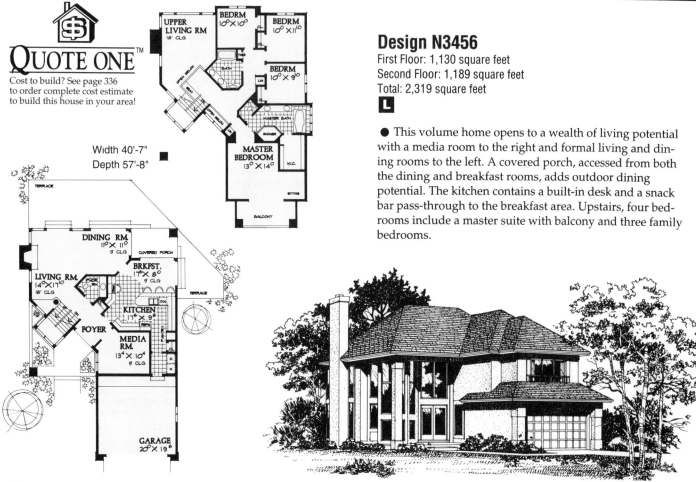

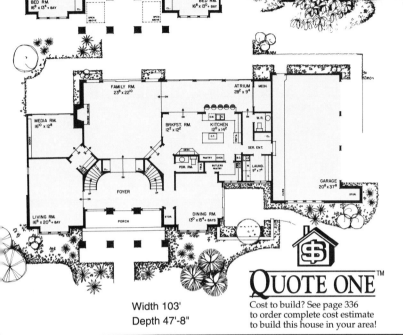

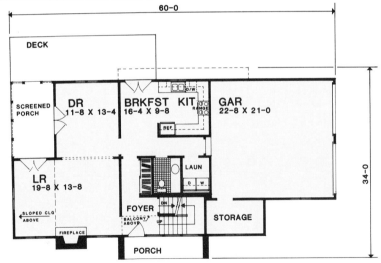

Width 103'
Depth 47'-8"

QUOTE ONE™

Cost to build? See page 336
to order complete cost estimate
to build this house in your area!

Design N3364

First Floor: 2,861 square feet
Second Floor: 1,859 square feet
Total: 4,720 square feet

L

● The impressive stonework facade of this contemporary home is as dramatic as it is practical—and it contains a grand floor plan. Notice the varying levels—a family room, a living room, a media room and an atrium are down a few steps from the elegant foyer. The large L-shaped kitchen is highlighted by an island work center and a pass-through snack bar. A double curved staircase leads to the second floor where four bedrooms and three full baths are found.

Design N4287

First Floor: 930 square feet
Second Floor: 1,362 square feet
Total: 2,292 square feet

L D

● This contemporary uses windows as a major part of its elegant design. Other special amenities include a convenient U-shaped kitchen, a screened porch and attached deck, and fireplace in the living room. All four bedrooms on the second floor have sloped ceilings.

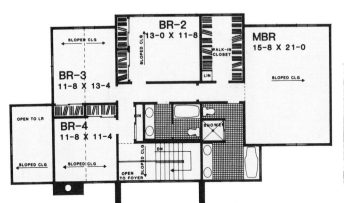

Design N3438

First Floor: 1,489 square feet
Second Floor: 741 square feet
Total: 2,230 square feet

L

● A unique farmhouse plan which provides a grand floor plan, this home is comfortable in country or suburban settings. Formal entertaining areas share first-floor space with family gathering rooms and work and service areas. The master suite is also on this floor for convenience and privacy. Upstairs is a guest bedroom, private bath and loft area that makes a perfect studio. Special features make this a great place to come home to.

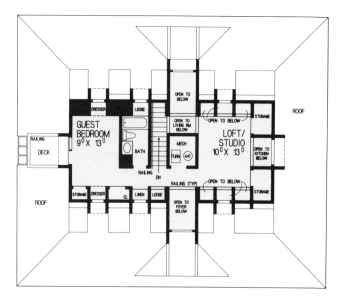

Cost to build? See page 336 to order complete cost estimate to build this house in your area!

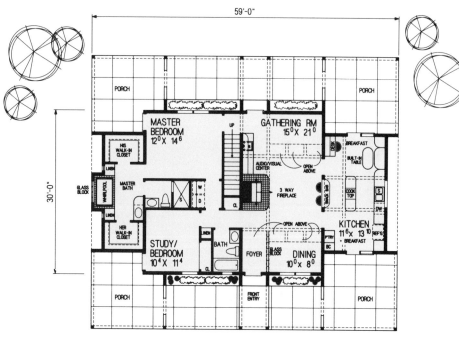

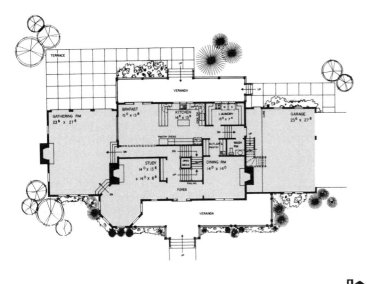

Design N3395

First Floor: 2,248 square feet
Second Floor: 2,020 square feet
Third Floor: 1,117 square feet
Total: 5,385 square feet

L **D**

● This home is a lovely example of classic
Queen Anne architecture. Its floor plan offers:
a gathering room with fireplace, a study with an
octagonal window area, a formal dining room
and a kitchen with attached breakfast room.
Bedrooms on the second floor include three
family bedrooms and a grand master suite. On
the third floor are a guest room with private
bath and sitting room and a game room with
attached library.

Width 94'-7"
Depth 53'-4"

QUOTE ONE™

Cost to build? See page 336
to order complete cost estimate
to build this house in your area!

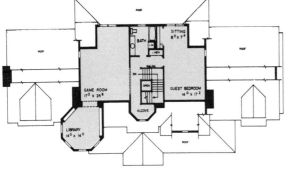

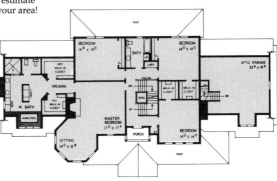

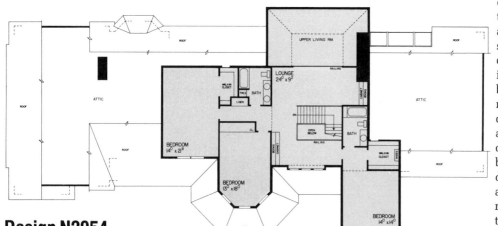

Design N2954

First Floor: 3,079 square feet
Second Floor: 1,461 square feet
Total: 4,540 square feet

L

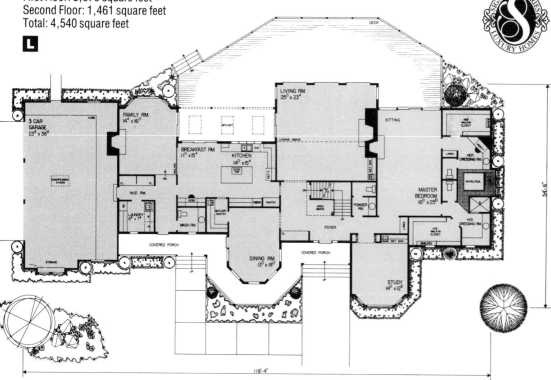

● This enchanting manor displays architectural elements typical of the Victorian Style: asymmetrical facade, decorative shingles and gables, and a covered porch. The two-story living room with fireplace and wet bar opens to the glass-enclosed rear porch with skylights. A spacious kitchen is filled with amenities, including an island cooktop, built-in desk, and butler's pantry connecting to the dining room. The master suite, adjacent to the study, opens to the rear deck. A cozy fireplace keeps the room warm on chilly evenings.

Separate His and Hers dressing rooms are outfitted with vanities and walk-in closets, and a luxurious whirlpool tub connects the baths. The second floor opens to a large lounge with built-in cabinets and bookshelves. Three bedrooms and two full baths complete the second-floor livability. The three-car garage contains disappearing stairs to an attic storage area.

114

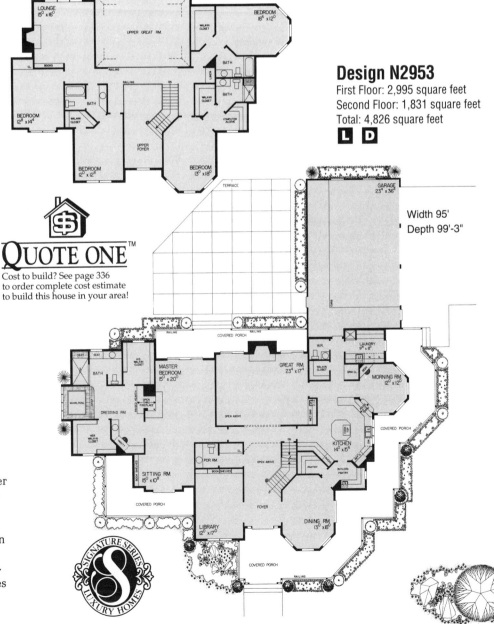

● A magnificent, finely wrought covered porch wraps around this impressive Victorian estate home. The gracious two-story foyer provides a direct view past the stylish bannister and into the great room with large central fireplace. To the left of the foyer is a bookshelf-lined library and to the right is a dramatic, octagonal-shaped dining room. The island cooktop completes a convenient work triangle in the kitchen, and a pass-through connects this room with the Victorian-style morning room. A butler's pantry, walk-in closet, and broom closet offer plenty of storage space. A luxurious master suite is located on the first floor and opens to the rear covered porch. A through-fireplace warms the bedroom, sitting room, and dressing room, which includes His and Hers walk-in closets. The step-up whirlpool tub is an elegant focal point to the master bath. Four uniquely designed bedrooms, three full baths, and a restful lounge with fireplace are located on the second floor. Who says you can't combine the absolute best of today's amenities with the quaint styling and comfortable warmth of the Victorian past!

Design N2953

First Floor: 2,995 square feet
Second Floor: 1,831 square feet
Total: 4,826 square feet

L **D**

QUOTE ONE™

Cost to build? See page 336 to order complete cost estimate to build this house in your area!

Width 95'
Depth 99'-3"

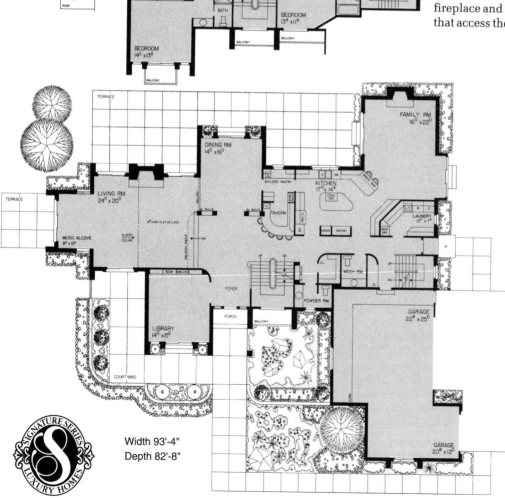

Design N2952

First Floor: 2,870 square feet
Second Floor: 2,222 square feet
Total: 5,092 square feet

● Semi-circular arches complement the strong linear roof lines and balconies of this exciting contemporary. The first floor is filled with well-planned amenities for entertaining and relaxing. The foyer opens to a step-down living room with a dramatic sloped ceiling, fireplace and three sliding glass doors that access the front courtyard and terrace. A tavern with built-in wine rack and an adjacent butler's pantry are ideal for entertaining. The family room features a fireplace, sliding glass door, and a handy snack bar. The kitchen allows meal preparation, cooking and storage within a step of the central work island. Three second-floor bedrooms, each with a private bath and balcony, are reached by either of two staircases. The master suite, with His and Hers baths and walk-in closets, whirlpool, and fireplace, adds the finishing touch to this memorable home.

Width 93'-4"
Depth 82'-8"

Design N2956

First Floor: 4,222 square feet
Second Floor: 1,726 square feet
Total: 5,948 square feet

● A curved staircase is the focal point of the foyer of this home. Two steps down from the foyer or dining room is the comfortable, two-story gathering room featuring a fireplace and two sliding glass doors. A large walk-in pantry, work island, snack bar, and view of the family room fireplace make the kitchen functional and comfortable. The master suite is secluded in its own wing. The bedroom, with a curved-hearth fireplace, and exercise room opens to the terrace through sliding glass doors. A media room with wet bar, accessible from the master bedroom and foyer, is the perfect place to relax. The second-floor stairs open to a lounge which overlooks the gathering room. Three additional bedrooms and a quiet study alcove on the second floor round out this gracious home.

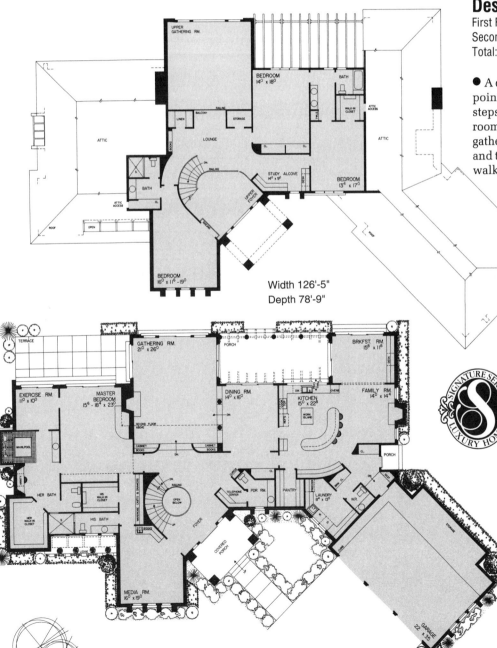

Width 126'-5"
Depth 78'-9"

Design N2940 First Floor: 4,786 square feet; Second Floor: 1,842 square feet; Total: 6,628 square feet
L D

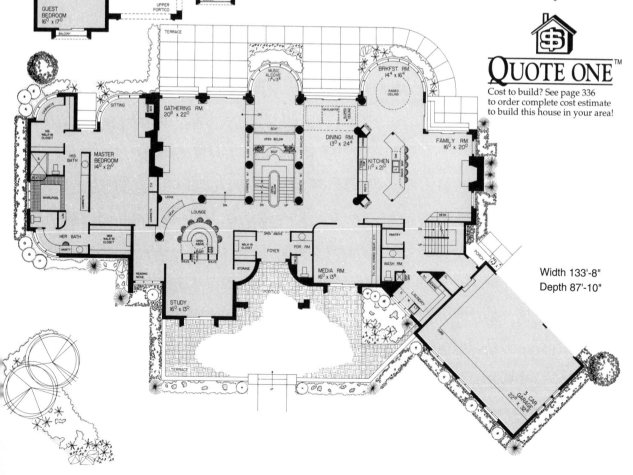

- Graceful window arches soften the massive chimneys and steeply gabled roof of this grand Norman manor. A two-story gathering room is two steps down from the adjacent lounge with impressive wet bar and semi-circular music alcove. The highly efficient galley-style kitchen overlooks the family room fireplace and spectacular windowed breakfast room. The master suite is a private retreat with fireplace and wood box tucked into the corner of its sitting room. Separate His and Hers baths and dressing rooms guarantee plenty of space and privacy. A large, built-in whirlpool tub adds the final touch. Upstairs, a second-floor balcony overlooks the gathering room below. There are also four additional bedrooms, each with private bath.

QUOTE ONE™
Cost to build? See page 336 to order complete cost estimate to build this house in your area!

Width 133'-8"
Depth 87'-10"

Design N2968 First Floor: 3,736 square feet
Second Floor: 2,264 square feet; Total: 6,000 square feet

L

● The distinctive covered entry to this stunning manor, flanked by twin turrets, leads to a gracious foyer with impressive fan lights. The plan opens from the foyer to a formal dining room, master study and step-down gathering room. The spacious kitchen has numerous amenities including an island workstation and built-in desk. The adjacent morning room and gathering room with wet bar and raised-hearth fireplace are bathed in light and open to the terrace for outdoor entertaining. The luxurious master suite has a wealth of amenities as well. The second floor features four bedrooms and an oversized activities room with fireplace and balcony. Unfinished attic space can be completed to your specifications.

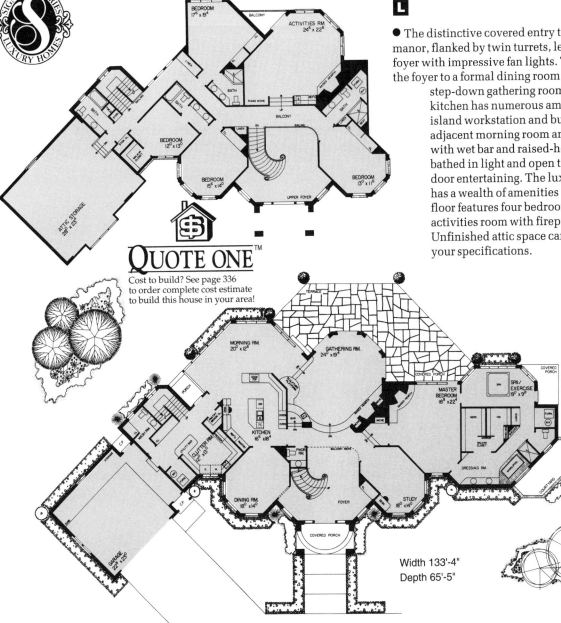

QUOTE ONE™

Cost to build? See page 336 to order complete cost estimate to build this house in your area!

Width 133'-4"
Depth 65'-5"

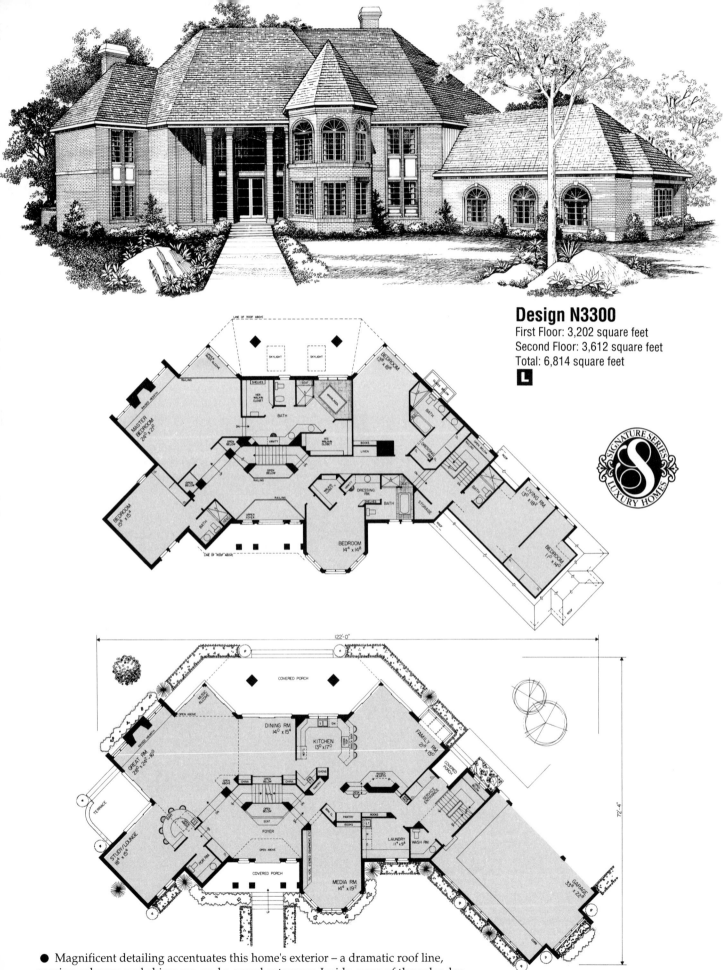

Design N3300

First Floor: 3,202 square feet
Second Floor: 3,612 square feet
Total: 6,814 square feet

● Magnificent detailing accentuates this home's exterior – a dramatic roof line, soaring columns and chimneys, and a grand entryway. Inside, none of the splendor is lost. Each of five bedrooms, one a private in-law suite, has its own full bath.

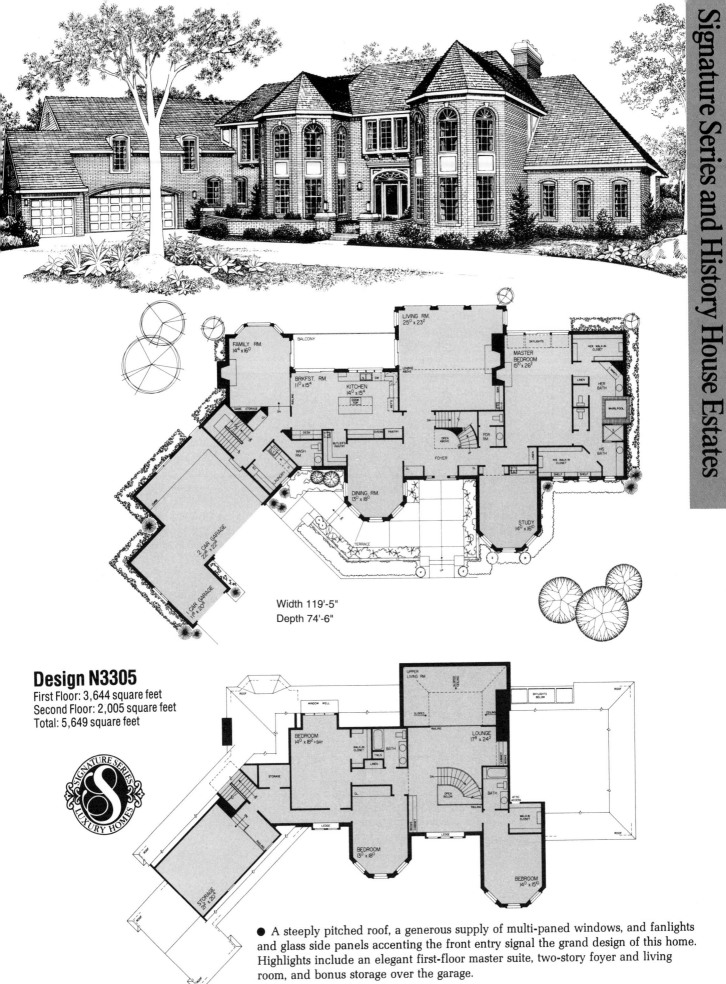

Width 119'-5"
Depth 74'-6"

Design N3305

First Floor: 3,644 square feet
Second Floor: 2,005 square feet
Total: 5,649 square feet

● A steeply pitched roof, a generous supply of multi-paned windows, and fanlights and glass side panels accenting the front entry signal the grand design of this home. Highlights include an elegant first-floor master suite, two-story foyer and living room, and bonus storage over the garage.

121

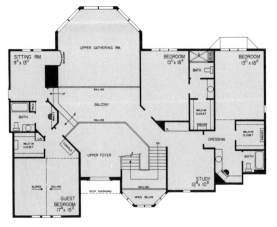

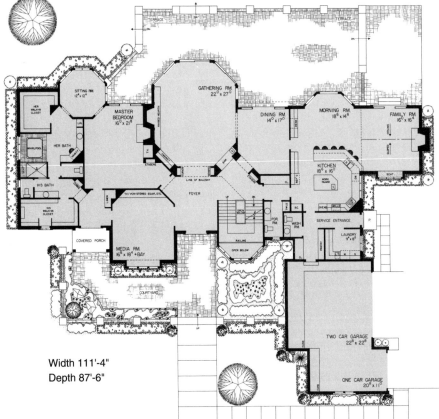

Width 111'-4"
Depth 87'-6"

Design N2951
First Floor: 4,195 square feet
Second Floor: 2,094 square feet
Total: 6,289 square feet

● A single prominent turret with two-story divided windows draws attention to this stately Tudor home. The open foyer allows an uninterrupted view into the impressive, two-story great room with wet bar, where a fireplace with raised hearth runs the entire length of one wall. The expansive kitchen, conveniently located near the service entrance, has a U-shaped work area and a snack bar that opens to the morning room. The adjacent sloped-ceiling family room has an additional fireplace and a comfortable window seat. A Victorian-inspired, octagon-shaped sitting room is tucked into the corner of the unique master bedroom. His and Hers baths and walk-in closets complete the impressive first-floor suite. Two bedrooms, a study, and a guest suite with private sitting room are located on the second floor. A magnificent second-floor bridge overlooks foyer and gathering room and provides extraordinary views to guests on the way to their bedroom.

Design N2955 First Floor: 3,840 square feet
Second Floor: 3,435 square feet; Total: 7,275 square feet

● A circular staircase housed in the turret makes an impressive opening statement in the two-story foyer of this Tudor. Two steps down lead to the elegant living room with music alcove or the sumptuous library with wet bar. The kitchen is a chef's delight with work island, full cooking counter and butler's pantry leading to a formal dining room. The second floor features four bedrooms, two with fireplaces, and each with private bath and abundant closet space. The master has an additional fireplace. Adjacent to the master bedroom is a nursery that would make an ideal exercise room.

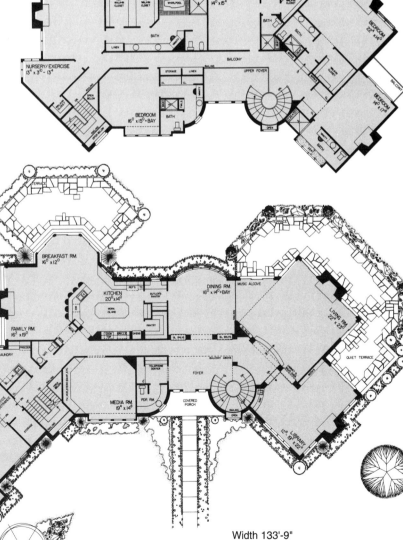

Width 133'-9"
Depth 85'-6"

Design N3301

First Floor: 3,425 square feet
Second Floor: 2,501 square feet
Total: 5,926 square feet

● Masterful use of space with a profusion of windows and terrace access are all employed in this Tudor treasure. A two-story foyer points the way directly to the living room which features a raised-hearth fireplace, huge bay window, and curved bar. The angular kitchen has a center island and is strategically placed with relationship to the formal dining room, the family room and its gracious fireplace, and a captivating breakfast room. A media room to the left of the foyer provides built-in space for an entertainment system. The sloped-ceiling master bedroom contains a third fireplace and another gigantic bay window. Its adjoining bath is divided into His and Hers dressing areas and closets, and centers around a relaxing whirlpool spa. Guests are easily accommodated in a full suite with its own living room and bath on the second floor. Three other bedrooms and a lounge on this floor share a balcony overlook to the living room below.

QUOTE ONE™

Cost to build? See page 336 to order complete cost estimate to build this house in your area!

Width 107'-1"
Depth 82'-4"

Design N2993

First Floor: 2,440 square feet
Second Floor: 2,250 square feet
Total: 4,690 square feet

L **D**

● This dramatically columned home delivers beautiful proportions and great livability on two levels. The main area of the house, the first floor, holds a gathering room, library, family room, dining room and gourmet kitchen. The master bedroom features a whirlpool tub and through fireplace. Two family bedrooms on the second floor share a full bath. A fourth bedroom is the perfect guest bedroom with its own private bath.

QUOTE ONE™

Cost to build? See page 336 to order complete cost estimate to build this house in your area!

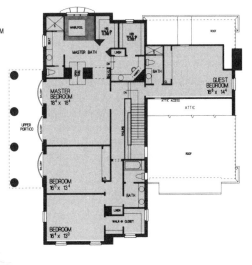

Design N3513

First Floor: 1,892 square feet
Second Floor: 1,295 square feet
Total: 3,187 square feet

● This grand entrance assures a sit-up-and-take-notice appearance. Curved steps lead to a raised front entry that makes a great impression with its rounded roof supported by stately columns. The soaring two-story foyer opens to a formal living room and dining room—each with a fireplace to warmly welcome guests. Informal living areas are situated to the rear of the plan. Here, a step-saving kitchen harmonizes well with the eating nook and family room providing easy access to the rear covered porch. Upstairs two secondary bedrooms—one with a dormer and one with balcony access—share a full bath. The gracious master suite features a built-in desk, a large walk-in closet and a dressing area. Note the unique master bath which provides space for a claw foot tub.

Cost to build? See page 336 to order complete cost estimate to build this house in your area!

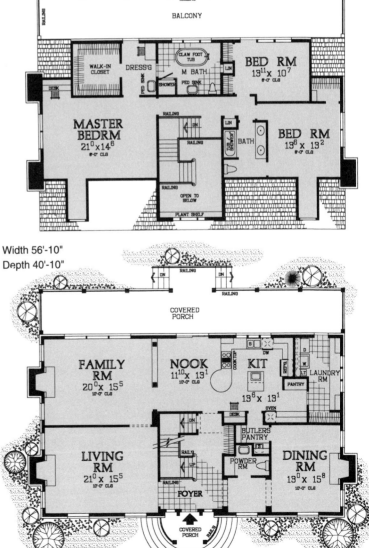

Width 56'-10"
Depth 40'-10"

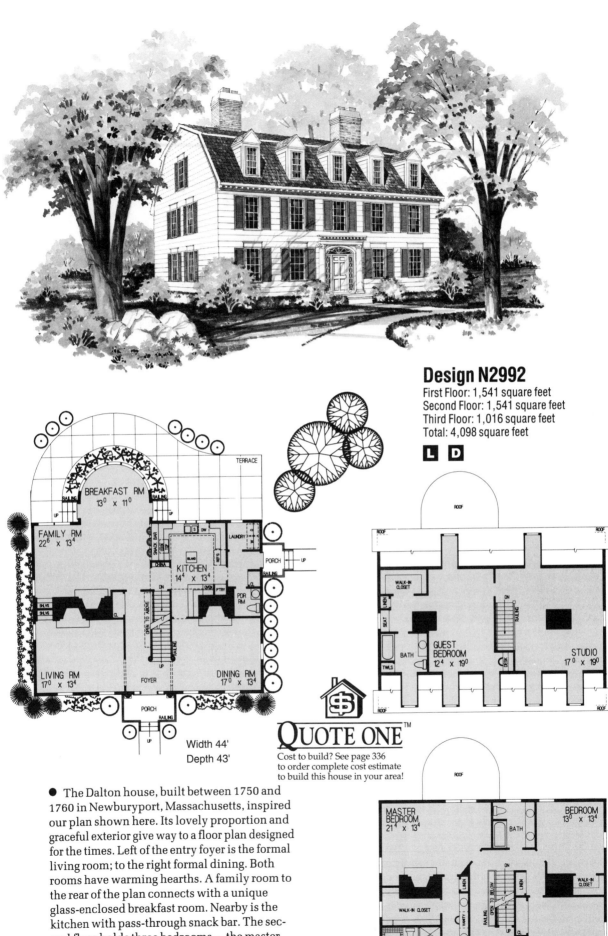

Design N2992

First Floor: 1,541 square feet
Second Floor: 1,541 square feet
Third Floor: 1,016 square feet
Total: 4,098 square feet

L D

TERRACE

BREAKFAST RM
13⁰ x 11⁰

FAMILY RM
22⁶ x 13⁴

KITCHEN
14⁴ x 13⁴

LAUNDRY

PORCH

PDR RM

LIVING RM
17⁰ x 13⁴

FOYER

DINING RM
17⁰ x 13⁴

PORCH

Width 44'
Depth 43'

WALK-IN CLOSET

BATH

GUEST BEDROOM
12⁴ x 19⁰

STUDIO
17⁰ x 19⁰

ROOF

Quote One™

Cost to build? See page 336 to order complete cost estimate to build this house in your area!

MASTER BEDROOM
21⁴ x 13⁴

BATH

BEDROOM
13⁰ x 13⁴

WALK-IN CLOSET

MASTER BATH

WHIRLPOOL

BEDROOM
17⁰ x 13⁴

● The Dalton house, built between 1750 and 1760 in Newburyport, Massachusetts, inspired our plan shown here. Its lovely proportion and graceful exterior give way to a floor plan designed for the times. Left of the entry foyer is the formal living room; to the right formal dining. Both rooms have warming hearths. A family room to the rear of the plan connects with a unique glass-enclosed breakfast room. Nearby is the kitchen with pass-through snack bar. The second floor holds three bedrooms — the master suite and two family bedrooms. On the third floor is a guest bedroom with private bath and studio.

Design N2989

First Floor: 1,972 square feet
Second Floor: 1,533 square feet
Total: 3,505 square feet

L

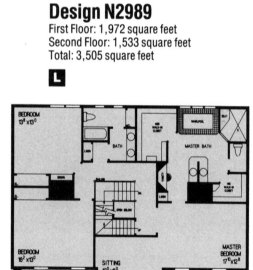

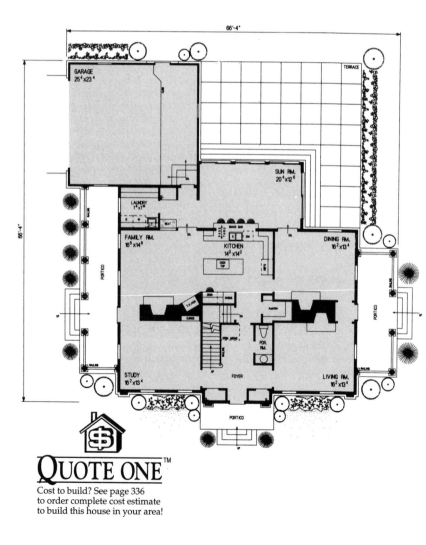

● This dramatic residence, patterned after one built in 1759 by Major John Vassall in Cambridge, offers a floor plan that is intriguing in its wealth of amenities. On the first floor are the formal living and dining rooms, each with fireplace. A front study connects to the family room with built-ins and another fireplace. Opening to the rear terrace is a most-welcome sun room with pass- through snack bar to the kitchen. Upstairs are three bedrooms. The master has a sitting room, double vanity, whirlpool tub, His and Hers closets, and built-in vanity. Two family bedrooms share a full bath.

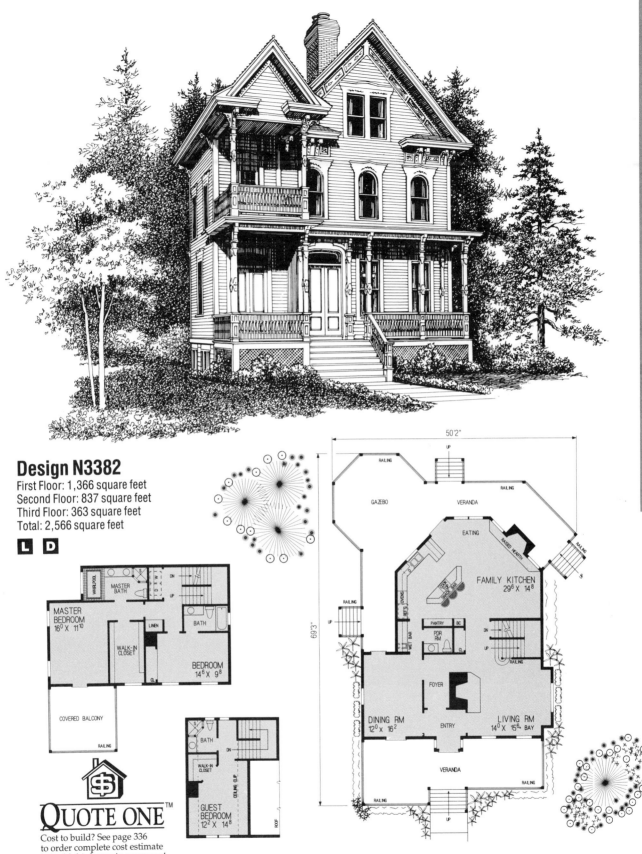

Design N3382

First Floor: 1,366 square feet
Second Floor: 837 square feet
Third Floor: 363 square feet
Total: 2,566 square feet

L **D**

QUOTE ONE™

Cost to build? See page 336
to order complete cost estimate
to build this house in your area!

● A simple but charming Queen Anne
Victorian, this enchanting three-story home
boasts delicately turned rails and decorated
columns on its covered front porch. Inside is a
floor plan that includes a living room with
fireplace and dining room that connects to the
kitchen via a wet bar. The adjoining family
room contains another fireplace. The second
floor holds two bedrooms, one a master suite
with grand bath. A tucked-away guest suite on
the third floor has a private bath.

Design N3512

First Floor: 1,983 square feet
Second Floor: 1,892 square feet
Total: 3,875 square feet

L **D**

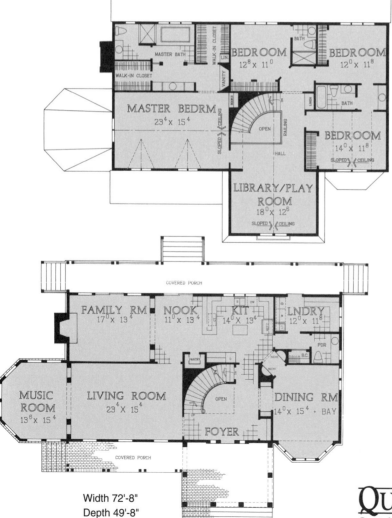

● A standing-seam metal roof, dramatic window treatment and an impressive portico provide gothic appeal with 20th-Century livability. To the left of the foyer is a formal living room sized to hold a congregation—perfect for enjoying a recital in the multi-windowed music room. A bay window enhances the formal dining room to the right. Columns provide a graceful entry to the spacious family room with a cozy fireplace and access to the covered porch. An eating nook—also with outdoor access—combines well with an efficient U-shaped kitchen, smartly designed to serve formal and informal living areas with equal ease. The second floor contains four bedrooms—one a master suite—three baths, and a library/playroom. The room-to-stretch master bedroom features a master bath highlighted with two walk-in closets and a relaxing tub.

Width 72'-8"
Depth 49'-8"

QUOTE ONE™
Cost to build? See page 336 to order complete cost estimate to build this house in your area!

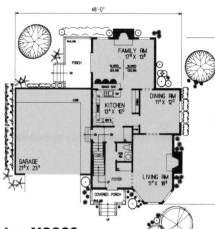

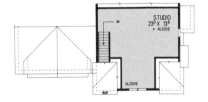

QUOTE ONE™

Cost to build? See page 336
to order complete cost estimate
to build this house in your area!

Design N3383

First Floor: 995 square feet
Second Floor: 1,064 square feet
Third Floor: 425 square feet
Total: 2,484 square feet

L **D**

● This delightful Victorian cottage features
exterior details that perfectly complement the
convenient plan inside. Note the central placement of the kitchen, near to the dining room
and the family room. Two fireplaces keep
things warm and cozy. Three second-floor bedrooms include a master suite with bay window
and two family bedrooms, one with an alcove
and walk-in closet. Use the third-floor studio as
a study, office or playroom for the children.

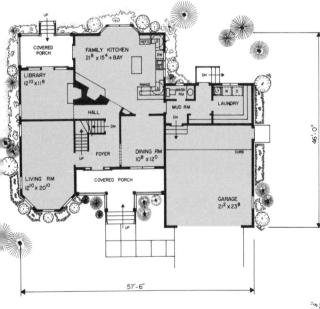

Design N3384

First Floor: 1,399 square feet
Second Floor: 1,123 square feet
Total: 2,522 square feet

L **D**

QUOTE ONE™

Cost to build? See page 336
to order complete cost estimate
to build this house in your area!

● Classic Victorian styling comes to the forefront in this Queen Anne. The interior boasts
comfortable living quarters for the entire family. On opposite sides of the foyer are the formal
dining and living rooms. To the rear is a country-
style island kitchen with attached family room.
A small library shares a covered porch with this
informal gathering area and also has its own
fireplace. Three bedrooms on the second floor
include a master suite with grand bath. The two
family bathrooms share a full bath.

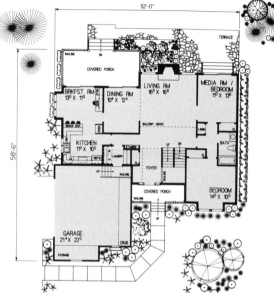

● This two-story farmhouse will be a delight for those who work at home. The second floor has a secluded master bedroom and a studio. A U-shaped kitchen with snack bar and breakfast area with bay window are only the first of the eating areas, which extend to a formal dining room and a covered rear porch for dining al fresco. The two-story living room features a cozy fireplace. A versatile room to the back could serve as a media room or a third bedroom.

Design N3390

First Floor: 1,508 square feet
Second Floor: 760 square feet
Total: 2,268 square feet

L   D

QUOTE ONE™

Cost to build? See page 336
to order complete cost estimate
to build this house in your area!

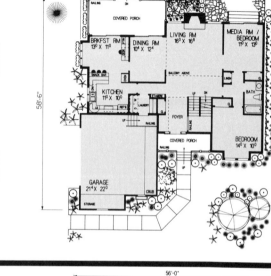

Design N3385

First Floor: 1,096 square feet
Second Floor: 900 square feet
Total: 1,996 square feet

L   D

QUOTE ONE™

Cost to build? See page 336
to order complete cost estimate
to build this house in your area!

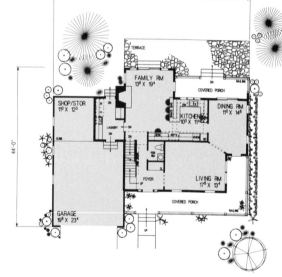

● Covered porches front and rear are complemented by a grand plan for family living. A formal living room and attached dining room provide space for entertaining guests. The large family room with fireplace is a gathering room for everyday use. Four bedrooms occupy the second floor. The master suite features two lavatories, a window seat and three closets. One of the family bedrooms has its own private balcony and could be used as a study.

Design N2974 First Floor: 911 square feet
Second Floor: 861 square feet; Total: 1,772 square feet

L

● Victorian houses are well known for their orientation on narrow building sites. And when this occurs nothing is lost to captivating exterior styling. This house is but 38 feet wide. Its narrow width belies the tremendous amount of livability found inside. And, of course, the ubiquitous porch/veranda contributes mightily to style as well as livability. The efficient, U-shape kitchen is flanked by the informal breakfast room and formal dining room. The rear living area is spacious and functions in an exciting manner with the outdoor areas. Bonus recreational, hobby and storage space is offered by the basement and the attic.

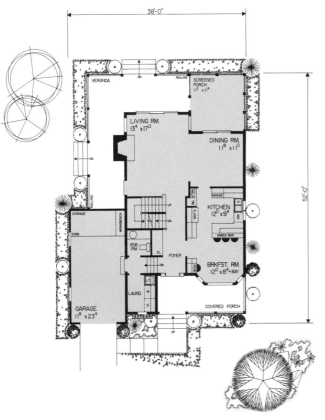

QUOTE ONE™

Cost to build? See page 336 to order complete cost estimate to build this house in your area!

Design N2971 First Floor: 1,766 square feet
Second Floor: 1,519 square feet; Total: 3,285 square feet

L

● The stately proportions and the exquisite detailing of Victorian styling are exciting, indeed. Like so many Victorian houses, interesting roof lines set the character with this design. Observe the delightful mixture of gable roof, hip roof, and the dramatic turret. Horizontal siding, wood shingling, wide fascia, rake and corner boards make a strong statement. Of course, the delicate detailing of the windows, railings, cornices and front entry is most appealing to the eye. Inside, a great four-bedroom family living plan.

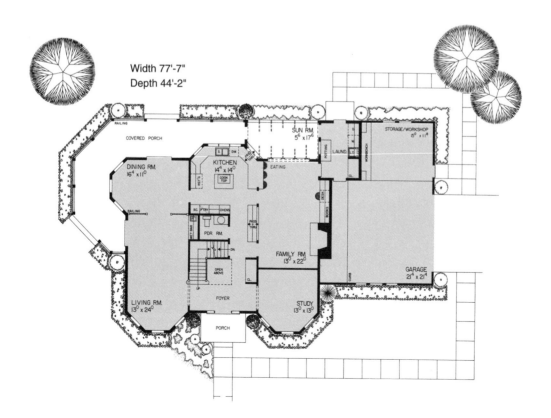

Width 77'-7"
Depth 44'-2"

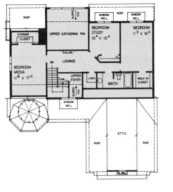

● A grand facade makes this Victorian stand out. Inside, guests and family are well accommodated: gathering room with terrace access, fireplace and attached formal dining room; split-bedroom sleeping arrangements. The master suite contains His and Hers walk-in closets, a separate shower and whirlpool tub and a delightful bay-windowed area. Upstairs there are three more bedrooms (one could serve as a study, one as a media room), a full bath and an open lounge area overlooking the gathering room.

Design N3393

First Floor: 1,449 square feet
Second Floor: 902 square feet
Total: 2,351 square feet

L **D**

QUOTE ONE™

Cost to build? See page 336
to order complete cost estimate
to build this house in your area!

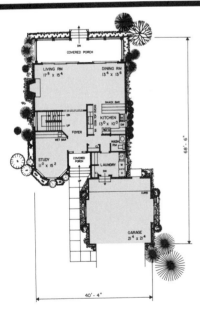

Design N3389

First Floor: 1,161 square feet
Second Floor: 1,090 square feet
Third Floor: 488 square feet
Total: 2,739 square feet

L **D**

QUOTE ONE™

Cost to build? See page 336
to order complete cost estimate
to build this house in your area!

● A Victorian turret accents the facade of this compact three-story. Downstairs rooms include a grand-sized living room/dining room combination. The U-shaped kitchen has a snack-bar pass-through to the dining room. Just to the left of the entry foyer is a private study. On the second floor are three bedrooms and two full baths. The master bedroom has a whirlpool spa and large walk-in closet. The third floor is a perfect location for a guest bedroom with private bath.

Design N2973

First Floor: 1,269 square feet
Second Floor: 1,227 square feet
Total: 2,496 square feet

L

● A most popular feature of the Victorian house has always been its covered porches. In addition to being an appealing exterior design feature, covered porches have their practical side, too. They provide wonderful indoor-outdoor living relationships. Notice sheltered outdoor living facilities for the various formal and informal living and dining areas of the plan. This home has a myriad of features to cater to the living requirements of the growing, active family.

Width 70'
Depth 44'-5"

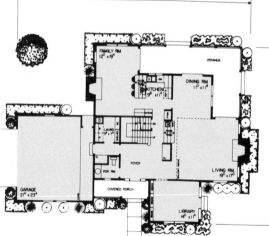

Design N2972

First Floor: 1,432 square feet
Second Floor: 1,108 square feet
Total: 2,540 square feet

L

● The spacious foyer of this Victorian is prelude to a practical and efficient interior. The formal living and dining area is located to one side of the plan. The more informal area of the plan includes the fine U-shaped kitchen which opens to the big family room. Just inside the entrance from the garage is the laundry; a closet and the powder room are a few steps away. The library will enjoy its full measure of privacy. Upstairs is the three-bedroom sleeping zone with a fireplace.

Design N3309

First Floor: 1,375 square feet
Second Floor: 1,016 square feet
Total: 2,391 square feet

L

● Covered porches, front and back, are a fine preview to the livable nature of this Victorian. Living areas are defined in a family room with fireplace, formal living and dining rooms, and a kitchen with breakfast room. An ample laundry room, garage with storage area, and powder room round out the first floor. Three second floor bedrooms are joined by a study and two full baths.

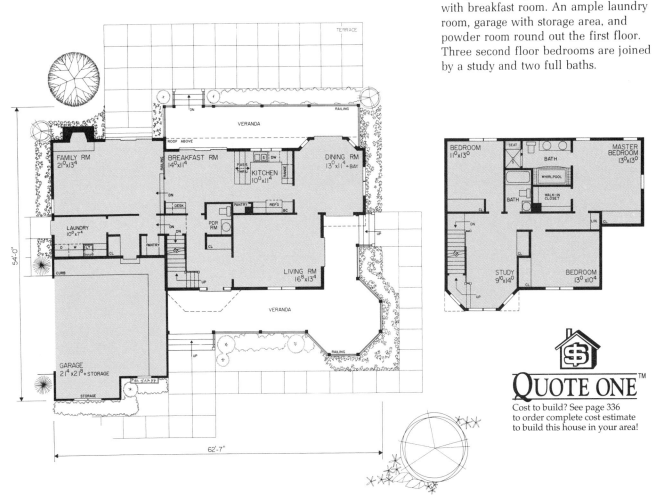

Quote One

Cost to build? See page 336 to order complete cost estimate to build this house in your area!

Design N3615

First Floor: 1,355 square feet
Second Floor: 582 square feet
Total: 1,937 square feet

L

● A portico makes a strong architectural statement and provides shelter for this home's front entrance. To the left of the foyer is the formal dining room which is but a step from the angular kitchen. The great room has a high volume ceiling. Its raised-hearth fireplace is flanked by doors to the deck. To the right of the foyer is the master suite. The master bath is compartmented and includes a walk-in closet, a whirlpool tub and access to the rear deck. The second floor holds two bedrooms and features a balcony overlooking the great room.

QUOTE ONE™
Cost to build? See page 336
to order complete cost estimate
to build this house in your area

Width 65'
Depth 55'-8"

Design N3394

First Floor: 1,531 square feet
Second Floor: 1,307 square feet
Third Floor: 664 square feet
Total: 3,502 square feet

L   D

QUOTE ONE™
Cost to build? See page 336
to order complete cost estimate
to build this house in your area!

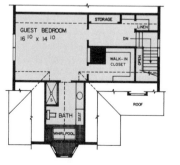
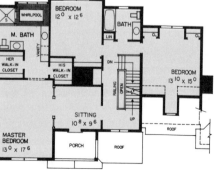

● The Folk Victorian is an important and delightful interpretation. And this version offers the finest in modern floor plans. The formal living areas are set off by a family room which connects the main house to the service areas. The second floor holds three bedrooms and two full baths. A sitting area in the master suite separates it from family bedrooms. On the third floor is a guest bedroom with gracious bath and large walk-in closet.

Design N3386

First Floor: 1,683 square feet
Second Floor: 1,388 square feet
Third Floor: 808 square feet
Total: 3,879 square feet

L **D**

QUOTE ONE™

Cost to build? See page 336
to order complete cost estimate
to build this house in your area!

● This beautiful Folk Victorian has all the
properties of others in its class. Living areas
include a formal Victorian parlor, a private
study and large gathering room. The formal
dining room has its more casual counterpart in
a bay-windowed breakfast room. Both are near
the well-appointed kitchen. Five bedrooms
serve family and guest needs handily. Three
bedrooms on the second floor include a luxurious master suite. For outdoor entertaining, there
is a covered rear porch leading to a terrace.

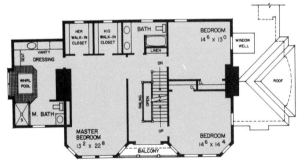

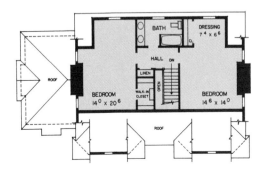

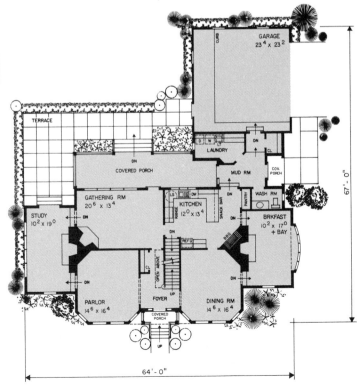

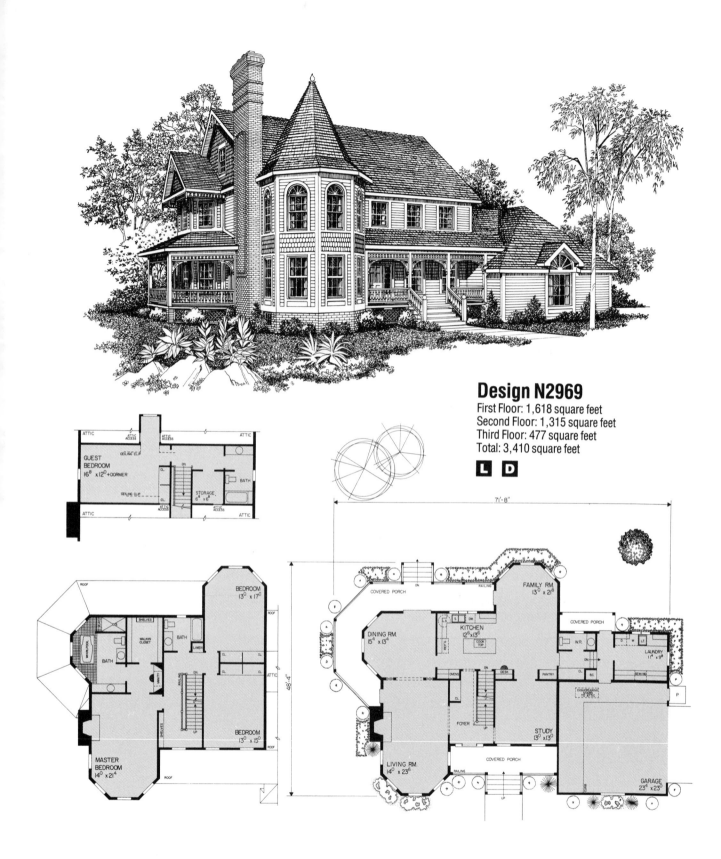

Design N2969

First Floor: 1,618 square feet
Second Floor: 1,315 square feet
Third Floor: 477 square feet
Total: 3,410 square feet

L **D**

● What could beat the charm of a tur-reted Victorian with covered porches to the front, side and rear? This deli-cately detailed exterior houses an outstanding family oriented floor plan. Projecting bays make their contribution to the exterior styling. In addition, they provide an extra measure of livability

to the living, dining and family rooms, plus two of the bedrooms. The efficient kitchen, with its island cooking station, functions well with the dining and family rooms. A study provides a quiet first floor haven for the family's less active pursuits. Upstairs there are three big bedrooms and a fine master bath.

The third floor provides a guest suite and huge bulk storage area (make it a cedar closet if you wish). This house has a basement for the development of further recreational and storage facili-ties. Don't miss the two fireplaces, large laundry and attached two-car garage. A great investment.

Design N2970 First Floor: 1,538 square feet
Second Floor: 1,526 square feet; Third Floor: 658 square feet
Total: 3,722 square feet

L

● A porch, is a porch, is a porch. But, when it wraps around to a side, or even two sides, of the house, we have called it a veranda. This charming Victorian features a covered outdoor living area on all four sides! It even ends at a screened porch which features a sun deck above. This interesting plan offers three floors of livability. And what livability it is! Plenty of formal and informal living facilities to go along with the potential of five bedrooms. The master suite is just that. It is adjacent to an interesting sitting room. It has a sun deck and excellent bath/personal care facilities. The third floor will make a wonderful haven for the family's student members.

QUOTE ONE™
Cost to build? See page 336
to order complete cost estimate
to build this house in your area!

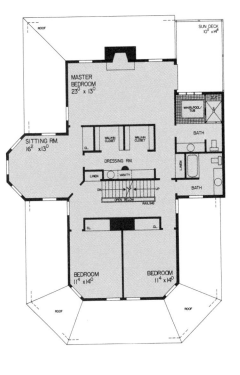

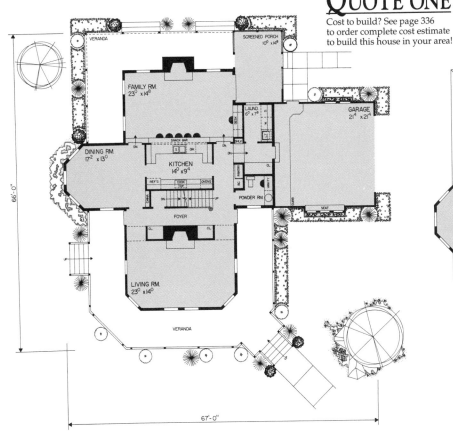

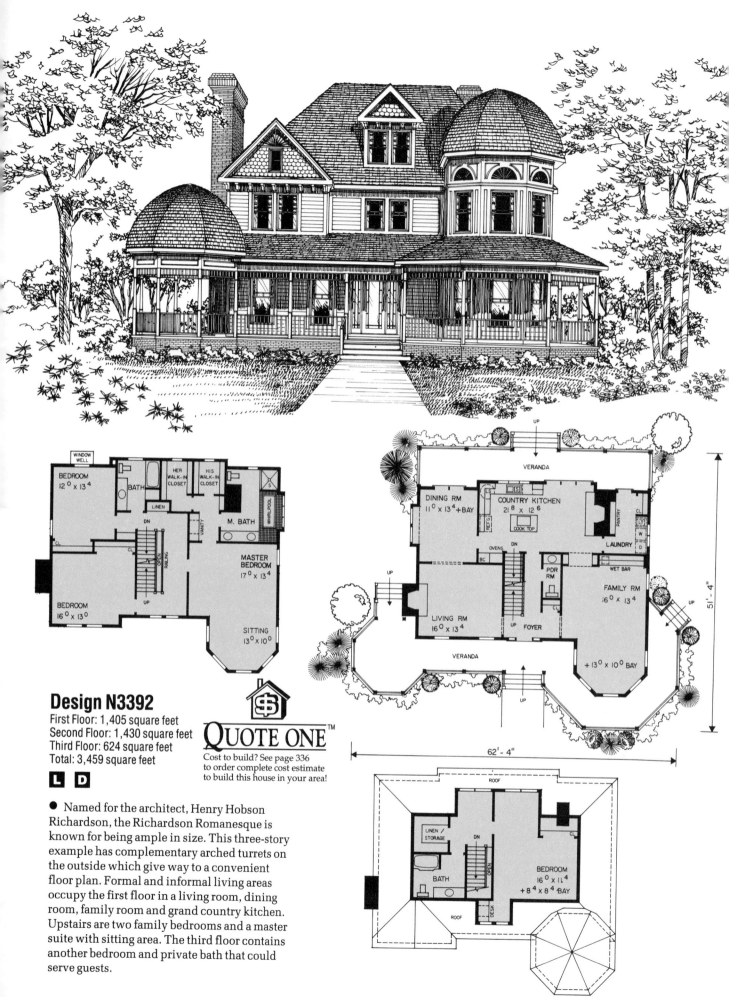

Design N3392

First Floor: 1,405 square feet
Second Floor: 1,430 square feet
Third Floor: 624 square feet
Total: 3,459 square feet

L **D**

QUOTE ONE™

Cost to build? See page 336
to order complete cost estimate
to build this house in your area!

● Named for the architect, Henry Hobson
Richardson, the Richardson Romanesque is
known for being ample in size. This three-story
example has complementary arched turrets on
the outside which give way to a convenient
floor plan. Formal and informal living areas
occupy the first floor in a living room, dining
room, family room and grand country kitchen.
Upstairs are two family bedrooms and a master
suite with sitting area. The third floor contains
another bedroom and private bath that could
serve guests.

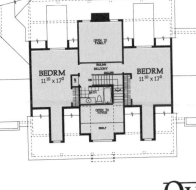

QUOTE ONE™

Cost to build? See page 336
to order complete cost estimate
to build this house in your area!

Design N3614

First Floor: 2,300 square feet
Second Floor: 812 square feet
Total: 3,112 square feet

L D

● If you're looking for the real McCoy—lightly influenced by classic style—you need look no further. Inside, the foyer opens to formal living and dining rooms. The kitchen—bordered by a snack bar—unites the breakfast room with the family room. The first-floor master suite is filled with amenities that include a raised-hearth fireplace, a sitting room, bookshelves and a unique master bath with a relaxing whirlpool tub. Tucked behind the kitchen is a guest suite. A private bath and a parlor with a raised-hearth fireplace will make visiting family and guests feel like royalty. The second floor contains two family bedrooms and a full bath.

Width 83'
Depth 71'-6"

QUOTE ONE™

Cost to build? See page 336
to order complete cost estimate
to build this house in your area!

Width 93'-6"
Depth 61'

Design N3608

First Floor: 2,347 square feet
Second Floor: 1,087 square feet
Total: 3,434 square feet

L

● Dutch gable roof lines and a gabled wraparound porch with star-burst trim provide an extra measure of farmhouse style. The foyer opens from the study or guest bedroom on the left that leads to the master suite, to the formal dining room on the right and to the massive great room in the center of the home, where a warming fireplace creates a cozy centerpiece. The kitchen conveniently combines with the great room, the breakfast nook and the dining room. The master suite includes access to the covered patio, a spacious walk-in closet and a master bath with a whirlpool tub.

143

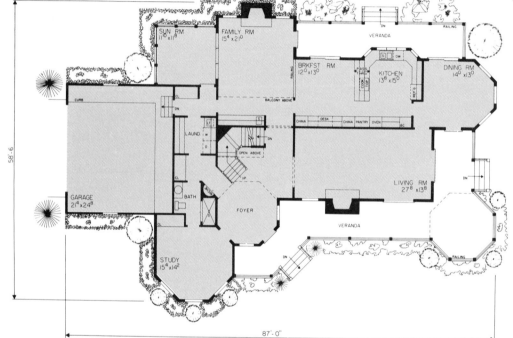

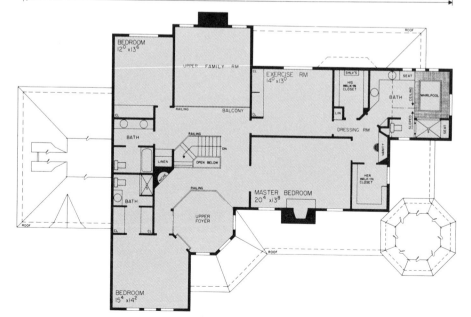

Design N3304

First Floor: 2,102 square feet
Second Floor: 1,971 square feet
Total: 4,073 square feet

L

● Victorian style is displayed in most exquisite proportions in this three-bedroom, four-bath home. From verandas, both front and rear, to the stately turrets and impressive chimney stack, this is a beauty. Inside is a great lay-out with many thoughtful amenities. Besides the large living room, formal dining room, and two-story family room, there is a cozy study for private time. A gourmet kitchen with built-ins has a pass-through counter to the breakfast room. The master suite on the second floor includes many special features: whirlpool spa, His and Hers walk-in closets, exercise room, and fireplace. There are two more bedrooms, each with a full bath, on the second floor.

QUOTE ONE™

Cost to build? See page 336 to order complete cost estimate to build this house in your area!

Quote One™

Cost to build? See page 336
to order complete cost estimate
to build this house in your area!

Design N3308

First Floor: 2,515 square feet
Second Floor: 1,708 square feet
Third Floor: 1,001 square feet
Total: 5,224 square feet

L

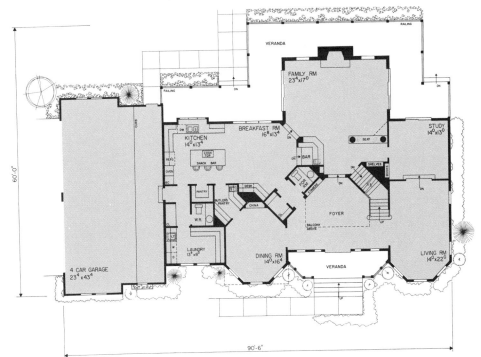

● Uniquely shaped rooms and
a cache of amenities highlight
this three-story beauty. Downstairs rooms accommodate both
formal and informal entertaining and also provide a liberal
share of work space in the
kitchen and laundry. The second floor has two bedrooms and
a full bath plus a master suite
with His and Hers closets and
whirlpool bath. An exercise
room on the third floor has its
own sauna and bath, while a
guest room on this floor is complemented by a charming alcove
and another full bath.

Design N3462

First Floor: 1,395 square feet
Second Floor: 813 square feet
Total: 2,208 square feet

L

Width 53'-8"
Depth 57'

QUOTE ONE™

Cost to build? See page 336
to order complete cost estimate
to build this house in your area!

● Get off to a great start with this handsome family farmhouse. Distinct formal and informal living zones provide space for any occasion. The central kitchen serves the large family room. The master bedroom is on the first floor and comes complete with double closets and master bath with double-bowl vanity, whirl-pool tub and separate shower. Upstairs, three family bedrooms extend fabulous livability.

Design N3443

First Floor: 1,211 square feet
Second Floor: 614 square feet
Total: 1,825 square feet

L **D**

● The master suite in this house is on a level all its own. The 21-foot bed-room includes a sitting area and a bath with walk-in closet, dual vanities, separate tub and shower and a com-partmented toilet. A second bedroom or optional den, with a full bath near-by, is located on the first floor. The formal living and dining rooms have sloped ceilings separated by a plant shelf, and bay windows. The family room features a snack bar to the kitchen and patio access. The garage contains a hobby shop.

QUOTE ONE™

Cost to build? See page 336
to order complete cost estimate
to build this house in your area!

Width 57'
Depth 44'-4"

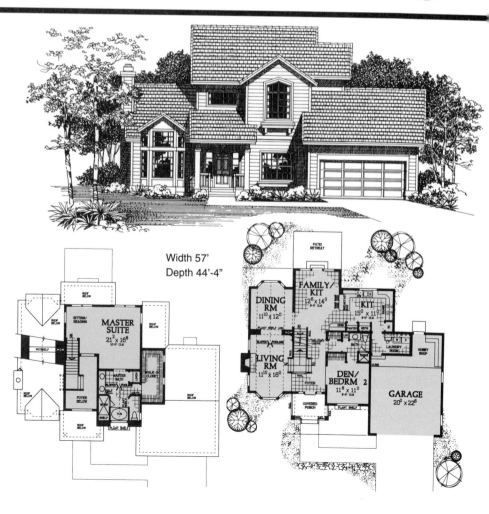

Design N3461

First Floor: 1,391 square feet
Second Floor: 611 square feet
Total: 2,002 square feet

L

● A Palladian window set in a dormer provides a nice introduction to this 1½-story country home. The two-story foyer draws on natural light and a pair of columns to set a comfortable, yet elegant mood. The living room, to the left, presents a grand space for entertaining. From full-course dinners to family suppers, the dining room will serve its purpose well. The kitchen delights with an island work station and openness to the keeping room. Here, a raised-hearth fireplace provides added comfort. Sleeping accommodations are comprised of four bedrooms, one a first-floor master suite. With a luxurious private bath, including dual lavatories, this room will surely be a favorite retreat. Upstairs, three secondary bedrooms meet the needs of the growing family.

Cost to build? See page 336
to order complete cost estimate
to build this house in your area!

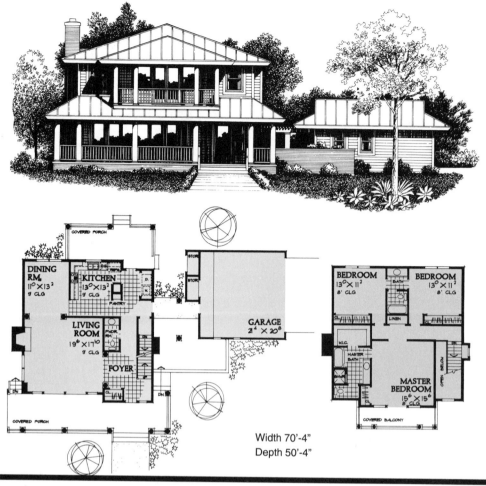

Design N3469

First Floor: 1,066 square feet
Second Floor: 1,006 square feet
Total: 2,072 square feet

L

● Our neo-classic farmhouse offers plenty of room for delightful diversions; a sheet-metal roof adds old-fashioned charm. Inside, a large living area with a fireplace connects to a formal dining room. The fully functional kitchen, the powder room and the utility room round out the first floor. The second floor provides well-arranged sleeping quarters—a large master bedroom and two family bedrooms. A mud yard separates the garage from the main house.

QUOTE ONE™

Cost to build? See page 336 to order complete cost estimate to build this house in your area!

Width 70'-4"
Depth 50'-4"

Width 65'
Depth 51'-8"

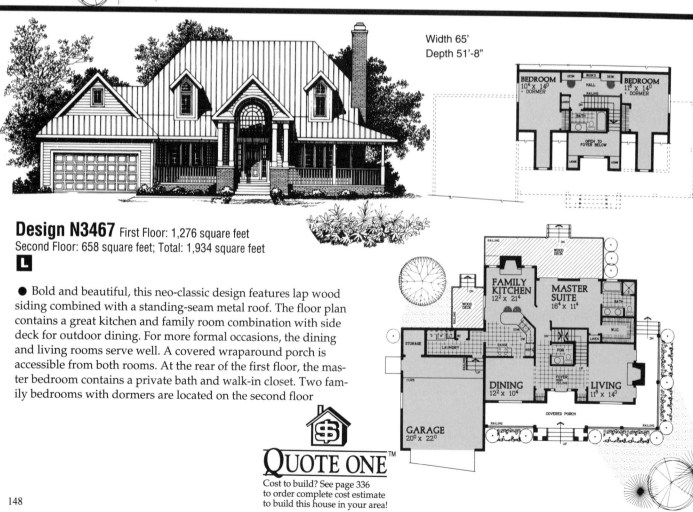

Design N3467
First Floor: 1,276 square feet
Second Floor: 658 square feet; Total: 1,934 square feet

L

● Bold and beautiful, this neo-classic design features lap wood siding combined with a standing-seam metal roof. The floor plan contains a great kitchen and family room combination with side deck for outdoor dining. For more formal occasions, the dining and living rooms serve well. A covered wraparound porch is accessible from both rooms. At the rear of the first floor, the master bedroom contains a private bath and walk-in closet. Two family bedrooms with dormers are located on the second floor

QUOTE ONE™

Cost to build? See page 336 to order complete cost estimate to build this house in your area!

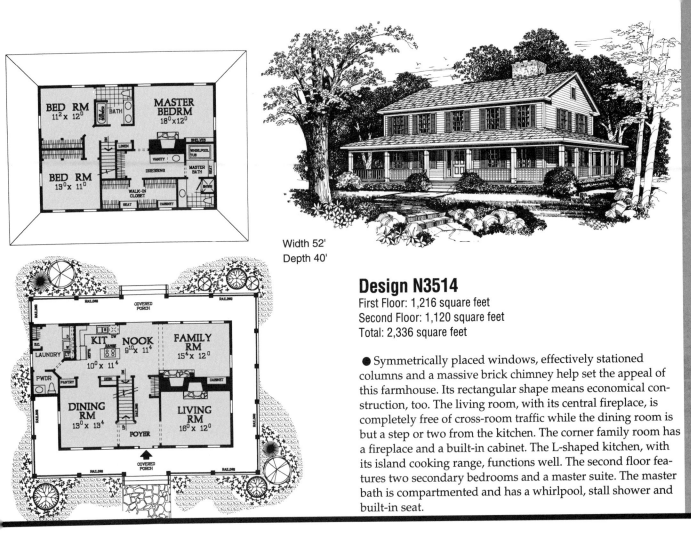

Width 52'
Depth 40'

Design N3514

First Floor: 1,216 square feet
Second Floor: 1,120 square feet
Total: 2,336 square feet

● Symmetrically placed windows, effectively stationed columns and a massive brick chimney help set the appeal of this farmhouse. Its rectangular shape means economical construction, too. The living room, with its central fireplace, is completely free of cross-room traffic while the dining room is but a step or two from the kitchen. The corner family room has a fireplace and a built-in cabinet. The L-shaped kitchen, with its island cooking range, functions well. The second floor features two secondary bedrooms and a master suite. The master bath is compartmented and has a whirlpool, stall shower and built-in seat.

Design N2908

First Floor: 1,427 square feet
Second Floor: 1,153 square feet
Total: 2,580 square feet

WIDTH 70'
DEPTH 34'

L D

● This Early American farmhouse offers plenty of modern comfort with its covered front porch with pillars and rails, double chimneys, building attachment, and four upstairs bedrooms.

QUOTE ONE™

Cost to build? See page 336 to order complete cost estimate to build this house in your area!

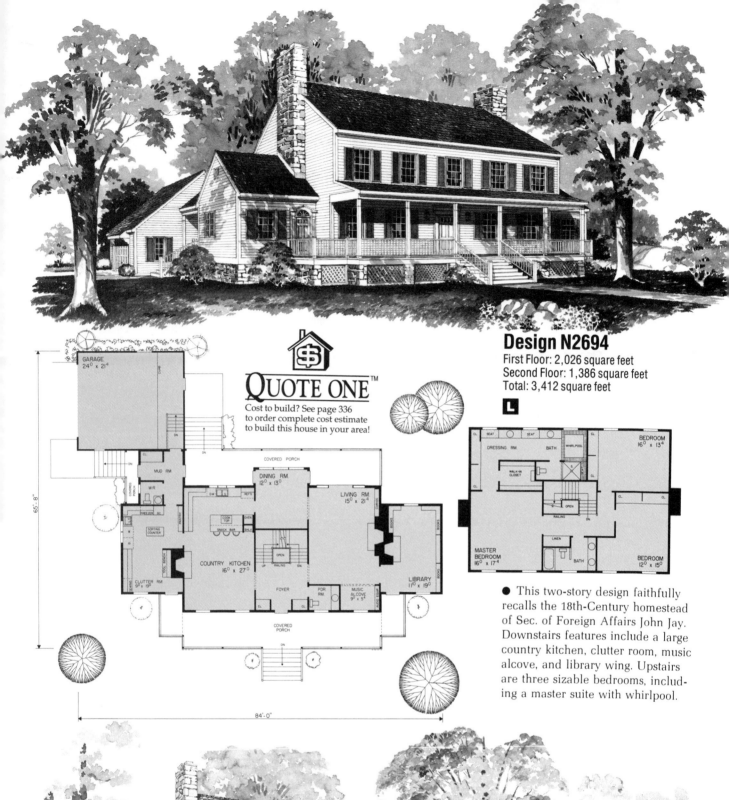

Design N2694

First Floor: 2,026 square feet
Second Floor: 1,386 square feet
Total: 3,412 square feet

L

● This two-story design faithfully
recalls the 18th-Century homestead
of Sec. of Foreign Affairs John Jay.
Downstairs features include a large
country kitchen, clutter room, music
alcove, and library wing. Upstairs
are three sizable bedrooms, including a master suite with whirlpool.

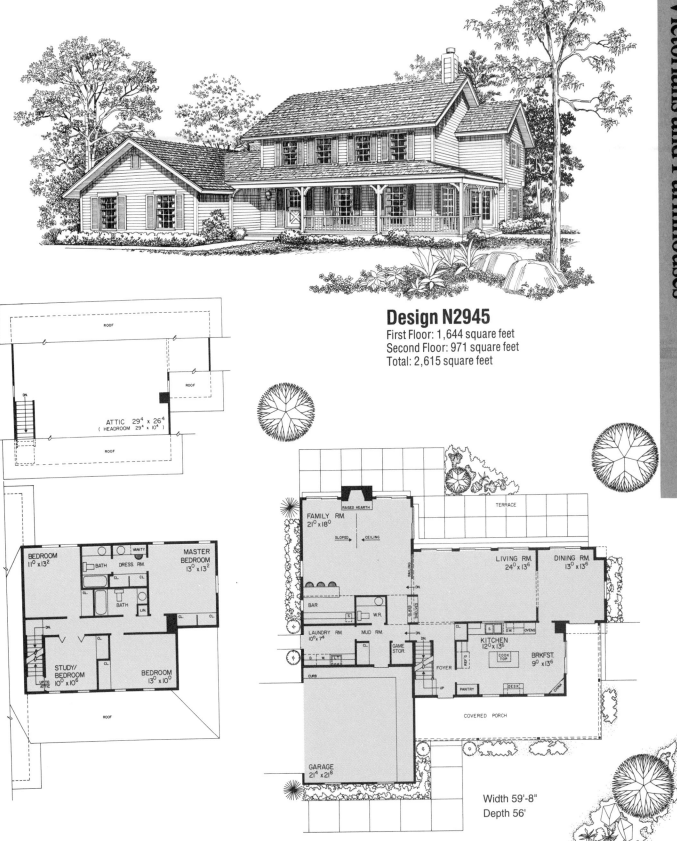

Design N2945

First Floor: 1,644 square feet
Second Floor: 971 square feet
Total: 2,615 square feet

ATTIC 29⁴ x 26⁴
(HEADROOM 29⁴ x 10⁴)

BEDROOM 11⁰ x13²

MASTER BEDROOM 13⁰ x 13²

BATH   DRESS. RM.

STUDY/ BEDROOM 10⁰ x 10⁶

BEDROOM 13⁰ x 10⁰

FAMILY RM. 21⁰ x 18⁰

RAISED HEARTH

SLOPED   CEILING

TERRACE

BAR

LIVING RM. 24⁰ x 13⁶

DINING RM. 13⁰ x 13⁶

W.R.

LAUNDRY RM. 10⁰ x 7⁸

MUD RM.

GAME STOR.

KITCHEN 12⁰ x 13⁶

BRKFST. 9⁰ x 13⁶

FOYER

PANTRY   DESK

COOK TOP

COVERED PORCH

GARAGE 21⁴ x 21⁸

Width 59'-8"
Depth 56'

● Here is a new floor plan designed to go with the almost identical exterior of one of Home Planners' most popular houses. A masterfully affordable design, this plan manages to include all the basics - and then adds a little more. Note the wraparound covered porch, large family room with raised-hearth fireplace and wet bar, spacious kitchen with island cook top, formal dining room, rear terrace, and extra storage on the first floor. Upstairs, the plan's as flexible as they come: three or four bedrooms (the fourth could easily be a study or playroom) and lots of unfinished attic just waiting for you to transform it into living space. This could make a fine studio, sewing room, home office, or just a place for the safe, dry storage of the family's paraphernalia, Christmas decorations, etc.

Design N2907

First Floor: 1,546 square feet
Second Floor: 1,144 square feet
Total: 2,690 square feet

L

● This traditional L-shaped farmhouse is
charming indeed with dormer windows and
covered porch supported by slender columns.
A spacious country kitchen with a bay provides
a convenient place for food preparation with its
central work island and size. There's a formal
dining room also adjacent to the kitchen. A rear
family room features its own fireplace, as does
a large living room in the front. All four bedrooms are isolated upstairs. Included is a large
master bedroom suite with its own bath, dressing room and abundant closet space.

Width 67'
Depth 51'-8"

Design N3325

First Floor: 1,595 square feet
Second Floor: 1,112 square feet
Total: 2,707 square feet

L **D**

● This four-bedroom farmhouse
plan is one of the most popular
styles in America today. The floor
plan begins with a foyer that introduces a grand living room. The
U-shaped kitchen has a central
island and a pass-through snack
bar that connects it to the breakfast
room. Nearby, the family room
delights with its warming hearth
and access to an entertainment
patio. A large utility area sits near
the garage. Upstairs, the master
bedroom suite includes two closets
and a private bath with a garden
tub and dual lavatories.

Width 63'-6"
Depth 48'

QUOTE ONE™

Cost to build? See page 336
to order complete cost estimate
to build this house in your area!

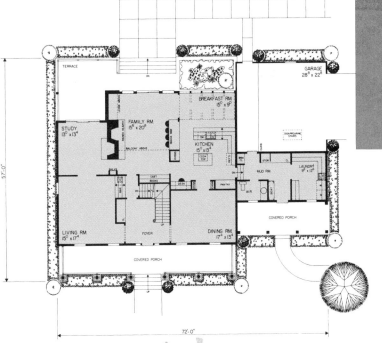

Design N2981

First Floor: 2,104 square feet
Second Floor: 2,015 square feet; Total: 4,119 square feet

L

• This formal two-story recalls a Louisiana plantation house, Land's End, built in 1857. The Ionic columns of the front porch and the pediment gable echo the Greek Revival style. Highlighting the interior is the bright and cheerful spaciousness of the informal family room area. It features a wall of glass stretching to the second story sloping ceiling. Enhancing the drama of this area is the adjacent glass area of the breakfast room. Note the "His/Her" areas of the master bedroom.

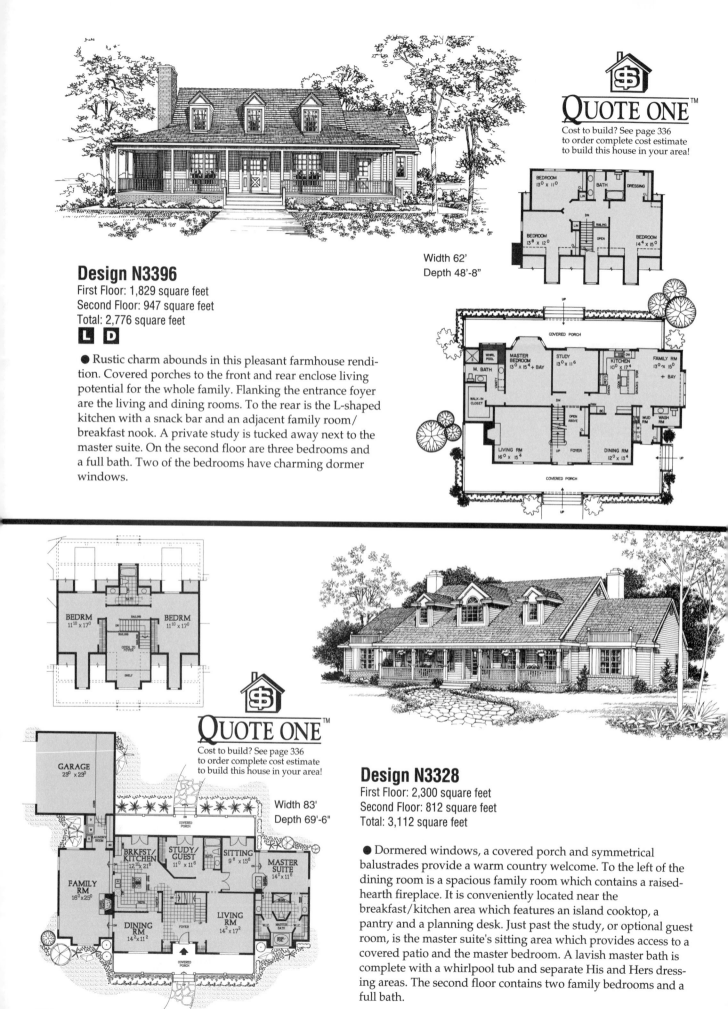

Design N3396

First Floor: 1,829 square feet
Second Floor: 947 square feet
Total: 2,776 square feet

L **D**

● Rustic charm abounds in this pleasant farmhouse rendition. Covered porches to the front and rear enclose living potential for the whole family. Flanking the entrance foyer are the living and dining rooms. To the rear is the L-shaped kitchen with a snack bar and an adjacent family room/breakfast nook. A private study is tucked away next to the master suite. On the second floor are three bedrooms and a full bath. Two of the bedrooms have charming dormer windows.

Width 62'
Depth 48'-8"

QUOTE ONE™
Cost to build? See page 336
to order complete cost estimate
to build this house in your area!

QUOTE ONE™
Cost to build? See page 336
to order complete cost estimate
to build this house in your area!

Width 83'
Depth 69'-6"

Design N3328

First Floor: 2,300 square feet
Second Floor: 812 square feet
Total: 3,112 square feet

● Dormered windows, a covered porch and symmetrical balustrades provide a warm country welcome. To the left of the dining room is a spacious family room which contains a raised-hearth fireplace. It is conveniently located near the breakfast/kitchen area which features an island cooktop, a pantry and a planning desk. Just past the study, or optional guest room, is the master suite's sitting area which provides access to a covered patio and the master bedroom. A lavish master bath is complete with a whirlpool tub and separate His and Hers dressing areas. The second floor contains two family bedrooms and a full bath.

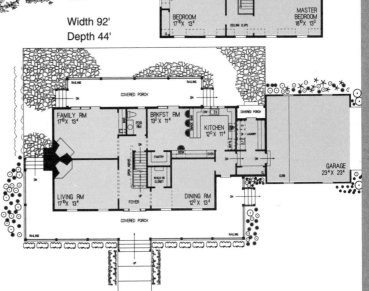

Width 92'
Depth 44'

Design N3398

First Floor: 1,533 square feet
Second Floor: 1,288 square feet
Total: 2,821 square feet

L **D**

● With its classic Farmhouse good-looks and just-right floor plan, this country residence has it all. The wraparound covered porch at the entry gives way to a long foyer with an open staircase. To the right and left are the formal dining room and the living room. More casual living areas are to the rear: a family room and U-shaped kitchen with an attached breakfast room. The second floor holds sleeping areas—two family bedrooms and a huge master suite with a walk-in closet and a pampering master bath.

QUOTE ONE™
Cost to build? See page 336
to order complete cost estimate
to build this house in your area!

Design N3606

First Floor: 1,969 square feet
Second Floor: 660 square feet
Total: 2,629 square feet
Bonus Room: 360 square feet

L **D**

● Varying roof planes, gables and dormers help create the unique character of this house. Inside, the great room gains attention with its high ceiling, fireplace/media center wall, view of the upstairs balcony and French doors to the sun room. In the U-shaped kitchen, an island work surface, a planning desk and a pantry are added conveniences. The master suite is spacious and can function with the home office, library or private sitting room. Its direct access to the huge raised veranda provides an ideal outdoor private haven for relaxation. The second floor highlights two bedrooms and a bath.

QUOTE ONE™
Cost to build? See page 336
to order complete cost estimate
to build this house in your area!

Width 90'-8"
Depth 80'-4"

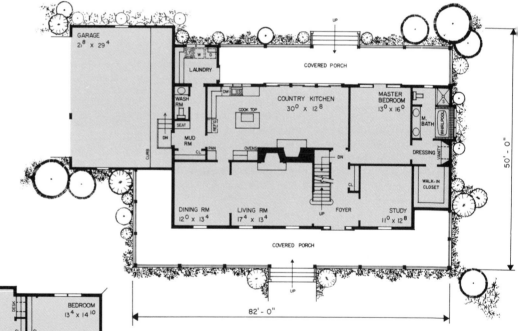

Design N3397

First Floor: 1,855 square feet
Second Floor: 1,241 square feet
Total: 3,096 square feet

L **D**

GARAGE
21⁸ x 29⁴

LAUNDRY

COVERED PORCH

UP

WASH RM

DW

COUNTRY KITCHEN
30⁰ x 12⁸

MASTER BEDROOM
13⁰ x 16⁰

COOK TOP

M. BATH

WHIRLPOOL

SEAT

MUD RM

REFG

PAN

CL

OVENS

DN

DRESSING

VANITY

CURB

DN

WALK-IN CLOSET

DINING RM
12⁰ x 13⁴

LIVING RM
17⁴ x 13⁴

CL

UP

FOYER

STUDY
11⁰ x 12⁸

COVERED PORCH

UP

50' - 0"

82' - 0"

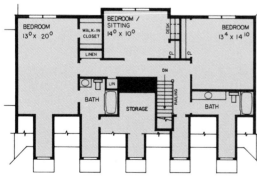

BEDROOM
13⁰ x 20⁰

WALK-IN CLOSET

BEDROOM / SITTING
14⁰ x 10⁰

DESK

BEDROOM
13⁴ x 14¹⁰

LINEN

CL

CL

DN

BATH

LIN

STORAGE

RAILING

BATH

● Five second-story dormers and a wide covered front porch add to the charm of this farmhouse design. Inside, the entry foyer opens to the left to a formal living room with fireplace and attached dining room. To the right is a private study. The back of the plan is dominated by a huge country kitchen featuring an island cook top. On this floor is the master suite with a large walk-in closet. The second floor holds three bedrooms (or two and a sitting room) with two full baths.

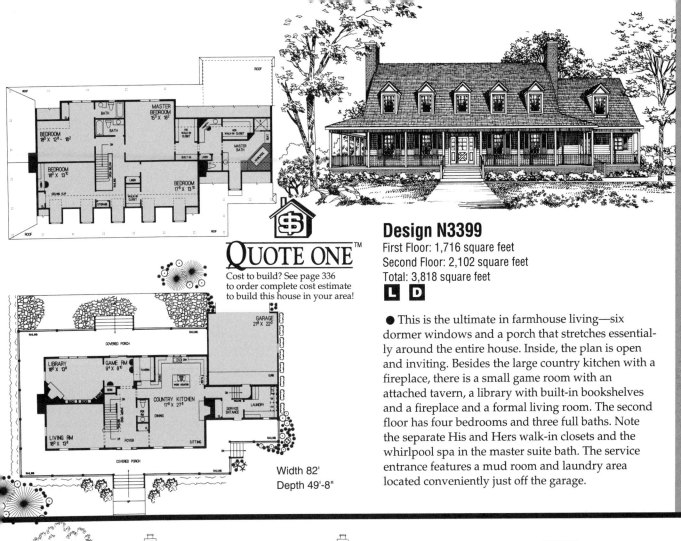

QUOTE ONE™

Cost to build? See page 336
to order complete cost estimate
to build this house in your area!

Design N3399

First Floor: 1,716 square feet
Second Floor: 2,102 square feet
Total: 3,818 square feet

L **D**

● This is the ultimate in farmhouse living—six dormer windows and a porch that stretches essentially around the entire house. Inside, the plan is open and inviting. Besides the large country kitchen with a fireplace, there is a small game room with an attached tavern, a library with built-in bookshelves and a fireplace and a formal living room. The second floor has four bedrooms and three full baths. Note the separate His and Hers walk-in closets and the whirlpool spa in the master suite bath. The service entrance features a mud room and laundry area located conveniently just off the garage.

Width 82'
Depth 49'-8"

Design N3324

First Floor: 1,762 square feet
Second Floor: 1,311 square feet
Total: 3,073 square feet

L **D**

QUOTE ONE™

Cost to build? See page 336
to order complete cost estimate
to build this house in your area!

Width 66'
Depth 47'-6"

● This home provides a perfect opportunity to share the comforts of traditional family living with in-home office space. The versatile plan allows for a well-positioned study off the foyer and a combination guest room/office near the laundry room—both with nearby facilities and excellent views. The large kitchen presents many possibilities for dining pleasures: a cozy meal in the breakfast nook; light eating and conversation at the bar; and evening meals in the dining room. The master bedroom provides spacious comfort with His and Hers walk-in closets and an impressive dressing area. Two family bedrooms share a large bathroom with plenty of linen space.

Design N2776

First Floor: 1,134 square feet
Second Floor: 874 square feet
Total: 2,008 square feet

L **D**

QUOTE ONE™

Cost to build? See page 336
to order complete cost estimate
to build this house in your area!

- This board-and-batten farmhouse design has all of the country charm of New England. Immediately off the front entrance is the delightful corner living room. The dining room with bay window is easily served by the U-shaped kitchen. Informal family living enjoyment resides in the family room which features a raised-hearth fireplace and sliding glass doors to the rear terrace. The second floor houses all of the sleeping facilities.

Design N3605

First Floor: 1,622 square feet
Second Floor: 900 square feet
Total: 2,522 square feet

L **D**

- This home's central foyer routes traffic most efficiently. Spaciousness is the by-word in the family living area. The fireplace is a commanding feature. French doors provide access to outdoor livability. The formal dining room features a bay window, a butler's pantry and adjacent space for china storage. A few steps away is the efficient, U-shaped kitchen. It is open to the informal breakfast nook area with its bay window and access to the covered porch. In the master bedroom, bonus wardrobe space will surely please. The children's sleeping requirements are adequately served by three bedrooms and two full baths.

Width 70'-6"
Depth 41'-5"

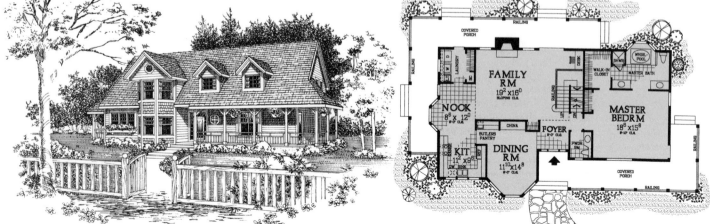

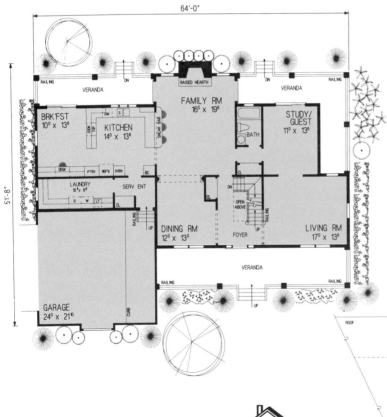

Design N3307

First Floor: 1,765 square feet
Second Floor: 1,105 square feet
Total: 2,870 square feet

L **D**

● This charming design brings together the best in historical styling and modern floor planning. Inside, the first-floor plan boasts formal living and dining areas on either side of the entry foyer, a study that could double as a guest room, a large family room with raised-hearth fireplace and snack bar pass-through, and a U-shaped kitchen with attached breakfast room. Two family bedrooms on the second floor share a full bath; the master bedroom has a thoughtfully appointed bath and large walk-in closet.

QUOTE ONE™

Cost to build? See page 336
to order complete cost estimate
to build this house in your area!

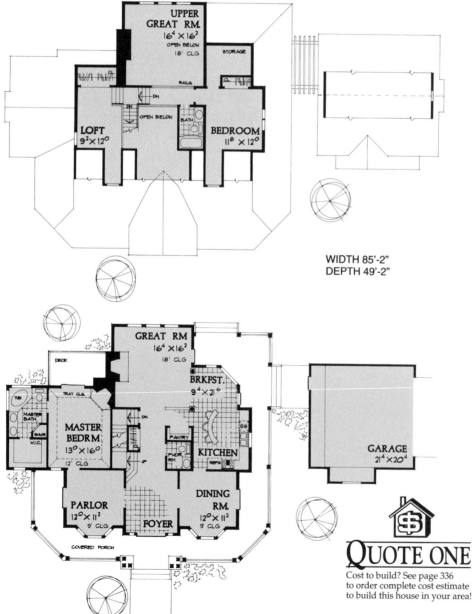

UPPER
GREAT RM.
16⁴ × 16²
OPEN BELOW
18' CLG

STORAGE

DN

RAIL.

CL

OPEN BELOW

LOFT
9² × 12⁰

BATH

BEDROOM
11⁸ × 12⁰

WIDTH 85'-2"
DEPTH 49'-2"

GREAT RM
16⁴ × 16²
18' CLG

DECK

BRKFST.
9⁴ × 21⁶

TRAY CLG.

TUB

MASTER
BATH

SHWR

W.I.C.

MASTER
BEDRM
13⁰ × 16⁰
12' CLG

DN

PANTRY

PWDR.
RM.

KITCHEN

REF.

GARAGE
21⁴ × 20⁴

UP

PARLOR
12⁰ × 11²
9' CLG

FOYER

DINING
RM.
12⁰ × 11²
9' CLG

COVERED PORCH

Design N3468

First Floor: 1,618 square feet
Second Floor: 510 square feet
Total: 2,128 square feet

L

● There's nothing lacking
in this contemporary farmhouse. A wraparound porch
ensures a favorite spot for
enjoying good weather. A
large great room sports a
fireplace and lots of natural
light. Grab a snack at the
kitchen island/snack bar or
in the bright breakfast room.
The vaulted foyer grandly
introduces the dining room
and parlor—the master bedroom is just off this room.
Inside it: tray ceiling, fireplace, luxury bath and walk-
in closet. Stairs lead up to a
quaint loft/bedroom—per-
fect for study or snoozing—a
full bath and an additional
bedroom. Designated storage
space also makes this one a
winner.

QUOTE ONE™

Cost to build? See page 336
to order complete cost estimate
to build this house in your area!

Design N3405
Square Footage: 3,144

In classic Santa Fe style, this home strikes a beautiful combination of historic exterior detailing and open floor planning on the inside. A covered porch running the width of the facade leads to an entry foyer that connects to a huge gathering room with fireplace and formal dining room. The family kitchen allows special space for casual gatherings. The right wing of the home contains two family bedrooms and full bath. The left wing is devoted to the master suite and guest room or study. Built-ins abound throughout the house.

Width 139'-10"
Depth 63'-8"

Quote One™

Cost to build? See page 336
to order complete cost estimate
to build this house in your area!

Design N2949
Square Footage: 2922

● Spanish and Western influences take center stage in a long, low stucco design. You'll enjoy the Texas-sized gathering room that opens to a formal dining area and has a snack bar through to the kitchen. More casual dining is accommodated in the nook. A luxurious master suite is graced by plenty of closet space and a soothing whirlpool spa. Besides another bedroom and full bath, there is a media room that could easily double as a third bedroom or guest room.

Width 82'
Depth 77'

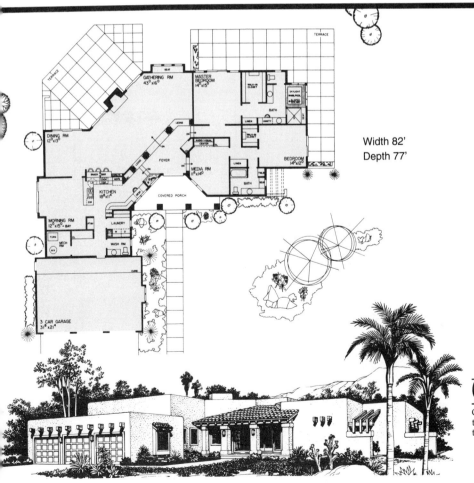

Quote One™

Cost to build? See page 336
to order complete cost estimate
to build this house in your area!

Design N3565

First Floor: 1,248 square feet
Second Floor: 1,012 square feet
Total: 2,260 square feet

L **D**

● Every detail of this plan
speaks of modern design. The
exterior is simple yet elegant,
while interior floor planning is
thorough yet efficient. The formal living and dining rooms are
to the left of the home, separated by columns. The living room
features a wall of windows and
a fireplace. The kitchen with
island cooktop is adjacent to the
large family room with terrace
access. A study with additional
terrace access completes the first
floor. The master bedroom features a balcony and a spectacular bath with whirlpool tub,
shower with seat, separate vanities and a walk-in closet. Two
family bedrooms share access to
a full bath. Also notice the three-
car garage.

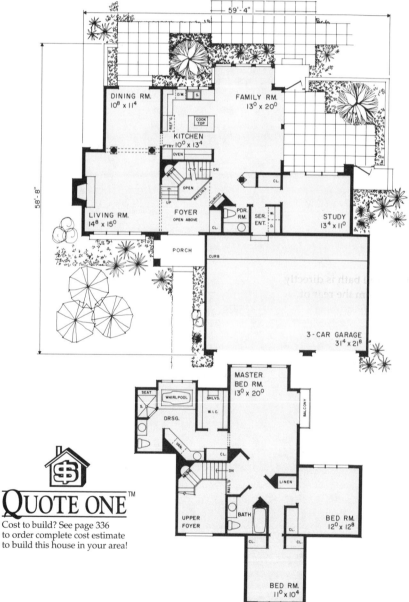

QUOTE ONE™

Cost to build? See page 336
to order complete cost estimate
to build this house in your area!

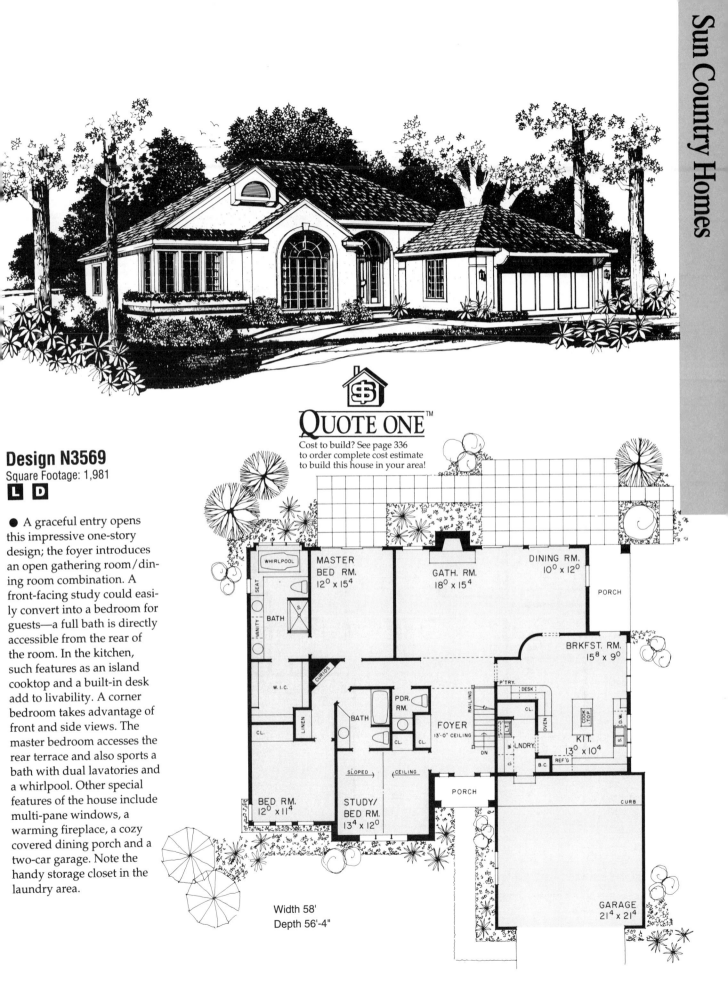

Design N3569

Square Footage: 1,981

L **D**

● A graceful entry opens this impressive one-story design; the foyer introduces an open gathering room/dining room combination. A front-facing study could easily convert into a bedroom for guests—a full bath is directly accessible from the rear of the room. In the kitchen, such features as an island cooktop and a built-in desk add to livability. A corner bedroom takes advantage of front and side views. The master bedroom accesses the rear terrace and also sports a bath with dual lavatories and a whirlpool. Other special features of the house include multi-pane windows, a warming fireplace, a cozy covered dining porch and a two-car garage. Note the handy storage closet in the laundry area.

QUOTE ONE™

Cost to build? See page 336 to order complete cost estimate to build this house in your area!

Width 58'
Depth 56'-4"

MASTER BED RM. 12⁰ x 15⁴

GATH. RM. 18⁰ x 15⁴

DINING RM. 10⁰ x 12⁰

PORCH

BRKFST. RM. 15⁸ x 9⁰

FOYER 13'-0" CEILING

KIT. 13⁰ x 10⁴

BED RM. 12⁰ x 11⁴

STUDY/ BED RM. 13⁴ x 12⁰

PORCH

GARAGE 21⁴ x 21⁴

Design N3421

Square Footage: 2,145

L

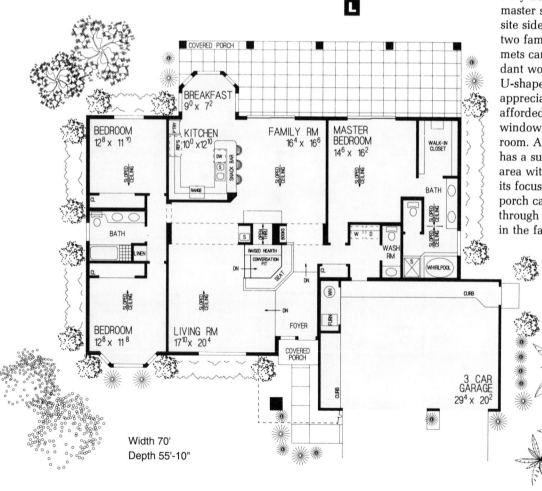

COVERED PORCH

BREAKFAST
9⁰ x 7²

BEDROOM
12⁸ x 11¹⁰

KITCHEN
10⁰ x 12¹⁰

PTRY

REFS

DW

S

SNACK BAR

RANGE

FAMILY RM
16⁴ x 16⁶

SLOPED CEILING

MASTER BEDROOM
14⁶ x 16²

SLOPED CEILING

WALK-IN CLOSET

BATH

CL

SLOPED CEILING

BATH

LINEN

S

OPEN SHELF

BOOKS

RAISED HEARTH

CONVERSATION PIT

DN

SEAT

DN

CL

W D

SLOPED CEILING

WASH RM

S

WHIRLPOOL

CL

SLOPED CEILING

BEDROOM
12⁸ x 11⁸

LIVING RM
17¹⁰ x 20⁴

SLOPED CEILING

DN

FOYER

WH

FURN

CURB

COVERED PORCH

CURB

3 CAR GARAGE
29⁴ x 20²

Width 70'
Depth 55'-10"

● Split-bedroom planning makes the most of a one-story design. In this case the master suite is on the opposite side of the house from two family bedrooms. Gourmets can rejoice at the abundant work space in the U-shaped kitchen and will appreciate the natural light afforded by the large bay window in the breakfast room. A formal living room has a sunken conversation area with a cozy fireplace as its focus. The rear covered porch can be reached through sliding glass doors in the family room.

Quote One™

Cost to build? See page 336 to order complete cost estimate to build this house in your area!

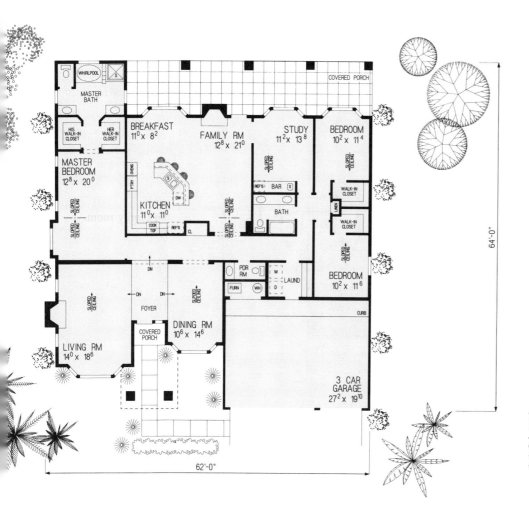

Design N3413

Square Footage: 2,517

L

● Though distinctly Southwest in design, this home
has some features that are
universally appealing. Note,
for instance, the central gallery, perpendicular to the
raised entry hall, and running almost the entire width
of the house. An L-shaped,
angled kitchen serves the
breakfast room and family
room in equal fashion.
Sleeping areas are found in
four bedrooms including an
optional study and exquisite
master suite.

Quote One™

Cost to build? See page 336
to order complete cost estimate
to build this house in your area!

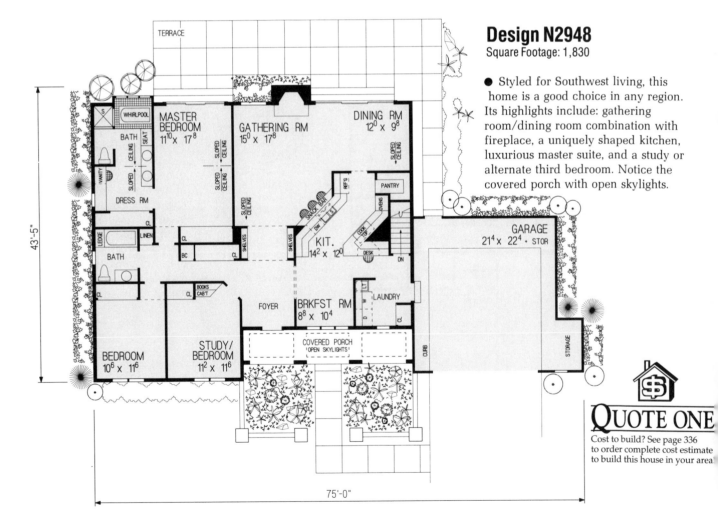

TERRACE

WHIRLPOOL

S

MASTER
BEDROOM
11¹⁰ x 17⁸

BATH
SEAT

VANITY

DRESS RM

LEDGE LINEN

CL

BATH

CL

BC

CL

BOOKS
CAB'T

CL

BEDROOM
10⁶ x 11⁶

STUDY/
BEDROOM
11² x 11⁶

FOYER

43'-5"

SLOPED CEILING

SLOPED CEILING

SLOPED CEILING

SLOPED CEILING

GATHERING RM
15⁰ x 17⁸

DINING RM
12⁰ x 9⁸

SLOPED CEILING

REF'S

PANTRY

KIT.
14² x 12⁰

DESK

DN

LAUNDRY

D W

CL

BRKFST RM
8⁸ x 10⁴

COVERED PORCH
(OPEN SKYLIGHTS)

CURB

GARAGE
21⁴ x 22⁴ + STOR

STORAGE

75'-0"

Design N2948
Square Footage: 1,830

● Styled for Southwest living, this
home is a good choice in any region.
Its highlights include: gathering
room/dining room combination with
fireplace, a uniquely shaped kitchen,
luxurious master suite, and a study or
alternate third bedroom. Notice the
covered porch with open skylights.

Design N2950
Square Footage 2,559

● A natural desert dweller, this stucco, tile-roofed beauty is equally comfortable in any clime. Inside, there's a well-planned design. Common living areas — gathering room, formal dining room, and breakfast room — are offset by a quiet study that could be used as a bedroom or guest room. A master suite features two walk-in closets, a double vanity, and whirlpool spa. The two-car garage has a service entrance; close by is an adequate laundry area and a pantry. Notice the warming hearth in the gathering room and the snack bar area for casual dining.

Quote One™

Cost to build? See page 336 to order complete cost estimate to build this house in your area!

Design N3422

Square Footage: 1,932

L

● An enclosed entry garden greets visitors to this charming Southwestern home. Inside, the foyer is flanked by formal and informal living areas—a living room and dining room to the right and a cozy study to the left. To the rear, a large family room, breakfast room and open kitchen have access to a covered porch and overlook the back yard. Notice the fireplace and bay window. The three-bedroom sleeping area includes a master with a spacious bath with whirlpool.

QUOTE ONE™
Cost to build? See page 336
to order complete cost estimate
to build this house in your area!

Width 50'
Depth 68'

Design N3419

Square Footage: 1,965

L

● This attractive, multi-gabled exterior houses a compact, livable interior. The entry foyer effectively routes traffic to all areas: left to the family room and kitchen, straight back to the dining room and living room, and right to the four-bedroom sleeping area. The spacious family room provides an informal gathering space while the living and dining rooms are perfect for formal occasions. The highlight of the sleeping area is the master bedroom with its whirlpool, walk-in closet and view of the back yard.

QUOTE ONE™
Cost to build? See page 336
to order complete cost estimate
to build this house in your area!

Width 56'
Depth 56'

Design N3322

First Floor: 1,860 square feet
Second Floor: 935 square feet
Total: 2,795 square feet

L **D**

● This cleverly designed Southwestern-style home takes its cue from the California Craftsman and Bungalow styles that have seen such an increase in popularity lately. Nonetheless, it is suited to just about any climate. Its convenient floor plan includes living and working areas on the first floor in addition to a master suite. The second floor holds two family bedrooms and a guest bedroom. Note the abundance of window area to the rear of the plan.

QUOTE ONE™

Cost to build? See page 336 to order complete cost estimate to build this house in your area!

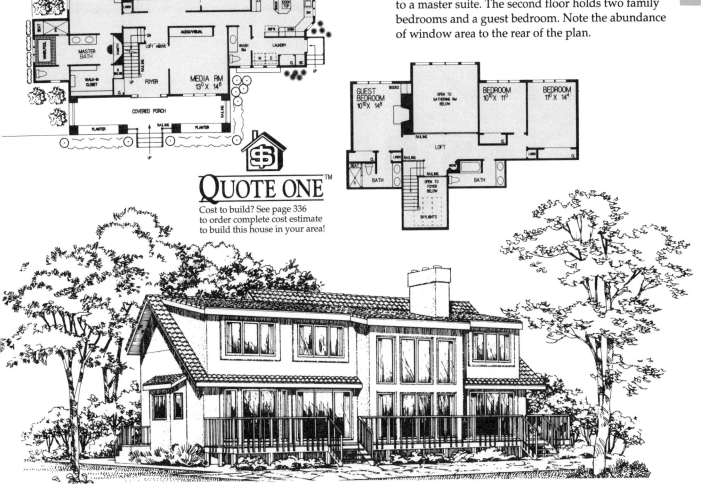

WIDTH 72'
DEPTH 57'-4"

COVERED PORCH

KITCHEN
14⁰ x 13²

BRKFST
9⁰ x 8⁶

PANTRY

MASTER
BEDROOM
13⁸ x 20⁶

MASTER
BATH

WALK-IN
CLOSET

VANITY

WALK-IN
CLOSET

DINING RM
12⁸ x 11⁸

BAR

FAMILY RM
21² x 15⁰

BEDROOM
12⁴ x 11⁶

FURN

LAUND

MECH RM

PDR
RM

FOYER

CURB

DN

COVERED
PORCH

LIVING RM
15⁴ x 12⁸

LIN

BATH

3 CAR
GARAGE
31⁴ x 21⁰

BEDROOM
12⁴ x 11⁸

BEDROOM
12⁴ x 11⁸

Design N3423
Square Footage: 2,577

● This spacious Southwestern home will be a pleasure to come home to. Immediately off the foyer are the dining room and step-down living room with bay window. The highlight of the four-bedroom sleeping area is the master suite with porch access and a whirlpool. The informal living area features an enormous family room with fireplace and bay-windowed kitchen and breakfast room.

QUOTE ONE™

Cost to build? See page 336
to order complete cost estimate
to build this house in your area!

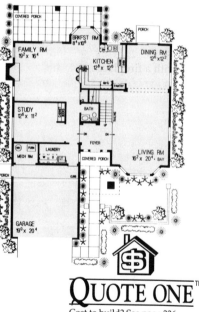

COVERED PORCH

FAMILY RM
19² x 16⁴

BRKFST RM
8⁴ x 10⁸

PORCH

KITCHEN
12⁸ x 12⁶

DINING RM
12⁶ x 12²

PANTRY

STUDY
12⁶ x 11²

BATH

FOYER

MECH RM

FURN

LAUNDRY

COVERED PORCH

LIVING RM
16² x 20⁴ bay

PORCH

CURB

GARAGE
19⁰ x 20⁴

BEDROOM
10⁸ x 10⁸

BEDROOM
10² x 12⁶

BATH

LINEN

BEDROOM
12⁸ x 11²

DN

UPPER LIVING RM

RAILING

RAILING

WHIRLPOOL

WALK-IN
CLOSET

UPPER FOYER

MASTER BATH

MASTER
BEDROOM
13⁰ x 13¹⁰

ROOF

ROOF

ROOF

Width 48'
Depth 65'-4"

Design N3427
First Floor: 1,574 square feet
Second Floor: 1,177 square feet
Total: 2,751 square feet

L

● Varying rooflines and unusual window treatments will make this home a standout anywhere. The transom-lit foyer opens onto a cozy study and a spacious living room with dramatic bay window. To the

QUOTE ONE™

Cost to build? See page 336
to order complete cost estimate
to build this house in your area!

rear, the kitchen easily serves the dining room and the bay-windowed breakfast room. The family room features a large fireplace. Upstairs are four bedrooms including a master with whirlpool bath.

Design N3639

First Floor: 2,137 square feet
Second Floor: 671 square feet
Total: 2,808 square feet

L

● This stucco home provides a wealth of livability for the entire family. Inside, formal living areas grab your attention with a dining room and an elegant living room that opens to a covered entertainment area outside. The family room—with a fireplace—delights with open views to the kitchen and breakfast nook. The nearby "recipe corner" includes a built-in desk. The laundry room is fully functional with a laundry tub and a broom closet. The two-car garage opens off this area. On the left side of the plan, the master bedroom suite delights with a full, private bath and a lanai perfect for a spa. A large den could easily double as a bedroom. Two bedrooms and a full bath are located upstairs.

QUOTE ONE™

Cost to build? See page 336 to order complete cost estimate to build this house in your area!

QUOTE ONE™

Cost to build? See page 336
to order complete cost estimate
to build this house in your area!

Design N3440

Square Footage: 2,290

L

● Pack 'em in! There's plenty of
room for everyone in this three-, or
optional four-bedroom home. The
expansive gathering room welcomes
family and guests with a through-
fireplace to the dining room, an
audio/visual center, and a door to
the outside. The kitchen includes a
wide pantry, a snack bar, and a separate eating area. Included in the
master suite: two walk-in closets,
shower, whirlpool tub and seat, dual
vanities, and linen storage.

Design N3430
Square Footage: 2,394

L

● This dramatic design benefits from open planning. The centerpiece of the living area is a sunken conversation pit which shares a through-fireplace with the family room. The living room and dining room share space beneath a sloped ceiling. The open kitchen features a snack bar and breakfast room and conveniently serves all living areas. Split zoning in the sleeping area places the private master suite to the left of the plan and three more bedrooms, including one with a bay window, to the right.

Width 72'
Depth 60'-6"

QUOTE ONE™
Cost to build? See page 336
to order complete cost estimate
to build this house in your area!

Design N3412
Square Footage: 2,150

L

● Although typically Southwestern in design, this home will bring style to any neighborhood. Huge bay windows flood the front living and dining rooms with plenty of natural light. An amenity-filled kitchen with attached family room will be the main gathering area, where the family works and relaxes together. Notice the fireplace, the island snack bar and walk-in pantry. A split sleeping zone separates the master suite with luxurious bath from the two family bedrooms. Also notice the covered porch off the family room.

QUOTE ONE™
Cost to build? See page 336
to order complete cost estimate
to build this house in your area!

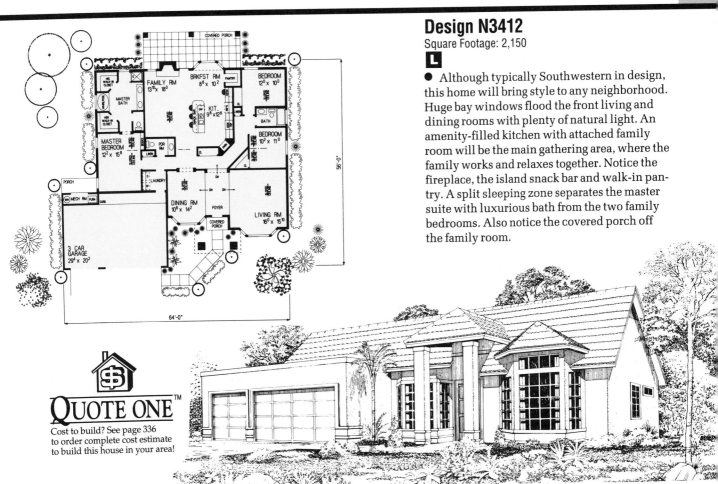

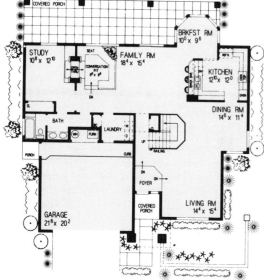

Width 54'
Depth 55'-4"

QUOTE ONE™
Cost to build? See page 336
to order complete cost estimate
to build this house in your area!

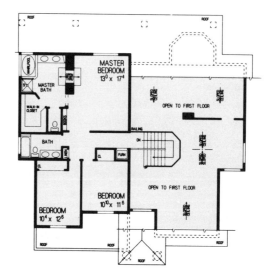

Design N3424

First Floor: 1,625 square feet
Second Floor: 982 square feet
Total: 2,607 square feet

L

● You'll find plenty about this Spanish design that will convince you that this is the home for your family. Enjoy indoor/outdoor living in the gigantic family room with covered patio access and a sunken conversation area sharing a through-fireplace with the study. An L-shaped kitchen has an attached, glass-surrounded breakfast room and is conveniently located next to the formal dining room/living room combination. Besides the opulent master suite on the second floor, there are two family bedrooms and a full bath.

Design N3449

First Floor: 1,336 square feet
Second Floor: 1,186 square feet
Total: 2,522 square feet

A covered porch leads inside to a wide, tiled foyer. A curving staircase makes an elegant statement in the open space between the living room and dining room. A through fireplace warms the nook and family room. Also look for a wet bar and glass shelves here. The master bedroom includes a sitting area, two closets and its own deck. Two family bedrooms share a full bath with dual vanities.

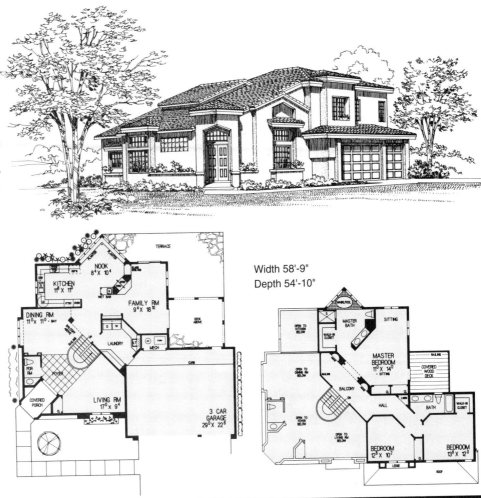

Width 58'-9"
Depth 54'-10"

QUOTE ONE™

Cost to build? See page 336 to order complete cost estimate to build this house in your area!

QUOTE ONE™

Cost to build? See page 336 to order complete cost estimate to build this house in your area!

Design N3323

First Floor: 1,923 square feet
Second Floor: 838 square feet
Total: 2,761 square feet

● Take a step down from the foyer to a gathering room with fireplace and reading alcove, to a media room or to a dining room with sliding glass doors to the terrace. The kitchen has an island range and eating space. Also on the first floor is a large master suite including a sitting area with terrace access, a walk-in closet and whirlpool. An elegant spiral staircase leads to two family bedrooms which share a full bath and a guest bedroom with private bath.

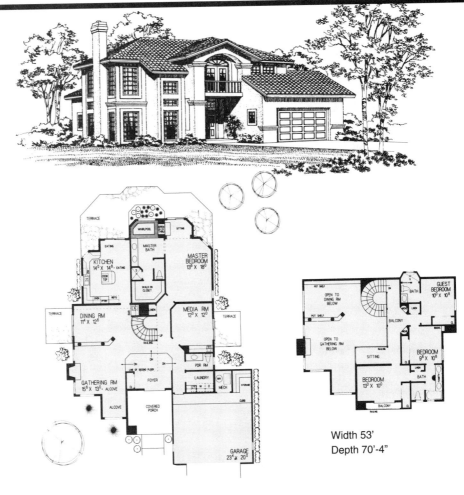

Width 53'
Depth 70'-4"

Design N3414

First Floor: 2,024 square feet
Second Floor: 1,144 square feet
Total: 3,168 square feet

L

QUOTE ONE™

Cost to build? See page 336
to order complete cost estimate
to build this house in your area!

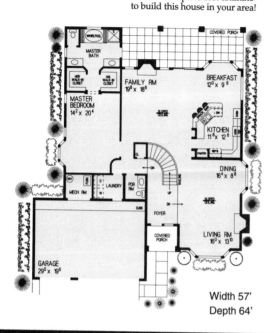

Width 57'
Depth 64'

● Though seemingly compact from the exterior, this home allows for "wide-open-spaces" living. The two-story entry connects directly to a formal living/dining area, a fitting complement to the more casual family room and cozy breakfast room. Split-bedroom planning puts the master suite on the first floor for utmost privacy. Up the curved staircase are three family bedrooms, a guest room with deck, and two full baths.

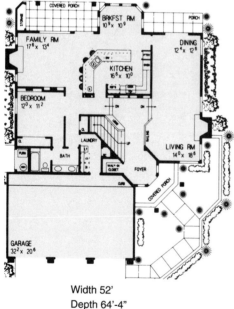

Width 52'
Depth 64'-4"

Design N3425

First Floor: 1,776 square feet
Second Floor: 1,035 square feet
Total: 2,811 square feet

● Here's a two-story Spanish design with an appealing, angled exterior. Inside is an interesting floor plan containing rooms with a variety of shapes. Formal areas are to the right of the entry tower: a living room with fireplace and

QUOTE ONE™

Cost to build? See page 336
to order complete cost estimate
to build this house in your area!

large dining room. The kitchen has loads of counter space and is complemented by a bumped-out breakfast room. Note the second fireplace in the family room, and the first-floor bedroom. Three second-floor bedrooms include a master suite with balcony.

176

Design N3435

First Floor: 1,946 square feet
Second Floor: 986 square feet
Total: 2,932 square feet

L

● Here's a grand Spanish Mission home designed for family living. Enter at the angled foyer which contains a curved staircase to the second floor. Family bedrooms are here along with a spacious guest suite. The master bedroom is found on the first floor and has a private patio and whirlpool overlooking an enclosed garden area. Besides a living room and dining room connected by a through-fireplace, there is a family room with casual eating space. There is also a library with large closet. You'll appreciate the abundant built-ins and interesting shapes throughout the house.

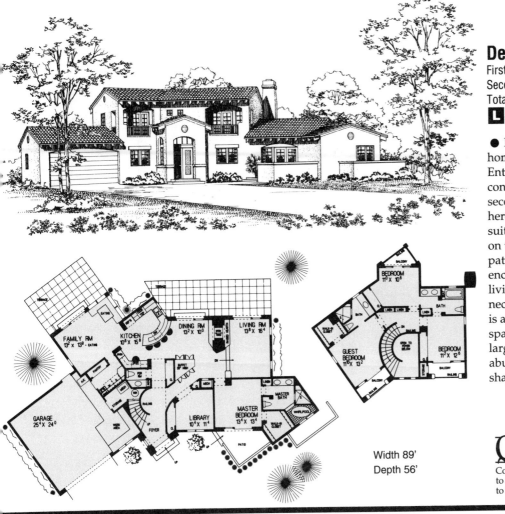

Width 89'
Depth 56'

QUOTE ONE™

Cost to build? See page 336 to order complete cost estimate to build this house in your area!

Design N3437

First Floor: 1,522 square feet
Second Floor: 800 square feet
Total: 2,322 square feet

L

● This two-story Spanish Mission-style home has character inside and out. The first-floor master suite features a fireplace and gracious bath with walk-in closet, whirlpool, shower, dual vanities and linen storage. A second fireplace serves both the gathering room and media room or library. The kitchen, with island cook top, includes a snack bar and an adjoining breakfast nook. Three bedrooms and two full baths occupy the second floor.

QUOTE ONE™

Cost to build? See page 336 to order complete cost estimate to build this house in your area!

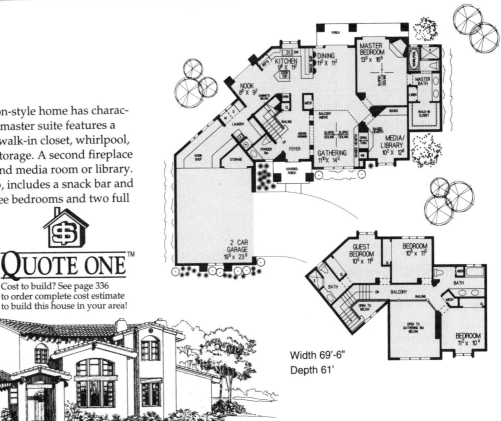

Width 69'-6"
Depth 61'

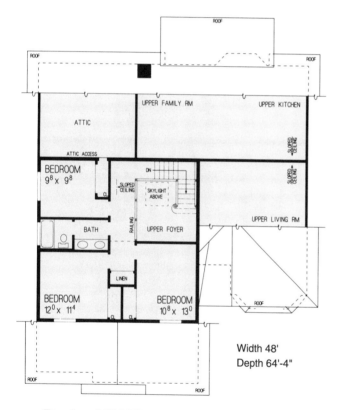

Width 48'
Depth 64'-4"

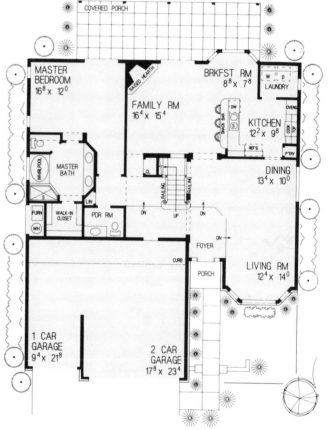

Design N3420 First Floor: 1,617 square feet
Second Floor: 658 square feet; Total: 2,275 square feet
L

● Here is a moderate-sized house with a wealth of amenities typical of much larger homes. Interesting window treatments include two bay windows, one in the living room and one in the breakfast room. In the kitchen there's a snack bar pass-through to the family room which boasts a corner raised-hearth fireplace. Also on this level, the master suite features a large bath with whirlpool and access to the rear covered porch. Upstairs are three more bedrooms and a shared bath. Notice the attic storage space.

Quote One™

Cost to build? See page 336
to order complete cost estimate
to build this house in your area!

Design N3432

First Floor: 1,966 square feet
Second Floor: 831 square feet
Total: 2,797 square feet

L

● Unique in nature, this two-story Santa Fe-style home is as practical as it is lovely. The facade is elegantly enhanced by a large entry court, overlooked by windows in the dining room and a covered patio from one of two family bedrooms. The entry foyer leads to living areas at the back of the plan: a living room with corner fireplace and a family room connected to the kitchen via a built-in eating nook. Upstairs, the master suite features a grand bath and large walk-in closet. The guest bedroom has a private bath. Every room in this home has its own outdoor area.

QUOTE ONE™

Cost to build? See page 336 to order complete cost estimate to build this house in your area!

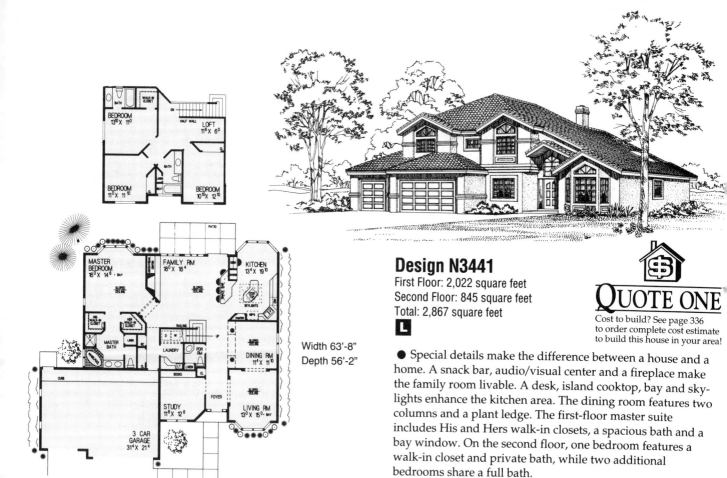

Design N3441

First Floor: 2,022 square feet
Second Floor: 845 square feet
Total: 2,867 square feet

L

Width 63'-8"
Depth 56'-2"

QUOTE ONE

Cost to build? See page 336
to order complete cost estimate
to build this house in your area!

● Special details make the difference between a house and a
home. A snack bar, audio/visual center and a fireplace make
the family room livable. A desk, island cooktop, bay and skylights enhance the kitchen area. The dining room features two
columns and a plant ledge. The first-floor master suite
includes His and Hers walk-in closets, a spacious bath and a
bay window. On the second floor, one bedroom features a
walk-in closet and private bath, while two additional
bedrooms share a full bath.

Design N3447

First Floor: 1,861 square feet
Second Floor: 1,039 square feet
Total: 2,900 square feet

L **D**

● Family activities of all types have a distinct place in this home.
The first floor contains a game room, along with a living room/dining
room combination with sloped ceiling. The family room is also on this
floor and has a cozy fireplace. The spacious, angled kitchen includes a
snack bar, walk-in pantry, and adjacent breakfast area with a bay. An
elegant staircase is accented by a niche and art gallery. The master bedroom features a private deck, two closets and a lavish bath. Two additional bedrooms share a full bath.

QUOTE ONE™

Cost to build? See page 336
to order complete cost estimate
to build this house in your area!

Width 64'
Depth 52'

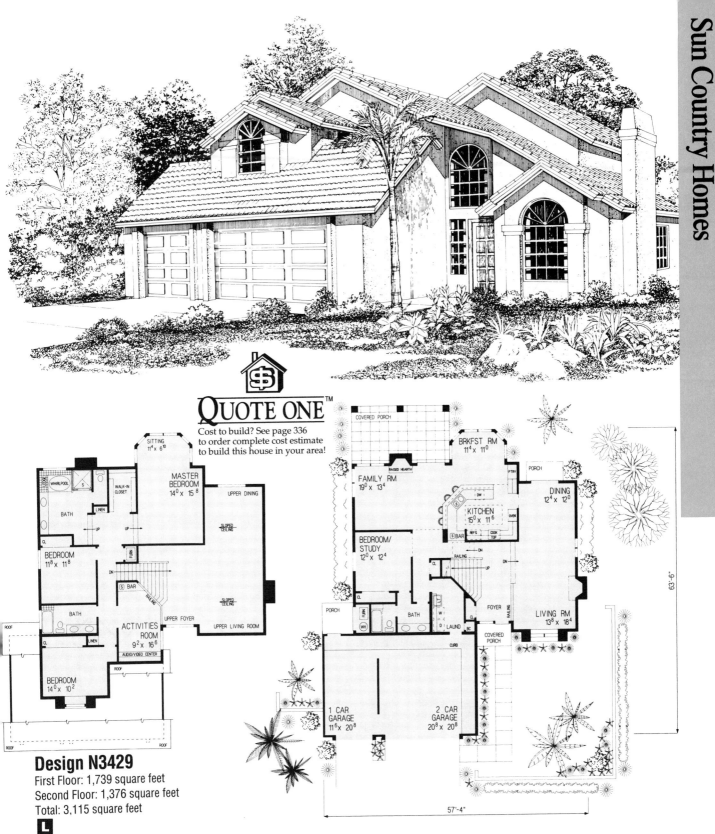

QUOTE ONE™

Cost to build? See page 336
to order complete cost estimate
to build this house in your area!

SITTING
11⁴ x 6¹⁰

WHIRLPOOL   S

WALK-IN
CLOSET

MASTER
BEDROOM
14⁰ x 15⁸

UPPER DINING

BATH   LINEN

UP   UP

FURN.

SLOPED
CEILING

BEDROOM
11⁸ x 11⁸

DN

S   BAR

RAILING

BATH

UPPER FOYER

SLOPED
CEILING

CL   LINEN

ACTIVITIES
ROOM
9² x 16⁶

UPPER LIVING ROOM

AUDIO/VIDEO CENTER

ROOF

BEDROOM
14⁰ x 10²

ROOF   ROOF

ROOF

COVERED PORCH

BRKFST RM
11⁴ x 11⁰

FAMILY RM
19⁰ x 13⁴

RAISED HEARTH

DW

KITCHEN
15⁰ x 11⁶

OVEN

PTRY

PORCH

DINING
12⁴ x 12⁰

S BAR

REF'S   COOK TOP

BEDROOM/
STUDY
12⁰ x 12⁴

RAILING   DN

CL   UP

DN

PORCH   FURN.

BATH

CL

W   D   LAUND.

BC

FOYER   RAILING

LIVING RM
13⁸ x 18⁴

WH

COVERED
PORCH

PORCH

CURB

1 CAR
GARAGE
11⁶ x 20⁸

2 CAR
GARAGE
20⁸ x 20⁸

63'-6"

57'-4"

Design N3429

First Floor: 1,739 square feet
Second Floor: 1,376 square feet
Total: 3,115 square feet

L

● From the dramatic open entry to the covered back porch, this home delivers a full measure of livability in Spanish design. Formal living areas (living room and dining room) have a counter-point in the family room and glassed-in breakfast room. The kitchen is a hub for both areas. Notice that the first-floor study has an adjacent bath, making it a fine guest room when needed. On the second floor, the activities room serves two family bedrooms and a grand master suite.

Design N2850

Main Level: 1,530 square feet
Upper Level: 984 square feet
Lower Level: 951 square feet
Total: 3,465 square feet

L D

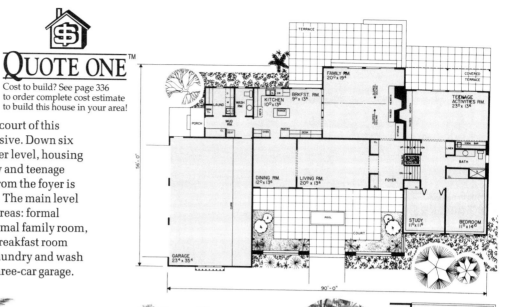

QUOTE ONE

Cost to build? See page 336
to order complete cost estimate
to build this house in your area!

● Entering through the entry court of this
Spanish design is very impressive. Down six
steps from the foyer is the lower level, housing
a bedroom and full bath, study and teenage
activities room. Six steps up from the foyer is
the upper-level bedroom area. The main level
has the majority of the living areas: formal
living and dining rooms, informal family room,
kitchen with accompanying breakfast room
and mud room consisting of laundry and wash
room. This home even has a three-car garage.

Design N2843

Upper Level: 1,861 square feet
Lower Level: 1,181 square feet
Total: 3,042 square feet

L

● Bi-level living will be enjoyed to its fullest in
this Spanish- styled design. There is a lot of
room for the various family activities. Informal
living will take place on the lower level in the
family room and lounge. The formal living and
dining rooms, sharing a through-fireplace, are
located on the upper level.

Design N3407

First Floor: 2,401 square feet
Second Floor: 927 square feet
Total: 3,328 square feet

L

● Honored traditions are echoed throughout this warm and inviting Santa Fe home. A large, two-story gathering room with a bee-hive fireplace provides a soothing atmosphere for entertaining or quiet interludes. A gallery leads to the kitchen and breakfast area. Abundant counter space and a work island will please the heartiest of cooks. A media room, with a full entertainment center, offers interesting angles. Nearby, the laundry room gains entry to the three-car garage. On the right side of the plan, the master suite revels in privacy. Bumped up to a study, this bedroom pleases with its own fireplace and a luxurious bath that sports dual lavatories, a whirlpool tub and a curved shower. On the second floor, three bedrooms and a reading loft leave room for all the kids.

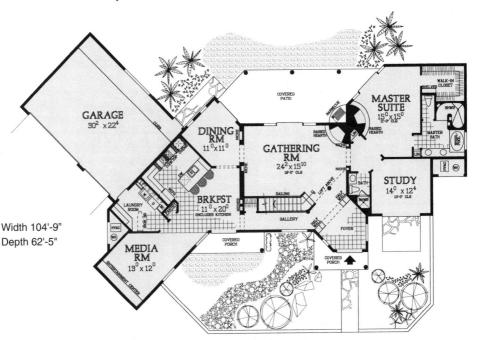

Width 104'-9"
Depth 62'-5"

Cost to build? See page 336
to order complete cost estimate
to build this house in your area!

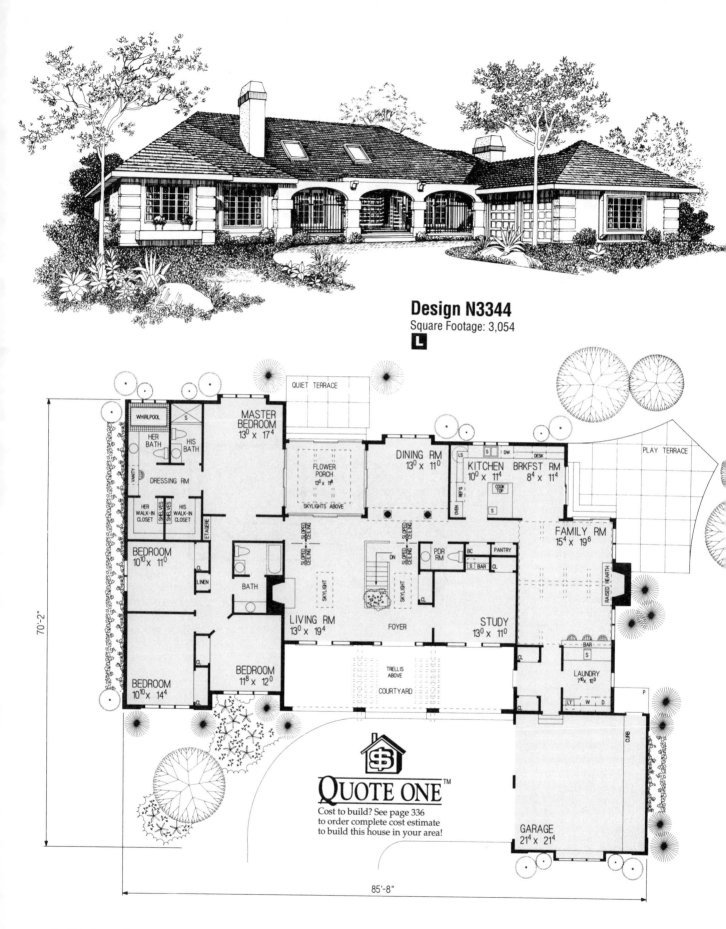

Design N3344

Square Footage: 3,054

L

QUIET TERRACE

MASTER BEDROOM
13⁰ x 17⁴

WHIRLPOOL   S

HER BATH   HIS BATH

DRESSING RM

VANITY

HER WALK-IN CLOSET   SHELVES   SHELVES   HIS WALK-IN CLOSET

FLOWER PORCH
13⁰ x 11⁰
SKYLIGHTS ABOVE

DINING RM
13⁰ x 11⁰

KITCHEN
10⁰ x 11⁴   BRKFST RM
8⁴ x 11⁴

LS   S   DW   DESK

REFG

COOK TOP

S

PLAY TERRACE

BEDROOM
10¹⁰ x 11⁰

ETAGERE

LINEN

BATH

SLOPED CEILING   SLOPED CEILING   SLOPED CEILING   SLOPED CEILING

SKYLIGHT   SKYLIGHT

DN

PDR RM   BC   PANTRY
S   BAR   CL

FAMILY RM
15⁴ x 19⁶

RAISED HEARTH

LIVING RM
13⁰ x 19⁴

FOYER

STUDY
13⁰ x 11⁰

CL

BAR
S

BEDROOM
11⁸ x 12⁰

CL

TRELLIS ABOVE

COURTYARD

CL

LAUNDRY
7⁰ x 10⁰

LT   W   D

BEDROOM
10¹⁰ x 14⁴

CL

70'-2"

P

Quote One™

Cost to build? See page 336
to order complete cost estimate
to build this house in your area!

GARAGE
21⁴ x 21⁴

85'-8"

● This home features interior planning for today's active family. Living areas include a living room with fireplace, a cozy study and family room with wet bar. Convenient to the kitchen is the formal dining room with attractive bay window overlooking the back yard. The four-bedroom sleeping area con-tains a sumptuous master suite. Also notice the cheerful flower porch with access from the master suite, living room and dining room.

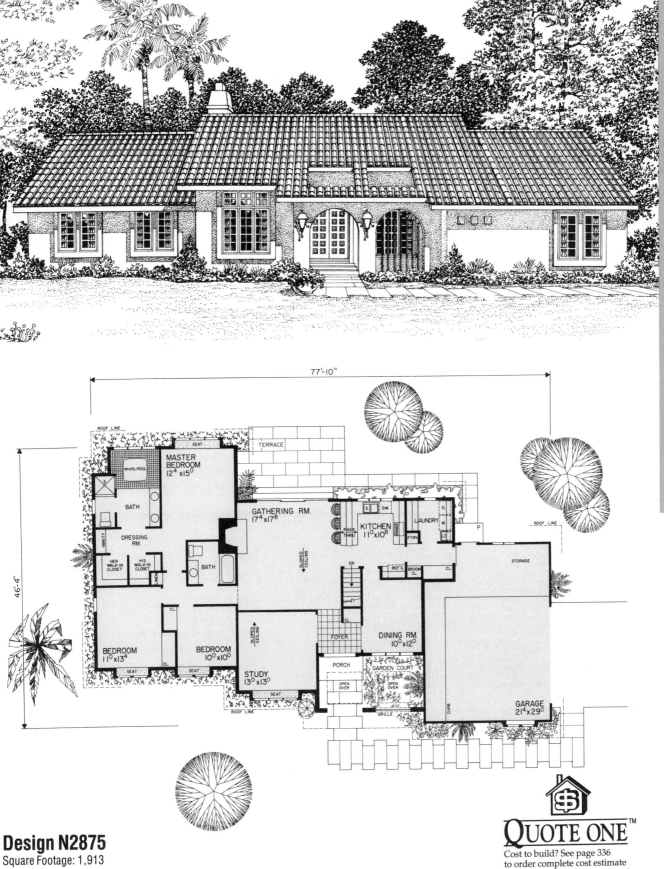

Design N2875
Square Footage: 1,913

● This elegant Spanish design incorporates excellent indoor-outdoor living relationships for modern families who enjoy the sun and comforts of a well-planned new home. Note the overhead openings for rain and sun to fall upon a front garden, while a twin arched entry leads to the front porch and foyer. Inside the floor plan features a modern kitchen with pass-thru to a large gathering room with fireplace. Other features include a dining room, laundry room, a study off the foyer, plus three bedrooms including master bedroom with its own whirlpool.

QUOTE ONE™
Cost to build? See page 336
to order complete cost estimate
to build this house in your area!

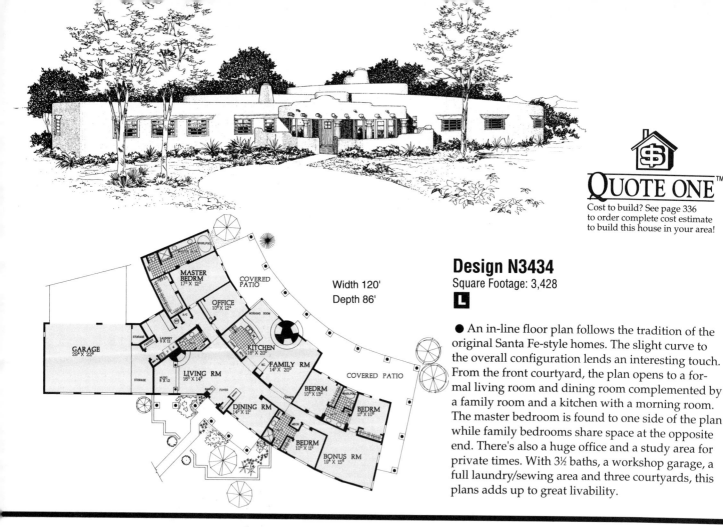

Design N3434

Square Footage: 3,428

L

● An in-line floor plan follows the tradition of the original Santa Fe-style homes. The slight curve to the overall configuration lends an interesting touch. From the front courtyard, the plan opens to a formal living room and dining room complemented by a family room and a kitchen with a morning room. The master bedroom is found to one side of the plan while family bedrooms share space at the opposite end. There's also a huge office and a study area for private times. With 3½ baths, a workshop garage, a full laundry/sewing area and three courtyards, this plans adds up to great livability.

Width 120'
Depth 86'

Design N3486

Square Footage: 2,000

● This home's distinctive roof lines complement varied stucco wall surfaces. The central foyer is dramatic with an eleven-foot ceiling, a skylight and a plant shelf. Just beyond an arched-ceiling passageway is the gathering room. Open planning between the kitchen and the breakfast room will make mealtimes a breeze. The sleeping wing is well-defined with its outstanding master suite, extra bedroom and study. In the master bath, twin lavatories, a stall shower and a whirlpool create a pampering atmosphere. French doors in the master bedroom lead to a rear terrace.

Width 75'
Depth 55'

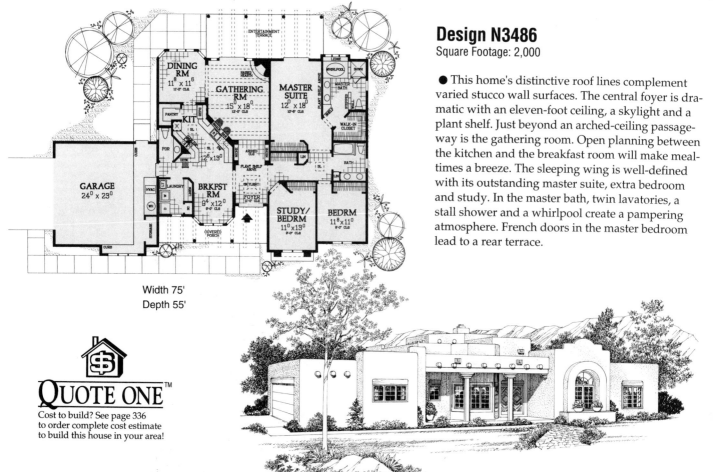

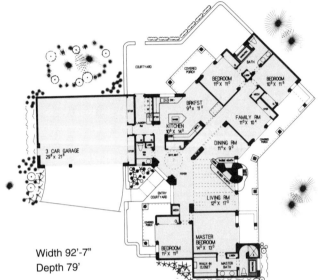

Width 92'-7"
Depth 79'

Design N3433
Square Footage: 2,350

L

● Santa Fe styling creates interesting angles in this one-story home. The master suite features a deluxe bath and a bedroom close at hand, perfect for a nursery, home office or exercise room. Fireplaces in the living room, dining room and covered porch create various shapes. Make note of the island range in the kitchen, extra storage in the garage, and covered porches on two sides.

QUOTE ONE™

Cost to build? See page 336 to order complete cost estimate to build this house in your area!

Design N3431
Square Footage: 1,907

● Graceful curves welcome you into the courtyard of this Santa Fe home. Inside, a gallery directs traffic to the work zone on the left or the sleeping zone on the right. Straight ahead lies a sunken gathering room with beamed ceiling and raised-hearth fireplace. A large pantry offers extra storage space for kitchen items. The covered rear porch is accessible from the dining room, gathering room and secluded master bedroom. Two family bedrooms share a compartmented bath. The study could serve as a guest room, media room or home office.

Width 61'-6"
Depth 67'-4"

QUOTE ONE™

Cost to build? See page 336 to order complete cost estimate to build this house in your area!

QUOTE ONE™
Cost to build? See page 336
to order complete cost estimate
to build this house in your area!

TERRACE

TERRACE

TERRACE

GATHERING RM.
26⁰ x22⁰

DINING RM.
15⁰ x12⁰

STUDY
14⁰ x10⁰

MORNING RM.
12⁰ x12⁰

MASTER BEDROOM
20⁰ x14⁰

ALCOVE

KITCHEN
15⁰ x12⁰

SITTING RM.
14⁰ x10⁴

BAR

FOYER

BATH

DRESSING RM.

MECH. RM.

WALK-IN CLOSET

COVERED PORCH

WASH RM.

LAUNDRY

STORAGE

BATH

BEDROOM
12⁰ x11⁰

COURTYARD

TERRACE

BEDROOM
15⁰ x12⁰

MECH.

GATE

3 CAR GARAGE
30⁰ x21⁴

Width 110'-7"
Depth 66'-11"

Design N2922
Square Footage: 3,505

● Loaded with custom features, this plan seems to have everything imaginable. There's an enormous sunken gathering room and cozy study. The country-style kitchen contains an efficient work area, as well as space for relaxing in the morning and sitting rooms. Two nice-sized bedrooms and a luxurious master suite round out the plan.

Design N3480
Square Footage: 1,845

● The inviting facade of this sun-country home introduces a most livable floor plan. Beyond the grand entry, a comfortable gathering room, with a central fireplace, shares sweeping, open spaces with the dining room. An efficiently patterned kitchen makes use of a large, walk-in pantry and a breakfast room. Nearby, a full laundry room rounds out the modern livability of this utilitarian area. Away from the hustle and bustle of the day, three bedrooms provide ample sleeping accommodations for the whole family. Two secondary bedrooms each enjoy full proportions and the convenience of a nearby full bath. In the master bedroom, look for double closets and a pampering bath with double lavs, a vanity and a whirlpool bath.

QUOTE ONE™
Cost to build? See page 336
to order complete cost estimate
to build this house in your area!

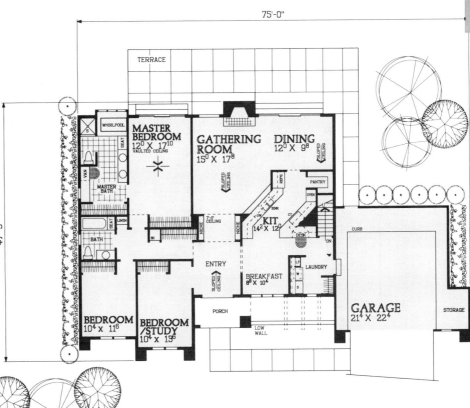

94'-6"

79'-11"

COVERED PATIO

COVERED REAR PORCH

PRIVATE PATIO

TRELLIS ABOVE

FAMILY ENTERTAINMENT PATIO

TRELLIS ABOVE

KIT
11⁰ x 10⁸
10'-0" CLG.

LIVING RM
15⁰ x 15⁹
11'-6" CLG.

WET BAR

STUDY
11⁶ x 11⁰

MASTER BEDRM
16⁸ x 14²
10'-0" CLG.

MBA

SEAT

WALK-IN CLOSET

NOOK
8⁸ x 9²
10'-0" CLG.

PANTRY

DINING RM
15⁰ x 11⁰
11'-6" CLG.

SLOPED CEILING

BEDRM
13² x 12⁶
10'-0" CLG.

LAUNDRY

FAMILY RM
12⁷ x 14⁰
10'-0" CLG.

FOYER

PDR

LINEN

BATH

WALK-IN CLOSET

WALK-IN CLOSET

STORAGE ROOM

WORK SHOP

HVAC

COVERED PATIO

COVERED PORCH

BEDRM
15² x 10¹⁰
10'-0" CLG.

HVAC

PRIVACY WALL

GARAGE
21⁹ x 29⁰

PRIVATE PATIO

CURB

PRIVACY WALL

Design N3436
Square Footage: 2,573

L

Quote One™

Cost to build? See page 336
to order complete cost estimate
to build this house in your area!

● Dress up the neighborhood with this dashing Spanish home. A front courtyard presents a delightful introduction to the inside living spaces. These excel with a central living room/dining room combination. A wet bar here makes entertaining easy. In the kitchen, a huge pantry and interesting angles are sure to please the house gourmet. A breakfast nook with a corner fireplace further enhances this area. Notice the laundry room nearby as well as the expansive work shop just off the three-car garage. The master bedroom makes room for a private bath with a whirlpool tub and dual lavatories; a walk-in closet adds to the modern amenities here. Two additional bedrooms make use of a Hollywood bath. Each bedroom is highlighted by a spacious walk-in closet.

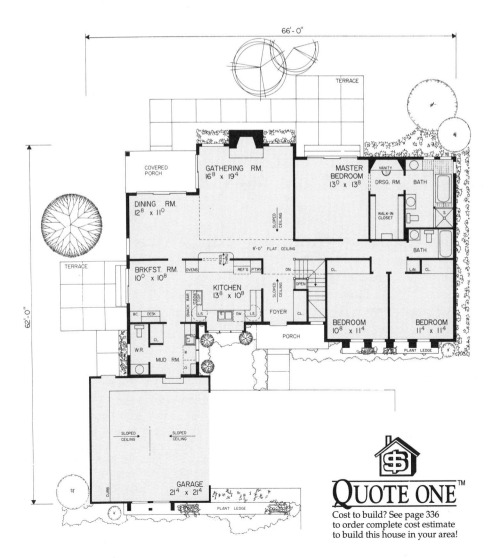

66'-0"

TERRACE

62'-0"

COVERED PORCH

GATHERING RM.
16⁸ x 19⁴

MASTER BEDROOM
13⁰ x 13⁸

VANITY

DRSG. RM.

BATH

DINING RM.
12⁸ x 11⁰

SLOPED CEILING

WALK-IN CLOSET

BATH

8'-0" FLAT CEILING

TERRACE

BRKFST. RM.
10⁰ x 10⁸

OVENS

PASS THRU

REF'G

PTRY

DN

CL.

L.IN.

CL.

KITCHEN
13⁸ x 10⁸

SNACK BAR

COOK TOP

SLOPED CEILING

OPEN

CL.

BEDROOM
10⁸ x 11⁴

BEDROOM
11⁴ x 11⁴

BC

DESK

LS

S

DW

LS

FOYER

CL.

PORCH

PLANT LEDGE

CL.

W.R.

MUD RM.

SLOPED CEILING

SLOPED CEILING

GARAGE
21⁴ x 21⁴

CURB

PLANT LEDGE

QUOTE ONE™

Cost to build? See page 336
to order complete cost estimate
to build this house in your area!

Design N2912
Square Footage: 1,864

● This modern design with smart Spanish styling incorporates careful zoning by room functions with lifestyle comfort. All three bedrooms, including a master bedroom suite, are isolated at one end of the one-story home for privacy and out of traffic patterns. Entry to a breakfast room and kitchen is possible through a mud room off the garage. That's good news for people carrying groceries from car to kitchen or people with muddy shoes during inclement weather. The modern kitchen includes a snack bar and cook top with multiple access to breakfast room, side foyer, and pass-thru to hallway. There's also a nearby formal dining room. A large rear gathering room features sloped ceiling and its own fireplace. Note the two-car garage and built-in plant ledge in front. Gabled end window treatment plus varied roof lines further enhance the striking appearance of this efficient design.

Design N3403
First Floor: 2,240 square feet
Second Floor: 660 square feet
Total: 2,900 square feet

L

QUOTE ONE™

Cost to build? See page 336
to order complete cost estimate
to build this house in your area!

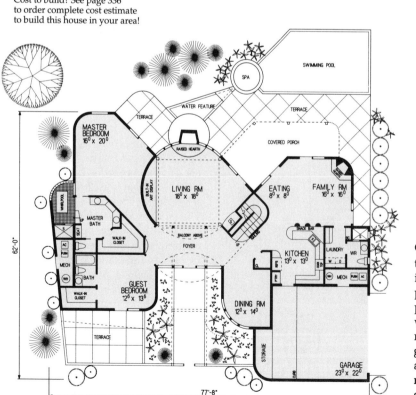

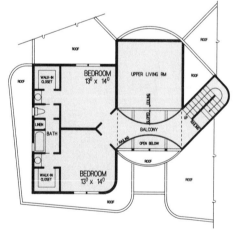

● There is no end to the distinctive features in
this Southwestern contemporary. Formal living areas are concentrated in the center of the
plan, perfect for entertaining. To the right of the
plan, the kitchen and family room function
well together as a working and living area. Also
note the separate laundry room. The optional
guest bedroom or den and the master bedroom
are located to the left of the plan. Upstairs, the
remaining two bedrooms are reached by a balcony overlooking the living room and share a
bath with twin vanities.

QUOTE ONE™

ost to build? See page 336
order complete cost estimate
build this house in your area!

Design N3316

First Floor: 1,111 square feet
Second Floor: 886 square feet
Total: 1,997 square feet

L

● Don't be fooled by a small-looking exterior. This plan offers three bedrooms and plenty of living space. Notice that the screened porch leads to a rear terrace with access to the breakfast room. A living room/dining room combination adds spaciousness to the first floor.

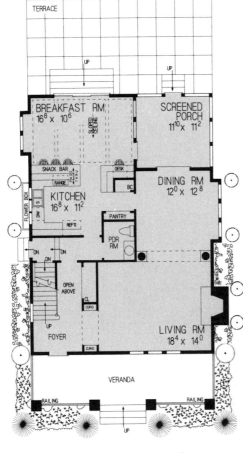

Width 34'-1"
Depth 50'

Design N2682

First Floor (Basic Plan): 976 square feet
First Floor (Expanded Plan): 1,230 square feet
Second Floor (Both Plans): 744 square feet
Total (Basic Plan): 1,720; Total (Expanded Plan): 1,974

L **D**

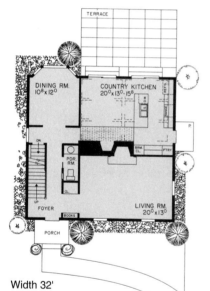

Width 32'
Depth 32'

DINING RM.
10⁸ x 12⁰

TERRACE

COUNTRY KITCHEN
20⁰ x 13⁰ -15⁸

PDR. RM.

FOYER

BOOKS

LIVING RM.
20⁰ x 13⁰

PORCH

BEDROOM
12¹⁰ x 9⁸

BEDROOM
12¹⁰ x 9⁸

ROOF

DN

LINEN

BATH

BATH

MASTER BEDROOM
11¹⁰ x 14⁰

ROOF

● Here is an expandable Colonial with a full measure of Cape Cod Charm. For those who wish to build the basic house, there is an abundance of low-budget livability. Twin fireplaces serve the formal living room and the informal country kitchen. Note the spaciousness of both areas. A dining room and powder room are also on the first floor of this basic plan. Upstairs three bedrooms and two full baths.

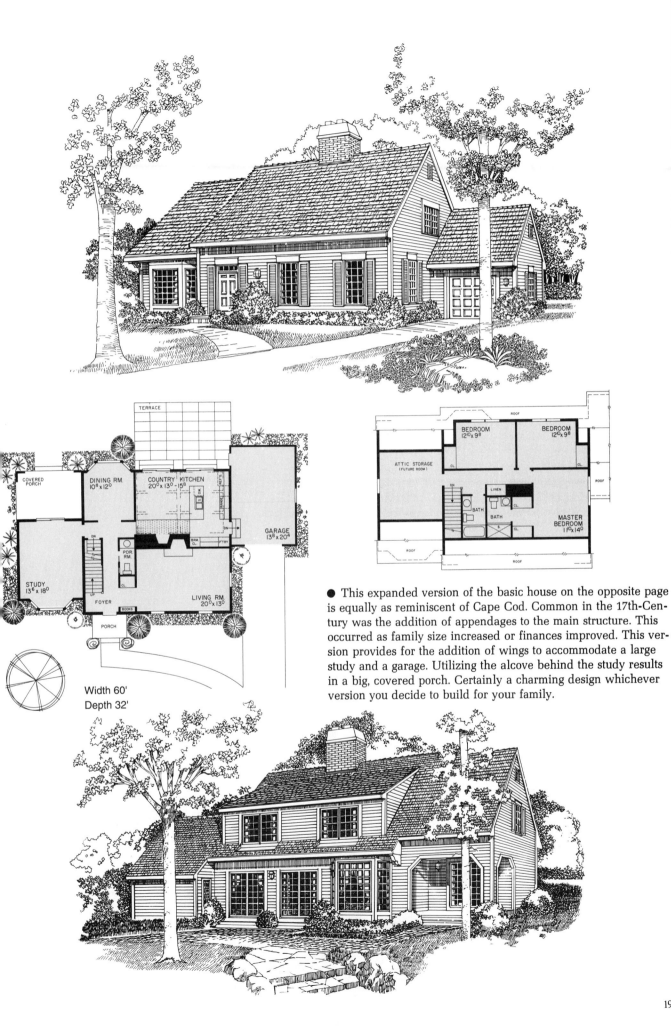

TERRACE

COVERED PORCH

DINING RM.
10⁸ x 12⁰

COUNTRY KITCHEN
20⁰ x 13⁰ - 15⁸

GARAGE
13⁸ x 20⁴

STUDY
13⁶ x 18⁰

PDR. RM.

FOYER

BOOKS

LIVING RM.
20⁰ x 13⁰

PORCH

Width 60'
Depth 32'

ROOF

BEDROOM
12¹⁰ x 9⁸

BEDROOM
12⁰ x 9⁸

ATTIC STORAGE
(FUTURE ROOM)

LINEN

BATH

BATH

MASTER BEDROOM
11⁰ x 14⁰

ROOF

ROOF

ROOF

● This expanded version of the basic house on the opposite page is equally as reminiscent of Cape Cod. Common in the 17th-Century was the addition of appendages to the main structure. This occurred as family size increased or finances improved. This version provides for the addition of wings to accommodate a large study and a garage. Utilizing the alcove behind the study results in a big, covered porch. Certainly a charming design whichever version you decide to build for your family.

Design N2657

First Floor: 1,217 square feet
Second Floor: 868 square feet
Total: 2,085 square feet

L

QUOTE ONE™

Cost to build? See page 336
to order complete cost estimate
to build this house in your area!

● Deriving its design from the traditional Cape Cod style, this facade features clap board siding,
small-paned windows and a
transom-lit entrance flanked by
carriage lamps. A central chimney
services two fireplaces, one in the
country-kitchen and the other in
the formal living room which is
removed from the disturbing flow
of traffic. The master suite is located to the left of the upstairs land-
ing. A full bathroom services two
additional bedrooms.

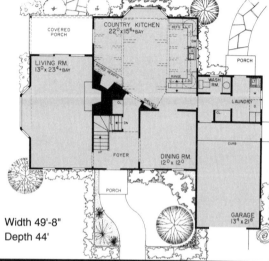

Width 49'-8"
Depth 44'

● Historically referred to as a "half house,"
this authentic adaptation has its roots in the
heritage of New England. With completion of
the second floor, the growing family doubles
their sleeping capacity. Notice that the overall
width of the house is only 44 feet. Take note of
the covered porch leading to the garage and
flower court.

QUOTE ONE™

Cost to build? See page 336
to order complete cost estimate
to build this house in your area!

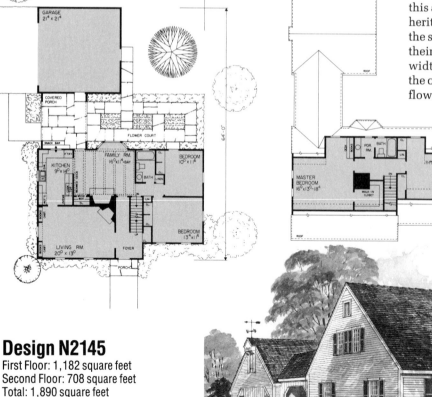

Design N2145

First Floor: 1,182 square feet
Second Floor: 708 square feet
Total: 1,890 square feet

L

● Captivating as a New England village! From the weather vane atop the garage to the roofed side entry and paned windows, this home is perfectly detailed. Inside, there is a lot of living space. An exceptionally large family room which is more than 29' by 13' including a dining area. The adjoining kitchen has a laundry just steps away. Two formal rooms are in the front.

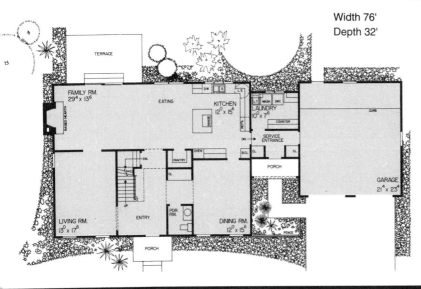

Width 76'
Depth 32'

Design N2596

First Floor: 1,489 square feet
Second Floor: 982 square feet
Total: 2,471 square feet

L D

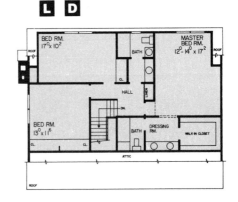

Design N2146

First Floor: 1,182 square feet
Second Floor: 708 square feet
Total: 1,890 square feet

L D

● Historically referred to as a "half house," this authentic adaptation has its roots in the heritage of New England. With completion of the second floor, the growing family doubles its sleeping capacity. Notice that both the family and living rooms have a fireplace. Don't overlook the many built-in units featured throughout the plan.

Design N2569 First Floor: 1,102 square feet
Second Floor: 764 square feet; Total: 1,866 square feet

L D

● What an enchanting updated version of the popular Cape Cod cottage. There are facilities for both formal and informal living pursuits. Note the spacious family area, the formal dining/living room, the first floor laundry and the efficient kitchen. The second floor houses the three bedrooms and two economically located baths.

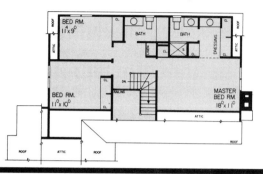

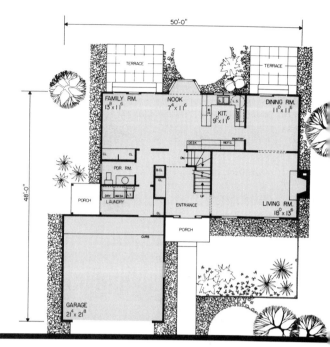

Design N2995

First Floor: 2,465 square feet
Second Floor: 617 square feet
Total: 3,082 square feet

L D

QUOTE ONE™

Cost to build? See page 336
to order complete cost estimate
to build this house in your area!

Width 120'-11"
Depth 52'-6"

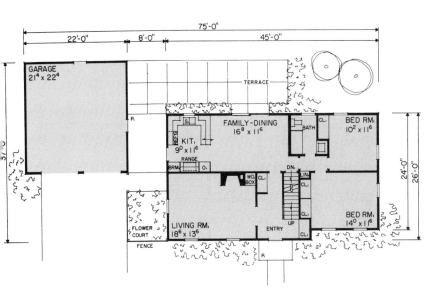

Design N3126

First Floor: 1,141 square feet
Second Floor: 630 square feet
Total: 1,771 square feet

L **D**

● This New England adaptation has a lot to offer. There is the U-shaped kitchen, family-dining room, four bedrooms, two full baths, fireplace, covered porch and two-car garage. A delightful addition to any neighborhood.

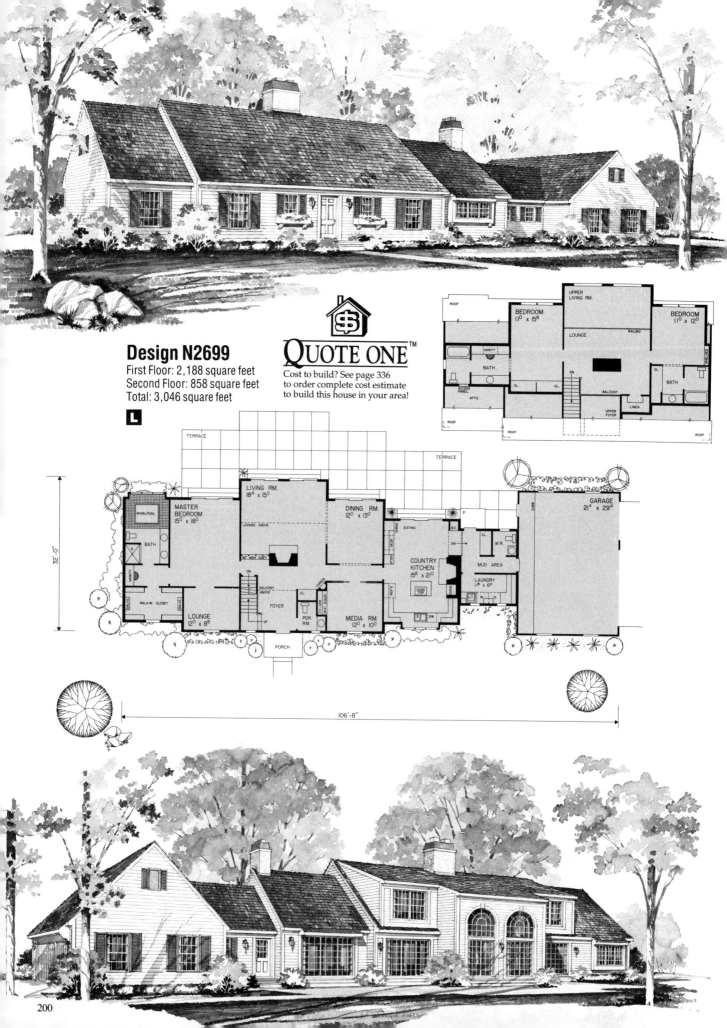

Design N2699

First Floor: 2,188 square feet
Second Floor: 858 square feet
Total: 3,046 square feet

L

QUOTE ONE™

Cost to build? See page 336
to order complete cost estimate
to build this house in your area!

Second floor labels:
ROOF
BEDROOM 11⁰ x 15⁸
UPPER LIVING RM.
BEDROOM 11⁰ x 12⁰
LOUNGE
RAILING
VANITY
BATH
ON.
SHELVES
CL.
BATH
ACCESS PANEL
ATTIC
CL.
CL.
BALCONY
LINEN
UPPER FOYER
ROOF
ROOF
ROOF

First floor labels:
TERRACE
TERRACE
LIVING RM. 18⁴ x 15⁰
DINING RM. 12⁰ x 13⁰
GARAGE 21⁴ x 29⁴
MASTER BEDROOM 15⁰ x 18⁰
WHIRLPOOL
LOUNGE ABOVE
CHINA
EATING
P.
BATH
CL.
W.R.
VANITY
36" HIGH CAB'T.
PTRY
DESK
B.C.
DN.
MUD AREA
COUNTRY KITCHEN 15⁸ x 21⁰
WALK-IN CLOSET
SHELVES
DN.
BALCONY ABOVE
CL.
REF'G.
COOK TOP
LAUNDRY 11⁸ x 6⁰
W. D.
LOUNGE 12⁰ x 8⁸
FOYER
TV. VCR HI-FI EQUIP.
PDR. RM.
MEDIA RM. 12⁰ x 10⁰
S
DW.
PORCH

32'-0"

106'-8"

200

Design N2615

First Floor: 2,563 square feet
Second Floor: 552 square feet
Total: 3,115 square feet

L **D**

● The exterior detailing of this design recalls 18th-Century New England architecture. Enter by way of the centered front door and you are greeted into the foyer. Directly to the right is the study or optional bedroom or to the left is the living room. This large formal room features sliding glass doors to the sun-drenched solarium. The beauty of the solarium will be appreciated from the master bedroom and the dining room along with the living room.

QUOTE ONE™
Cost to build? See page 336
to order complete cost estimate
to build this house in your area!

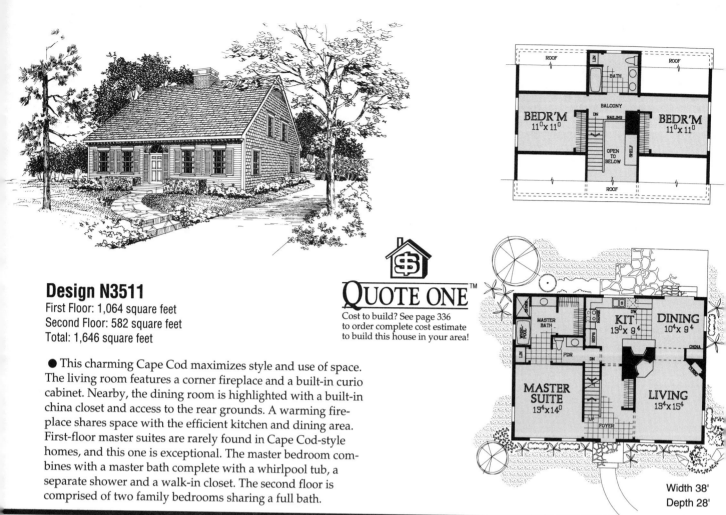

Design N3511

First Floor: 1,064 square feet
Second Floor: 582 square feet
Total: 1,646 square feet

● This charming Cape Cod maximizes style and use of space. The living room features a corner fireplace and a built-in curio cabinet. Nearby, the dining room is highlighted with a built-in china closet and access to the rear grounds. A warming fireplace shares space with the efficient kitchen and dining area. First-floor master suites are rarely found in Cape Cod-style homes, and this one is exceptional. The master bedroom combines with a master bath complete with a whirlpool tub, a separate shower and a walk-in closet. The second floor is comprised of two family bedrooms sharing a full bath.

QUOTE ONE™
Cost to build? See page 336 to order complete cost estimate to build this house in your area!

Width 38'
Depth 28'

Design N3318

First Floor: 1,557 square feet
Second Floor: 540 square feet
Total: 2,097 square feet

L **D**

● Details make the difference in this darling two-bedroom (or three-bedroom if you choose) bungalow. From covered front porch to covered rear porch, there's a fine floor plan. Living areas are to the rear: a gathering room with through-fireplace and pass-through to the kitchen and a formal dining room with porch access. To the front of the plan are a family bedroom and bath and a study. The study can also be planned as a guest bedroom with bath. Upstairs is the master bedroom with through-fireplace to the bath and a gigantic walk-in closet.

Alternate 1st Floor Plan

Width 48'
Depth 43'-8"

QUOTE ONE™
Cost to build? See page 336 to order complete cost estimate to build this house in your area!

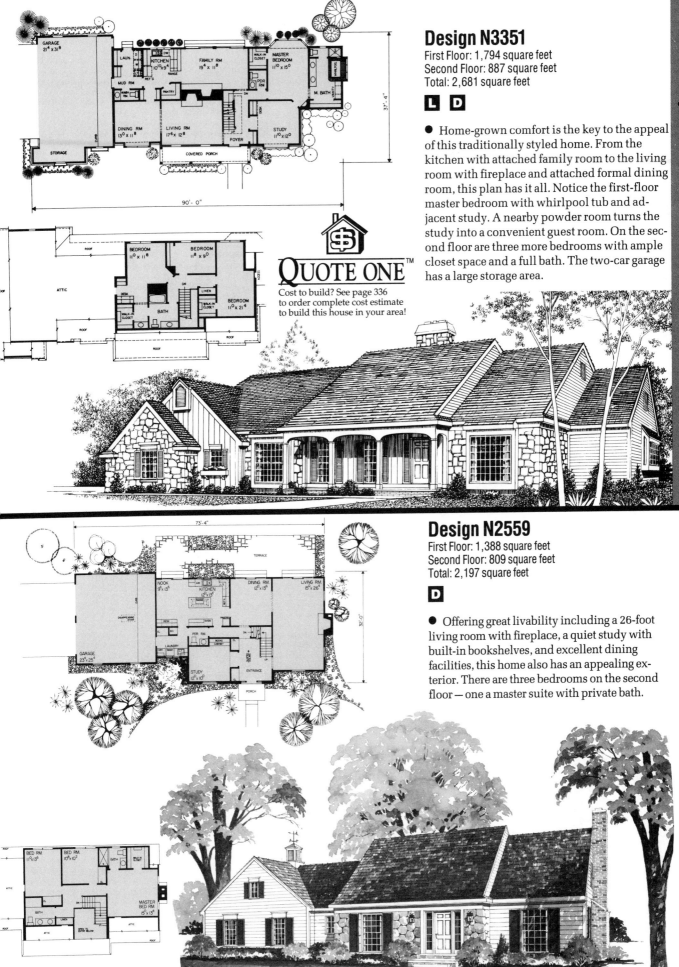

Design N3351

First Floor: 1,794 square feet
Second Floor: 887 square feet
Total: 2,681 square feet

L **D**

● Home-grown comfort is the key to the appeal of this traditionally styled home. From the kitchen with attached family room to the living room with fireplace and attached formal dining room, this plan has it all. Notice the first-floor master bedroom with whirlpool tub and adjacent study. A nearby powder room turns the study into a convenient guest room. On the second floor are three more bedrooms with ample closet space and a full bath. The two-car garage has a large storage area.

QUOTE ONE™

Cost to build? See page 336 to order complete cost estimate to build this house in your area!

Design N2559

First Floor: 1,388 square feet
Second Floor: 809 square feet
Total: 2,197 square feet

D

● Offering great livability including a 26-foot living room with fireplace, a quiet study with built-in bookshelves, and excellent dining facilities, this home also has an appealing exterior. There are three bedrooms on the second floor — one a master suite with private bath.

Design N3353

First Floor: 2,191 square feet
Second Floor: 874 square feet
Total: 3,065 square feet

L **D**

● This captivating 1½-story Southern Colonial provides the best in livability. On the first floor are the living room, dining room and private media room. A country kitchen with fireplace offers casual living space. The master suite is also located on this floor and has a lavish master bath with whirlpool spa. Upstairs are two family bedrooms, each with its own bath, and a central lounge overlooking the living room.

Design N2964

First Floor: 1,441 square feet
Second Floor: 621 square feet
Total: 2,062 square feet

● Tudor houses have their own unique exterior features. This outstanding two-story has a first-floor master bedroom plus two bedrooms with a lounge upstairs. The living room is dramatically spacious. It has a two-story sloping ceiling and large glass areas across the back. The open staircase to the upstairs has plenty of natural light as does the stairway to the basement recreation area.

Width 55'
Depth 59'-8"

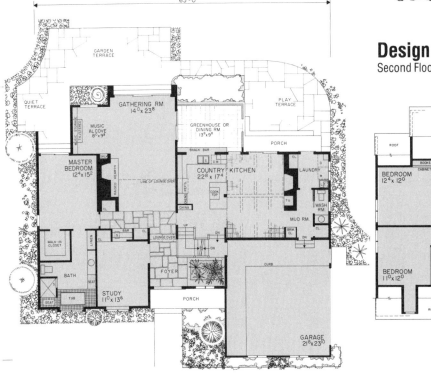

63'-0"

GARDEN TERRACE

QUIET TERRACE

GATHERING RM.
14⁰ x 23⁸

MUSIC ALCOVE
8⁰ x 9⁸

GREENHOUSE OR DINING RM.
13⁴ x 9⁸

PLAY TERRACE

PORCH

SNACK BAR

MASTER BEDROOM
12⁴ x 15²

COUNTRY KITCHEN
22⁸ x 17⁴

LAUNDRY

COOK TOP

LINE OF LOUNGE OVER

CHINA

WASH RM.

TV

WALK-IN CLOSET

BAR CL

LOUNGE OVER

MUD RM.

BRM CL

BATH

UP

DN

FOYER

CURB

STUDY
11⁰ x 13⁶

PORCH

GARAGE
21⁸ x 23¹⁰

TUB

Design N2883 First Floor: 1,919 square feet
Second Floor: 895 square feet; Total: 2,814 square feet

ROOF

ROOF

SLOPED CEILING

UPPER GREEN HOUSE

BOOKS
CABINET

BEDROOM
12⁴ x 12⁰

UPPER GATHERING RM.

RAILING

STUDIO BEDROOM
13⁶ x 11⁴

ROOF

LOUNGE
16⁸ x 12⁰

RAILING

CL

ATTIC STORAGE

CL

RAILING

DN

BEDROOM
11⁰ x 12⁰

CL

LINEN

BATH

UPPER FOYER

CEILING CLIP

ROOF

ROOF

ROOF

● A country-style home is part of America's fascination with the rural past. This home's emphasis of the traditional home is in its gambrel roof, dormers and fanlight windows. Having a traditional exterior from the street view, this home has window walls and a greenhouse, which opens the house to the outdoors in a thoroughly contemporary manner. The interior meets the requirements of today's active family. Like the country houses of the past, it has a gathering room for family get-togethers or entertaining. The adjacent two-story greenhouse doubles as the dining room. There is a pass-through snack bar to the country kitchen here. This country kitchen just might be the heart of the house with its two areas — work zone and sitting room. There are four bedrooms on the two floors — the master bedroom suite on the first floor; three more on the second floor. A lounge, overlooking the gathering room and front foyer, is also on the second floor.

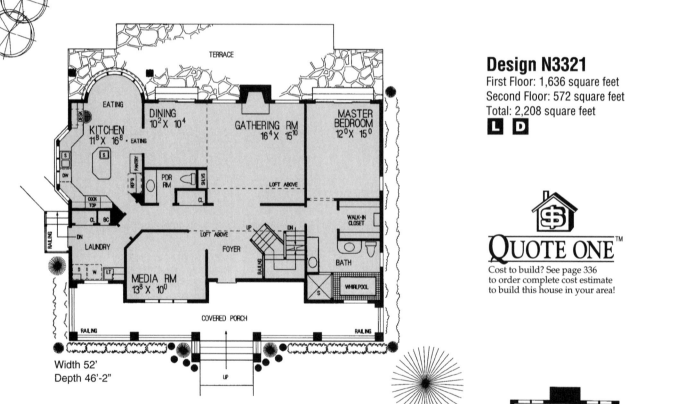

TERRACE

EATING

DINING
10² X 10⁴

KITCHEN
11⁸ X 16⁸ • Eating

GATHERING RM
16⁴ X 15¹⁰

MASTER BEDROOM
12⁰ X 15⁰

PANTRY

PDR RM

LOFT ABOVE

WALK-IN CLOSET

COOK TOP

CL BC

RAILING

DN LAUNDRY

LOFT ABOVE

UP DN

FOYER

RAILING

BATH

D W LT

MEDIA RM
13⁸ X 10⁰

WHIRLPOOL

COVERED PORCH

RAILING   RAILING

Width 52'
Depth 46'-2"

UP

Design N3321

First Floor: 1,636 square feet
Second Floor: 572 square feet
Total: 2,208 square feet

L **D**

QUOTE ONE™

Cost to build? See page 336
to order complete cost estimate
to build this house in your area!

● Cozy and completely functional, this 1½-story
bungalow has many amenities not often found in
homes its size. The covered porch at the front opens
at the entry to a foyer with an angled staircase. To
the left is a media room. To the rear is the gathering
room with its central fireplace. Attached to the gathering room is a formal dining room with rear terrace
access. The kitchen features a curved casual eating
area and an island work station. The right side of
the first floor is dominated by the master suite. It
has access to the rear terrace and a luxurious bath.
Upstairs are two family bedrooms connected by a
loft area overlooking the gathering room and foyer.

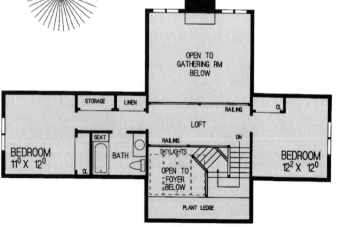

OPEN TO GATHERING RM BELOW

STORAGE LINEN

RAILING

LOFT

BEDROOM
11⁰ X 12⁰

SEAT

BATH

RAILING

SKYLIGHTS

DN

BEDROOM
12² X 12⁰

OPEN TO FOYER BELOW

PLANT LEDGE

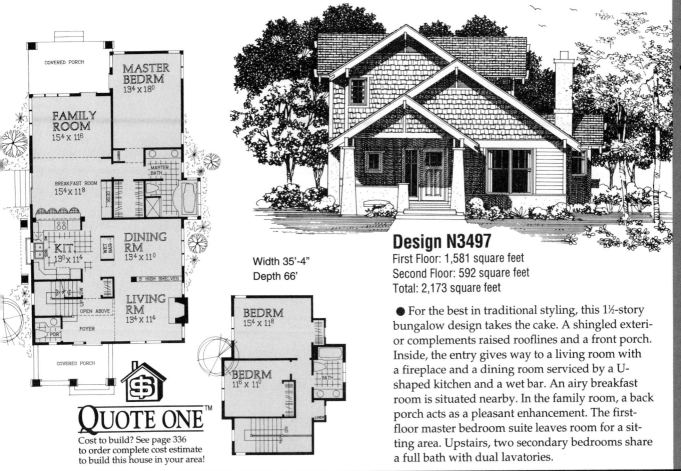

COVERED PORCH

MASTER BEDRM
13⁴ x 18⁰

FAMILY ROOM
15⁴ x 11⁸

BREAKFAST ROOM
15⁴ x 11⁸

MASTER BATH

KIT
13⁰ x 11⁴

WET BAR

DINING RM
13⁴ x 11⁰

5' HIGH SHELVES

OPEN ABOVE

LIVING RM
13⁴ x 11⁴

FOYER

PDR

COVERED PORCH

Width 35'-4"
Depth 66'

BEDRM
15⁴ x 11⁸

BEDRM
11⁶ x 11⁰

BATH

LINEN

QUOTE ONE™

Cost to build? See page 336
to order complete cost estimate
to build this house in your area!

Design N3497

First Floor: 1,581 square feet
Second Floor: 592 square feet
Total: 2,173 square feet

● For the best in traditional styling, this 1½-story bungalow design takes the cake. A shingled exterior complements raised rooflines and a front porch. Inside, the entry gives way to a living room with a fireplace and a dining room serviced by a U-shaped kitchen and a wet bar. An airy breakfast room is situated nearby. In the family room, a back porch acts as a pleasant enhancement. The first-floor master bedroom suite leaves room for a sitting area. Upstairs, two secondary bedrooms share a full bath with dual lavatories.

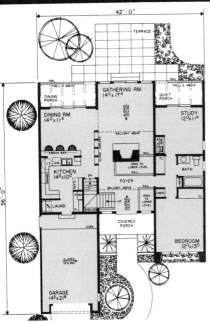

42'-0"

TERRACE

56'-0"

DINING PORCH

GATHERING RM
14⁰ x 17⁴

QUIET PORCH

DINING RM
14⁰ x 11⁴

STUDY
12⁰ x 11⁴

SNACK BAR

KITCHEN
14⁰ x 10⁰

BATH

FOYER

BALCONY ABOVE

LAUND

LINEN

COVERED PORCH

BEDROOM
12⁰ x 13⁰

SLOPED CEILING

GARAGE
14⁰ x 21⁸

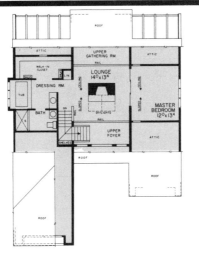

ATTIC

WALK-IN CLOSET

DRESSING RM

TUB

BATH

UPPER GATHERING RM

LOUNGE
14⁰ x 13⁴

ATTIC

MASTER BEDROOM
12⁰ x 13⁴

UPPER FOYER

ATTIC

ROOF

ROOF

ROOF

UNEX.

FUTURE FAMILY RM

UNEX.

BASEMENT

AIR COND

OPEN TO FIRST FLOOR

UNEXCAVATED

UNEX.

OPEN TO FIRST FLOOR

ACTIVITIES/ BASEMENT

Design N2887

First Floor: 1,338 square feet
Second Floor: 661 square feet
Total: 1,999 square feet

● This attractive contemporary 1½-story will be the envy of many. The kitchen offers a snack bar for those quick meals but also serves a nearby dining room. The gathering room has a fireplace and access to the rear terrace. There is also a study with wet bar and a private porch. Upstairs, the large master suite occupies the entire floor. It has an oversized tub, walk-in closet and open lounge with fireplace. Additional space in the lower level can be developed later.

Design N3313

First Floor: 1,482 square feet
Second Floor: 885 square feet
Total: 2,367 square feet

L

● Cozy living abounds in a first-floor living room and family room, dining room, and kitchen with breakfast room. Two fireplaces keep things warm. Three bedrooms upstairs have more than adequate closet space.

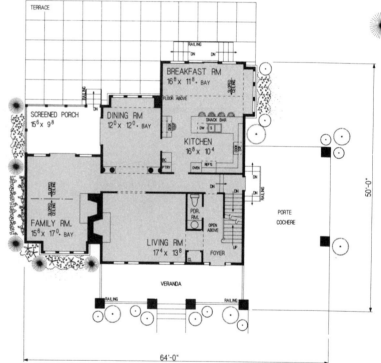

QUOTE ONE™

Cost to build? See page 336 to order complete cost estimate to build this house in your area!

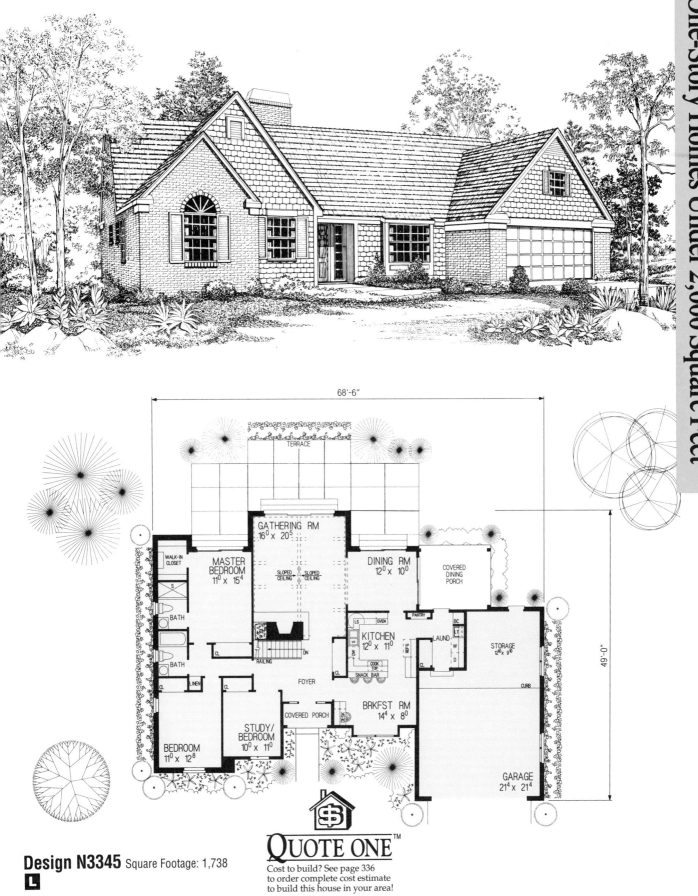

Design N3345 Square Footage: 1,738

L

QUOTE ONE™

Cost to build? See page 336 to order complete cost estimate to build this house in your area!

● This quaint shingled cottage offers an unexpected amount of living space in just over 1,700 square feet. The large gathering room with fireplace, dining room with covered porch, and kitchen with breakfast room handle formal parties as easily as they do the casual family get-together. Three bedrooms, one that could also serve as a study, are found in a separate wing of the house. Give special attention to the storage space in this home and the extra touches that set it apart from many homes of equal size.

Width 52'-8"
Depth 49'

Design N3454

Square Footage: 1,699

L **D**

● An efficient, spacious interior comes through in this compact floor plan. Through a pair of columns, an open living and dining room area creates a warm space for all sorts of living pursuits. Sliding glass doors guarantee a bright, cheerful interior while providing easy access to outdoor living. The L-shaped kitchen has an island work surface, a practical planning desk and an informal eating space. The breakfast area has access to an outdoor living area—perfect for enjoying a morning cup of coffee. Sleeping arrangements are emphasized by the master suite with its tray ceiling and sliding glass doors to the yard.

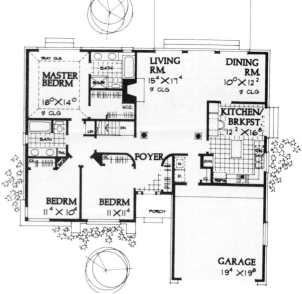

Design N3376

Square Footage: 1,999

L **D**

Width 60'
Depth 55'

● Small families or empty nesters will appreciate the layout of this traditional ranch. The foyer opens to the gathering room with fireplace and sloped ceiling. The dining room is open to the gathering room for entertaining ease and contains sliding doors to a rear terrace. The breakfast room also provides access to a covered porch for dining outdoors. The media room to the left of the home offers a bay window and a wet bar, or it can double as a third bedroom.

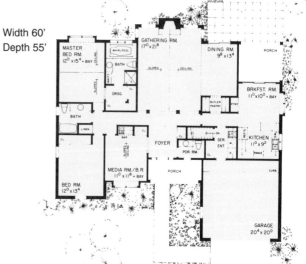

Quote One™

Cost to build? See page 336
to order complete cost estimate
to build this house in your area!

Design N3451

Square Footage: 1,560

L

● This split-bedroom plan includes
two bedrooms in only 1,560 square
feet. The master bedroom is to the rear
of the home and includes a private
bath. A family bedroom or study is to
the left of the home with a full bath.
The washer and dryer are placed
within easy reach of both bedrooms.
A spacious gathering room with a fireplace provides space for relaxing or
entertaining guests. A formal dining
room adjacent to the kitchen offers
access to a terrace for evening meals
outside.

46'-4"

55'-8"

TERRACE

DINING
13⁶ X 10⁴

MASTER
SUITE
18⁸ X 13⁰

GATHERING
ROOM
13⁸ X 15²

SNACK BAR

KIT
11⁶ X 10⁸

SLOPED CEILING

OVEN

PNTRY

MASTER
BATH

NICHE

NICHE

VANITY

FOYER

BATH

WHIRLPOOL

SHR

SEAT

LAUND

ENTRY

HVAC

WH

SLOPED CEILING

PORCH

CURB

BED/STUDY
14⁴ X 13⁸

GARAGE
19⁶ X 19⁸

Design N2929
Square Footage: 1,608

● This efficient floor plan caters to the needs of the small family. The angled kitchen is located in a space convenient to the garage, dining room, dining terrace and front door. The spacious living area has a dramatic fireplace and rear terrace access. A favorite spot will be the media room with built-in cabinets for the TV, VCR and stereo. Storage space abounds in the master bedroom and its adjacent bath has twin lavatories, a tub and stall shower. There's an extra bedroom for guests or for use as a nursery.

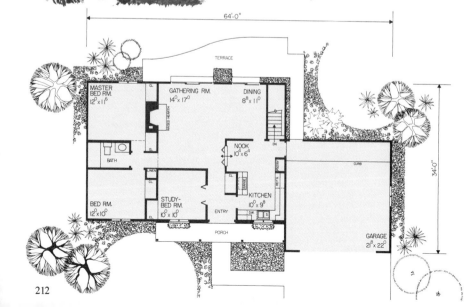

Design N2570
Square Footage: 1,176

L **D**

● This attractive Tudor offers a study which could double ideally as a guest room, sewing room or even serve as the TV room. The living area is a spacious L-shaped zone for formal living and dining. The efficient kitchen is handy to the front door and overlooks the front yard. It features a convenient breakfast nook for those informal meals. Handy to the entry from the garage and the yard are the stairs to the basement. Don't overlook the attractive front porch.

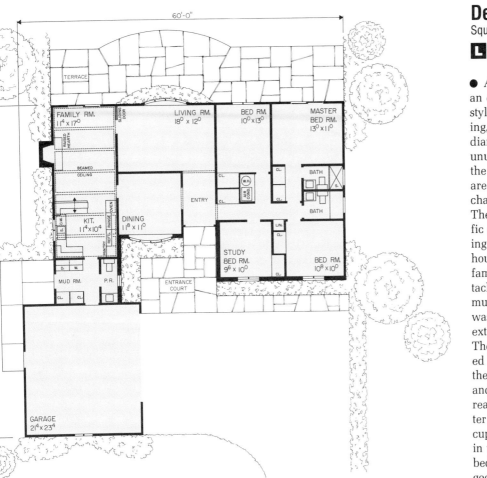

60'-0"

FAMILY RM.
11⁴ x 17⁰

RAISED HEARTH

BEAMED CEILING

SLIDING DOOR

LIVING RM.
18⁰ x 12⁰

BED RM.
10⁰ x 13⁰

MASTER BED RM.
13⁰ x 11⁰

BATH

BATH

ENTRY

W.H.

AIR COND

CL.

CL.

CL.

CL.

S.

TERRACE

KIT.
11⁴ x 10⁴

RANGE OVEN

REF'L.

PANTRY

DINING
11⁸ x 11⁰

STUDY
BED RM.
9⁶ x 10⁰

BED RM.
10⁸ x 10⁰

LIN.

CL.

CL.

D.

W.

MUD RM.

P.R.

CL.

CL.

ENTRANCE COURT

60'-0"

GARAGE
21⁴ x 23⁴

Design N2170
Square Footage: 1,646

L

● An L-shaped home with an enchanting Olde English styling. The wavy-edged siding, the simulated beams, the diamond lite windows, the unusual brick pattern and the interesting roof lines all are elements which set the character of authenticity. The center entry routes traffic directly to the formal living and sleeping zones of the house. Between the kitchen-family room area and the attached two-car garage is the mud room. Here is the washer and dryer with the extra powder room nearby. The family room is highlighted by the beamed ceilings, the raised hearth fireplace and sliding glass doors to the rear terrace. The work center with its abundance of cupboard space will be fun in which to function. Four bedrooms, two full baths and good closet space are features of the sleeping area.

QUOTE ONE™

Cost to build? See page 336
to order complete cost estimate
to build this house in your area!

Design N3488

Square Footage: 1,944

● As you enter the foyer, you are greeted by the sleeping zone on the right and the living zone on the left. A large kitchen connects to the breakfast area and includes a desk, a walk-in pantry, a spacious counter area with a snack bar that connects to the gathering room and entry to the formal dining room. The gathering room features a fireplace and access to the back-yard terrace. The master bedroom also accesses the terrace and features a master bath with a whirlpool tub and a separate shower. A study at the front of the home could be converted into an additional bedroom.

Width 72'-8"
Depth 47'-4"

Design N2728

Square Footage: 1,825

L **D**

● This lovely L-shaped English adaptation presents a wonderful face with impressive exterior features. Its floor plan adds livability for modern families. Note the fireplace — a focal point in the living/dining room area. The kitchen is strategically placed to serve the dining room and family room. In addition to the two full baths in the sleeping zone, there is a handy washroom at the entrance from the garage. Note the fine master bath.

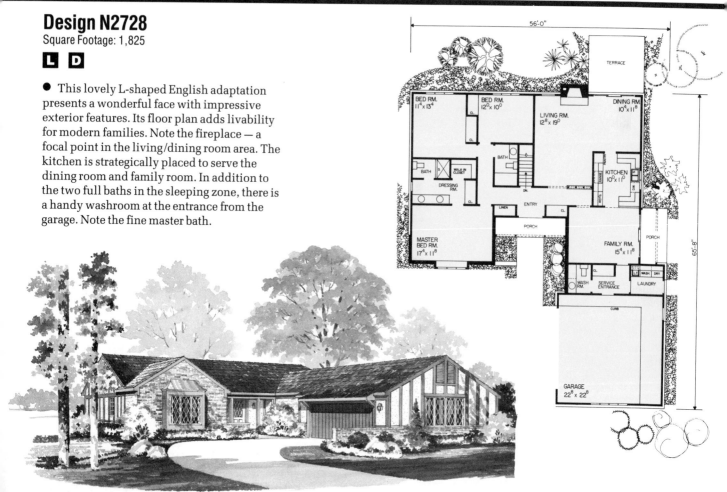

214

Design N2678
Square Footage: 1,971

L D

● A country kitchen is the center of living in this design. It boasts an island range with snack bar, pantry, broom closet, eating area with sliding glass doors leading to a covered porch, and an adjacent mud room with laundry facilities. There are also formal living and dining rooms plus three bedrooms and 2½ baths. Note the storage space in the garage.

Design N2607
Square Footage: 1,208

Width 58'-10"
Depth 41'-6"

L

● This English Tudor cottage has two sizable bedrooms, a full bath and extra washroom. The living and dining areas are spacious and overlook both the front and rear yard. In addition to the formal dining area with its built-in china cabinet, there is a delightful breakfast eating alcove in the kitchen. The U-shaped work area is wonderfully efficient.

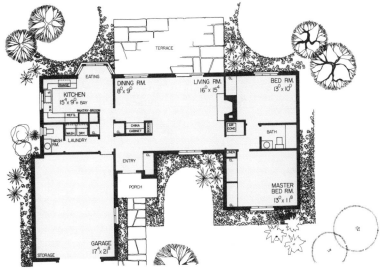

Design N2206
Square Footage: 1,769

L

● The charm of Tudor adaptations has become increasingly popular in recent years. And little wonder. Its freshness of character adds a unique touch to any neighborhood. This interesting one-story home will be a standout wherever you choose to have it built. The covered front porch leads to the formal front entry–the foyer. From this point traffic flows freely to the living and sleeping areas. The outstanding plan features a separate dining room, a beamed ceiling living room, an efficient kitchen and an informal family room.

Width 64'-10"
Depth 43'-11"

OPTIONAL BASEMENT

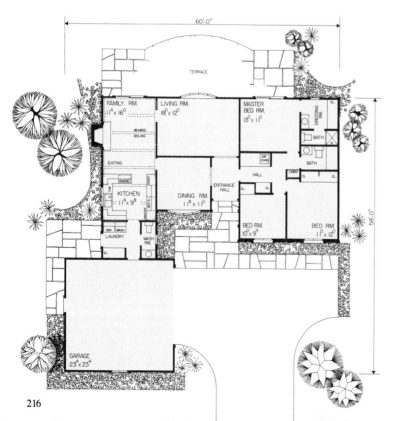

Design N2606
Square Footage: 1,499

L

● This modest sized house with its 1,499 square feet could hardly offer more in the way of exterior charm and interior livability. Measuring only 60 feet in width means it will not require a huge, expensive piece of property. The orientation of the garage and the front drive court are features which promote an economical use of property. In addition to the formal, separate living and dining rooms, there is the informal kitchen/family room area. Note the beamed ceiling, the fireplace, the sliding glass doors and the eating area of the family room.

OPTIONAL BASEMENT

Design N2737
Square Footage: 1,796

L

● You will be able to build this distinctive, modified U-shaped one-story home on a relatively narrow site. But, then, if you so wished, with the help of your architect and builder you may want to locate the garage to the side of the house. Inside, the living potential is just great. The interior U-shaped kitchen handily services the dining and family rooms and nook. A rear covered porch functions ideally with the family room while the formal living room has its own terrace. Three bedrooms and two baths highlight the sleeping zone (or make it two bedrooms and a study). Notice the strategic location of the washroom, laundry, two storage closets and the basement stairs.

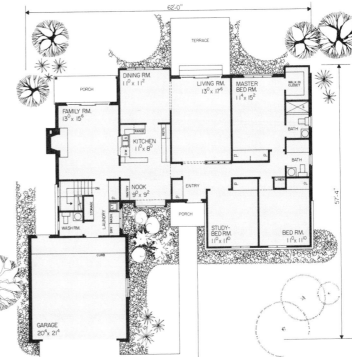

Design N2802
Square Footage: 1,729

L D

● The three exteriors shown at the left house the same, efficiently planned one-story floor plan shown below. Be sure to notice the design variations in the window placement and roof pitch. The Tudor design to the left is delightful. Half-timbered stucco and brick comprise the facade of this English Tudor variation of the plan. Note authentic bay window in the front bedroom.

Design N2803
Square Footage: 1,679

L D

● Housed in varying facades, this floor plan is very efficient. The front foyer leads to each of the living areas. The sleeping area of two, or optional three, bedrooms is ready to serve the family. Then there is the gathering room. This room is highlighted by its size, 16 x 20 feet. A contemporary mix of fieldstone and vertical wood siding characterizes this exterior. The absence of columns or posts gives a modern look to the covered porch.

Design N2804
Square Footage: 1,674

L D

● Stuccoed arches, multi-paned windows and a gracefully sloped roof accent the exterior of this Spanish-inspired design. Like the other two designs, the interior kitchen will efficiently serve the dining room, covered dining porch and breakfast room with great ease. Blueprints for all three designs include details for an optional non-basement plan.

QUOTE ONE™

Cost to build? See page 336 to order complete cost estimate to build this house in your area!

OPTIONAL NON-BASEMENT

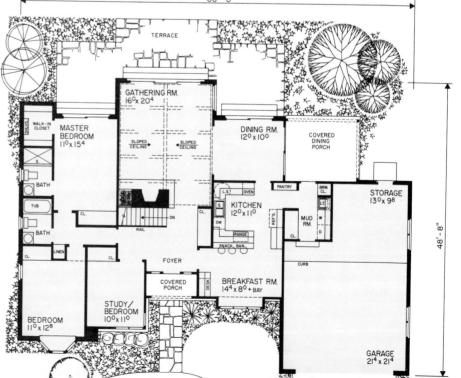

Design N2805
Square Footage: 1,547

L D

● Three completely different exterior facades share one compact, practical and economical floor plan. The major design variations are roof pitch, window placement and garage openings. Each design will hold its own when comparing the three exteriors. The design on the left is a romantic stone-and-shingle cottage design. This design, along with the other two designs presented here, is outstanding.

Design N2806
Square Footage: 1,584

L D

● This Tudor version of the plan is also very appealing. The living/dining room expands across the rear of the plan and has direct access to the covered porch. Notice the built-in planter adjacent to the open staircase leading to the basement.

Design N2807
Square Footage: 1,576

L D

● The contemporary version may be your choice. In addition to living/dining areas, there is a breakfast room that overlooks the covered porch. A desk, snack bar and mud room house laundry facilities and are near the U-shaped kitchen. The master bedroom has a private bath.

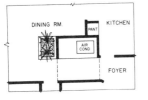

QUOTE ONE™

Cost to build? See page 336 to order complete cost estimate to build this house in your area!

OPTIONAL NON-BASEMENT

Design N2941

Square Footage: 1,842

D

● Here is a basic floor plan which goes with each of the differently styled exteriors. The Early American version above is charming, indeed. Horizontal siding, stone, window boxes, a dovecote, a picket fence and a garden court enhance its appeal. Note the covered entrance.

Design N2942

Square Footage: 1,834

D

● The Tudor exterior above will be the favorite of many. Stucco, simulated timber work and diamond-lite windows set its unique character. Each of the delightful exteriors features eye-catching roof lines. Inside, there is an outstanding plan to cater to the living patterns of the small family, empty nesters, or retirees.

Design N2943

Square Footage: 1,834

D

● The Contemporary optional exterior above features vertical siding and a wide overhanging roof with exposed rafter ends. The foyer is spacious with sloped ceiling and a dramatic open staircase to the basement recreation area. Other ceilings in the house are also sloped. The breakfast, dining and media rooms are highlights, along with the laundry, the efficient kitchen, the snack bar and the master bath.

QUOTE ONE™

Cost to build? See page 336 to order complete cost estimate to build this house in your area!

Width 58'-2"
Depth 59'-9"

Quote One™

Cost to build? See page 336 to order complete cost estimate to build this house in your area!

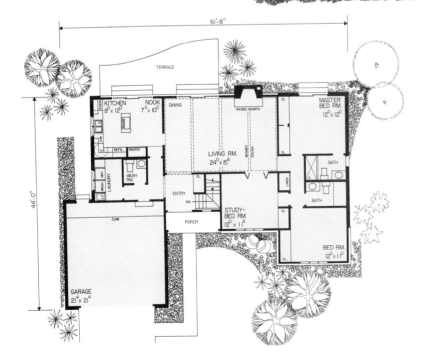

Design N2565
Square Footage: 1,540

L **D**

● This modest sized floor plan has much to offer in the way of livability. It may function as either a two or three bedroom home. The living room is huge and features a fine, raised hearth fireplace. The open stairway to the basement is handy and will lead to what may be developed as the recreation area. In addition to the two full baths, there is an extra wash room. Adjacent is the laundry room and the service entrance from the garage. The blueprints you order for this design will show details for each of the three delightful elevations above. Which is your favorite? The Tudor, the Colonial or the Contemporary?

Design N1305
Square Footage: 1,382

D

● Order blueprints for any one of the three exteriors shown on these two pages and you will receive details for building the outstanding floor plan at right. In less than 1,400 square feet there are three bedrooms, two full baths, a separate dining room, a formal living room, a fine kitchen overlooking the rear yard, and an informal family room. In addition, there is the attached two-car garage. Note the location of the stairs when this plan is built with a basement. Each of the exteriors is predominantly brick — the front of Design N1305 features both stone and vertical boards and battens with brick on the other three sides. Design N1382 and Design N1383 both have double front doors.

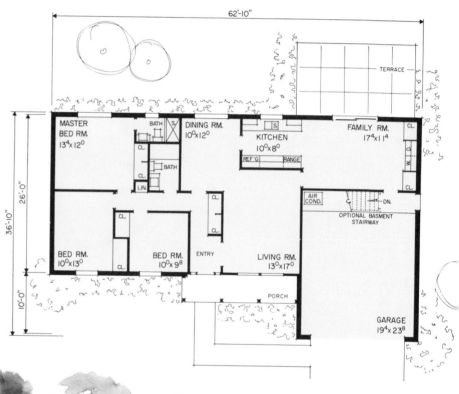

Design N1382
Square Footage: 1,382

D

Design N1383
Square Footage: 1,382

D

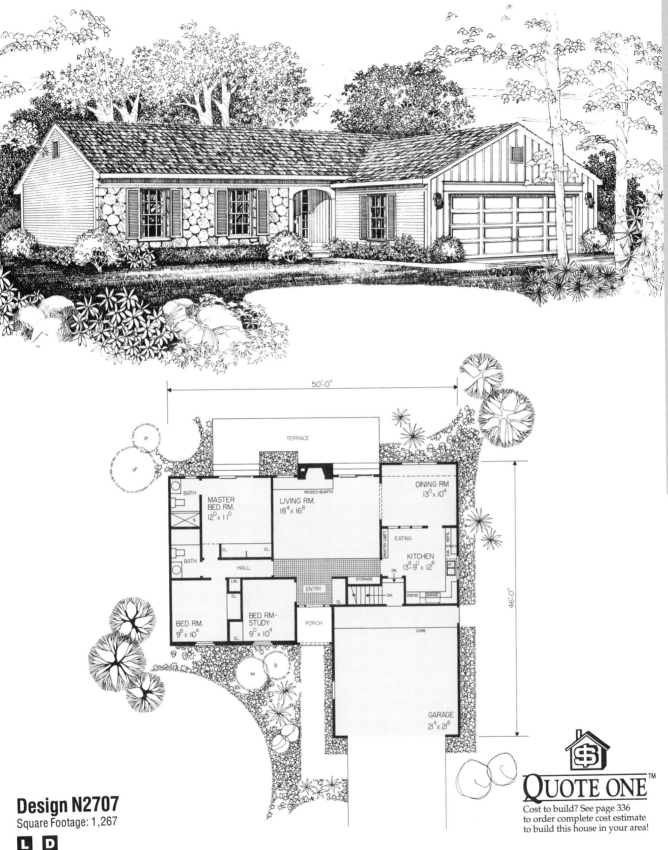

50'-0"

TERRACE

46'-0"

RAISED HEARTH

| BATH | MASTER BED RM. 12⁰ x 11⁰ | LIVING RM. 18⁴ x 16⁸ | DINING RM. 13⁰ x 10⁴ |

EATING

KITCHEN 13-9⁸ x 12⁸

PANTRY CAB'T

REFR.

BATH

HALL

CL. CL.

DN.

OVENS RANGE

LIN.

STORAGE

ENTRY

CL.

DN.

BED RM. 9⁸ x 10⁴

CL.

BED RM-STUDY 9⁰ x 10⁴

PORCH

CURB

GARAGE 21⁴ x 21⁸

QUOTE ONE™

Cost to build? See page 336
to order complete cost estimate
to build this house in your area!

Design N2707
Square Footage: 1,267

L **D**

● Here is a charming Early American adaptation that will serve as a picturesque and practical retirement home. Also, it will serve admirably those with a small family in search of an efficient, economically built home. The living area, highlighted by the raised hearth fireplace, is spacious. The kitchen features eating space and easy access to the garage and basement. The dining room is adjacent to the kitchen and views the rear yard. Then, there is the basement for recreation and hobby pursuits. The bedroom wing offers three bedrooms and two full baths. Don't miss the sliding doors to the terrace from the living room and the master bedroom. Storage units are plentiful including a pantry cabinet in the eating area of the kitchen. This plan will be efficient and livable.

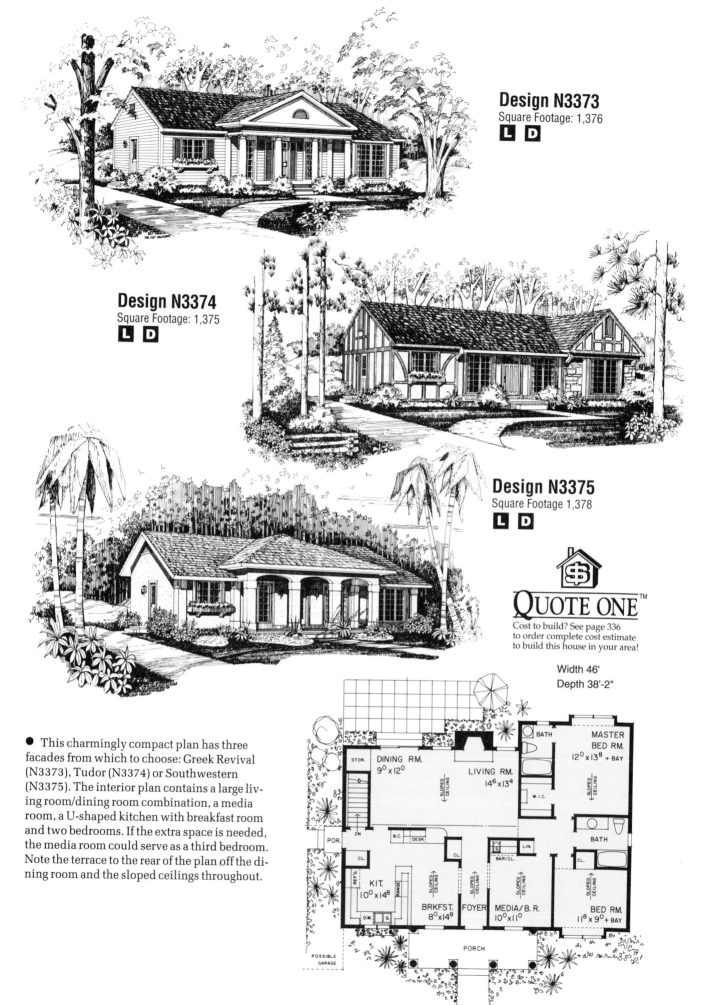

Design N3373
Square Footage: 1,376
L **D**

Design N3374
Square Footage: 1,375
L **D**

Design N3375
Square Footage 1,378
L **D**

Quote One™
Cost to build? See page 336
to order complete cost estimate
to build this house in your area!

Width 46'
Depth 38'-2"

● This charmingly compact plan has three
facades from which to choose: Greek Revival
(N3373), Tudor (N3374) or Southwestern
(N3375). The interior plan contains a large living room/dining room combination, a media
room, a U-shaped kitchen with breakfast room
and two bedrooms. If the extra space is needed,
the media room could serve as a third bedroom.
Note the terrace to the rear of the plan off the dining room and the sloped ceilings throughout.

BATH

MASTER
BED RM.
12⁰x13⁸ + BAY

STOR.

DINING RM.
9⁰x12⁰

LIVING RM.
14⁶x13⁴

SLOPED CEILING

W.I.C.

SLOPED CEILING

POR.

DN

B.C.   DESK

CL.

CL.

LIN.

S

BAR/CL.

BATH

CL.

REF'G.

KIT.
10⁰x14⁸

RANGE

SLOPED CEILING

SLOPED CEILING

SLOPED CEILING

SLOPED CEILING

D.W.   S.

BRKFST.
8⁰x14⁸

FOYER

MEDIA/ B. R.
10⁰x11⁰

BED RM.
11⁸x9⁰ + BAY

POSSIBLE
GARAGE

PORCH

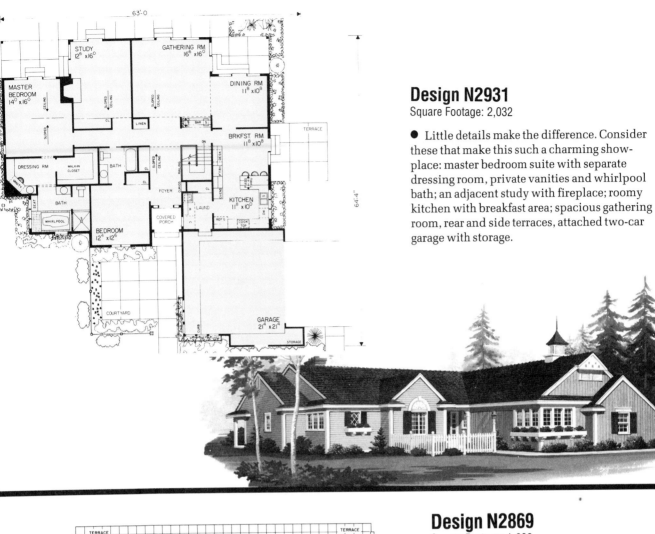

Design N2931
Square Footage: 2,032

● Little details make the difference. Consider these that make this such a charming show-place: master bedroom suite with separate dressing room, private vanities and whirlpool bath; an adjacent study with fireplace; roomy kitchen with breakfast area; spacious gathering room, rear and side terraces, attached two-car garage with storage.

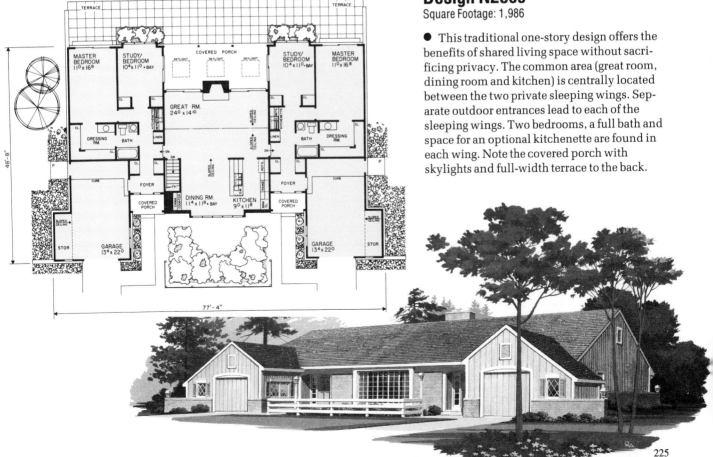

Design N2869
Square Footage: 1,986

● This traditional one-story design offers the benefits of shared living space without sacrificing privacy. The common area (great room, dining room and kitchen) is centrally located between the two private sleeping wings. Separate outdoor entrances lead to each of the sleeping wings. Two bedrooms, a full bath and space for an optional kitchenette are found in each wing. Note the covered porch with skylights and full-width terrace to the back.

Design N3350
Square Footage: 1,777

L **D**

● Though smaller in size, this traditional one-story provides a family-oriented floor plan that leaves nothing out. Besides the formal living room (or study if you prefer) and dining room, there's a gathering room with fireplace, snack bar, and sliding glass doors to the rear terrace. The U-shaped kitchen is in close proximity to the handy utility area just off the garage. Of particular note is the grand master bedroom with garden whirlpool tub, walk-in closet and private terrace. The sleeping area is completed with two family bedrooms to the front.

OPTIONAL NON-BASEMENT

QUOTE ONE™

Cost to build? See page 336
to order complete cost estimate
to build this house in your area!

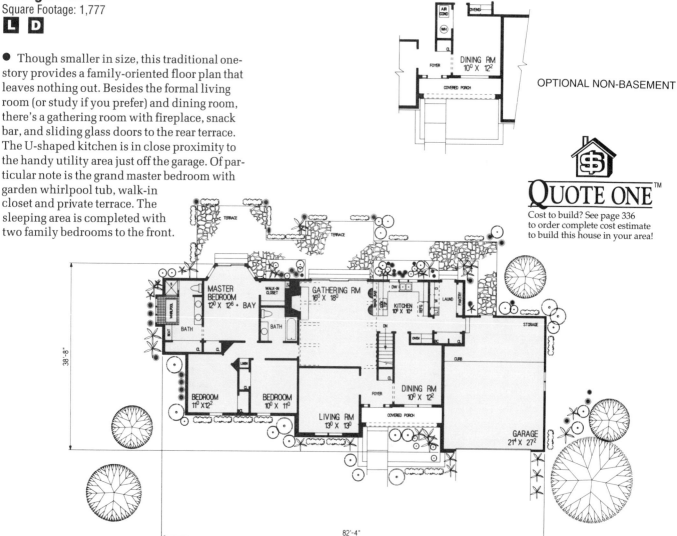

QUOTE ONE™
Cost to build? See page 336
to order complete cost estimate
to build this house in your area!

Design N2505
Square Footage: 1,366

L **D**

● This design offers you a choice of
three distinctively different exteriors.
Which is your favorite? Blueprints
show details for all three optional
elevations. A study of the floor plan
reveals a fine measure of livability. In
less than 1,400 square feet there are
features galore. An excellent return on
your construction dollar. In addition to
the two eating areas and the open
planning of the gathering room, the
indoor-outdoor relationships are of
great interest. The basement may be
developed for recreational activities.
Be sure to note the storage potential,
particularly the linen closet, the pantry,
the china cabinet and the broom closet.

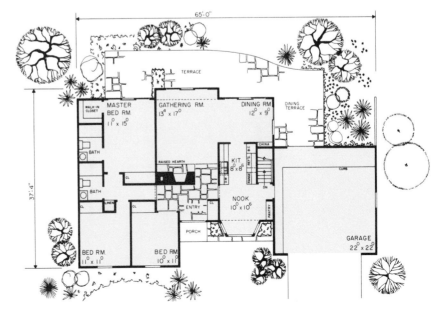

Design N1920
Square Footage: 1,600

L

● This home offers a charming exterior with a truly great floor plan. The covered front porch at the entrance heralds outstanding features inside. The sleeping zone has three bedrooms and two full baths. Each of the bedrooms has its own walk-in closet. Note the efficient U-shaped kitchen with the family room and dining room to each side. There is also a laundry with wash room just off the garage. Blueprints for this design include details for both basement and non-basement construction.

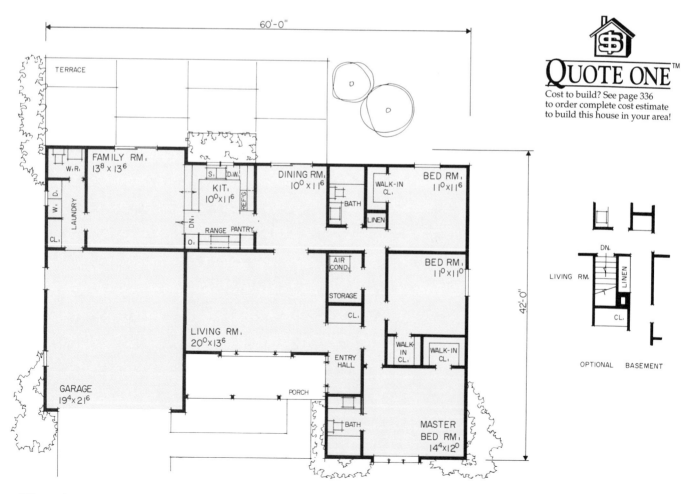

QUOTE ONE™
Cost to build? See page 336 to order complete cost estimate to build this house in your area!

OPTIONAL BASEMENT

Design N1323
Square Footage: 1,344

L **D**

● Incorporated in the set of blueprints for this design are details for building each of the three charming, traditional exteriors. Each of the three alternate exteriors has a distinction all its own. A study of the floor plan reveals fine livability. There are two full baths, a fine family room, an efficient work center, a formal dining area, bulk storage facilities and sliding glass doors to the quiet and living terraces. The laundry is strategically located near the kitchen.

QUOTE ONE™
Cost to build? See page 336 to order complete cost estimate to build this house in your area!

Design N1829

Square Footage: 1,800

L D

● All the charm of a traditional heritage is wrapped up in this U-shaped home with its narrow, horizontal siding, delightful window treatment and high-pitched roof. The massive center chimney, the bay window and the double front doors are plus features. Inside, the living potential is outstanding. The sleeping wing is self-contained and has four bedrooms and two baths. The large family and living rooms cater to divergent age groups.

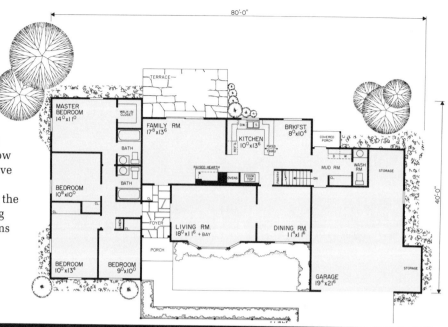

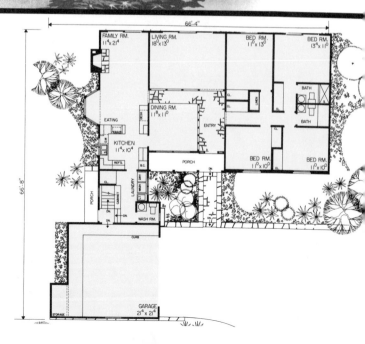

Design N2533

Square Footage: 1,897

● The distinctive appeal of the traditional L-shaped ranch home is hard to beat. Notice the delightful window and door treatment, covered front porch, vertical siding and the fieldstone. The center entrance with slate floor routes traffic effectively. The four-bedroom sleeping wing highlights two full baths. The formal living and dining rooms act as a buffer between the sleeping area and the family room/kitchen area. The family room has sliding glass doors, a fireplace and large bay window.

Design N1113
Square Footage: 1,008

L D

● A cozy plan, but just right for a small family or empty nesters. An ample living room/dining room area leads the way to a rear kitchen overlooking a terrace. Two full baths serve three bedrooms—one a master suite. The kitchen includes informal eating space. Stairs lead to a full basement that may be developed as desired.

QUOTE ONE™
Cost to build? See page 336 to order complete cost estimate to build this house in your area!

Width 71'
Depth 43'-5"

Design N3487

Square Footage: 1,835

L

● A cozy covered porch invites you into the foyer with the sleeping area on the right and the living area to the left and straight ahead. From the front-facing breakfast room, enter the efficient kitchen with its corner laundry room, large pantry, snack bar pass-through to the gathering room and entry to the dining area. The gathering room and dining room feature an impressive fireplace and access to the rear terrace. Terrace access is also available from the master bedroom with a master bath that includes a whirlpool tub and a separate shower. A study at the front of the house can also be converted into a third bedroom.

Design N3490

Square Footage: 1,970

L **D**

● A projecting two-car garage narrows the overall width of this house, thus permitting the utilization of a smaller, less expensive building site. Efficient traffic patterning characterizes the interior. Open planning results in a spacious kitchen area with a convenient U-shaped work space and a generous informal eating area. A study may function as a home office or sewing room. In the master bedroom, a sloped ceiling and sliding glass doors to the patio will be appreciated. In the master bath, a garden tub, a stall shower, two lavatories, a walk-in closet and a linen closet assure fine livability.

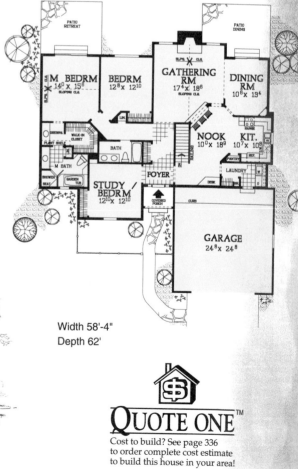

Width 58'-4"
Depth 62'

232

Design N3460
Square Footage: 1,389

L

● A double dose of charm, this special farmhouse plan offers two elevations in its blueprint package—one showcases a delightful wraparound porch. Though rooflines and porch options are different, the floor plan is basically the same and very livable. A formal living room/dining room combination has a warming fireplace and a delightful bay window. The kitchen separates this area from the more casual family room. In the kitchen, you'll find an efficient snack bar that services the family room, as well as a pantry for additional storage space. Three bedrooms include two family bedrooms served by a full bath, and a lovely master suite with its own private bath with separate lavatories. Notice the location of the washer and dryer—convenient to all of the bedrooms.

QUOTE ONE™

Cost to build? See page 336 to order complete cost estimate to build this house in your area!

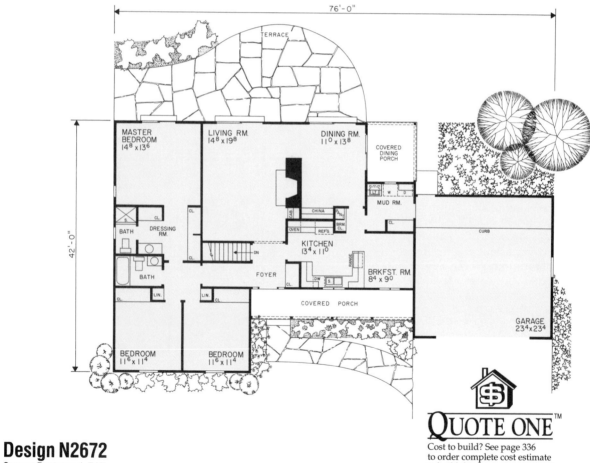

Design N2672
Square Footage: 1,717

L **D**

● The traditional appearance of this one-story is emphasized by its covered porch, multi-paned windows, narrow clapboard and vertical wood siding. Not only is the exterior eye-appealing but the interior has an efficient plan and is very livable. The front U-shaped kitchen will work with the breakfast room and mud room, which houses the laundry facilities. An access to the garage is here. Outdoor dining can be enjoyed on the covered porch adjacent to the dining room. Both of these areas, the porch and dining room, are convenient to the kitchen. Sleeping facilities consist of three bedrooms and two full baths. Note the three sets of sliding glass doors leading to the terrace.

Quote One™
Cost to build? See page 336 to order complete cost estimate to build this house in your area!

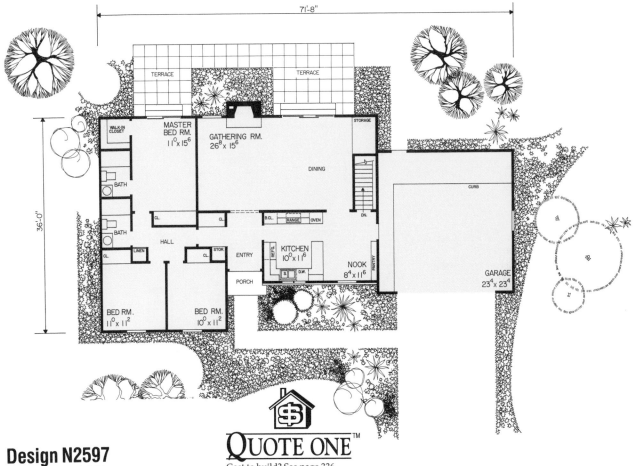

71'-8"

36'-0"

TERRACE   TERRACE

WALK-IN CLOSET

MASTER BED RM.
11⁰ x 15⁶

GATHERING RM.
26⁸ x 15⁶

STORAGE

BATH

DINING

CURB

BATH

CL.   CL.

B.CL.   RANGE   OVEN

DN.

LINEN   HALL   CL.   STOR.   ENTRY

REFG.   KITCHEN
10⁰ x 11⁶

PANTRY

GARAGE
23⁴ x 23⁴

PORCH   S   D.W.   NOOK
8⁴ x 11⁶

BED RM.
11⁰ x 11²

BED RM.
10⁰ x 11²

Quote One™

Cost to build? See page 336
to order complete cost estimate
to build this house in your area!

Design N2597
Square Footage: 1,515

L **D**

● Whether it be a starter house you are after, or one in which to spend your retirement years, this pleasing frame home will provide a full measure of pride in ownership. The contrast of vertical and horizontal lines, the double front doors and the coach lamp post at the garage create an inviting exterior. Efficiently planned, the floor plan functions in an orderly manner. The 26-foot gathering room has a delightful view of the rear yard and will take care of those formal dining occasions. There are two full baths serving the three bedrooms. Additional features include: plenty of storage facilities, two sets of glass doors to the terraces, a fireplace in the gathering room, a basement and an attached two-car garage to act as a buffer against the wind.

Design N1946

Square Footage: 1,632

● This basic exterior may have two different floor plans. For a three-bedroom home order blueprints for N1945; for a four-bedroom house order N1946.

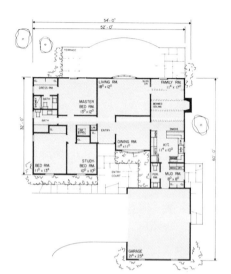

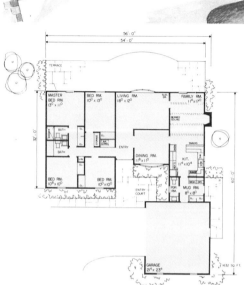

Design N1327

Square Footage: 1,392

● This design overcomes the restrictions of a narrow building site. It has four bedrooms and two baths. Notice the efficient traffic patterns established between the living and family rooms and the kitchen. An optional basement plan is included with the blueprint order.

OPTIONAL BASEMENT PLAN

Design N3466
Square Footage: 1,800

● Small but inviting, this one-story ranch-style farm-house is the perfect choice for a small family or empty-nesters. It's loaded with amenities even the most particular homeowner can appreciate. For example, the living room and dining room each have plant shelves, sloped ceilings and built-ins to enhance livability. The living room also sports a warming hearth. The master bedroom contains a well-appointed bath with dual vanity and walk-in closet. The additional bedroom has its own bath with linen storage. The kitchen is separated from the breakfast nook by a clever bar area. Access to the two-car garage is through a laundry area with washer/dryer hookup space.

QUOTE ONE™
Cost to build? See page 336 to order complete cost estimate to build this house in your area!

Width 89'
Depth 46'-2"

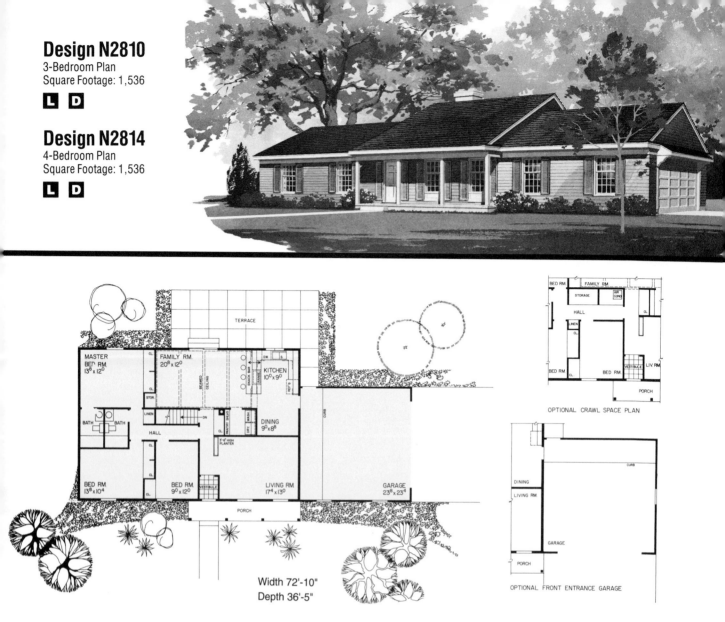

Design N2810
3-Bedroom Plan
Square Footage: 1,536

L **D**

Design N2814
4-Bedroom Plan
Square Footage: 1,536

L **D**

OPTIONAL CRAWL SPACE PLAN

OPTIONAL FRONT ENTRANCE GARAGE

Width 72'-10"
Depth 36'-5"

● The designs on these two pages are particularly energy-efficient. All exterior walls employ the use of 2x6 stud construction to permit the installation of extra thick insulation. The high cornice design also allows for more ceiling insulation. Efficiency is also evident at the air-lock vestibule which restricts the flow of outside air to the interior. Also, the basic rectangle shape of the house is very economical to build. Note the back-to-back plumbing plan, centrally located furnace, minimal window and door openings and modest size. **Design N2810 is available with our Quote One™ Cost Estimate Service. Please see page 336 for details.**

Design N2811
3-Bedroom Plan
Square Footage: 1,581

L **D**

Design N2815
4-Bedroom Plan
Square Footage: 1,581

L **D**

Design N2812
3-Bedroom Plan
Square Footage: 1,581

L **D**

Design N2816
4-Bedroom Plan
Square Footage: 1,581

L **D**

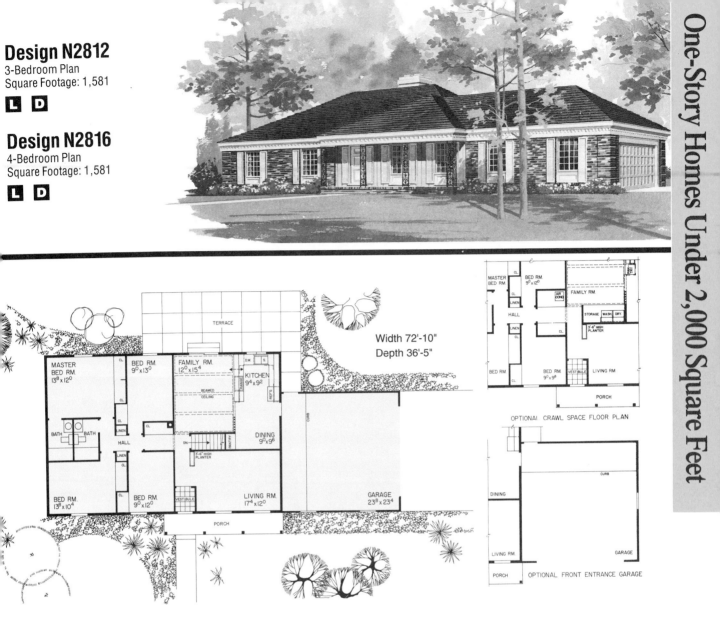

Width 72'-10"
Depth 36'-5"

MASTER BED RM. 13⁸ x 12⁰

BED RM. 9⁰ x 13⁰

FAMILY RM. 12⁰ x 15⁴

KITCHEN 9⁴ x 9²

BEAMED CEILING

TERRACE

BATH   BATH

HALL

BED RM. 13⁸ x 10⁴

BED RM. 9⁰ x 12⁰

VESTIBULE

DINING 9⁰ x 9⁶

LIVING RM. 17⁴ x 12⁰

GARAGE 23⁸ x 23⁴

PORCH

OPTIONAL CRAWL SPACE FLOOR PLAN

MASTER BED RM.

BED RM. 9⁰ x 12⁰

FAMILY RM.

HALL

STORAGE WASH. DRY.

BED RM.

BED RM. 9⁰ x 9⁸

VESTIBULE

LIVING RM.

PORCH

OPTIONAL FRONT ENTRANCE GARAGE

DINING

CURB

LIVING RM.

GARAGE

PORCH

● Within 1,536 square feet there is outstanding livability and a huge variety of options from which to choose: the cozy, front-porch farmhouse adaptation; the pleasing Southern Colonial version, the French creation, or the rugged Western facade. There are also three- or four-bedroom options. If you wish to order blueprints for the hip-roofed design with three bedrooms, specify Design N2812; for the four-bedroom option specify N2816. To order blueprints for the three-bedroom Southern Colonial, request Design N2811, for the four-bedroom, order N2815. The three- bedroom farmhouse is Design N2810; the four-bedroom option is N2814. The three-bedroom Western ranch is Design N2813; the four- bedroom option is N2817.

Design N2813
3-Bedroom Plan
Square Footage: 1,536

L **D**

Design N2817
4-Bedroom Plan
Square Footage: 1,536

L **D**

239

Design N2911

Square Footage: 1,233

● A low-budget home can be a showplace too!
Exquisite proportion, fine detailing, projecting
wings and interesting roof lines help provide
the appeal of this modest one-story. Each of the
bedrooms has excellent wall space and wardrobe storage potential. The master bath features
a vanity, twin lavatories, stall shower plus a
whirlpool. Another full bath is located near the
second bedroom. The spacious gathering room/
dining room area has a fireplace and access to
outdoor terraces. The design has blueprints for
two kitchen plans.

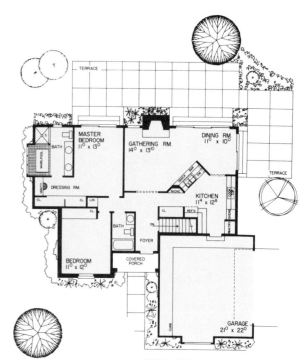

Width 50'
Depth 47'-8"

Design N2603

Square Footage: 1,949

L **D**

● Surely it would be difficult to beat the appeal of this traditional one-story home. Its slightly modified U-shape with the two front facing gables, the bay window, the covered front porch and the interesting use of exterior materials all add to the exterior charm. Besides, there are three large bedrooms serviced by two full baths and three walk-in closets. The excellent kitchen is flanked by the formal dining room and the informal family room. Don't miss the pantry, the built-in oven and the pass-thru to the snack bar. The handy first floor laundry is strategically located to act as a mud room. The extra wash room is but a few steps away. The sizable living room highlights a fireplace and a picture window. Note the location of the basement stairs.

Quote One™

Cost to build? See page 336 to order complete cost estimate to build this house in your area!

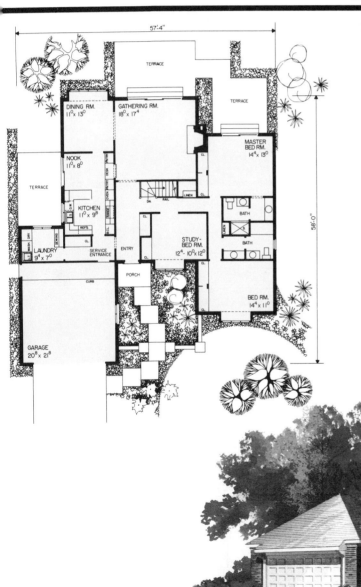

Design N2738

Square Footage: 1,898

● Impressive architecture is apparent in this three-bedroom home. The U-shaped kitchen and breakfast room are located near the formal dining room and hearth-warmed gathering room. Three (or make it two with a study) bedrooms and two baths are in the sleeping wing. Note the dining terrace off the nook and living terrace off the gathering room and master bedroom.

Design N3442

Square Footage: 1,273

L **D**

● This is a superb home-building candidate for those with a narrow, relatively inexpensive building site. Inside, the rounded corners of the foyer add appeal and foster a feeling of spaciousness. Separate formal and informal dining areas are achieved through the incorporation of a breakfast bar. The spacious living room features a sloped ceiling, a central fireplace and cheerful windows. The master suite has a sloped ceiling and a high shelf for plants or other decor items.

Width 40'-8"
Depth 59'

QUOTE ONE™

Cost to build? See page 336 to order complete cost estimate to build this house in your area!

Design N3465

Square Footage: 1,410

L

QUOTE ONE™

Cost to build? See page 336 to order complete cost estimate to build this house in your area!

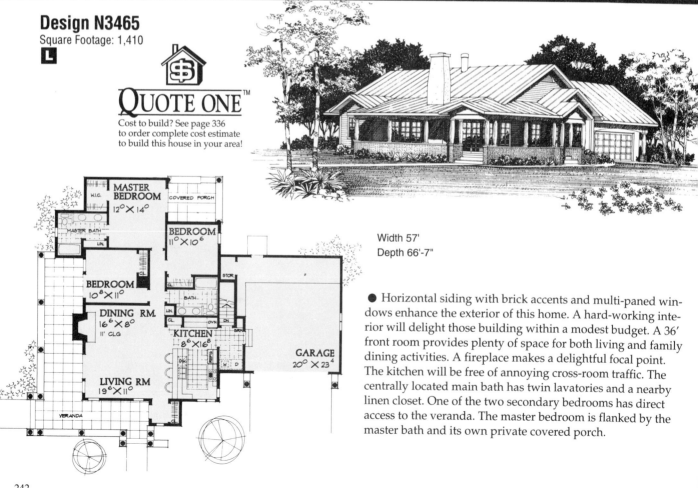

Width 57'
Depth 66'-7"

● Horizontal siding with brick accents and multi-paned windows enhance the exterior of this home. A hard-working interior will delight those building within a modest budget. A 36' front room provides plenty of space for both living and family dining activities. A fireplace makes a delightful focal point. The kitchen will be free of annoying cross-room traffic. The centrally located main bath has twin lavatories and a nearby linen closet. One of the two secondary bedrooms has direct access to the veranda. The master bedroom is flanked by the master bath and its own private covered porch.

Design N3481A

Square Footage: 1,901

● In just under 2,000 square feet, this pleasing one-story home bears all the livability of houses twice its size. A combined living and dining room offers elegance for entertaining; with two elevations to choose from, the living room can either support an octagonal bay or a bumped-out nook. The U-shaped kitchen finds easy access to the breakfast nook and rear family room; sliding glass doors lead from the family room to a back stoop. The master bedroom has a quaint potshelf and a private bath with a spa tub, a double-bowl vanity, a walk-in closet and a compartmented toilet. With two additional family bedrooms—one may serve as a den if desired—and a hall bath with dual lavatories, this plan offers the best in accommodations. Both elevations come with the blueprint package.

Design N3481B

Square Footage: 1,908

Width 42'
Depth 63'-6"

Cost to build? See page 336
to order complete cost estimate
to build this house in your area!

243

Design N1389
Square Footage: 1,488

D

● Your choice of exterior goes with this outstanding floor plan. If you like French Provincial, Design N1389 is your choice. If you prefer the simple, straightforward lines of contemporary plans, Design N1387 will be your favorite. For the warmth of Colonial adaptations, the charming exterior of Design N1388 is perfect. Note the differences in the three plans: window treatment, roof lines and other details.

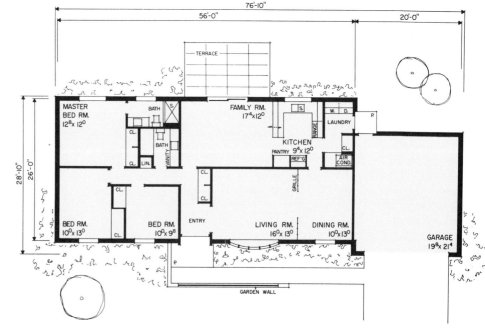

Design N1387
Square Footage: 1,488

D

Design N1388
Square Footage: 1,488

D

Design N1380
Square Footage: 1,399

L **D**

Design N1381
Square Footage: 1,399

L **D**

● These two stylish exteriors have the same practical, L-shaped floor plan. Design N1380 is characterized by the pediment gables and the masses of brick. Design N1381 is captivating because of its hip-roof, panelled shutters and lamp post. Inside, there is an abundance of liva-bility. The formal living and dining area is spacious, and the U-shaped kitchen is efficient. There is informal eating space, a separate laundry and a fine family room. The blueprints include details for building either with or without a basement.

Design N1896
Square Footage: 1,690

● Complete family livability is provided by this exceptional floor plan. Further, this design has a truly delightful traditional exterior. The fine layout features a center entrance hall with storage closet in addition to the wardrobe closet. Then, there is the formal, front living room and the adjacent, separate dining room. The U-shaped kitchen has plenty of counter and cupboard space. There is even a pantry. The family room functions with the kitchen and is but a step from the outdoor terrace. The mud room has space for storage and laundry equipment. The extra wash room is nearby. The large family will find those four bedrooms and two full baths just the answer to sleeping and bath accommodations.

Design N1890
Square Footage: 1,628

● The pediment gable and columns help set the charm of this modestly sized home. Here is graciousness normally associated with homes twice its size. The pleasant symmetry of the windows and the double front doors complete the picture. Inside, each square foot is wisely planned to assure years of convenient living. There are three bedrooms, each with twin wardrobe closets. There are two full baths economically grouped with the laundry and heating equipment. A fine feature.

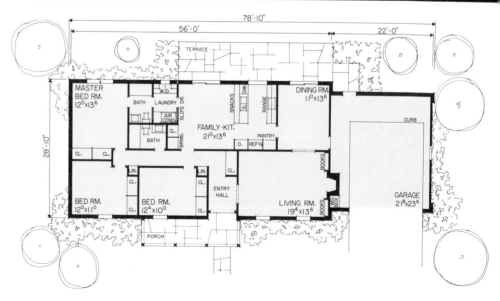

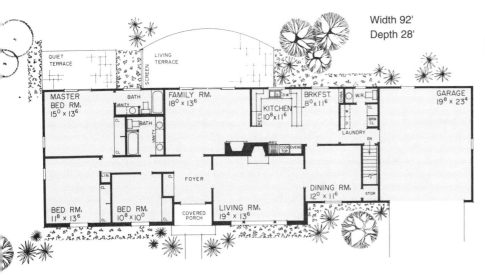

Width 92'
Depth 28'

QUIET TERRACE

LIVING TERRACE

SCREEN

MASTER BED RM. 15⁰ x 13⁶

BATH
VANITY

BATH
VANITY

CL

CL

FAMILY RM. 18⁰ x 13⁶

KITCHEN 10⁸ x 11⁶

REF'S

D W

BRKFST. 8⁰ x 11⁶

CHINA

W.R.

CL

W
D

BRM CL

GARAGE 19⁸ x 23⁴

LAUNDRY

BBQ
COOK TOP
OVENS

DN

FOYER

LIN
CL

CL

CL

BED RM. 11⁸ x 13⁶

BED RM. 10⁸ x 10⁰

CL

COVERED PORCH

LIVING RM. 19⁴ x 13⁶

DINING RM. 12⁰ x 11⁶

STOR

Design N1325
Square Footage: 1,942

L D

● The large front entry hall permits direct access to the formal living room, the sleeping area and the informal family room. Both of the living areas have a fireplace. When formal dining is the occasion of the evening the separate dining room is but a step from the living room. The U-shaped kitchen is strategically flanked by the family room and the breakfast areas.

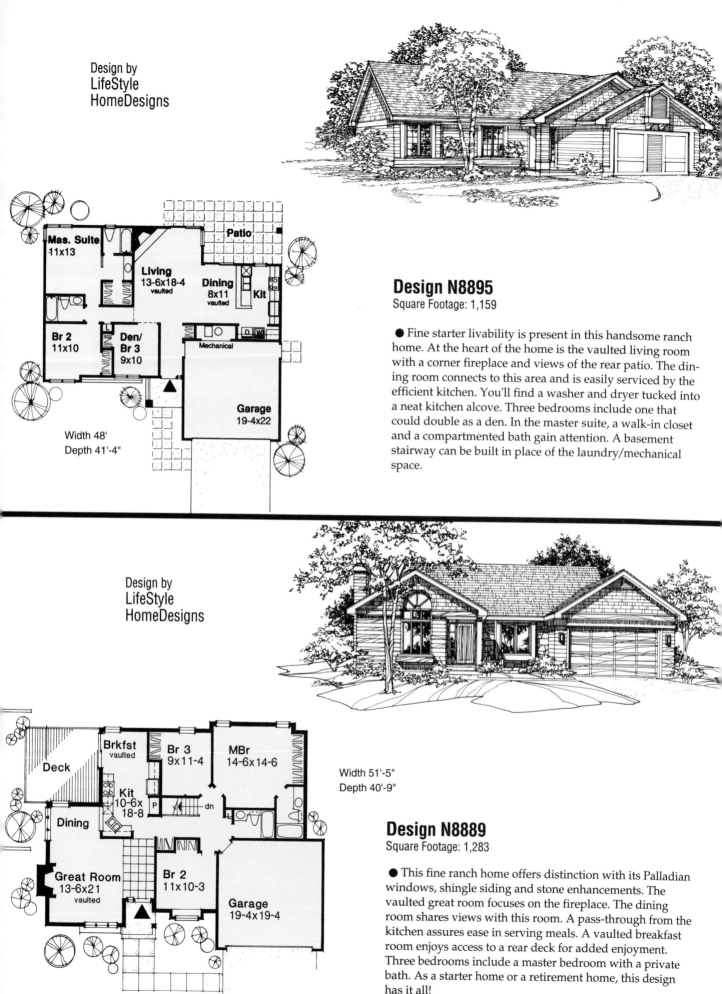

Design by
LifeStyle
HomeDesigns

Mas. Suite
11x13

Patio

Living
13-6x18-4
vaulted

Dining
8x11
vaulted

Kit

Br 2
11x10

Den/
Br 3
9x10

Mechanical

D W

Garage
19-4x22

Width 48'
Depth 41'-4"

Design N8895
Square Footage: 1,159

● Fine starter livability is present in this handsome ranch home. At the heart of the home is the vaulted living room with a corner fireplace and views of the rear patio. The dining room connects to this area and is easily serviced by the efficient kitchen. You'll find a washer and dryer tucked into a neat kitchen alcove. Three bedrooms include one that could double as a den. In the master suite, a walk-in closet and a compartmented bath gain attention. A basement stairway can be built in place of the laundry/mechanical space.

Design by
LifeStyle
HomeDesigns

Deck

Brkfst
vaulted

Br 3
9x11-4

MBr
14-6x14-6

Kit
10-6x
18-8

P

dn

Dining

Great Room
13-6x21
vaulted

Br 2
11x10-3

Garage
19-4x19-4

Width 51'-5"
Depth 40'-9"

Design N8889
Square Footage: 1,283

● This fine ranch home offers distinction with its Palladian windows, shingle siding and stone enhancements. The vaulted great room focuses on the fireplace. The dining room shares views with this room. A pass-through from the kitchen assures ease in serving meals. A vaulted breakfast room enjoys access to a rear deck for added enjoyment. Three bedrooms include a master bedroom with a private bath. As a starter home or a retirement home, this design has it all!

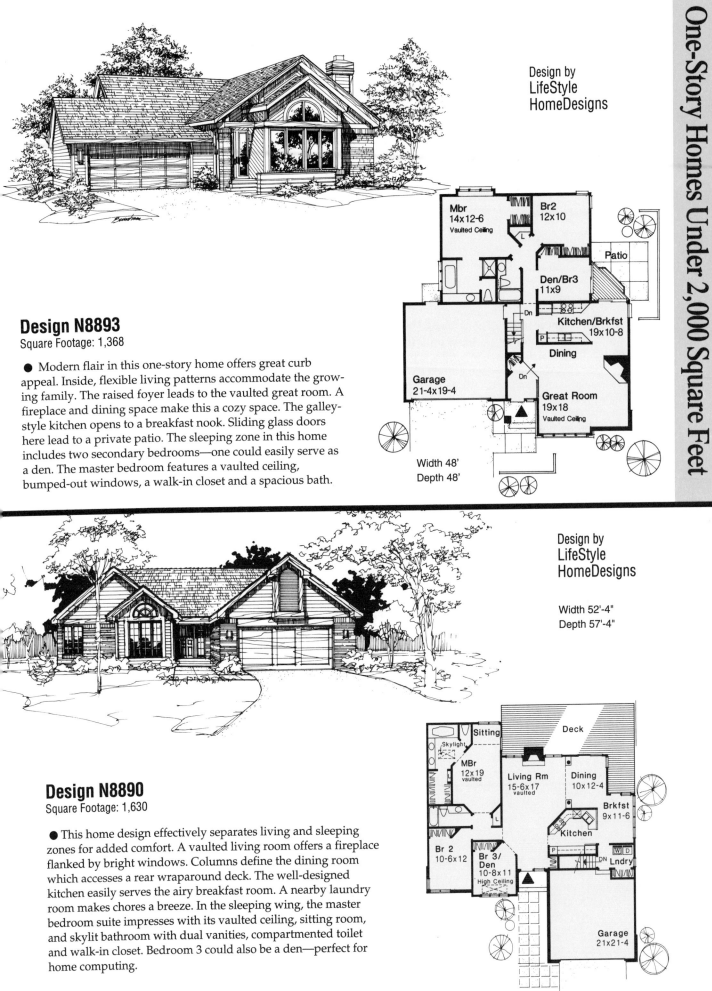

Design by
LifeStyle
HomeDesigns

Mbr
14x12-6
Vaulted Ceiling

Br2
12x10

Patio

Den/Br3
11x9

Kitchen/Brkfst
19x10-8

Dining

Garage
21-4x19-4

Great Room
19x18
Vaulted Ceiling

Width 48'
Depth 48'

Design N8893
Square Footage: 1,368

● Modern flair in this one-story home offers great curb appeal. Inside, flexible living patterns accommodate the growing family. The raised foyer leads to the vaulted great room. A fireplace and dining space make this a cozy space. The galley-style kitchen opens to a breakfast nook. Sliding glass doors here lead to a private patio. The sleeping zone in this home includes two secondary bedrooms—one could easily serve as a den. The master bedroom features a vaulted ceiling, bumped-out windows, a walk-in closet and a spacious bath.

Design by
LifeStyle
HomeDesigns

Width 52'-4"
Depth 57'-4"

Sitting

Skylight

Deck

MBr
12x19
vaulted

Living Rm
15-6x17
vaulted

Dining
10x12-4

Brkfst
9x11-6

Kitchen

Br 2
10-6x12

**Br 3/
Den**
10-8x11
High Ceiling

Lndry

Garage
21x21-4

Design N8890
Square Footage: 1,630

● This home design effectively separates living and sleeping zones for added comfort. A vaulted living room offers a fireplace flanked by bright windows. Columns define the dining room which accesses a rear wraparound deck. The well-designed kitchen easily serves the airy breakfast room. A nearby laundry room makes chores a breeze. In the sleeping wing, the master bedroom suite impresses with its vaulted ceiling, sitting room, and skylit bathroom with dual vanities, compartmented toilet and walk-in closet. Bedroom 3 could also be a den—perfect for home computing.

Design by
LifeStyle
HomeDesigns

Spa · Patio · Deck

M. Suite
12—8x17
vaulted

Dining
11—8x11—8
vaulted

Screen
Porch
11—8x11—8

Living Room
15x22
high ceiling

Kit/Brkfst
18x15

Stor

DN

Den/Office
14x13—4
high ceiling

Br 2
10—4x12

Garage
21x19—4

Width 60'
Depth 55'-4"

Design N8888
Square Footage: 1,850

● For all the room you need, this design takes precedence. A front den or office is highlighted by a massive brick fireplace and lots of bright windows. Use this space, too, to accommodate house guests. The living room also features a fireplace. The gourmet kitchen enjoys an island and a sunny breakfast nook. The formal dining room opens to the rear deck and spa. Two bedrooms are situated on the left side of the plan. In the master bedroom suite, large proportions, deck access and a luxury bath are popular enhancements. A large walk-in closet and a linen closet assure you meet storage needs.

Enhanced Plan

● All the charm of a traditional country home is wrapped up in this economical ranch. The three-bedroom plan can also serve as two bedrooms plus a study or playroom. The kitchen and family room combination offers plenty of space for family gatherings. A one- or two-car garage may be attached. Other options include a front porch with railing, a rear deck with railing, a box bay window and a fireplace.

The blueprints for this house show how to build both a basic, low-cost version and an enhanced, upgraded version. Blueprints and a complete lumber and materials package are also available for this home at your local 84 Lumber dealer.

Design N3700
Square Footage: 1,317

Width 66'
Depth 34'-5"

DECK · RAILING

2 CAR
GARAGE
19⁸ X 21⁴

OPT.
FIREPLACE

EATING

FAMILY KITCHEN
24² X 13¹⁰

SNACK
BAR

LINE OF
OPTIONAL
1 CAR
GARAGE

BATH

MASTER
BEDROOM
11⁸ X 13¹⁰

BATH

PANTRY

CL

HALF
WALL

LIVING ROOM
15² X 13²

STUDY/
BEDROOM
9¹⁰X 9⁶

ENTRY

DN

BEDROOM
11⁴ X 10⁶

HALF
WALL

OPT. BAY WINDOW

COVERED PORCH

RAILING

Basic Plan

Enhanced Plan

Design N3701
Square Footage: 1,130

● Traditional charm is an apt description of this economical ranch home. The master bedroom offers a full bath plus ample closet space. A full-size bath adjoins the other two bedrooms. The kitchen is designed to serve as an eat-in kitchen for this efficient home. Options include a one- or two-car garage, a front porch, a rear deck with a railing, a box-bay window and a fireplace.

The blueprints for this house show how to build both a basic, low-cost version and an enhanced, upgraded version. Blueprints and a complete lumber and materials package are also available for this home at your local 84 Lumber dealer.

Width 60'
Depth 28'

Basic Plan

Design N3704
Square Footage: 1,492

● The comfort and charm of this lovely ranch home are surprisingly affordable. Featuring an old-fashioned front porch, this three-bedroom home includes two full baths. A large dining area and a pantry adjoin a large work area to form a country kitchen. Livability can be enhanced with the optional one- or two-car garage, a rear deck with a railing, two angle-bay windows and a fireplace.

The blueprints for this house show how to build both a basic, low-cost version and an enhanced, upgraded version. Blueprints and a complete lumber and materials package are also available for this home at your local 84 Lumber dealer.

Enhanced Plan

Width 72'
Depth 28'

Basic Plan

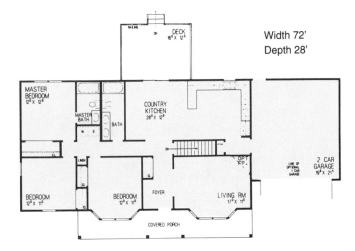

251

Design N2917

Square Footage: 1,813

L

● Here's an attractive design with many of today's most-asked-for features: gathering room with fireplace, separate formal dining room, roomy kitchen with equally spacious breakfast area, and three bedrooms including a master suite with huge walk-in closet and two private vanities. One other plus: a great-to-stretch-out-on terrace leading to the backyard.

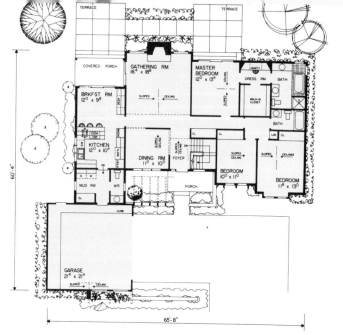

Design N2902

Square Footage: 1,632

L

● A sun space highlights this passive solar design. It has access from the kitchen, dining room and garage. Three skylights illuminate the interior — one in the kitchen, one in the laundry and one in the master bath. The living room/dining room has a sloped ceiling, fireplace and two sets of sliding glass doors to the terrace. Three bedrooms and two baths are found in the sleeping wing. The area of the sunspace is 216 square feet not included in the above total.

QUOTE ONE™

Cost to build? See page 336 to order complete cost estimate to build this house in your area!

Width 59'
Depth 56'-8"

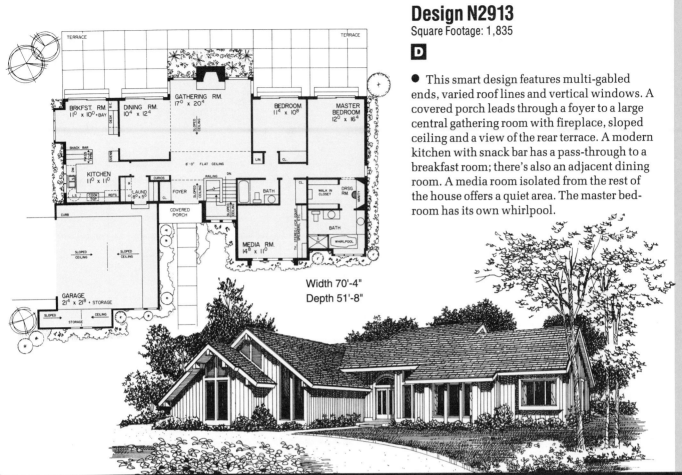

Design N2913
Square Footage: 1,835

D

● This smart design features multi-gabled ends, varied roof lines and vertical windows. A covered porch leads through a foyer to a large central gathering room with fireplace, sloped ceiling and a view of the rear terrace. A modern kitchen with snack bar has a pass-through to a breakfast room; there's also an adjacent dining room. A media room isolated from the rest of the house offers a quiet area. The master bedroom has its own whirlpool.

Width 70'-4"
Depth 51'-8"

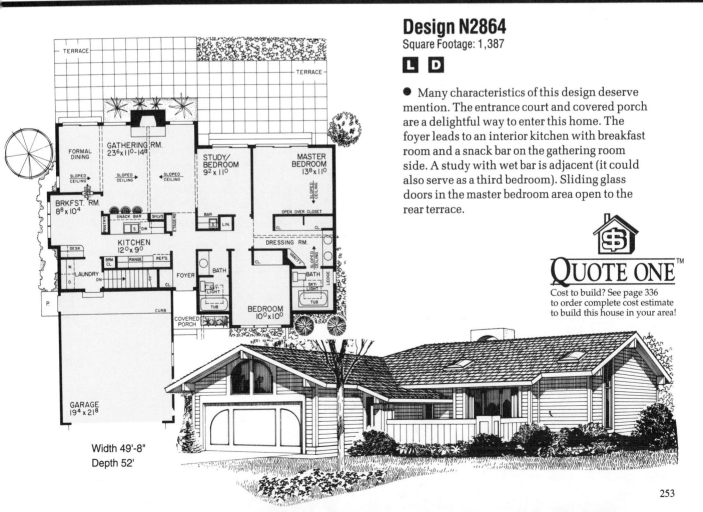

Design N2864
Square Footage: 1,387

L **D**

● Many characteristics of this design deserve mention. The entrance court and covered porch are a delightful way to enter this home. The foyer leads to an interior kitchen with breakfast room and a snack bar on the gathering room side. A study with wet bar is adjacent (it could also serve as a third bedroom). Sliding glass doors in the master bedroom area open to the rear terrace.

Quote One™
Cost to build? See page 336 to order complete cost estimate to build this house in your area!

Width 49'-8"
Depth 52'

Design N2871

Living Area: 1,824 square feet
Greenhouse Area: 81 square feet
Total: 1,905 square feet

D

Quote One™

Cost to build? See page 336 to order complete cost estimate to build this house in your area!

● A greenhouse off the dining room and living room provides a cheerful focal point for this comfortable three-bedroom home. The spacious living room features a cozy fireplace and sloped ceiling. In addition to the dining room, there's a less formal breakfast room just off the modern kitchen. Stairs just off the foyer lead down to a recreation room. The master bedroom suite opens to a terrace. The mud room and washroom off the garage allow rear entry to the house during inclement weather.

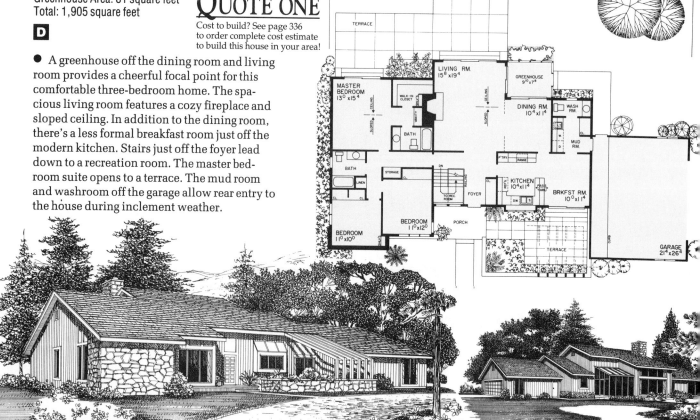

Design N2824

Square Footage: 1,550

● Low maintenance and economy in building are the outstanding exterior features of this sharp one-story design. The entrance opens to a charming courtyard garden and covered walk to the front porch. Sliding glass doors are featured in each of the main rooms for easy access to the outdoors. A sun porch is tucked between the study and gathering rooms. Optional non-basement details are included with the blueprints for this design.

OPTIONAL NON-BASEMENT

254

QUOTE ONE™

st to build? See page 336
order complete cost estimate
build this house in your area!

68'-0"

GATHERING RM.
13⁸ x 18⁸

DINING RM.
13⁰ x 11⁰

MASTER BEDROOM
16⁰ x 12⁰

40'-5"

BATH
BATH
WALK-IN CLOSET
RAISED HEARTH
KITCHEN
9⁰ x 12⁰
CHINA
STORAGE WORK BENCH STORAGE
CURB
SNACK BAR
LINEN
PDR RM.
FOYER
BREAKFAST
9⁰ x 9⁰
GARAGE
23⁴ x 23⁴
BEDROOM
11⁴ x 12⁰
BEDROOM
10⁰ x 11⁰
COVERED PORCH

Design N2671
Square Footage: 1,589

L D

● The rustic exterior of this one-story home features vertical wood siding. The entry foyer is floored with flagstone and leads to the three areas of the plan: sleeping, living and work center. The sleeping area has three bedrooms including a master with sliding glass doors to the rear terrace. The living area, consisting of gathering and dining rooms, also has access to the terrace. The work center is efficiently planned. It houses the kitchen with snack bar, breakfast room with built-in china cabinet and stairs to the basement.

TERRACE

GATHERING RM.
17⁰ x 17⁴

DINING
12⁰ x 13⁶

MASTER BED RM.
11⁰ x 17⁰

STUDY
11⁰ x 10²

STORAGE

THRU FIREPLACE
RAISED HEARTH
SLOPED CEILING

DESK
OVEN
PNTRY

WALK-IN CLOSET
BATH
BATH
KITCHEN
11⁰ x 11⁶
LAUNDRY
STORAGE
10⁴ x 8⁴

LINEN
FOYER
BREAKFAST
8⁸ x 11⁶
CURB

BED RM.
11⁰ x 13⁶
BED RM.
11⁰ x 10⁰
COVERED PRIVACY COURT
GARAGE
22⁸ x 22⁴

Width 73'-6"
Depth 52'-2"

Design N2795
Square Footage: 1,952

● This three-bedroom design leaves no room for improvement. To the left of the entry foyer is the sleeping wing equipped with three bedrooms and two baths. Straight ahead is the gathering room with through-fireplace to the dining room. To the right of this area is the work center. It includes a breakfast room, U-shaped kitchen and laundry.

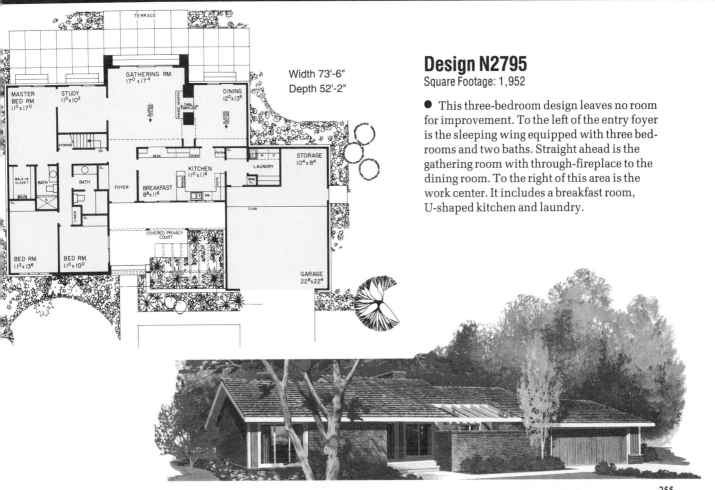

● This is most certainly an outstanding contemporary design. Study the exterior carefully before your journey to inspect the floor plan. The vertical lines are carried from the siding to the paned windows to the garage door. The front entry is recessed so the overhanging roof creates a covered porch.

Note the planter court with privacy wall. The floor plan is just as outstanding. The rear gathering room has a sloped ceiling, raised hearth fireplace, sliding glass doors to the terrace and a snack bar with pass-thru to the kitchen. In addition to the gathering room, there is the living room/study. This

room could be utilized in a variety of ways depending on your family's choice. The formal dining room is convenient to the U-shaped kitchen. Three bedrooms and two closely located baths are in the sleeping wing. This plan includes details for the construction of an optional basement.

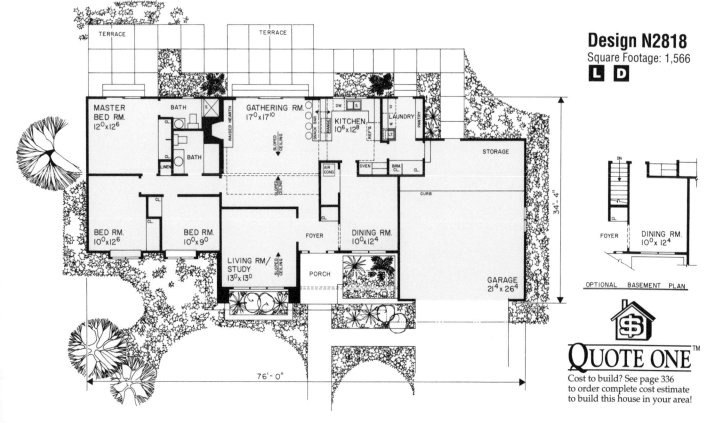

Design N2818
Square Footage: 1,566

L D

OPTIONAL BASEMENT PLAN

QUOTE ONE™
Cost to build? See page 336
to order complete cost estimate
to build this house in your area!

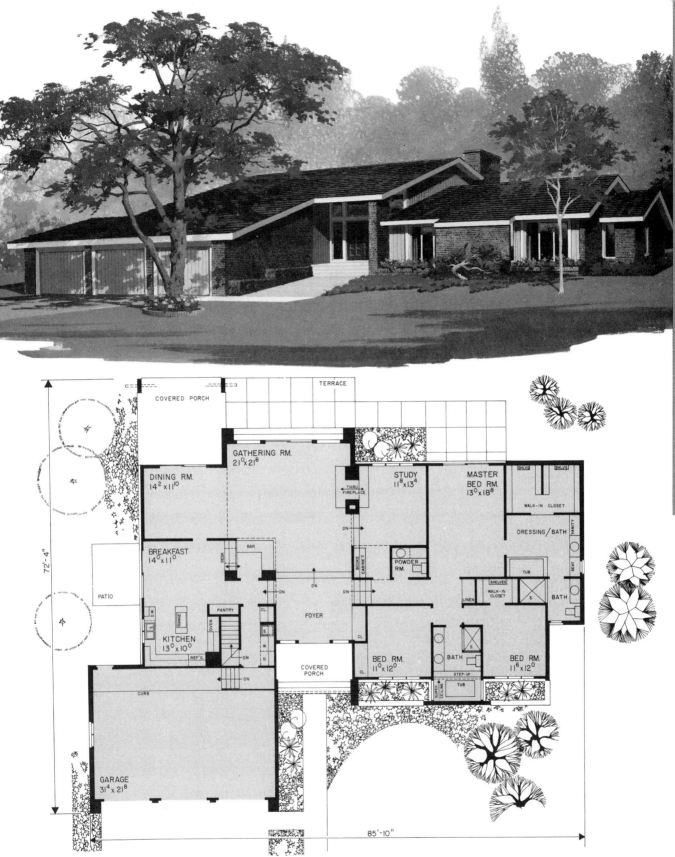

DINING RM.
$14^2 \times 11^{10}$

GATHERING RM.
$21^0 \times 21^6$

TERRACE

COVERED PORCH

STUDY
$11^6 \times 13^4$

MASTER BED RM.
$13^0 \times 18^8$

WALK-IN CLOSET

DRESSING/BATH

THRU FIREPLACE

BREAKFAST
$14^0 \times 11^0$

BAR

DESK

BOOKS

CABINET

POWDER RM.

TUB

SHELVES

WALK-IN CLOSET

LINEN

BATH

FOYER

KITCHEN
$13^0 \times 10^0$

RANGE

PANTRY

OVEN

REF'G.

PATIO

BATH

BED RM.
$11^0 \times 12^0$

STEP-UP

TUB

BED RM.
$11^6 \times 12^0$

SLOPED CEILING

COVERED PORCH

GARAGE
$31^4 \times 21^8$

CURB

72'-4"

85'-10"

Design N2789 Square Footage: 2,732

L **D**

● An attached three car garage! What a fantastic feature of this three bedroom contemporary design. And there's more. As one walks up the steps to the covered porch and through the double front doors the charm of this design will be overwhelming. Inside, a large foyer greets all visitors and leads them to each of the three areas, each down a few steps. The living area has a large gathering room with fireplace and a study adjacent on one side and the formal dining room on the other. The work center has an efficient kitchen with island range, breakfast room, laundry and built-in desk and bar. Then there is the sleeping area. Note the raised tub with sloped ceiling.

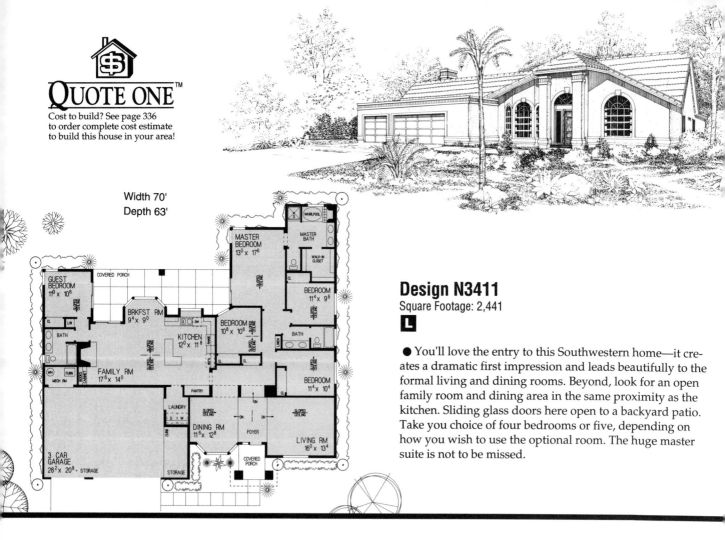

Width 70'
Depth 63'

Design N3411

Square Footage: 2,441

L

● You'll love the entry to this Southwestern home—it creates a dramatic first impression and leads beautifully to the formal living and dining rooms. Beyond, look for an open family room and dining area in the same proximity as the kitchen. Sliding glass doors here open to a backyard patio. Take you choice of four bedrooms or five, depending on how you wish to use the optional room. The huge master suite is not to be missed.

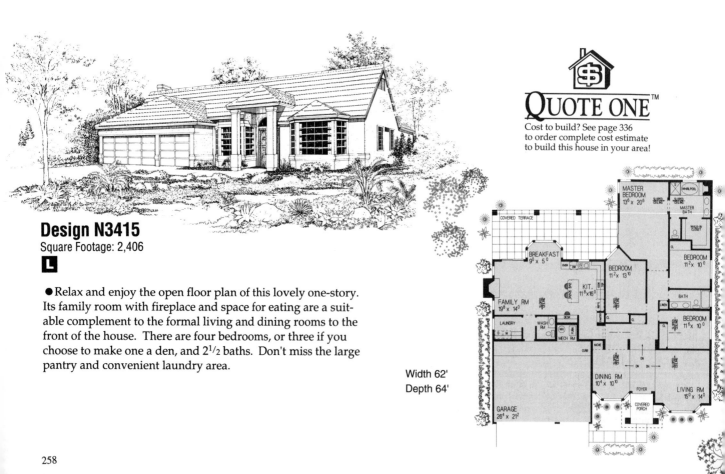

Design N3415

Square Footage: 2,406

L

● Relax and enjoy the open floor plan of this lovely one-story. Its family room with fireplace and space for eating are a suitable complement to the formal living and dining rooms to the front of the house. There are four bedrooms, or three if you choose to make one a den, and 2¹/₂ baths. Don't miss the large pantry and convenient laundry area.

Width 62'
Depth 64'

Design N3560

Square Footage: 2,189

L

● Simplicity is the key to the stylish good looks of this home's facade. A walled garden entry and large window areas appeal to outdoor enthusiasts. Inside, the kitchen forms the hub of the plan. It opens directly off the foyer and contains an island counter and a work counter with eating space on the living area side. A sloped ceiling, fireplace, and sliding glass doors to a rear terrace are highlights in living area. The master bedroom also sports sliding glass doors to the terrace. Its dressing area is enhanced with double walk-in closets and lavatories. A whirlpool tub and seated shower are additional amenities. Two family bedrooms are found on the opposite side of the house. They share a full bath with twin lavatories.

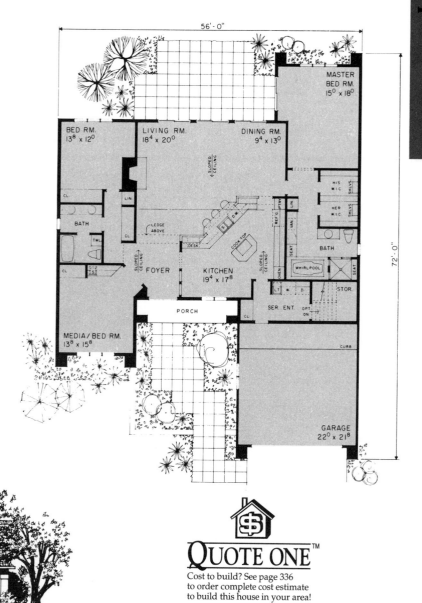

QUOTE ONE™

Cost to build? See page 336
to order complete cost estimate
to build this house in your area!

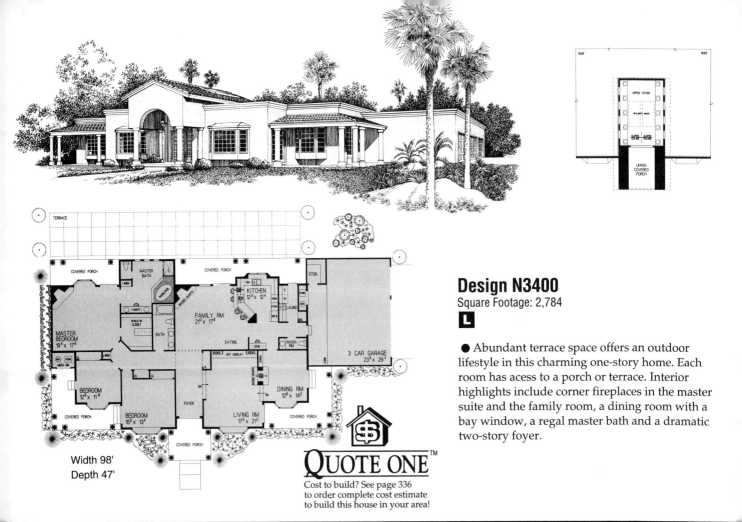

Design N3400
Square Footage: 2,784

L

● Abundant terrace space offers an outdoor lifestyle in this charming one-story home. Each room has acess to a porch or terrace. Interior highlights include corner fireplaces in the master suite and the family room, a dining room with a bay window, a regal master bath and a dramatic two-story foyer.

Width 98'
Depth 47'

QUOTE ONE™

Cost to build? See page 336
to order complete cost estimate
to build this house in your area!

QUOTE ONE™

Cost to build? See page 336
to order complete cost estimate
to build this house in your area!

Width 77'-4"
Depth 74'-8"

Design N3475
Square Footage: 3,286

L

● The tiled, hipped roof with varying roof planes and wide overhangs sets off this Spanish design. In the sunken living room, a curved, raised-hearth fireplace acts as a focal point. The U-shaped kitchen contains an island work surface, breakfast bar, pantry and broom closet. An informal nook extends to include the family room and will cater to family activities. Opposite the formal living room is the separate dining room. Its expanse of glass looks out on the garden court. A major floor-planning feature of this design is found in the sleeping arrangements; notice the complete separation of the parents' and children's bedroom facilities.

Design N2670

Square Footage: 3,058
Lounge: 279 square feet

L

● A centrally located interior atrium is one of the most interesting features of this Spanish design. The atrium has a built-in seat and will bring light to its adjacent rooms: the living room, the dining room and the breakfast room. Beyond the foyer, sunken one step, is a tiled reception hall that includes a powder room. This area leads to the sleeping wing and up one step to the family room with its raised-hearth fireplace and sliding glass doors to the rear terrace. Overlooking the family room is a railed lounge which can be used for various activities. Sleeping areas include a master suite and three family bedrooms.

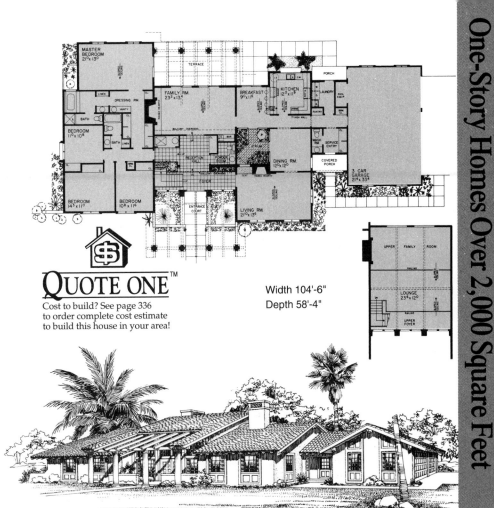

QUOTE ONE™

Cost to build? See page 336 to order complete cost estimate to build this house in your area!

Width 104'-6"
Depth 58'-4"

Design N3329

Square Footage: 2,968

L

● Projecting wood beams, called vigas, add a decorative touch to this Santa Fe exterior. To the left of the foyer rests a living room with a corner fireplace and a music alcove. Past the formal dining room on the right is the family room with a fireplace and outdoor access. The kitchen offers yet another fireplace, along with a snack bar and an adjacent morning room. The master bedroom is placed to the left of the home. The master bath includes a whirlpool tub and a separate shower. At the opposite end of the home are three family bedrooms, two full baths and a study with a built-in bookcase.

QUOTE ONE™

Cost to build? See page 336 to order complete cost estimate to build this house in your area!

Width 120'
Depth 76'

261

Design N3357
Square Footage: 2,913

L **D**

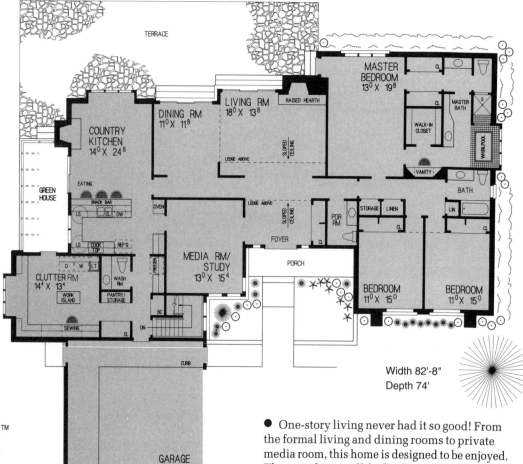

TERRACE

COUNTRY KITCHEN
14⁰ X 24⁸

DINING RM
11⁰ X 11⁸

LIVING RM
18⁰ X 13⁸

RAISED HEARTH

MASTER BEDROOM
13⁰ X 19⁸

MASTER BATH

WALK-IN CLOSET

WHIRLPOOL

GREEN HOUSE

EATING

SNACK BAR

LS S DW

LEDGE ABOVE

SLOPED CEILING

VANITY

BATH

LS

COOK TOP

REF'G

LEDGE ABOVE

SLOPED CEILING

PDR RM

STORAGE LINEN

LIN

D W LT

WASH RM

FREEZER

MEDIA RM/ STUDY
13⁰ X 15⁴

FOYER

CL

PORCH

CLUTTER RM
14⁴ X 13⁴

WORK ISLAND

PANTRY/ STORAGE

BEDROOM
11⁰ X 15⁰

BEDROOM
11⁰ X 15⁰

SEWING

CL

BC

DN

CURB

Width 82'-8"
Depth 74'

GARAGE
23⁶ X 23⁸

QUOTE ONE™

Cost to build? See page 336
to order complete cost estimate
to build this house in your area!

● One-story living never had it so good! From
the formal living and dining rooms to private
media room, this home is designed to be enjoyed.
The greenhouse off the kitchen adds 147 square
feet to the plan. It offers access to the clutter
room where gardening or hobby activities can
take place. A the opposite end of the house are
a master bedroom with generous bath and two
family bedrooms. Notice the wealth of built-ins
throughout the house.

Design N3368
Square Footage: 2,720

L **D**

QUOTE ONE™

Cost to build? See page 336
to order complete cost estimate
to build this house in your area!

● Roof lines are the key to the interesting exterior of this design. Their configuration allows for sloped ceilings in the gathering room and large foyer. The master bedroom suite has a huge walk-in closet, garden whirlpool and

separate shower. Two family bedrooms share a full bath. One of these bedrooms could be used as a media room with pass-through wet bar. Note the large kitchen with conversation bay and the wide terrace to the rear.

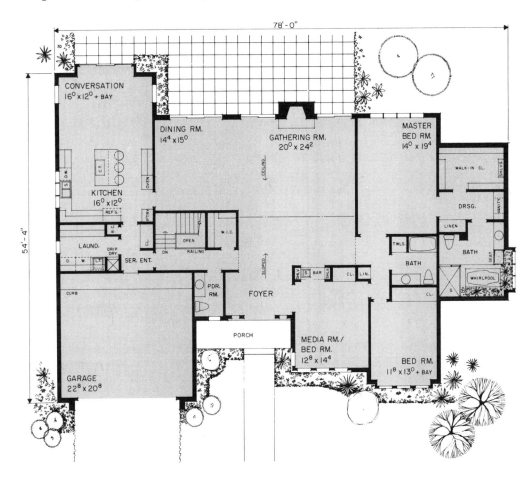

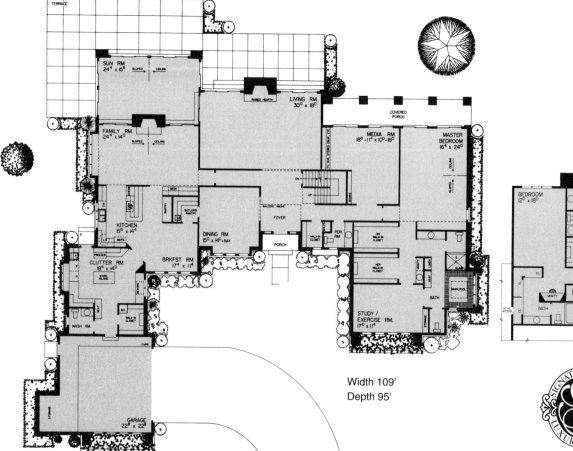

TERRACE

SUN RM.
24⁴ x 15⁸   SLOPED   CEILING

LIVING RM.
30⁰ x 18⁰   RAISED HEARTH

COVERED
PORCH

FAMILY RM.
24⁴ x 14⁰   SLOPED   CEILING

MEDIA RM.
18⁰ -11⁴ x 10⁰-18⁰

MASTER
BEDROOM
16⁴ x 24⁰   CEILING

KITCHEN
15⁶ x 14⁴

DEN

PANTRY

BUTLER'S
PANTRY

DINING RM.
15⁰ x 14⁰ + BAY

FOYER

HIS
WALK-IN
CLOSET

FREEZER

CLUTTER RM.
18⁴ x 14⁰   WORK ISLAND

BRKFST. RM.
17⁴ x 11⁴

PORCH

WALK-IN
CLOSET

PDR.
RM.

HER
WALK-IN
CLOSET

VANITY

WHIRLPOOL

WALK-IN
CLOSET

WASH. RM.

BATH

STORAGE

STUDY /
EXERCISE RM.
17⁰ x 11⁴

STORAGE

GARAGE
22⁸ x 22⁸

Width 109'
Depth 95'

BEDROOM
12⁰ x 18⁰   BATH

BEDROOM
12⁰ x 18⁰

WALK-IN
CLOSET

ATTIC
ACCESS

CL

DN.

OPEN
BELOW

ATTIC
ACCESS

VANITY   LINEN

BATH

BALCONY

SLOPED
CEILING

UPPER
FOYER

Design N2938
First Floor: 4,518 square feet
Second Floor: 882 square feet
Total: 5,400 square feet
L

● A semi-circular fanlight and side-lights grace the entrance of this striking contemporary. The lofty foyer, with balcony above, leads to an elegant, two-story living room with fireplace. The family room, housing a second fireplace, leads to a glorious sunroom; both have dramatic sloped ceilings.

The kitchen and breakfast room are conveniently located for access to the informal family room or to the formal dining room via the butler's pantry. The large adjoining clutter room with work island offers limitless possibilities for the seamstress, hobbyist, or indoor gardener. An executive-sized, first-

floor master suite offers privacy and relaxation; the bath with whirlpool tub and dressing area with twin walk-in closets open to a study that could double as an exercise room. Two second-floor bedrooms with private baths and walk-in closets round out the livability in this gracious home.

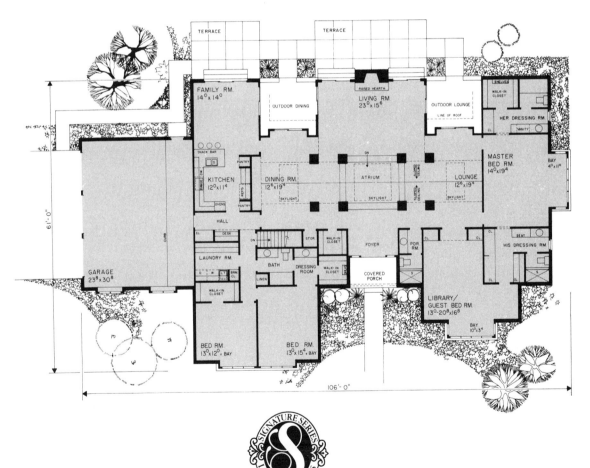

TERRACE   TERRACE

FAMILY RM.
14⁰x14⁰

OUTDOOR DINING

RAISED HEARTH

LIVING RM.
23⁰x15⁶

OUTDOOR LOUNGE

LINE OF ROOF

SHELVES

WALK-IN CLOSET

HER DRESSING RM.

VANITY

SNACK BAR

PANTRY

KITCHEN
12⁰x11⁴

RANGE

OVENS

REF'S

DINING RM.
12⁶x19⁴

SKYLIGHT

ATRIUM

SKYLIGHT

SLOPING CEILING

LOUNGE
12⁶x19⁴

SKYLIGHT

MASTER BED RM.
14⁰x19⁴

BAY
4⁰x11⁴

HALL

CL   DESK

LAUNDRY RM.

D   W

BRM

CL

BATH

DRESSING ROOM

STOR

WALK-IN CLOSET

WALK-IN CLOSET

FOYER

PDR RM.

COVERED PORCH

CL

CL

SEAT

HIS DRESSING RM.

S

LINEN

WALK-IN CLOSET

BED RM.
13⁰x12⁰ + BAY

BED RM.
13⁰x15⁴ + BAY

LIBRARY/ GUEST BED RM.
13⁰-20⁸x16⁸

BAY
10⁰x3⁴

GARAGE
23⁸x30⁸

61'-0"

106'-0"

Design N2791
Square Footage: 3,809

● The use of vertical paned windows and the hipped roof highlight the exterior of this unique design. Upon entrance one will view a charming sunken atrium with skylight above plus a skylight in the dining room and one in the lounge. Formal living will be graciously accommodated in the living room. It features a raised-hearth fireplace, two sets of sliding glass doors to the rear terrace plus two more sliding doors, one to an outdoor dining terrace and the other to an outdoor lounge. Informal living will be enjoyed in the family room with snack bar and in the large library. All will praise the fine planning of the master suite. It features a bay window, His and Hers dressing room with private baths and an abundance of closet space.

Design N2858
Square Footage: 2,231

● This sun oriented design was created to face the south. By doing so, it has minimal northern exposure. It has been designed primarily for the more temperate U.S. latitudes using 2 x 6 wall construction. The morning sun will brighten the living and dining rooms along with the adjacent terrace. Sun enters the garden room by way of the glass roof and walls. In the winter, the solar heat gain from the garden room should provide relief from high energy bills. Solar shades allow you to adjust the amount of light that you want to enter in the warmer months. Interior planning deserves mention, too. The work center is efficient. The kitchen has a snack bar on the garden room side and a serving counter to the dining room. The breakfast room with laundry area is also convenient to the kitchen. Three bedrooms are on the northern wall. The master bedroom has a large tub and a separate shower with a four foot square skylight above. When this design is oriented toward the sun, it should prove to be energy efficient and a joy to live in.

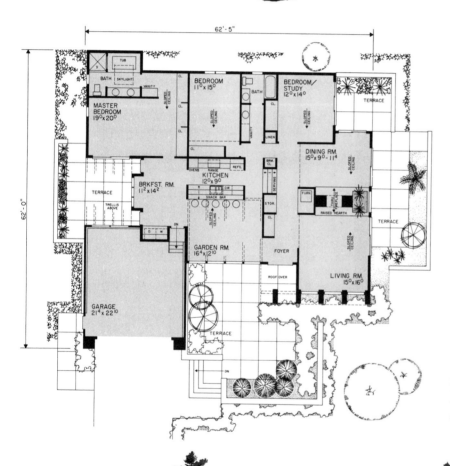

Design N2857
Square Footage: 2,982

● You'll applaud the many outstanding features of this home. Notice first the master bedroom. It has His and Hers baths, each with a large walk-in closet, sliding glass doors to a private terrace, and an adjacent study. Two family bedrooms are separate from the master for total privacy. The gathering room is designed for entertaining. It has its own balcony and a fireplace as a focal point. The U-shaped kitchen is efficient and has an attached breakfast room and snack bar pass-through to the dining room.

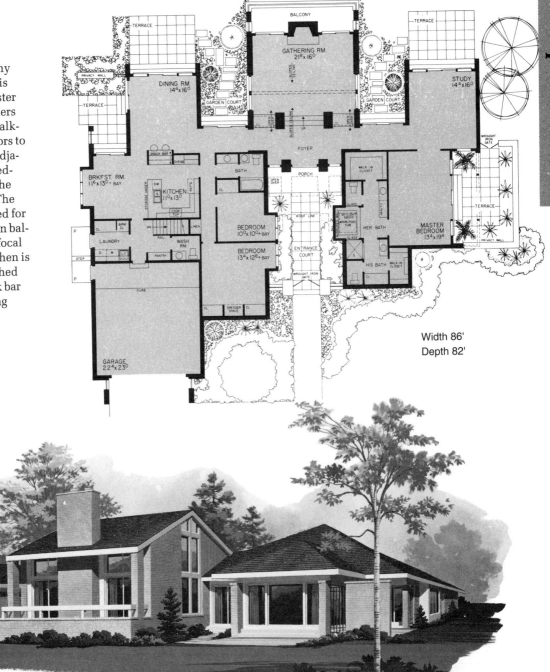

Width 86'
Depth 82'

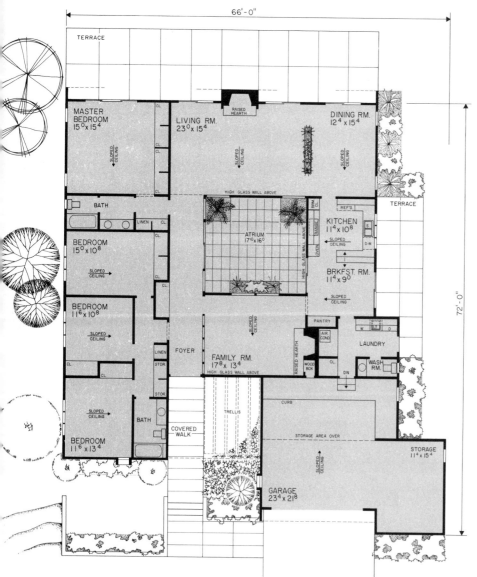

66'-0"

TERRACE

MASTER BEDROOM
15⁰ x 15⁴

LIVING RM.
23⁰ x 15⁴
SLOPED CEILING

RAISED HEARTH

DINING RM.
12⁴ x 15⁴
SLOPED CEILING

TERRACE

SLOPED CEILING

CL

BATH

LINEN CL

HIGH GLASS WALL ABOVE

BEDROOM
15⁰ x 10⁸
SLOPED CEILING

ATRIUM
17¹⁰ x 16⁰

HIGH GLASS WALL ABOVE

REF'G.

KITCHEN
11⁴ x 10⁸

OVEN RANGE D.W.

SLOPED CEILING

BRKFST. RM.
11⁴ x 9⁰
SLOPED CEILING

BEDROOM
11⁶ x 10⁸
SLOPED CEILING

CL

72'-0"

PANTRY

AIR COND.

LAUNDRY
W D

FOYER

SLOPED CEILING

LINEN STOR.

CL

STOR.

FAMILY RM.
17⁸ x 13⁴
HIGH GLASS WALL ABOVE

RAISED HEARTH

WOOD BOX

CL

DN

WASH RM.

BATH

BEDROOM
11⁶ x 13⁴
SLOPED CEILING

COVERED WALK

TRELLIS

CURB

STORAGE AREA OVER

SLOPED CEILING

STORAGE
11⁴ x 15⁴

GARAGE
23⁴ x 21⁸

Design N2135
Square Footage: 2,495 (Excluding Atrium)

● For those seeking a new experience in home ownership. The proud
occupants of this contemporary home
will forever be thrilled at their choice
of such a distinguished exterior and
such a practical and exciting floor
plan. The variety of shed roof planes
contrast dramatically with the simplicity of the vertical siding. Inside
there is a feeling of spaciousness re-
sulting from the sloping ceilings. The
uniqueness of this design is further
enhanced by the atrium. Open to the
sky, this outdoor area, indoors, can be
enjoyed from all parts of the house.
The sleeping zone has four bedrooms, two baths and plenty of closets. The informal living zone has a
fine kitchen and breakfast room. The
formal zone consists of a large living-
dining area with fireplace.

BRKFST. RM.

FAM. RM.

PANTRY

W D

LAUNDRY

WOOD BOX

DN

DN

W.R.

GARAGE

CURB

OPTIONAL PARTIAL BASEMENT

Design N2832

Square Footage: 2,805 (Excluding Atrium)

D

● The advantage of passive solar heating is a significant highlight of this contemporary design. The huge skylight over the atrium provides shelter during inclement weather, while permitting natural light to enter below. The stone floor of this area absorbs an abundance of heat from the sun during the day and permits the circulation of warm air to other areas at night. Sloping ceilings highlight each of the major rooms: three bedrooms, formal living and dining rooms and the study. Broad expanses of roof can accommodate solar panels, if desired, to complement this design.

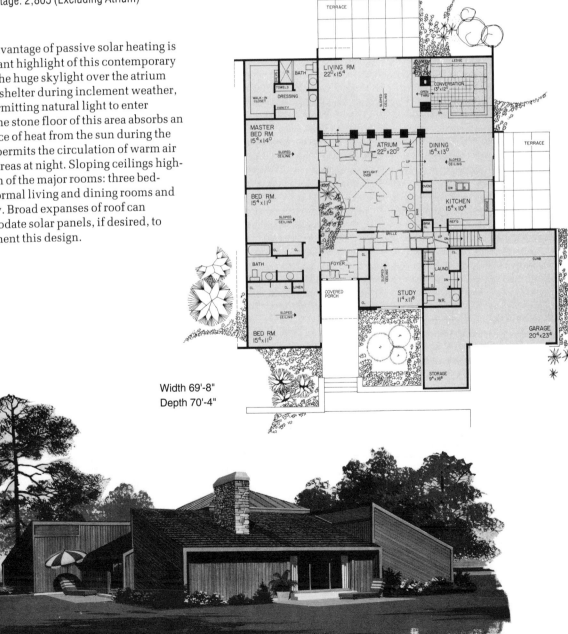

Width 69'-8"
Depth 70'-4"

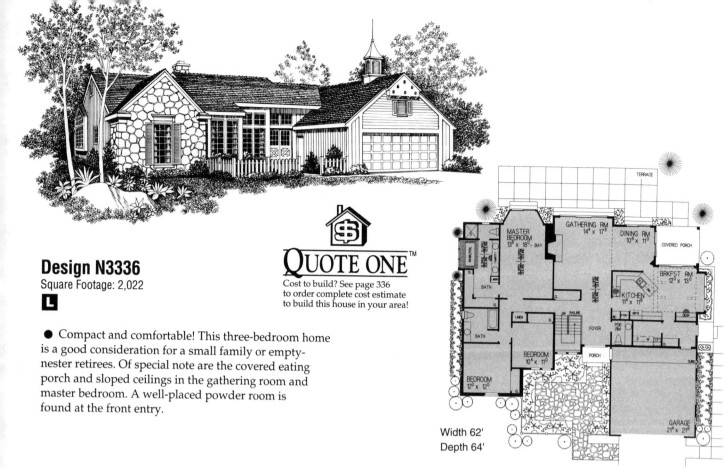

Design N3336
Square Footage: 2,022

● Compact and comfortable! This three-bedroom home is a good consideration for a small family or empty-nester retirees. Of special note are the covered eating porch and sloped ceilings in the gathering room and master bedroom. A well-placed powder room is found at the front entry.

QUOTE ONE™
Cost to build? See page 336 to order complete cost estimate to build this house in your area!

Width 62'
Depth 64'

Design N3489
Square Footage: 2,415

L **D**

● Twin niches in the hallway enhance this traditional home's central foyer. Open planning characterizes the kitchen, family room and gathering/dining room areas. The angular kitchen is efficient with its walk-in pantry and snack-bar pass-through to the gathering room. Double doors open to the spacious master suite. In the master bath, a huge walk-in closet, a whirlpool, a stall shower, a compartmented toilet and a linen closet will be appreciated. The children's bedroom wing has three sizeable bedrooms. In the two-car garage, a handy storage closet relieves clutter.

QUOTE ONE™
Cost to build? See page 336 to order complete cost estimate to build this house in your area!

Width 74'
Depth 54'

Design N3327

Square Footage: 2,881

L **D**

● The high, massive hipped-roof of this home creates an impressive facade while varying roof planes and projecting gables further enhance appeal. A central, high-ceilinged foyer routes traffic efficiently to the sleeping, formal and informal zones of the house. Note the sliding glass doors that provide access to outdoor living facilities. A built-in china cabinet and planter unit are fine decor features. In the angular kitchen, a high ceiling and efficient work patterning set the pace. The conversation room may act as a multi-purpose room. For TV time, a media room caters to audio-visual activities. Sleeping quarters take off with the spacious master bedroom; here you'll find a tray ceiling and sliding doors to the rear yard. An abundance of wall space for effective and flexible furniture arrangement further characterizes the room. Two sizable bedrooms serve the children or guests.

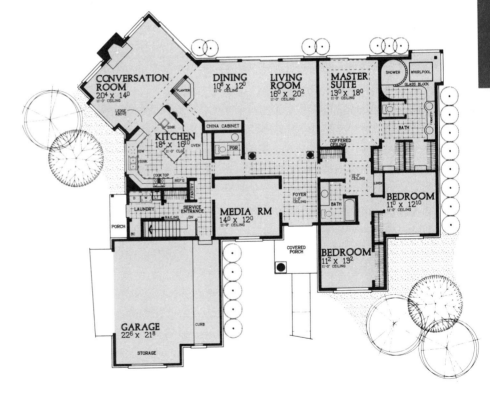

Width 77'-11"
Depth 73'-11"

QUOTE ONE™

Cost to build? See page 336
to order complete cost estimate
to build this house in your area!

Design N3600/N3601

Square Footage: 2,258/2,424

L

● This unique one-story plan seems tailor-made for a small family or for empty-nesters. Formal areas are situated well for entertaining—living room to the right and formal dining room to the left. A large family room is found to the rear. It has access to a rear wood deck and is warmed in the cold months by a welcome hearth. The U-shaped kitchen features an attached morning room for casual meals. It is near the laundry and a wash room. Bedrooms are private in both the two- and three-bedroom versions of this plan; the master suite remains pampering with a walk-in closet and fine bath. Notice the nearby office with its private porch.

Design N3601

QUOTE ONE™

Cost to build? See page 336 to order complete cost estimate to build this house in your area!

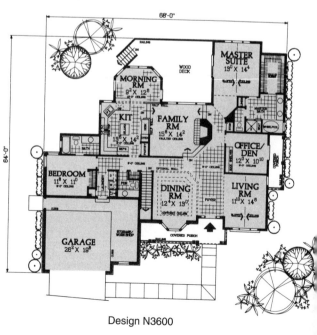

Design N3600

Rear Elevation N3600

Design N2867 Square Footage: 2,388

L

● A live-in relative would be very comfortable in this home. This design features a self-contained suite (473 sq. ft.) consisting of a bedroom, bath, living room and kitchenette with dining area. This suite is nestled behind the garage away from the main areas of the house. The rest of this traditional, one-story house, faced with fieldstone and vertical wood siding, is also very livable. One whole wing houses the four family bedrooms and bath facilities. The center of the plan has a front, U-shaped kitchen and breakfast room. The formal dining room and large gathering room will enjoy the view, and access to, the backyard. The large, covered porch will receive much use.

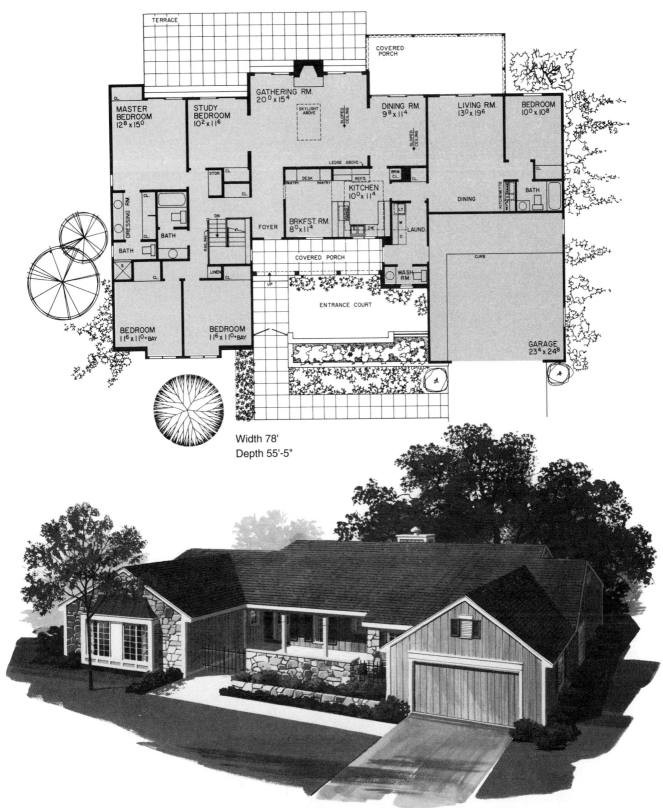

Width 78'
Depth 55'-5"

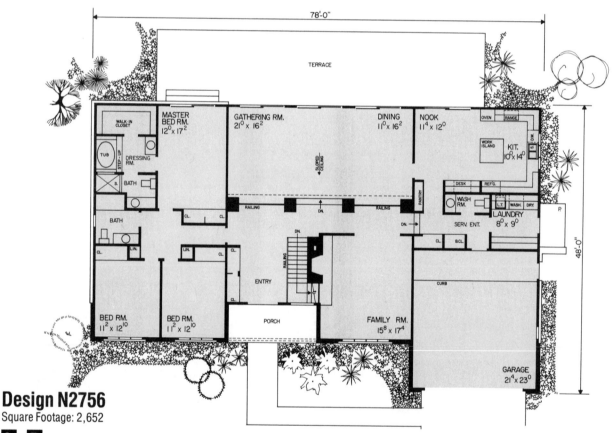

Design N2756

Square Footage: 2,652

L **D**

● This one-story, contemporary design is bound to serve your family well. It will assure the best in contemporary living with its many fine features. Notice the bath with tub and stall shower, dressing room and walk-in closet featured with the master bedroom. Two more family bedrooms are adjacent. The sunken gathering room/dining room is highlighted by the sloped ceiling and sliding glass doors to the large, rear terrace. This formal area is a full 32' x 16'. Imagine the great furniture placement that can be done in this area. In addition to the gathering room, there is an informal family room with a fireplace. You will enjoy the efficient kitchen and get much use out of the work island, pantry and built-in desk. Note the service entrance with washroom and laundry.

Design N2181
Square Footage: 2,612

L **D**

● This home is the complete picture of charm. The interior features are outstanding. It is possible to substitute brick or even siding when building this home.

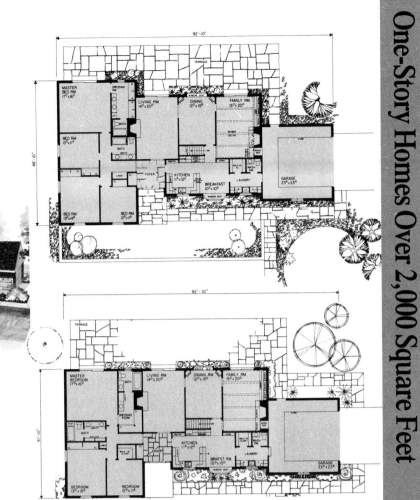

Design N2675
Square Footage: 2,478

D

● Many extra features have been designed into this delightfully traditional home. If you like this design but need a four-bedroom home, order design N2181 above.

Design N2766
Square Footage: 2,711

D

● A sizable master bedroom has a dressing area featuring two walk-in closets, a twin lavatory and compartmented bath. There are also two family bedrooms sharing a full bath. A third bedroom can also be used as a study. Formal living and dining rooms are separated by a through-fireplace. A spacious kitchen/nook is cheerfully informal with a sun room just a step away through sliding glass doors. Be sure to note the number of sizable closets.

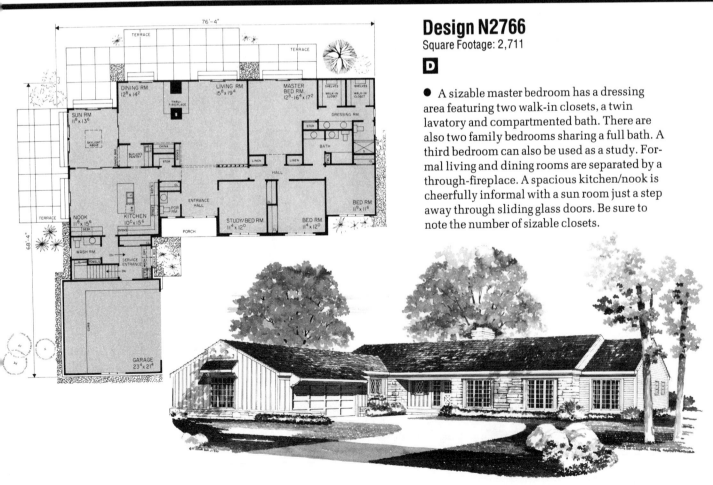

275

Design N2256
Square Footage: 2,632

● This refreshing contemporary home has a
unique exterior that is enhanced by a great floor
plan. The central focus is the large living room
with raised-hearth fireplace. To the right is the
formal dining room and island kitchen with
informal eating space. To the left are three family bedrooms — the master has a gigantic walk-
in closet. All are tied together with a long hallway. Don't miss the wide terrace at the rear of
the plan.

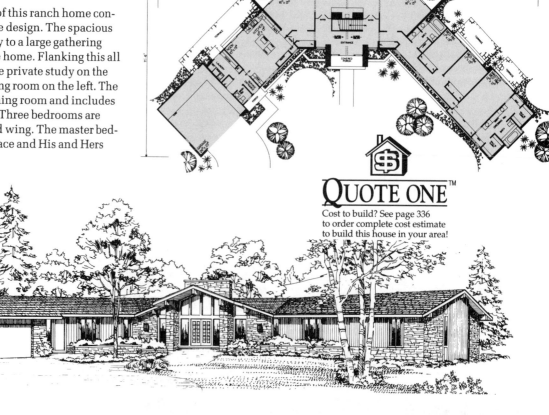

Design N2534
Square Footage: 3,262

● The angular wings of this ranch home con-
tribute to its distinctive design. The spacious
entrance hall gives way to a large gathering
room — the heart of the home. Flanking this all
purpose area are a more private study on the
right and a formal dining room on the left. The
kitchen adjoins the dining room and includes
informal eating space. Three bedrooms are
found in the right-hand wing. The master bedroom has a private terrace and His and Hers
walk-in closets.

Design N2879 Living Area Including Atrium: 3,173 square feet
Upper Lounge/Balcony: 267 square feet
Total: 3,440 square feet

● This plush modern design seems to have it all, including an upper lounge, upper family room, and upper foyer. There's also an atrium with skylight centrally located downstairs. A modern kitchen with snack bar service to a breakfast room also enjoys its own greenhouse window. A deluxe master bedroom includes its own whirlpool and bay window. Three other bedrooms also are isolated at one end of the house downstairs to allow privacy and quiet. A spacious family room in the rear enjoys its own raised-hearth fireplace and view of a rear covered terrace. A front living room with its own fireplace looks out upon a side garden court and the central atrium. There's also a formal dining room situated between the kitchen and living room, plus a three-car garage, covered porches, and sizable laundry with washroom just off the garage.

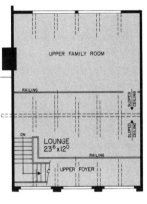

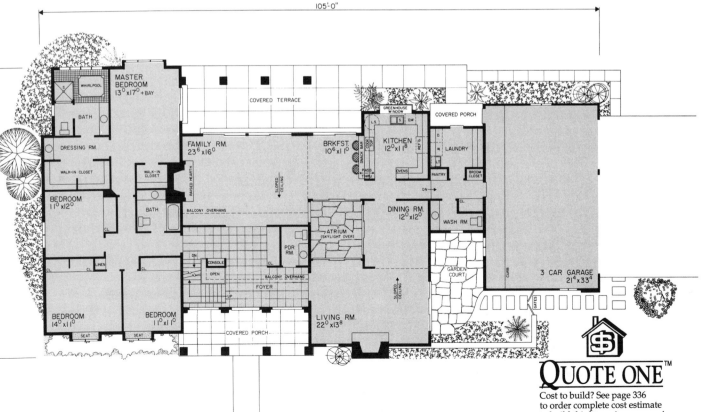

QUOTE ONE™
Cost to build? See page 336 to order complete cost estimate to build this house in your area!

277

Design N2767

Square Footage: 3,000

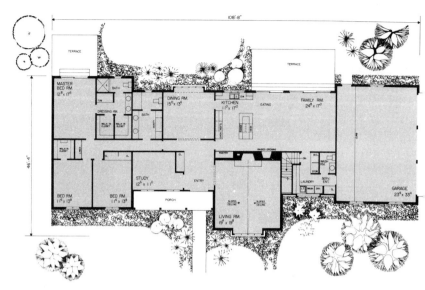

● This home has all the amenities to assure a comfortable lifestyle. Large impressive living areas accommodate both formal and informal occasions. There are three large bedrooms, two full baths with twin lavatories, walk-in closets and a fine study. The kitchen features an island work center with range and desk. The two fireplaces warm their surroundings. Two separate terraces offer a variety of uses. Note the laundry, wash room and three-car garage.

Design N2768

Square Footage: 3,436

● Besides its elegant traditionally styled exterior with long covered front porch, this home has an exceptionally livable interior. There is an outstanding four-bedroom, two-bath sleeping wing. The efficient kitchen with island range is flanked by the formal dining room and informal breakfast nook. Separated by a through-fireplace are the living and family rooms which overlook the rear yard. There's even a potential live-in facility that could also be used as a hobby room or sewing room.

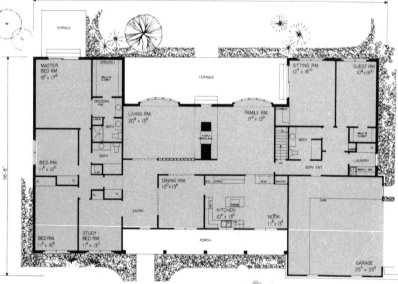

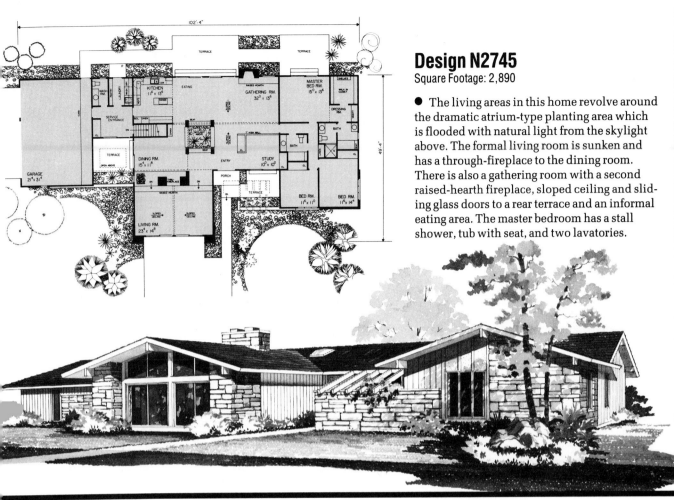

Design N2745
Square Footage: 2,890

● The living areas in this home revolve around the dramatic atrium-type planting area which is flooded with natural light from the skylight above. The formal living room is sunken and has a through-fireplace to the dining room. There is also a gathering room with a second raised-hearth fireplace, sloped ceiling and sliding glass doors to a rear terrace and an informal eating area. The master bedroom has a stall shower, tub with seat, and two lavatories.

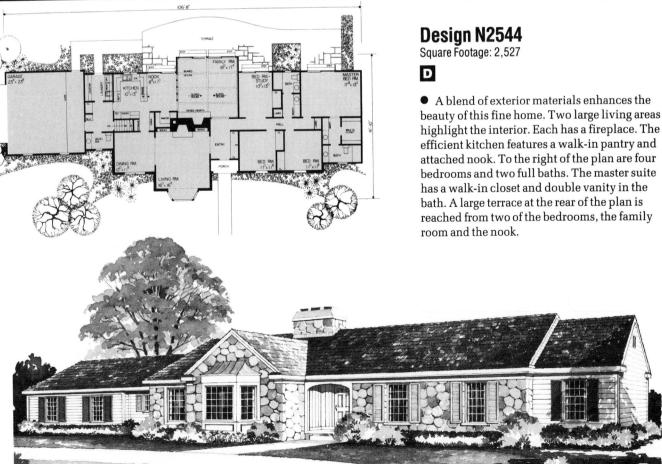

Design N2544
Square Footage: 2,527

D

● A blend of exterior materials enhances the beauty of this fine home. Two large living areas highlight the interior. Each has a fireplace. The efficient kitchen features a walk-in pantry and attached nook. To the right of the plan are four bedrooms and two full baths. The master suite has a walk-in closet and double vanity in the bath. A large terrace at the rear of the plan is reached from two of the bedrooms, the family room and the nook.

Design N2778

Square Footage: 2,761

D

● No matter what the occasion, family and friends alike will enjoy the sizable gathering room in this home. This room has a through-fireplace to the study and two sets of sliding glass doors to the large, rear terrace. Indoor/outdoor living also can be enjoyed from the dining room, study and master bedroom. There is also a covered porch accessible through sliding glass doors in the dining room and breakfast nook.

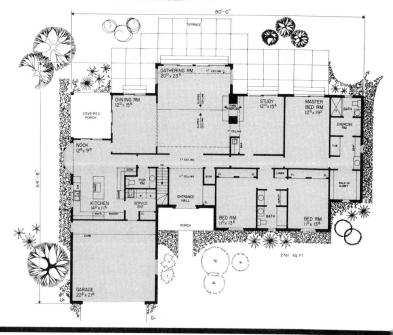

Design N1786

Square Footage: 2,370

● This is an extremely appealing design, highlighted by its brick masses, its window detailing, its interesting shape and its inviting covered front entrance. The foyer is centrally located and but a step or two from all areas. The bedroom wing is distinctly defined. The quiet, sunken living room is off by itself. There is even a separate formal dining room. The family room has a fireplace and is adjacent to the U-shaped kitchen. Just off the garage is the mud room with washroom for quick clean-ups.

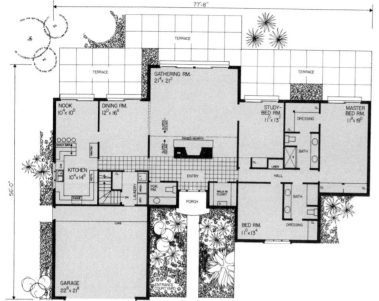

Design N2594
Square Footage: 2,294

D

● A spectacular foyer offers double entry to the heart of this home — a large gathering room complete with raised-hearth fireplace and sliding glass doors onto the terrace. There is also a formal dining room. A well-located study (or third bedroom) offers space for undisturbed work. The kitchen features a snack bar and breakfast nook with sliding glass doors onto the terrace. In the master bedroom suite there are sliding glass doors to the terrace and a dressing room with entry to the bath. Another bedroom is located to the front of the plan.

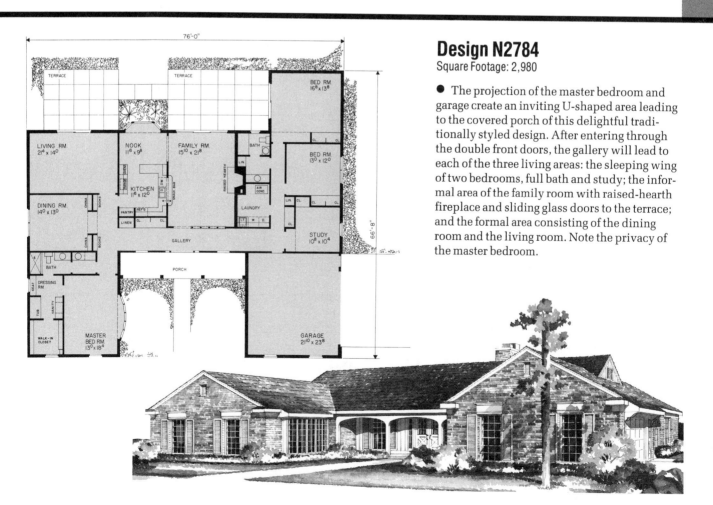

Design N2784
Square Footage: 2,980

● The projection of the master bedroom and garage create an inviting U-shaped area leading to the covered porch of this delightful traditionally styled design. After entering through the double front doors, the gallery will lead to each of the three living areas: the sleeping wing of two bedrooms, full bath and study; the informal area of the family room with raised-hearth fireplace and sliding glass doors to the terrace; and the formal area consisting of the dining room and the living room. Note the privacy of the master bedroom.

281

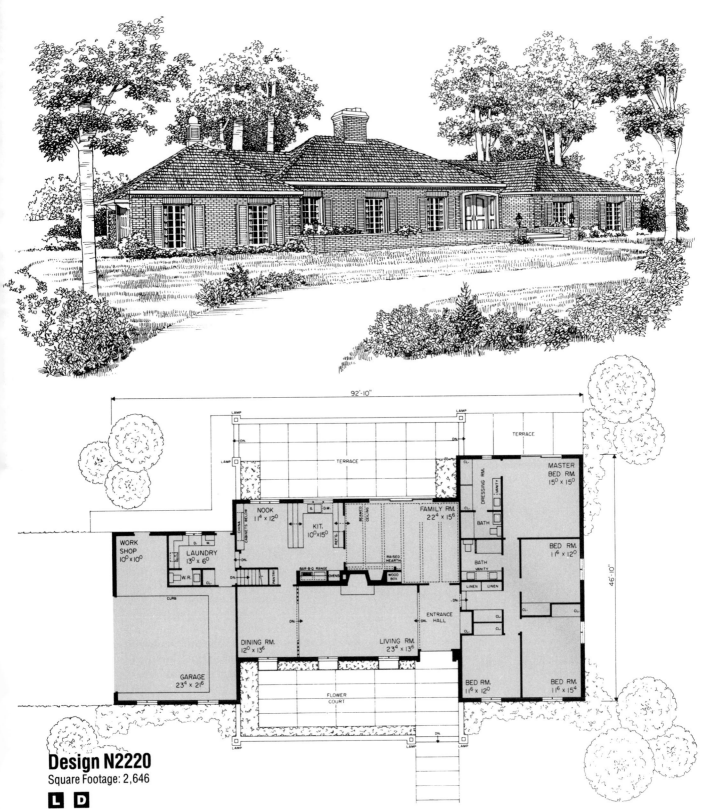

Design N2220

Square Footage: 2,646

L **D**

● The gracious formality of this home is reminiscent of a popularly accepted French styling. The hip-roof, the brick quoins, the cornice details, the arched window heads, the distinctive shutters, the recessed double front door and the massive center chimney, and the de-lightful flower court are all features which set the dramatic appeal of this home. This floor plan is a favorite of many. The four bedroom, two bath sleeping wing is a zone by itself. Further, the formal living and dining rooms are ideally located. For enter-taining they function well together and look out upon the pleasant flower court. Overlooking the raised living terrace at the rear are the family and breakfast rooms and work center. Don't miss the laundry, extra wash room and work shop in garage.

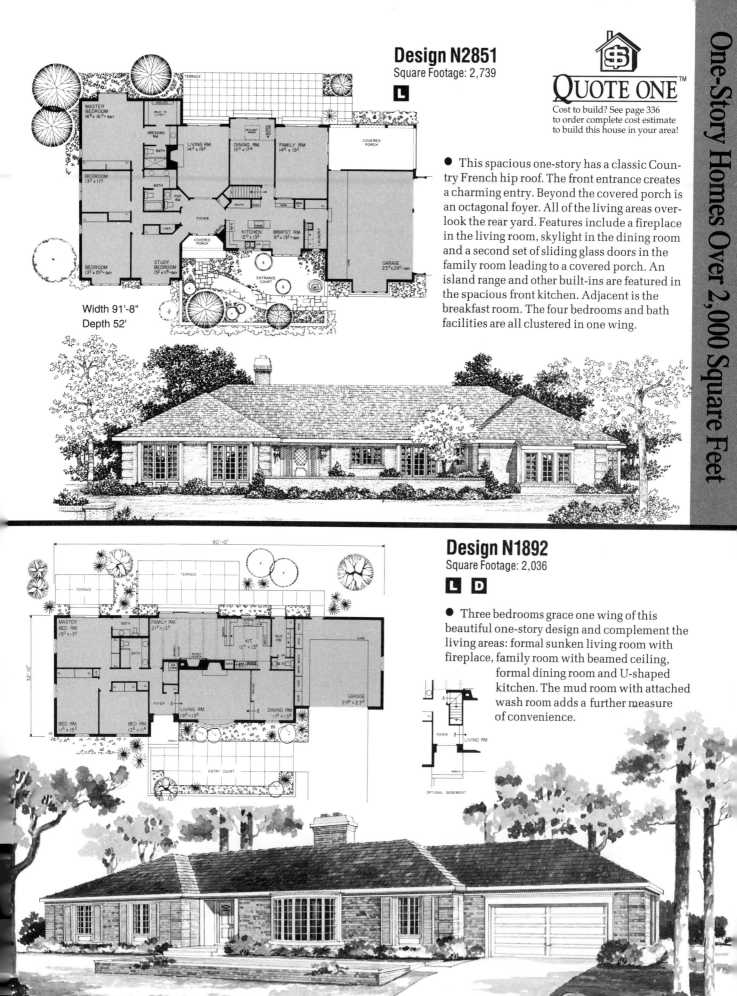

Design N2851
Square Footage: 2,739

L

QUOTE ONE™
Cost to build? See page 336
to order complete cost estimate
to build this house in your area!

● This spacious one-story has a classic Country French hip roof. The front entrance creates a charming entry. Beyond the covered porch is an octagonal foyer. All of the living areas overlook the rear yard. Features include a fireplace in the living room, skylight in the dining room and a second set of sliding glass doors in the family room leading to a covered porch. An island range and other built-ins are featured in the spacious front kitchen. Adjacent is the breakfast room. The four bedrooms and bath facilities are all clustered in one wing.

Width 91'-8"
Depth 52'

Design N1892
Square Footage: 2,036

L **D**

● Three bedrooms grace one wing of this beautiful one-story design and complement the living areas: formal sunken living room with fireplace, family room with beamed ceiling, formal dining room and U-shaped kitchen. The mud room with attached wash room adds a further measure of convenience.

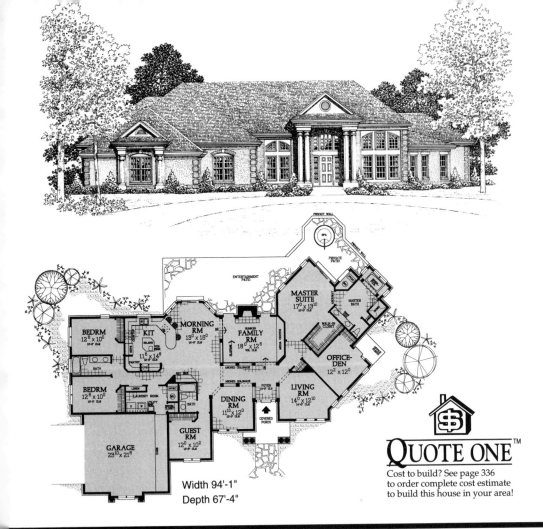

Design N3612
Square Footage: 2,946

L

● Double columns make a grand entrance into this stately traditional home. Formal occasions may be shared in the living and dining rooms found to the front of the plan. The rear of the design is reserved for casual times. Here, a gourmet kitchen combines with a morning room and a family room with a built-in media center, providing the perfect spot for family gatherings. Bedrooms are split, with two family bedrooms, a hall bath and a guest room with a full bath occupying the left wing. On the right, a sumptuous master suite featuring a lavish bath shares space with an adjacent office-den.

Width 94'-1"
Depth 67'-4"

Quote One™
Cost to build? See page 336
to order complete cost estimate
to build this house in your area!

Design N2779
Square Footage: 3,225

L D

● This French design is surely impressive. The exterior is highlighted with a hip roof, paned-glass windows, brick privacy wall and double front doors. The inside is just as appealing. Note the unique placement of rooms and features: formal dining room with butler's pantry, sizable parlor, gathering room with fireplace and sliding glass doors, and an adjacent study. The U-shaped kitchen has an island range, snack bar, breakfast nook and pantry.

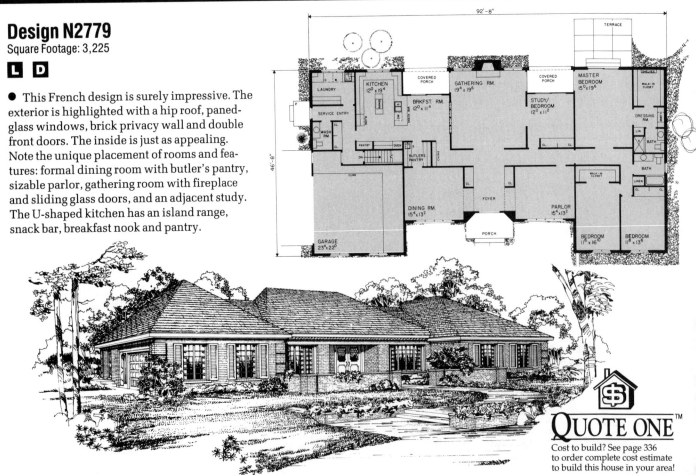

Quote One™
Cost to build? See page 336
to order complete cost estimate
to build this house in your area!

Design N2693
Square Footage: 3,462

● This elegant Georgian manor is reminiscent of historic Rose Hill, built 1818 in Lexington, Kentucky. It is typical of the classic manors with Greek Revival features built in Kentucky as the 19th Century dawned. Note the classical portico of four Ionic columns plus the fine proportions. Also noteworthy is the updated interior, highlighted by a large country kitchen with fireplace and an efficient work center that includes an island cooktop. The country kitchen leads directly into a front formal dining room, just off the foyer. On the other side of the foyer is a front living room. A large library is located in the back of the house. It features built-in bookcases plus a fireplace, one of four fireplaces.

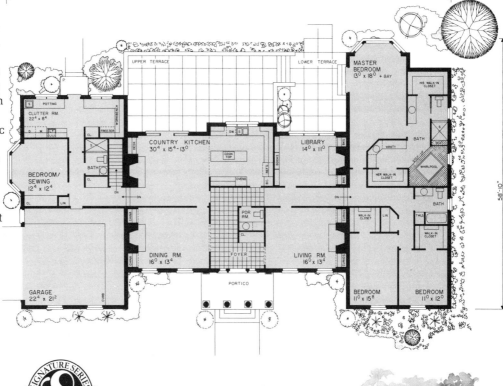

Design N3632
Square Footage: 2,539

L

● An open courtyard takes center-stage in this graceful Mediterranean-style home. Art collectors will appreciate the gallery that enhances the entry. To the right of the gallery is a dining room and an adjacent country kitchen designed with an island snack bar and a large pantry. The centrally located family-great room supplies the nucleus for formal and informal entertaining. A raised-hearth fire-place and built-in media centers add a special touch. The sleeping wing features a master suite located to the rear for privacy. Here, you may relax in the sitting room or retire to the master bath. Two family bedrooms share a hall bath.

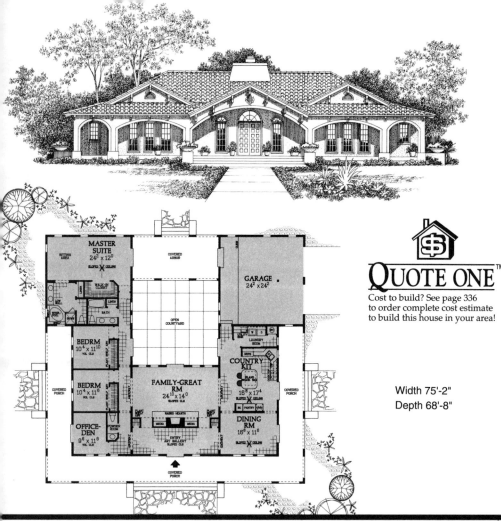

QUOTE ONE™

Cost to build? See page 336 to order complete cost estimate to build this house in your area!

Width 75'-2"
Depth 68'-8"

Design N3630
Square Footage: 3,034

L

● A grand entry enhances the exterior of this elegant stucco home. The office located at the front of the plan makes this design ideal for a home-based business. Formal areas combine to provide lots of space for entertaining. The kitchen, complete with a snack bar and a breakfast nook, opens to the family room which connects to the media room. The private master suite includes two retreats—one is a multi-windowed sitting area, the other contains a spa for outdoor enjoyment. Be sure to also notice the walk-in closet and the luxurious bath. Two family bedrooms share a full bath.

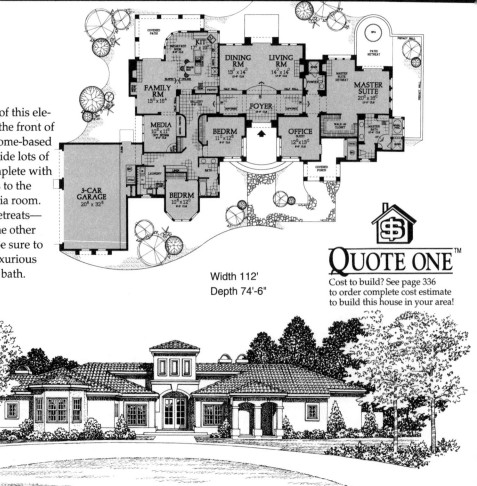

Width 112'
Depth 74'-6"

QUOTE ONE™

Cost to build? See page 336 to order complete cost estimate to build this house in your area!

Design N3559

Square Footage: 2,916

L D

● Intricate details make the most of this lovely one-story: high, varied rooflines, circle and half-circle window detailing, multi-pane windows and a solid chimney stack. The floor plan caters to comfortable living. Besides the living room/dining room area to the rear, there is a large conversation area with fireplace and plenty of windows. The kitchen is separated from living areas by an angled snack-bar counter. A media room to the front of the plan provides space for more private activities. Three bedrooms grace the right side of the plan. The master suite features a tray vaulted ceiling and sliding glass doors to the rear terrace. The dressing area is graced by His and Hers walk-in closets, a double-bowl lavatory and a compartmented commode. The shower area is highlighted with glass block and is sunken down one step. A garden whirlpool finishes off the area.

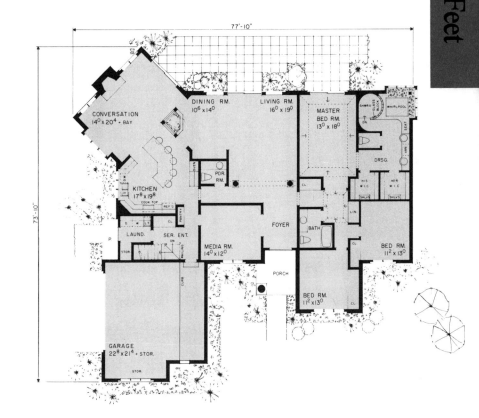

QUOTE ONE™

Cost to build? See page 336
to order complete cost estimate
to build this house in your area!

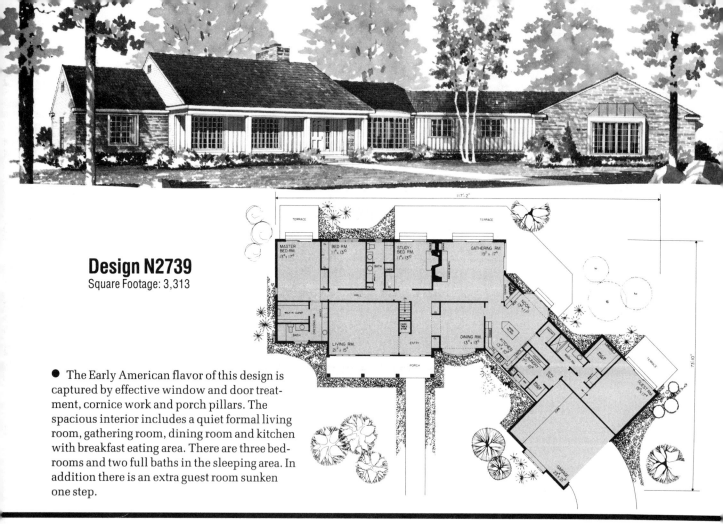

Design N2739

Square Footage: 3,313

● The Early American flavor of this design is captured by effective window and door treatment, cornice work and porch pillars. The spacious interior includes a quiet formal living room, gathering room, dining room and kitchen with breakfast eating area. There are three bedrooms and two full baths in the sleeping area. In addition there is an extra guest room sunken one step.

Design N2783

Square Footage: 3,210

L

● The configuration of this traditional design is outstanding. The garage and bedroom wing on one side and the master bedroom on the other create an inviting U-shaped entry court.

The gathering room has access to the rear terrace along with the dining room, family room and rear bedroom. Note interior kitchen which is adjacent to each of the major rooms.

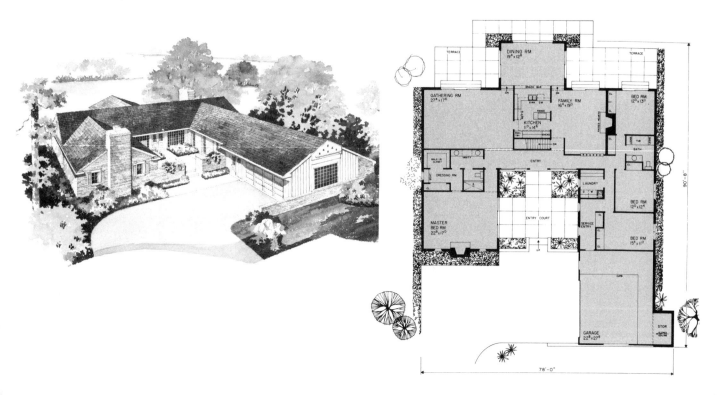

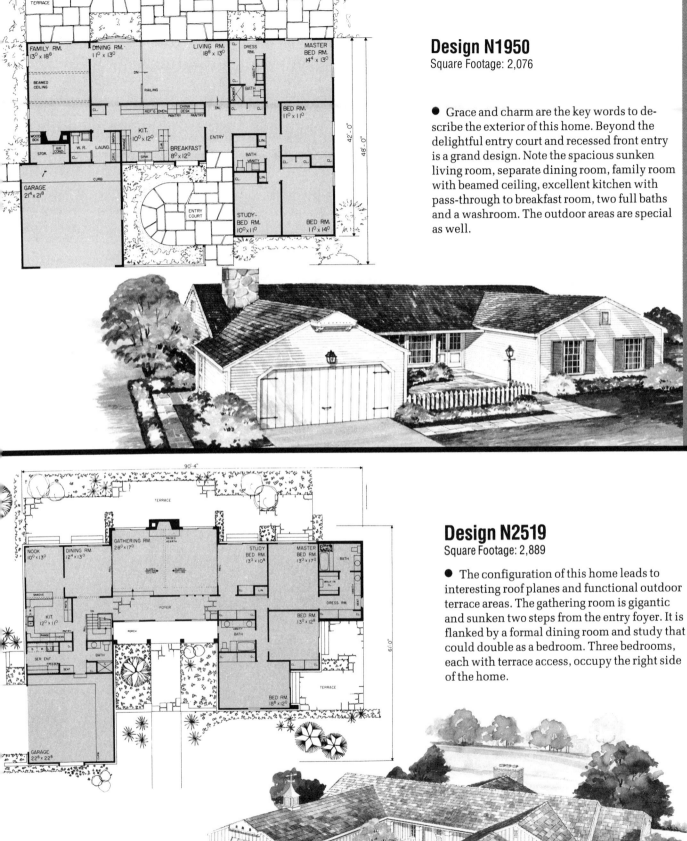

Design N1950
Square Footage: 2,076

● Grace and charm are the key words to describe the exterior of this home. Beyond the delightful entry court and recessed front entry is a grand design. Note the spacious sunken living room, separate dining room, family room with beamed ceiling, excellent kitchen with pass-through to breakfast room, two full baths and a washroom. The outdoor areas are special as well.

Design N2519
Square Footage: 2,889

● The configuration of this home leads to interesting roof planes and functional outdoor terrace areas. The gathering room is gigantic and sunken two steps from the entry foyer. It is flanked by a formal dining room and study that could double as a bedroom. Three bedrooms, each with terrace access, occupy the right side of the home.

Design N2888
Square Footage: 3,018

L

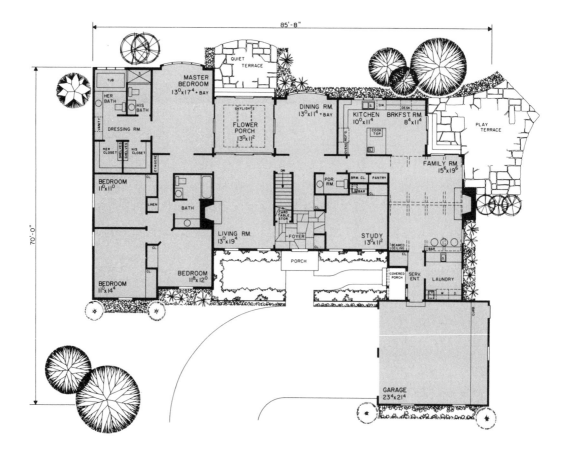

● This is an outstanding Early American design for the 20th-Century. The exterior detailing with narrow clap boards, multi-paned windows and cupola are the features of yesteryear. Interior planning, though, is for today's active family. Formal living room, in- formal family room plus a study are present. Every activity will have its place in this home. Picture yourself working in the kitchen. There's enough counter space for two or three helpers. Four bedrooms are in the private area. Stop and imagine your daily routine if you occupied the master bedroom. Both you and your spouse would have plenty of space and privacy. The flow- er porch, accessible from the master bedroom, living and dining rooms, is a very delightful "plus" feature. Study this design's every detail.

Design N2916
Square Footage: 2,129

L

● The covered front porch of this Early Ameri-can-styled house, provides a shelter for the inviting panelled front door. Inside, the plan offers wonderful formal and informal living patterns. The country kitchen has a beamed ceiling and a fireplace. The U-shaped work center is most efficient. There are two dining areas — an informal eating space and a formal dining room. The more formal gathering room is spacious and sports a sloped ceiling and two sets of sliding glass doors to the rear terrace.

QUOTE ONE™
Cost to build? See page 336 to order complete cost estimate to build this house in your area!

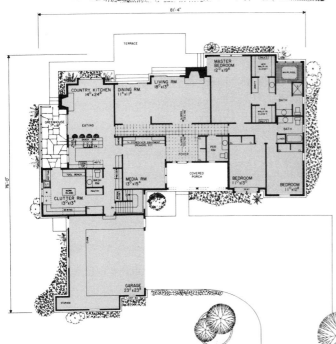

Design N2880
Living Area: 2,758 square feet
Greenhouse: 149 square feet
Total: 2,907 square feet

L D

QUOTE ONE™
Cost to build? See page 336 to order complete cost estimate to build this house in your area!

● This comfortable traditional home offers plenty of modern livability. A clutter room off the two-car garage is the perfect space for a workbench, sewing and hobbies. Across the hall is a media room and nearby is the country kitchen with attached greenhouse. There are also formal dining and living rooms, a covered porch, and three bedrooms including a master suite.

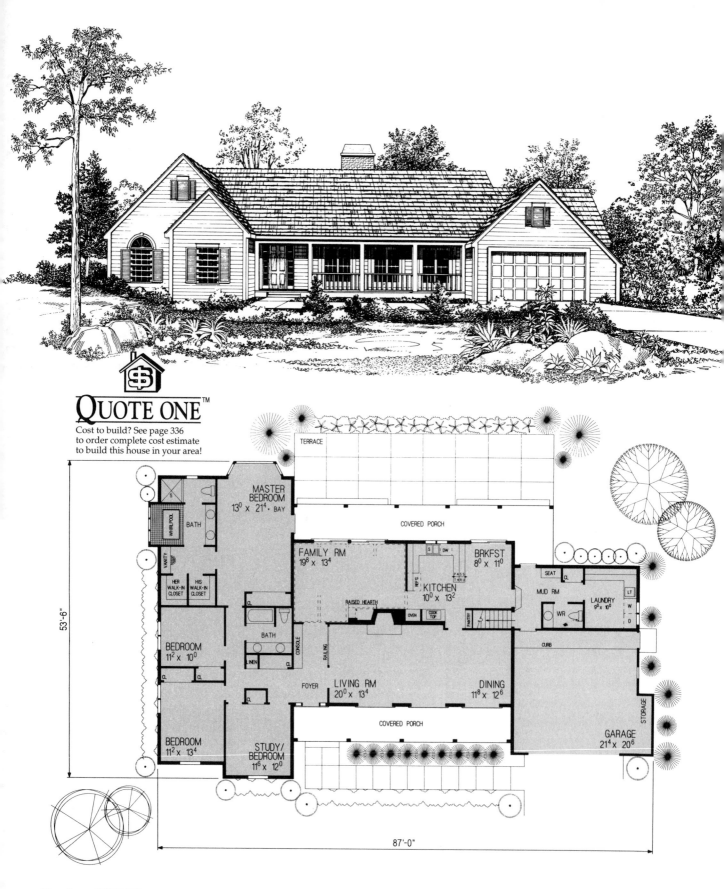

QUOTE ONE™

Cost to build? See page 336
to order complete cost estimate
to build this house in your area!

TERRACE

MASTER
BEDROOM
13⁰ x 21⁴ · BAY

WHIRLPOOL

BATH

VANITY

HER
WALK-IN
CLOSET

HIS
WALK-IN
CLOSET

COVERED PORCH

FAMILY RM
19⁸ x 13⁴

S   DW

PASS
THRU

BRKFST
8⁰ x 11⁰

SEAT   CL

KITCHEN
10⁰ x 13²

MUD RM

LAUNDRY
9⁰ x 10⁰

LT

W
D

WR

CL

BATH

RAISED HEARTH

OVEN   COOK
TOP

PANTRY

BEDROOM
11² x 10⁰

CONSOLE

RAILING

CURB

LINEN   CL

FOYER

LIVING RM
20⁰ x 13⁴

DINING
11⁸ x 12⁶

STORAGE

CL

BEDROOM
11² x 13⁴

STUDY/
BEDROOM
11⁶ x 12⁰

COVERED PORCH

GARAGE
21⁴ x 20⁶

53'-6"

87'-0"

Design N3348 Square Footage: 2,549

L

● Covered porches front and rear will
be the envy of the neighborhood when
this house is built. The interior plan
meets family needs perfectly in well-
zoned areas: a sleeping wing with four
bedrooms and two baths, a living zone
with formal and informal gathering
space, and a work zone with U-shaped
kitchen and laundry with washroom.
The two-car garage has a huge storage
area.

Design N3332

Square Footage: 2,168

L

● Nothing completes a traditional-style home quite as well as a country kitchen with fireplace. Notice also the sloped-ceiling living room and well-appointed master suite. A handy washroom is near the laundry, just off the garage.

QUOTE ONE™

Cost to build? See page 336 to order complete cost estimate to build this house in your area!

TERRACE

LIVING RM
20⁸ x 17⁴

SLOPED CEILING ← → SLOPED CEILING

DN
PORCH

DINING RM
11⁸ x 11⁴

TERRACE

MASTER BEDROOM
12⁴ x 17⁶

WALK-IN CLOSET

WHIRLPOOL

BATH

SEAT

S

RAISED HEARTH

WOOD BOX

PANTRY

BC

WASH RM

W D

CL

LAUNDRY
9² x 8⁴

46'-0"

BATH

LINEN

CL

STOR.

DN

FOYER

CLOS.

CLOS.

PASS THRU

SNACK BAR

DW

REF.

CURB

DN

COUNTRY KITCHEN
22⁴ x 13⁰

RANGE

BEDROOM
11⁴ x 11⁰

CL CL

DESK

BEDROOM
11⁴ x 11⁴

UP

COVERED PORCH

GARAGE
21⁴ x 21⁴

76'-4"

QUOTE ONE™
Cost to build? See page 336
to order complete cost estimate
to build this house in your area!

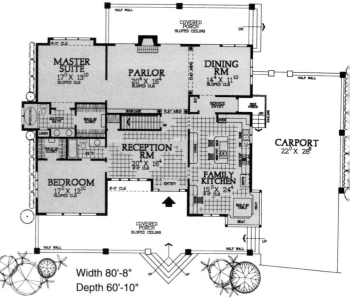

Width 80'-8"
Depth 60'-10"

Design N3498
Square Footage: 2,135

● You'll savor the timeless style of this charming bungalow design. Inside, livability excels with a side-facing kitchen attached to a pleasant morning room with an interesting bumped-out nook. Or use the island snack bar for meals on the go. A formal dining room rests to the rear of the plan and enjoys direct access to a back porch. The parlor, with a central fireplace, also has access to this outdoor living area. The master bedroom offers large dimensions and a private bath with a walk-in closet, dual vanities and a bumped-out tub. An additional bedroom may also serve as a study.

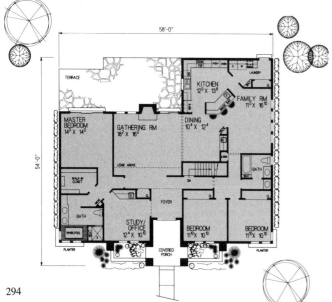

QUOTE ONE™
Cost to build? See page 336
to order complete cost estimate
to build this house in your area!

Design N3319
Square Footage: 2,274

L **D**

● This attractive bungalow design separates the master suite from family bedrooms and puts casual living to the back in a family room. The formal living and dining areas are centrally located and have access to a rear terrace, as does the master suite. The kitchen sits between formal and informal living areas. The two family bedrooms are found to the front of the plan. A home office or study opens off the family foyer and the master suite.

Design N3636/N3637

Square Footage: 2,626/3,278

L

● This adaptation reflects Frank Lloyd Wright's purest Prairie style. Note the access provided to the central, open courtyard from the family/great room, country kitchen, bedroom, master suite and guest suite. Open planning combines the country kitchen with a snack bar and a formal dining room. Amenities that enhance the master suite include a sitting area,

a walk-in closet and a luxurious master bath. The left wing of Design N3636 contains the sleeping quarters and an office/den. The larger version, Design N3637, offers split planning with family bedrooms, a guest suite and a formal living room located on the left and the master suite on the right. Plans for a detached garage are included with the blueprints for Design N3637.

QUOTE ONE™

Cost to build? See page 336 to order complete cost estimate to build this house in your area!

Design N3636

Width 75'-10"
Depth 69'-4"

Design N3637

Garage Plan G201

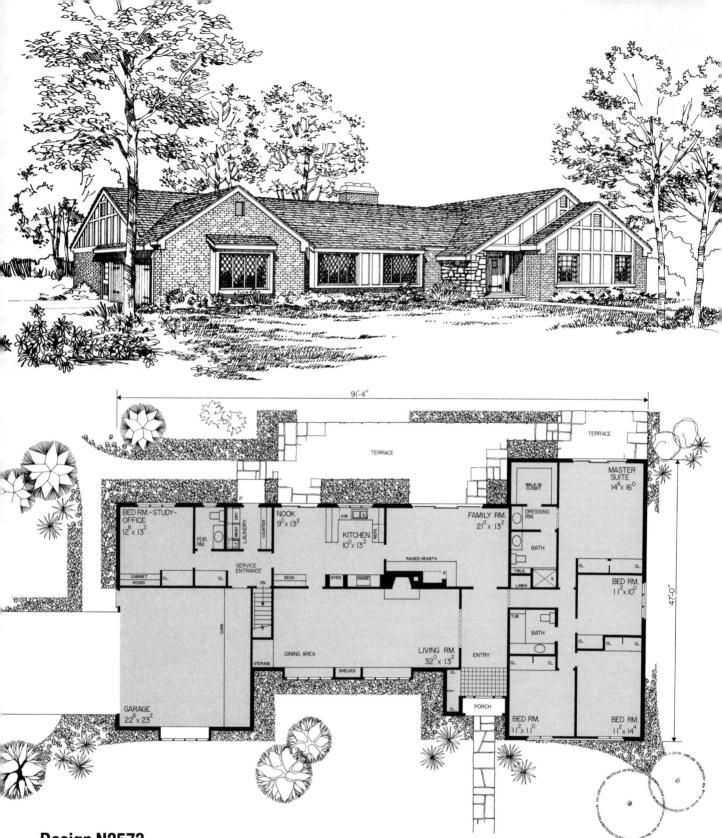

The floor plan labels read:

TERRACE

TERRACE

91'-4"

BED RM.-STUDY-OFFICE 12⁸ x 13²

PDR. RM.

WASH DRY

LAUNDRY

COUNTER

P

NOOK 9⁰ x 13²

D.W.

KITCHEN 10⁰ x 13²

REF'G.

FAMILY RM. 21⁰ x 13²

DRESSING RM.

WALK-IN CLOSET

MASTER SUITE 14⁶ x 16⁰

47'-0"

CABINET BOOKS

CL

CL

SERVICE ENTRANCE

DESK

DN.

RAISED HEARTH

OVEN RANGE

BATH

TWLS.

S

LINEN

CL

BED RM. 11⁵ x 10⁰

CL CL CL

CURB

STORAGE

DINING AREA

SHELVES

LIVING RM. 32⁰ x 13²

ENTRY

TUB

BATH

CL

CL

GARAGE 22⁸ x 23²

PORCH

BED RM. 11² x 11⁰

BED RM. 11² x 14⁴

Design N2573

Square Footage: 2,747

L **D**

● A Tudor ranch! Combining brick and wood for an elegant look. It has a living/dining room measuring 32' by 13', large indeed. It is fully appointed with a traditional fireplace and built-in shelves, flanked by diagonally paned windows. There's much more! There is a family room with a raised hearth fireplace and sliding glass doors that open onto the terrace. A U-shaped kitchen has lots of built-ins . . . a range, an oven, a desk. Plus a separate breakfast nook. The sleeping facilities consist of three family bedrooms plus an elegant master bedroom suite. A conveniently located laundry with a folding counter is in the service entrance. Adjacent to the laundry is a washroom. The corner of the plan has a study or make it a fifth bedroom if you prefer.

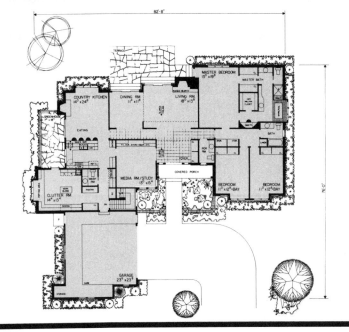

Design N2961
Square Footage: 2,919

● This is an interesting and charming one-story. Contributing to the appeal: varying roof planes, cornice detailing, brick exterior and accents of stucco and beam-work. Inside, the spacious foyer with slate floor routes traffic effectively. Highlights here include a media room, clutter room, country kitchen, formal living room, dining room and large master bedroom with its luxurious master bath. Be sure to notice the glass-walled greenhouse.

Design N2877
Square Footage: 2,612

L **D**

● Here's a dramatic Post-Modern exterior with a popular plan featuring an outstanding master bedroom suite. The bedroom itself is spacious, has a sloped ceiling, a large walk-in closet and sliding glass doors to the terrace. Along with this bedroom, there are three more served by a full bath. The living area of this plan has the formal areas in the front and informal areas in the rear. Both have a fireplace. The roomy work center is efficiently planned.

Width 84'-8"
Depth 53'-8"

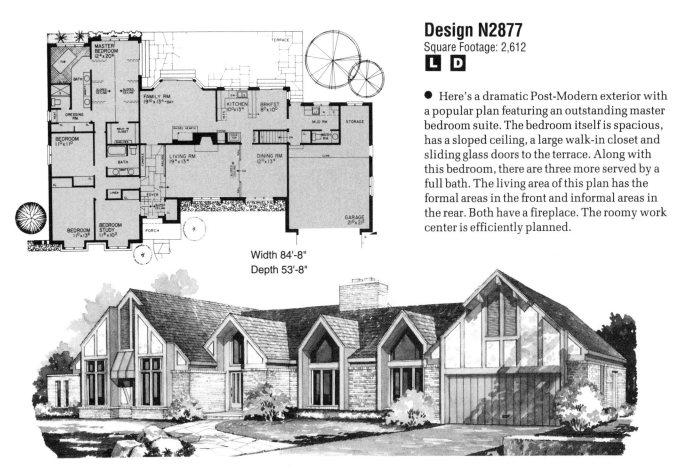

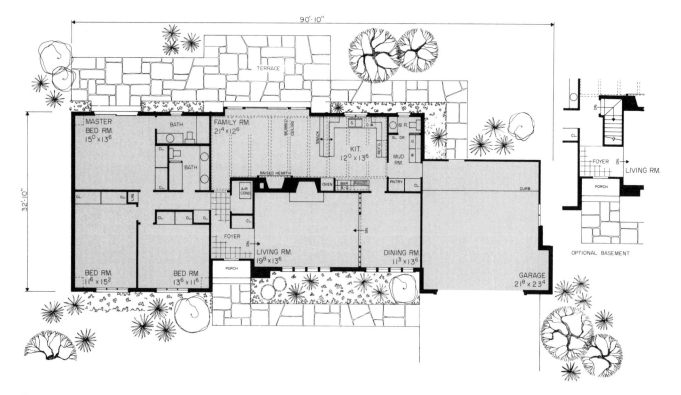

Design N2318
Square Footage: 2,029

L

● Warmth and charm are characteristics of Tudor adaptations. This modest sized home with its twin front-facing gabled roofs represents a great investment. While it will be an exciting and refreshing addition to any neighborhood, its appeal will never grow old.

The covered, front entrance opens to the center foyer. Traffic patterns flow in an orderly and efficient manner to the three main zones — the formal dining zone, the sleeping zone and the informal living zone. The sunken living room with its fireplace is separated

from the dining room by an attractive trellis divider. A second fireplace, along with beamed ceiling and sliding glass doors, highlights the family room. Note snack bar, mud room, cooking facilities, two full baths and optional basement.

Design N2962
Square Footage: 2,112

● A Tudor exterior with an efficient floor plan is favored by many. Each of the three main living zones in this plan are within a few steps of the foyer for easy traffic flow. Open planning and plenty of glass create a nice environment for the living/dining area. The L-shaped kitchen with island range and work surface is delightfully open to the large breakfast room. Nearby is the step-saving laundry. The sleeping zone has the flexibility of functioning as a two- or three-bedroom area. Notice the economical back-to-back plumbing.

QUOTE ONE™
Cost to build? See page 336 to order complete cost estimate to build this house in your area!

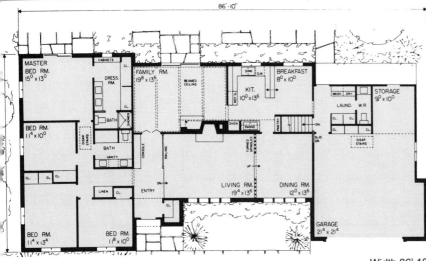

Design N1989
Square Footage: 2,282

L **D**

● High style abounds in this picturesque, ground-hugging design. The plan calls for a sunken living room and separate dining room. Overlooking the rear yard is an informal family room with beamed ceiling. Note the proximity of the kitchen and breakfast room. A master bedroom suite is one of four bedrooms found to the left of the entry foyer.

Width 86'-10"
Depth 48'-10"

Design N3346

Square Footage: 2,032

L

● This home boasts a delightful Tudor exterior with a terrific interior floor plan. Though compact, there's plenty of living space: large study with fireplace, gathering room, dining room, and breakfast room. The master bedroom has an attached bath with whirlpool tub. Note the double walk-in closets.

QUOTE ONE™

Cost to build? See page 336 to order complete cost estimate to build this house in your area!

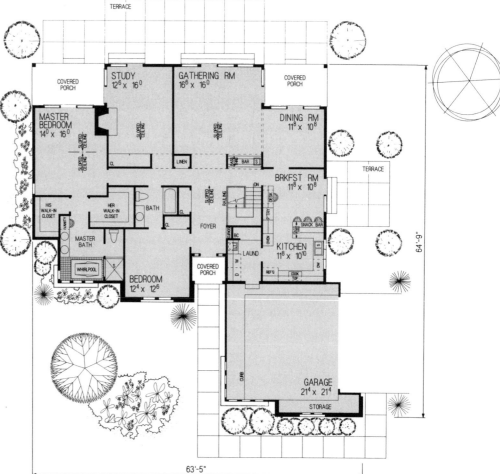

Design N3603

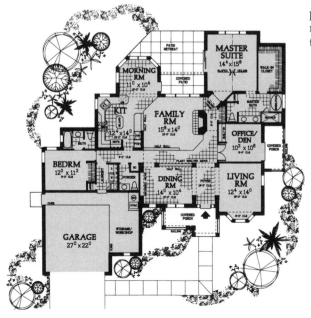

Design N3602

Width 70'
Depth 67'-4"

Design N3602/N3603
Square Footage: 2,312/2,520

L

● This lovely one-story home fits right into sunny regions. Its stucco exterior with easily accessed outdoor living areas makes it an all-time favorite. Inside, the floor plan accommodates empty-nester lifestyles. There is plenty of room for both formal and informal entertaining: living room, dining room, family room and morning room. A quiet office or den provides a getaway for quieter pursuits. Sleeping areas are split with the master bedroom and bath on one side and a secondary bedroom and bath on the other. Other special features include a warming hearth in the family room, a private porch off the den and a grand rear deck. Design N3603 provides a three-bedroom option.

QUOTE ONE™
Cost to build? See page 336 to order complete cost estimate to build this house in your area!

Design N2142
Square Footage: 2,450

D

● Adaptations of Old English homes have enjoyed great popularity. This design is no exception. Notice the up-to-date floor planning inside: formal living and dining rooms to the right, family room and kitchen/breakfast room at center, sleeping wing to the left. Notice the two terrace areas, raised-hearth fireplace, and conveniently located powder room.

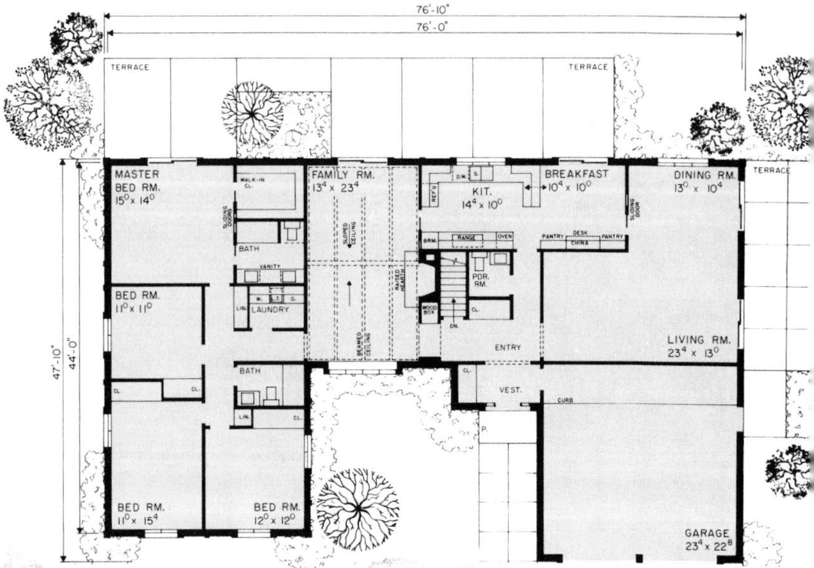

Design N2515
Square Footage: 2,363

D

● The brick veneer of this house is effectively complemented by beam work, stucco and window treatment. The interior plan is equally engaging. The kitchen, nook and dining room overlook the front yard. The laundry is around the corner. A sloping, beamed ceiling and raised-hearth fireplace are highlights of the family room. Like the living room and master bedroom, it functions with the rear terrace. Wood posts separate the living room and hall.

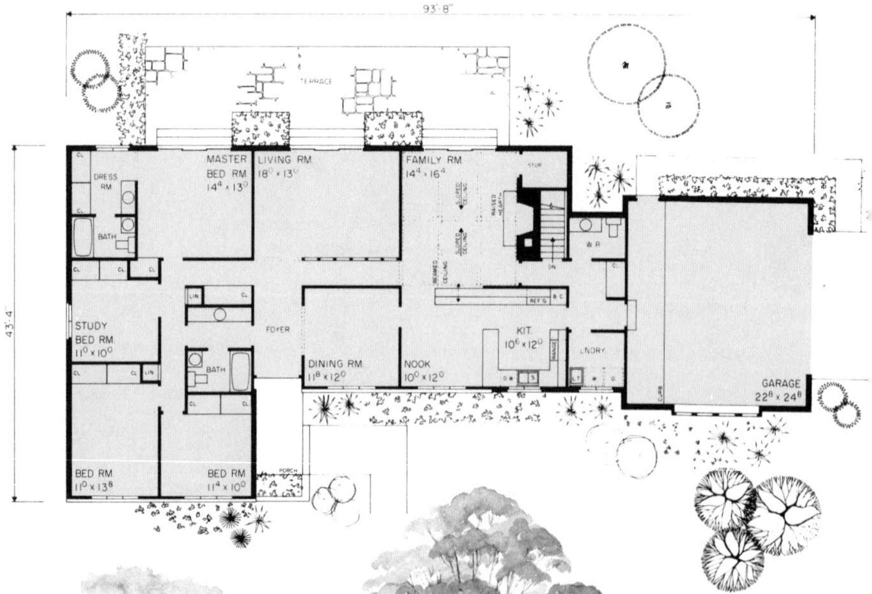

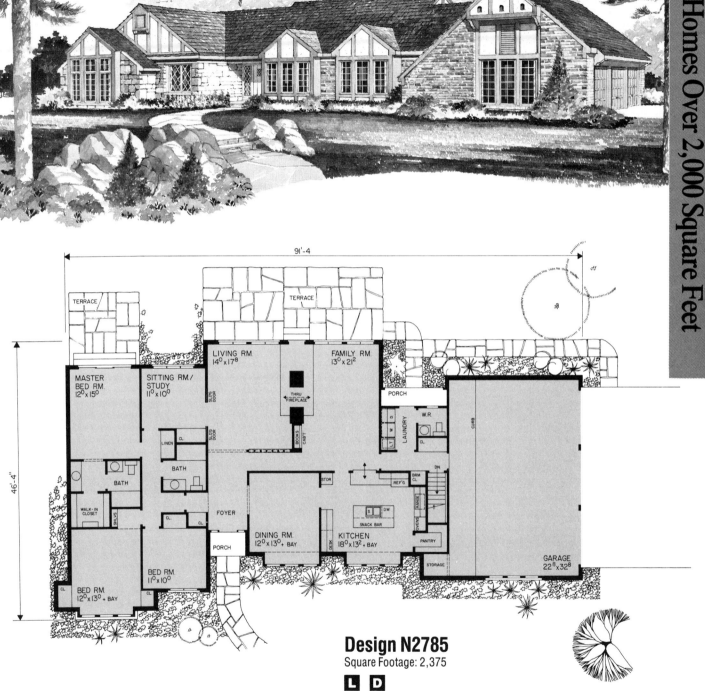

Design N2785
Square Footage: 2,375

L D

Exceptional Tudor design! Passers-by will take a second glance at this fine home wherever it may be located. And the interior is just as pleasing. As one enters the foyer and looks around, the plan will speak for itself in the areas of convenience and efficiency.

Cross room traffic will be avoided. There is a hall leading to each of the three bedrooms and study of the sleeping wing and another leading to the living room, family room, kitchen and laundry with washroom. The formal dining room can be entered from both

the foyer and the kitchen. Efficiency will be the by-word when describing the kitchen. Note the fine features: a built-in desk, pantry, island snack bar with sink and pass-thru to the family room. The fireplace will be enjoyed in the living and family rooms.

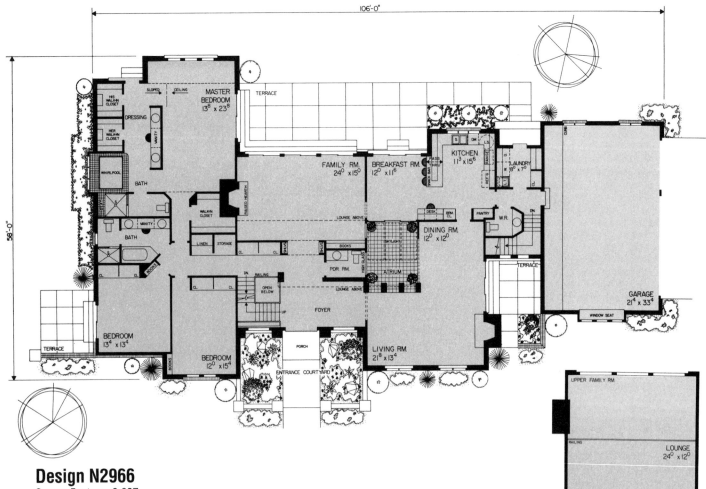

Design N2966
Square Footage: 3,687

● This Tudor adaptation is as dramatic inside as it is outside. As a visitor approaches the front courtyard there is much that catches the eye. The interesting roof lines, the appealing window treatment, the contrasting exterior materials and their textures, the inviting panelled front door and the massive twin chimneys with their protruding clay pots. Inside, the spacious foyer with its sloping ceiling looks up into the balcony-type lounge. It also looks down the open stairwell to the lower level area. From the foyer, traffic flows conveniently to other areas. The focal point of the living zone is the delightful atrium. Both the formal living room and the informal family room feature a fireplace. Each of the full baths highlights a tub and shower, a vanity and twin lavatories. Note the secondary access to the basement adjacent to the door to three car garage. Lounge adds an additional 284 sq. ft.

Design N2926

First Floor: 1,570 square feet; Second Floor: 598 square feet
Lower Level: 1,080 square feet; Total: 3,248 square feet

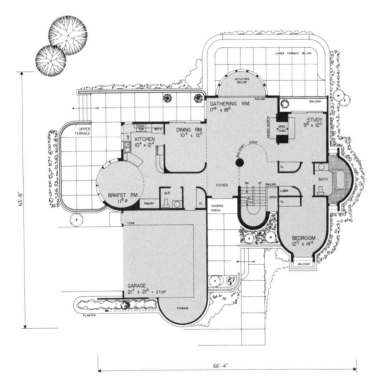

● This striking Contemporary design offers plenty of leisure living on three levels including an activities room with bar, exercise room with sauna, two gathering rooms, circular glass windows, and skylights. Note the outstanding master bedroom suite with skylight over the bath, adjoining lounge, and adjacent upper gathering room.

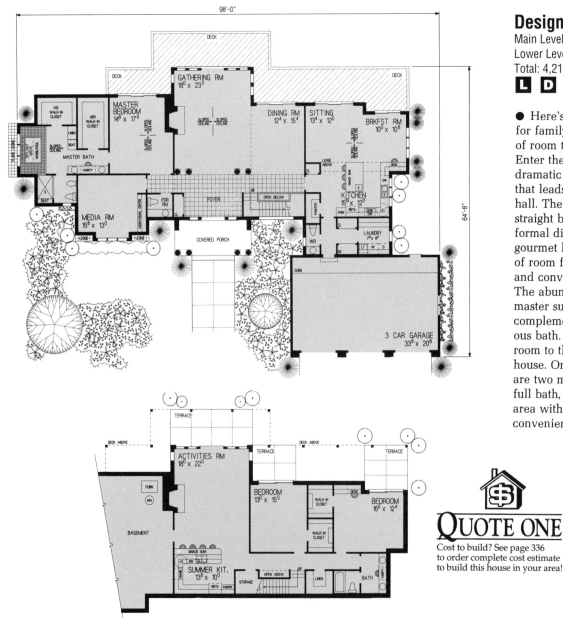

Design N3311

Main Level: 2,662 square feet
Lower Level: 1,548 square feet
Total: 4,210 square feet

L **D**

● Here's a hillside haven
for family living with plenty
of room to entertain in style.
Enter the main level from a
dramatic columned portico
that leads to a large entry
hall. The gathering room is
straight back and adjoins a
formal dining area. A true
gourmet kitchen with plenty
of room for casual eating
and conversation is nearby.
The abundantly appointed
master suite on this level is
complemented by a luxuri-
ous bath. Note the media
room to the front of the
house. On the lower level
are two more bedrooms, a
full bath, a large activity
area with fireplace and a
convenient summer kitchen.

QUOTE ONE™

Cost to build? See page 336
to order complete cost estimate
to build this house in your area!

Design N3361

Main Level: 3,548 square feet
Lower Level: 1,036 square feet
Total: 4,584 square feet

L

QUOTE ONE™

Cost to build? See page 336
to order complete cost estimate
to build this house in your area!

● Here's a dandy hillside home that can easily accommodate the largest of families and is perfect for both formal and informal entertaining. Straight back from the entry foyer is a grand gathering room/dining room combination. It is complemented by the breakfast room and a front-facing media room. The sleeping wing contains three bedrooms and two full baths. On the lower level is an activities room with summer kitchen and a fourth bedroom that makes the perfect guest room.

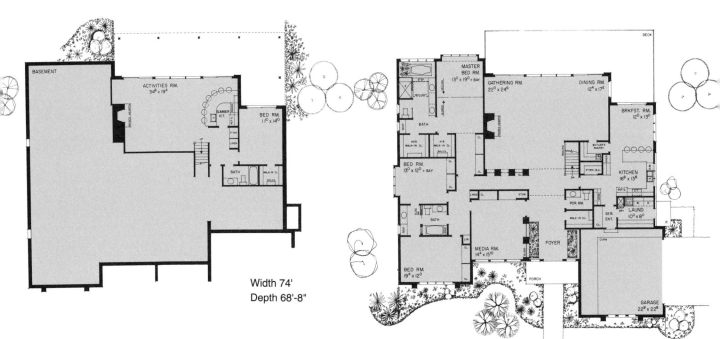

Width 74'
Depth 68'-8"

Design N2841

Main Level: 1,044 square feet
Upper Level: 851 square feet
Lower Level: 753 square feet
Total: 2,648 square feet

L

● This spacious tri-level with traditional stone exterior offers excellent comfort and zoning for the modern family. A main-floor gathering area is continued above with two-story appeal. The lower level offers an activities room with raised-hearth in addition to an optional bunk room with bath. A modern kitchen on the main level features a handy snack bar in addition to a dining room. A study on the main level could be used as a bedroom. The master bedroom is located on the upper level along with a rectangular bunk room with its own balcony.

QUOTE ONE™

Cost to build? See page 336 to order complete cost estimate to build this house in your area!

Design N3360

Upper Level: 2,673 square feet
Lower Level: 1,389 square feet
Total: 4,062 square feet

L

● This plan has the best of both worlds — a traditional exterior and a modern multi-level floor plan. The central foyer routes traffic effectively to all areas: the kitchen, gathering room, sleeping area, media room and the stairs leading to the lower level. Highlights include a master bedroom suite with luxurious bath and a lower-level activities room with fireplace and kitchen. Also note the bedroom on this level.

Width 60'
Depth 72'

Design N3366

Main Level: 1,638 square feet
Upper Level: 650 square feet
Lower Level: 934 square feet
Total: 3,222 square feet

L

● There is much more to this design than
meets the eye. While it may look like a 1½-story
plan, bonus recreation and hobby space in the
walk-out basement adds almost 1,000 square
feet. The first floor holds living and dining
areas as well as the master bedroom suite. Two
family bedrooms on the second floor are connected by a balcony area that overlooks the
gathering room below. Notice the covered
porch beyond the breakfast and dining rooms.

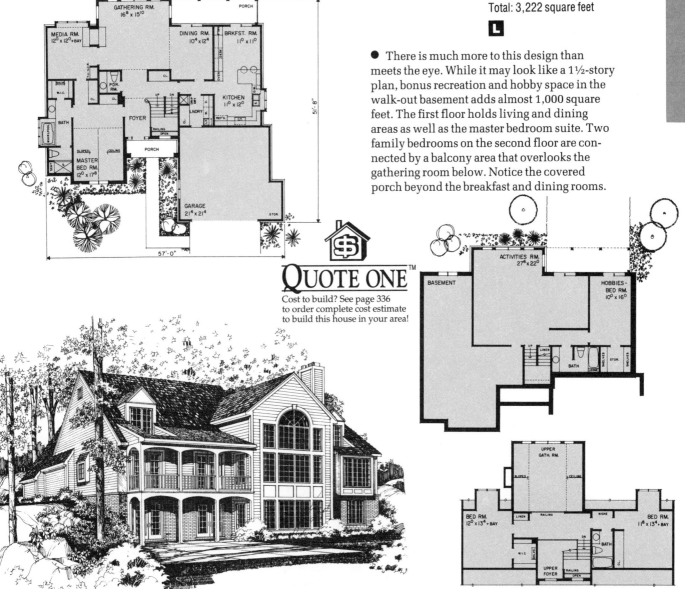

QUOTE ONE™

Cost to build? See page 336
to order complete cost estimate
to build this house in your area!

Design N2944

Main Level: 1,545 square feet
Upper Level: 977 square feet
Lower Level: 933 square feet
Total: 3,455 square feet

● This eye-catching contemporary features
three stacked levels of livability. The main
level has a fine U-shaped kitchen which is
flanked by the informal breakfast room and formal dining room. The living room is dramatic
with a sloped ceiling that extends through the
upper level. A two-way fireplace can be enjoyed from the dining room, living room and
media room. Upstairs, the balcony serves as the
connecting link for the three bedrooms. The
lower level offers a huge activities room plus
lounge. Note the bar and fireplace.

Width 44'
Depth 70'-4"

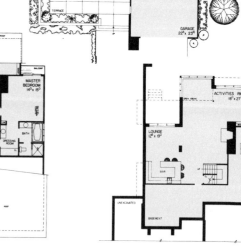

Design N2679

Main Level: 1,179 square feet
Upper Level: 681 square feet
Family Room Level: 643 square feet
Lower Level: 680 square feet
Total: 3,183 square feet

● This spacious contemporary offers space for
the large or growing family. The main level
includes a breakfast room in addition to a formal dining room. Adjacent is a sloped-ceiling
living room with raised-hearth. The upper level
features an isolated master bedroom suite with
adjoining study or sitting room and balcony.
The family-room level includes a long family
room with adjoining terrace on one end and an
adjoining bar with washroom at the other end.
Two other bedrooms are positioned in the
lower level, each with its own terrace.

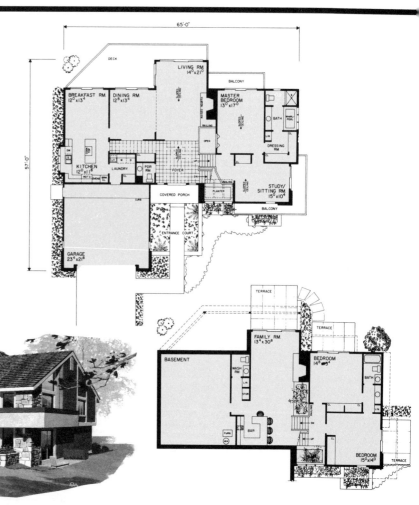

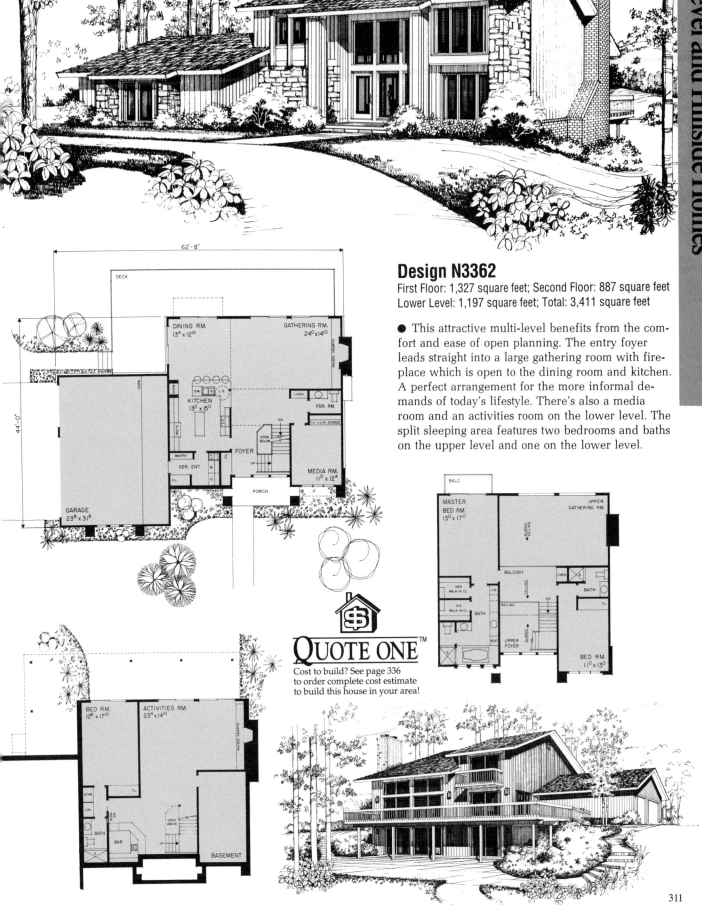

DECK

62'-8"

44'-0"

DINING RM.
13⁴ x 12¹⁰

GATHERING RM.
24⁰ x 14¹⁰

RAISED HEARTH

KITCHEN
13⁰ x 15⁰

OVEN
D.W. S.S. L.S.

LINEN

PDR. RM.

T.V.-V.C.R.-STEREO

REFRIG.

PANTRY

FOYER

OPEN BELOW

DN

SER. ENT.

CL.

UP

MEDIA RM.
11⁰ x 12⁴

GARAGE
23⁸ x 31⁸

PORCH

Design N3362

First Floor: 1,327 square feet; Second Floor: 887 square feet
Lower Level: 1,197 square feet; Total: 3,411 square feet

● This attractive multi-level benefits from the comfort and ease of open planning. The entry foyer leads straight into a large gathering room with fireplace which is open to the dining room and kitchen. A perfect arrangement for the more informal demands of today's lifestyle. There's also a media room and an activities room on the lower level. The split sleeping area features two bedrooms and baths on the upper level and one on the lower level.

QUOTE ONE™

Cost to build? See page 336 to order complete cost estimate to build this house in your area!

BALC.

MASTER
BED RM.
13⁰ x 17⁰

SLOPED CEILING

UPPER
GATHERING RM.

HER
WALK-IN CL.

LIN.

BALCONY

CEILING

LINEN

BATH

HIS
WALK-IN CL.

BATH

RAILING

DN

CL.

SEAT

UPPER
FOYER

SLOPED

BED RM.
11⁰ x 13⁰

BED RM.
12⁸ x 17¹⁰

ACTIVITIES RM.
23⁴ x 14¹⁰

PLANTER BOX

STOR.

CL.

LIN.

OPEN
ABOVE

BATH

BAR

UP

BASEMENT

Design N2901

Main Level: 1,449 square feet
Upper Level: 665 square feet
Master Bedroom Level: 448 square feet
Activities Room Level: 419 square feet
Total: 2,981 square feet

L

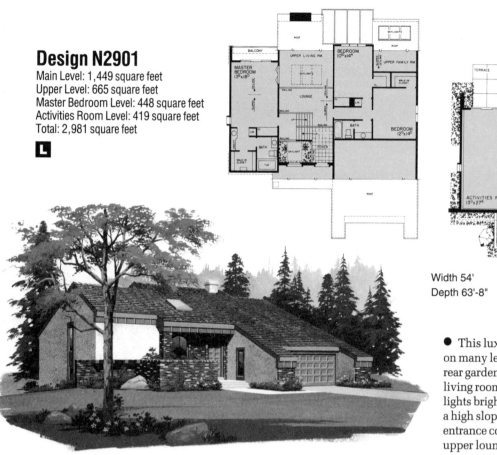

Width 54'
Depth 63'-8"

● This luxurious three-bedroom offers comfort on many levels. Its modern design incorporates a rear garden room and conversation pit in the living room/dining room area. There are skylights brightening the adjacent family room with a high sloped ceiling. Other features include an entrance court, activities room, modern kitchen, upper lounge and master bedroom.

Design N1850

Main Level: 1,456 square feet
Lower Level: 728 square feet
Total: 2,184 square feet

● A perfect rectangle, this split-level is comparatively inexpensive to build and very appealing to live in. It features a large upper-level living room with a fireplace, a formal dining room, three bedrooms (with two full baths nearby) and an outdoor deck. Another fireplace warms the family room on the lower level, which also has a full bath and room for a study or a fourth bedroom.

Width 54'-8"
Depth 28'

QUOTE ONE™

Cost to build? See page 336 to order complete cost estimate to build this house in your area!

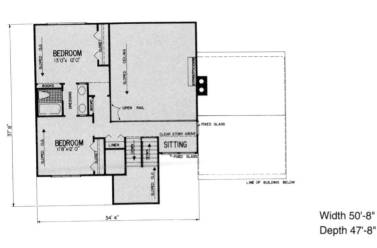

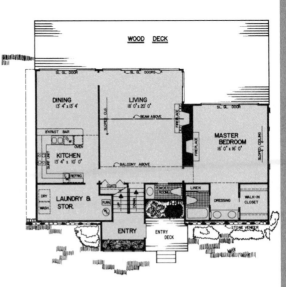

Width 50'-8"
Depth 47'-8"

Design N4115

Main Level: 1,494 square feet
Upper Level: 597 square feet
Total: 2,091 square feet

● Here is a home that's moderately sized without sacrificing livability. Just off the entry is a large, two-story living room. There's also a dining room with a breakfast bar/pass-through to the kitchen. To the rear is an enormous deck for sunning and relaxing. A split-sleeping area features two upper-level bedrooms and a main-level master bedroom. Notice the fireplace and sloped ceilings.

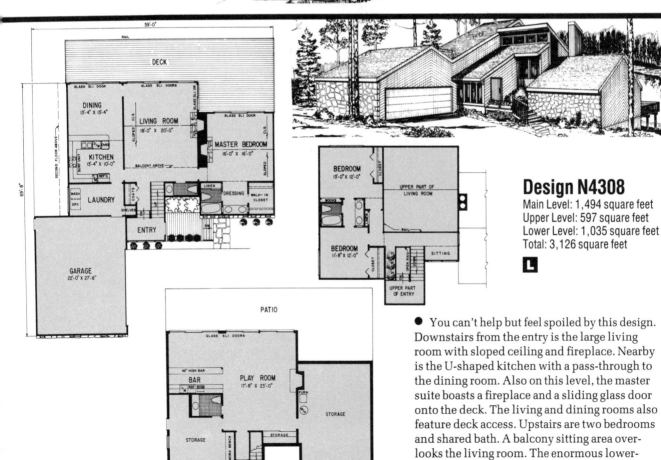

Design N4308

Main Level: 1,494 square feet
Upper Level: 597 square feet
Lower Level: 1,035 square feet
Total: 3,126 square feet

L

● You can't help but feel spoiled by this design. Downstairs from the entry is the large living room with sloped ceiling and fireplace. Nearby is the U-shaped kitchen with a pass-through to the dining room. Also on this level, the master suite boasts a fireplace and a sliding glass door onto the deck. The living and dining rooms also feature deck access. Upstairs are two bedrooms and shared bath. A balcony sitting area overlooks the living room. The enormous lower-level playroom includes a fireplace, a large bar and sliding glass doors to the patio.

Design N2511

Main Level: 1,043 square feet
Upper Level: 703 square feet
Lower Level: 794 square feet
Total: 2,540 square feet

L D

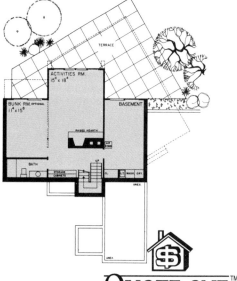

QUOTE ONE™

Cost to build? See page 336
to order complete cost estimate
to build this house in your area!

● Rustic yet contemporary, this design on three
levels is a real beauty. Living areas include a
gathering room, study (or optional bedroom),
dining room and activities room in the basement. There are two bunk rooms — upper level
and lower level — and terrace space for any
outdoor activity.

Design N2716

Main Level: 1,013 square feet
Upper Level: 885 square feet
Lower Level: 1,074 square feet
Total: 2,972 square feet

L

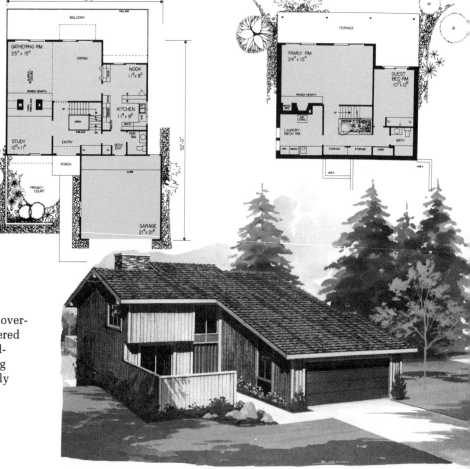

● This plan has a genuine master suite — overlooking the gathering room through shuttered
windows. The gathering room has a raised-
hearth fireplace, sloped ceiling and sliding
glass doors onto the main balcony. A family
room and study also have fireplaces. The
kitchen features plenty of built-ins and a
separate dining nook.

52'-0"

DECK

COVERED TERRACE | SKYLIGHT ABOVE

DINING RM. 12⁰ x 12¹⁰

KITCHEN 11⁰ x 11⁶

BRKFST. RM. 10⁰ x 16⁰

GATHERING RM. 17⁶ x 15⁰

RAISED HEARTH

SLOPED CEILING

SLOPED CEILING

BRM. CL. REFS. OVEN

WALK-IN CLOSET

PANTRY

CONVERSATION AREA

BAR

UP DN

LAUND.

48'-0"

STUDY 11⁰ x 11⁸

QUIET TERRACE

SLOPED CEILING

DN

FOYER

PDR. RM.

CURB

COURT

PORCH

GARAGE 21⁰ x 21⁸

QUOTE ONE™

Cost to build? See page 336
to order complete cost estimate
to build this house in your area!

Design N2823

Main Level: 1,370 square feet
Upper Level: 927 square feet
Total: 2,297 square feet

L **D**

MASTER BEDROOM 12⁰ x 14⁸

NURSERY / SITTING RM. 10⁸ x 7⁸

BEDROOM 10⁰ x 13⁶

CL

LINEN

RAILING

DN

VANITY

WALK-IN CLOSET

OPEN

RAILING

CL

BATH

BATH

BEDROOM 10⁰ x 11²

ATTIC

● The street view of this contemporary design features a small courtyard entrance as well as a private
terrace off the study. Inside the livability will be
outstanding. This design features spacious first-floor
activity areas that flow smoothly into each other. In
the gathering room a raised-hearth fireplace creates a
dramatic focal point. An adjacent covered terrace,
featuring a skylight, is ideal for outdoor dining and
could be screened in later for an additional room.

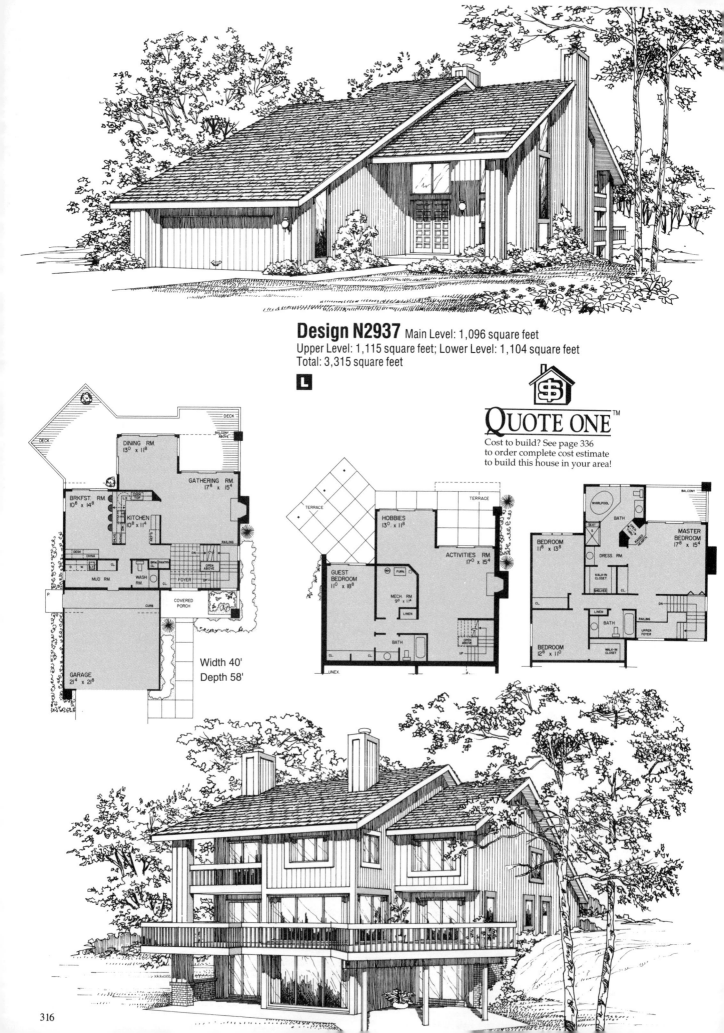

Design N2937 Main Level: 1,096 square feet
Upper Level: 1,115 square feet; Lower Level: 1,104 square feet
Total: 3,315 square feet

L

QUOTE ONE™

Cost to build? See page 336
to order complete cost estimate
to build this house in your area!

Width 40'
Depth 58'

Design N2828

First Floor: 817 square feet—Living Area; Foyer & Laundry: 261 square feet
Second Floor: 852 square feet—Living Area; Foyer & Storage: 214 square feet; Total: 2,144 square feet

STORAGE
12⁸ x 8⁰

FUTURE BAR

ACTIVITIES RM.
23⁰ x 24⁸

STORAGE
12⁸ x10⁰

FURN.

FURN.

UNEXCAVATED

CL.

UP

WASH. RM.

UNEX.

BASEMENT PLAN

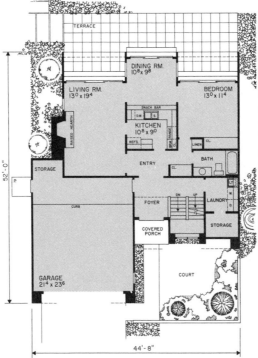

TERRACE

DINING RM.
10⁸ x 9⁸

LIVING RM.
13⁰ x 19⁴

BEDROOM
13⁰ x 11⁴

SNACK BAR

D.W. S

KITCHEN
10⁸ x 9⁰

REF'S.

BRM RANGE

RAISED HEARTH

CL.

LINEN

CL.

BATH

ENTRY

STORAGE

52'-0"

CURB

DN   UP

FOYER

LAUNDRY
W
D

COVERED PORCH

STORAGE

GARAGE
21⁴ x 23⁶

COURT

P

44'-8"

BALCONY

BEDROOM/
LOUNGE
10⁸ x 10⁴

BALCONY

MASTER
BEDROOM
13⁰ x 21⁸

BEDROOM
13⁰ x 11⁴

SLOPED CEILING

OPTIONAL FIREPLACE

BATH

CL.

LINEN

SKYLIGHT

BATH

CL.

SLOPED CEILING

CL.

CL.

LINEN

SKYLIGHTS

DN

SEWING/
HOBBIES

UPPER FOYER

SLOPED CEILING

● A fine contemporary design in two stories, this home also extends its livability to the basement where bonus space could be converted later to an activities or hobby room. On the first floor, living areas revolve around a central kitchen with snack bar in the dining room. The first-floor bedroom could also serve as a study, family room or library. Note the raised-hearth fireplace in the living room. Upstairs are three bedrooms, or two and a lounge, and a sewing or hobby room. Two long balconies here overlook the terrace below.

Design N2786

Main Level: 871 square feet
Upper Level: 1,132 square feet
Lower Level: 528 square feet
Total: 2,531 square feet

● Bay windows in both the formal living room and formal dining room add much appeal to this traditional tri-level. The interior livability is outstanding. An abundance of built-ins in the kitchen create an efficient work center. Features include an island range, pantry, broom closet, desk and breakfast room with sliding glass doors to the rear terrace. The lower level houses an informal family room, wash room and laundry. Note the walk-in closet in the master bedroom suite.

Width 54'
Depth 44'-5"

Design N2787

Main Level: 976 square feet
Upper Level: 1,118 square feet
Lower Level: 524 square feet
Total: 2,618 square feet

L D

● Main, upper and lower levels serve the residents of this home. The family room with raised-hearth fireplace, laundry and wash room are on the lower level. Formal living and dining rooms, a kitchen and breakfast room are on the main level. The upper level holds three bedrooms and a study (or four bedrooms, if desired) and two baths.

Width 58'
Depth 45'-4"

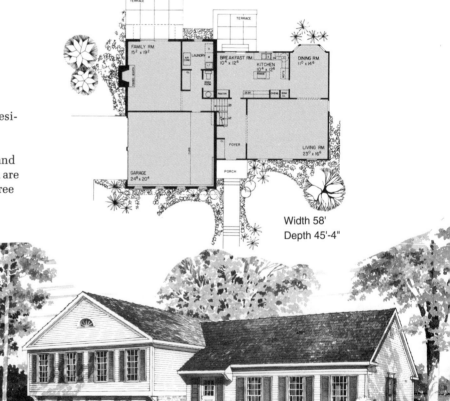

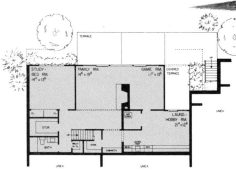

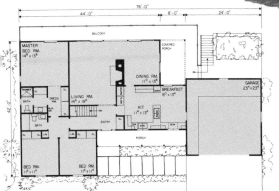

Design N1974

Main Level: 1,680 square feet
Lower Level: 1,344 square feet
Total: 3,024 square feet

● You would never guess from looking at the front of this traditional design that it possessed such a strikingly different exterior to the back. Yet its configuration means great hillside living. The most popular outdoor area will be the balcony. Inside, the formal living and dining room will serve formal functions while the informal family room on the lower level meets everyday needs.

Design N2769

Main Level: 1,898 square feet
Lower Level: 1,134 square feet
Total: 3,032 square feet

● This traditional hillside design has fine architectural styling. Its floor plan allows for split sleeping areas and a separation of formal and informal living areas.

Design N2608

Main Level: 728 square feet; Upper Level: 874 square feet
Lower Level: 310 square feet; Total: 1,912 square feet

L D

● Here is tri-level livability with a fourth
basement level for bulk storage and, per-
haps, a shop area. There are four bedrooms,
a handy laundry, two eating areas, formal
and informal living areas and two fireplaces.
Sliding glass doors in the formal dining room
and the family room open to a terrace. The
U-shaped kitchen has a built-in range/oven
and storage pantry. The breakfast nook overlooks the family room.

QUOTE ONE™

Cost to build? See page 336
to order complete cost estimate
to build this house in your area!

Width 56'-8"
Depth 36'-5"

Design N2628

Main Level: 649 square feet; Upper Level: 672 square feet
Lower Level: 624 square feet; Total: 1,945 square feet

L D

● Traditional, yet contemporary! With lots of
extras, too. Like a wet bar and game storage in
the family room. A beamed ceiling, too, and a
sliding glass door onto the terrace. In short, a
family room designed to make your life easy
and enjoyable. There's more. A living room
with a traditionally styled fireplace and built-
in bookshelves. And a dining room with a sliding glass door that opens to a second terrace.
Here's the appropriate setting for those times
when you want a touch of elegance.

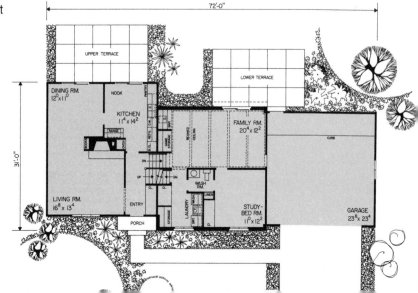

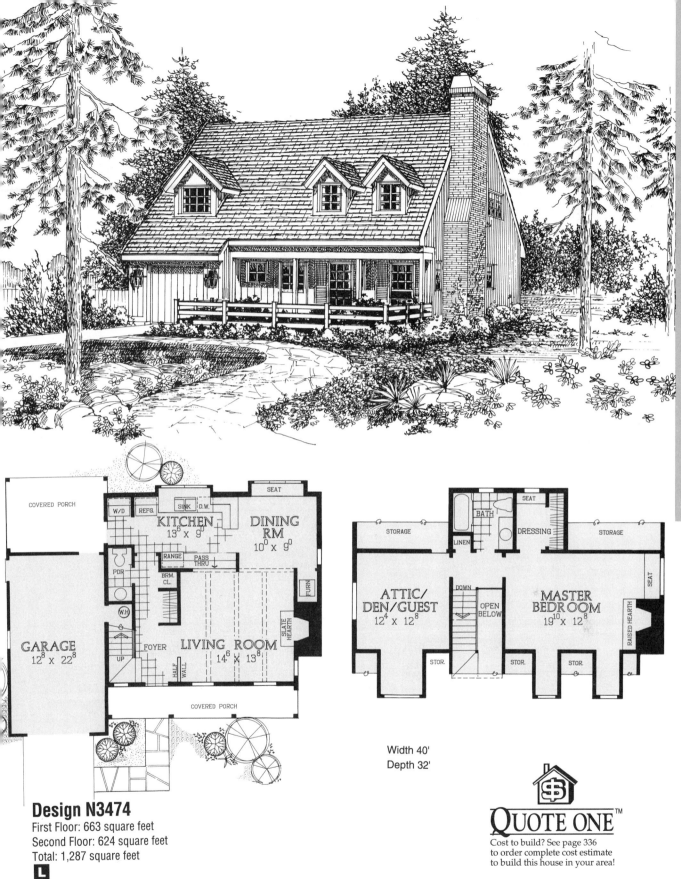

COVERED PORCH

W/D | REFG. | SINK | D.W.

SEAT

KITCHEN
13⁶ x 9⁰

DINING
RM
10⁰ x 9⁰

RANGE

PASS
THRU

BRM.
CL.

PDR

W.H.

FURN

GARAGE
12⁸ x 22⁸

FOYER

UP

HALF
WALL

LIVING ROOM
14⁶ x 13⁸

SLATE
HEARTH

COVERED PORCH

STORAGE

SEAT

BATH

LINEN

DRESSING

STORAGE

ATTIC/
DEN/GUEST
12⁴ x 12⁸

DOWN

OPEN
BELOW

MASTER
BEDROOM
19¹⁰ x 12⁸

RAISED HEARTH

SEAT

STOR.

STOR.

STOR.

STOR.

Width 40'
Depth 32'

Quote One™

Cost to build? See page 336
to order complete cost estimate
to build this house in your area!

Design N3474

First Floor: 663 square feet
Second Floor: 624 square feet
Total: 1,287 square feet

L

● This rustic cabin is a delight. A spacious living room
with a beam ceiling and warming fireplace greets you as
you enter the foyer via the inviting covered porch. The
adjoining dining room offers a picturesque window seat
and convenience to the large kitchen with its window

sink, pass-through to the living room and access to the
powder room and rear covered porch. A roomy master
bedroom featuring a fireplace and a walk-in closet with
a seat and an attic den or guest room complete the second floor. Notice all the upstairs storage space available.

Design N2488 First Floor: 1,113 square feet; Second Floor: 543 square feet; Total: 1,656 square feet

D

Quote One™

Cost to build? See page 336
to order complete cost estimate
to build this house in your area!

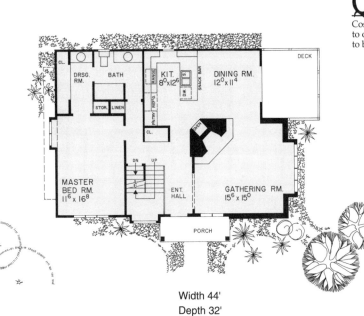

Width 44'
Depth 32'

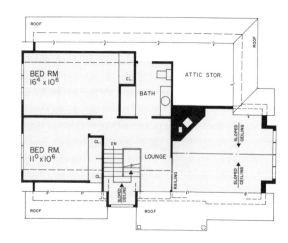

● A cozy cottage for the young at heart! Whether called upon to serve the young active family as a leisure-time retreat at the lake, or the retired couple as a quiet haven in later years, this charming design will perform well. As a year round second home, the up-stairs with its two sizable bedrooms, full bath and lounge area looking down into the gathering room below, will ideally accommodate the younger generation. When called upon to function as a retirement home, the second floor will cater to the visiting family members and friends. Also, it will be available for use as a home office, study, sewing room, music area, the pursuit of hobbies, etc. Of course, as an efficient, economical home for the young, growing family, this design will function well.

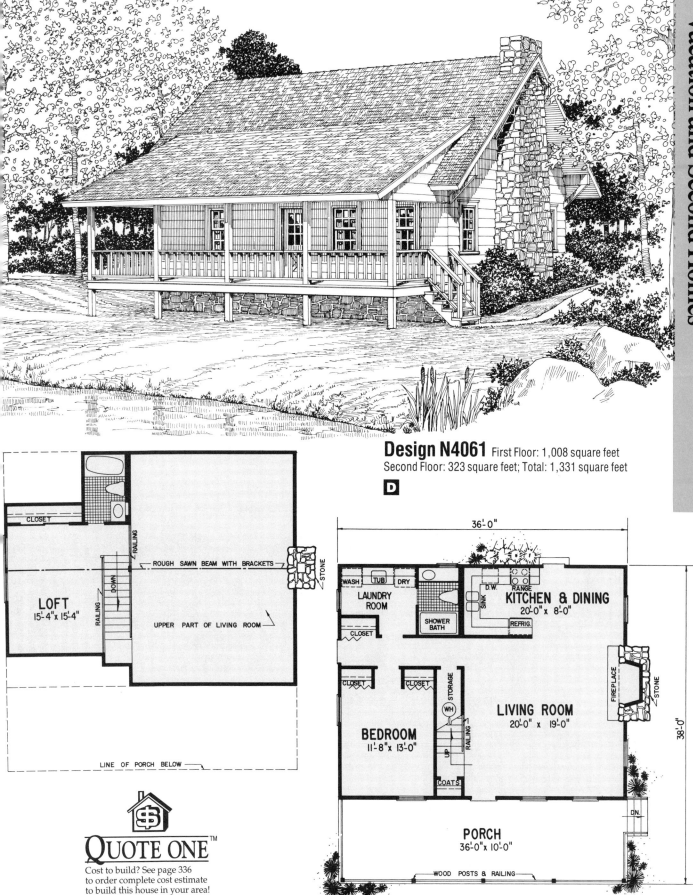

Design N4061 First Floor: 1,008 square feet
Second Floor: 323 square feet; Total: 1,331 square feet

D

CLOSET

LOFT
15'-4" x 15'-4"

RAILING

DOWN

ROUGH SAWN BEAM WITH BRACKETS

STONE

UPPER PART OF LIVING ROOM

LINE OF PORCH BELOW

WASH TUB DRY

LAUNDRY ROOM

D.W. RANGE

SINK

KITCHEN & DINING
20'-0" x 8'-0"

SHOWER BATH

CLOSET

REFRIG.

36'-0"

CLOSET CLOSET

STORAGE

WH

RAILING

UP

BEDROOM
11'-8" x 13'-0"

LIVING ROOM
20'-0" x 19'-0"

FIREPLACE

STONE

38'-0"

COATS

DN.

PORCH
36'-0" x 10'-0"

WOOD POSTS & RAILING

QUOTE ONE™

Cost to build? See page 336
to order complete cost estimate
to build this house in your area!

● This charming farmhouse design will be economical to build and a pleasure to occupy. Like most vacation homes, this design features an open plan. The large living area includes a living room and dining room and a massive stone fireplace. A partition separates the kitchen from the living room. Also downstairs are a bedroom, full bath, and laundry room. Upstairs is a spacious sleeping loft overlooking the living room. Don't miss the large front porch — this will be a favorite spot for relaxing.

QUOTE ONE™

Cost to build? See page 336
to order complete cost estimate
to build this house in your area!

Width 40'
Depth 57'-4"

Design N3453

Square Footage: 1,442

L

● This volume home impresses with its stately rooflines and stucco exterior. The front porch opens to an eleven-foot ceiling in the foyer. Straight ahead, an elegant living room serves as a prelude to the dramatic circular dining bay. Here, family and guests alike will revel in the fine views out the back of the house. The kitchen, with its advantageous snack bar, offers an abundance of counter and cabinet space. The media room, with its closet space and access to a full hall bath, could easily convert to a bedroom. In the master bedroom you'll find a lengthy closet in addition to a stunning bath. Glass block provides privacy to the toilet and shower while the spa tub delights in its well-illuminated nook. Dual lavatories complete the amenities in this room.

QUOTE ONE™

Cost to build? See page 336
to order complete cost estimate
to build this house in your area!

Width 51'-6"
Depth 59'-6"

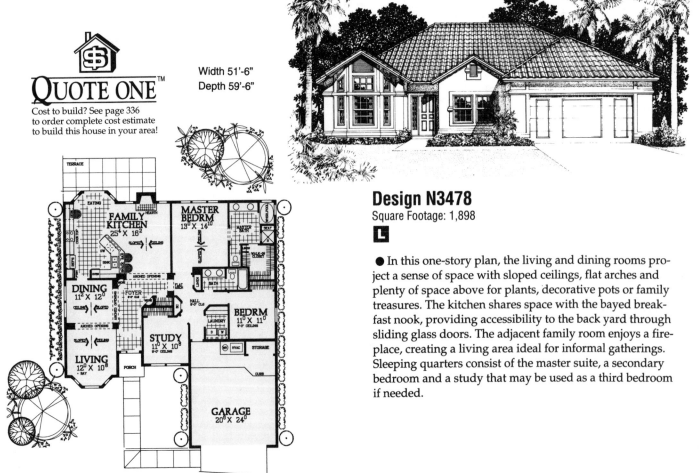

Design N3478

Square Footage: 1,898

L

● In this one-story plan, the living and dining rooms project a sense of space with sloped ceilings, flat arches and plenty of space above for plants, decorative pots or family treasures. The kitchen shares space with the bayed breakfast nook, providing accessibility to the back yard through sliding glass doors. The adjacent family room enjoys a fireplace, creating a living area ideal for informal gatherings. Sleeping quarters consist of the master suite, a secondary bedroom and a study that may be used as a third bedroom if needed.

Design N3416
Square Footage: 1,375

Here's a Southwestern design that will be economical to build and a pleasure to occupy. The front door opens into a spacious living room with corner fireplace and dining room with coffered ceiling. The nearby kitchen serves both easily. A few steps away is the cozy media room with built-in space for audio/visual equipment. Down the hall are two bedrooms and two baths; the master features a whirlpool. A guest room is found around the entry court and includes a fireplace and sloped ceiling.

Width 44'
Depth 52'-4"

QUOTE ONE™
Cost to build? See page 336 to order complete cost estimate to build this house in your area!

Design N4153
First Floor: 893 square feet
Second Floor: 549 square feet
Total: 1,442 square feet

L **D**

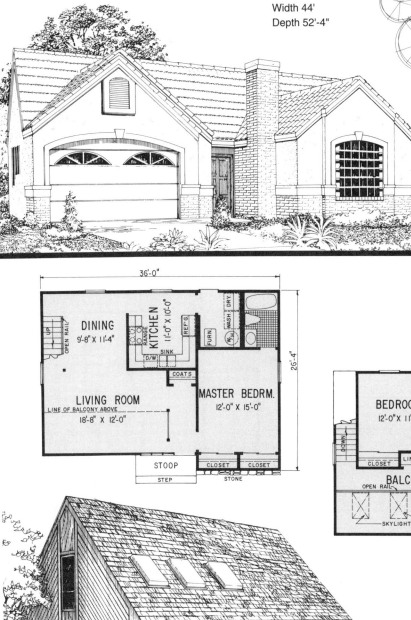

● The rectangular shape of this design will make it an economical and easy-to-build choice for those wary of high construction costs. The first floor benefits from the informality of open planning: the living room and dining room combine to make one large living space. The partitioned kitchen is convenient. Also downstairs is the master bedroom and bath. The second floor houses two large bedrooms, a full bath and a balcony over the living room. Notice the skylights.

Design N4125 Entry Level: 1,089 square feet
Upper Level: 508 square feet; Total: 1,597 square feet

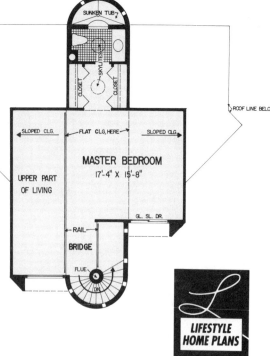

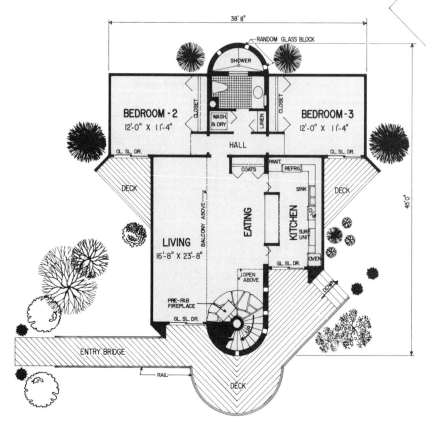

● Geometrical design elements are used to striking effect in this appealing contemporary. Several entrances lead into the open living and eating area. A pass-through to the kitchen saves steps in serving and cleaning up. Two rear bedrooms each have a private deck. A large circular tower encloses a spiral staircase leading up to the balcony master suite. Notice the semicircular sunken tub in the bath.

Design N3341 First Floor: 1,055 square feet
Second Floor: 981 square feet; Total: 2,036 square feet

L

● Designed for the empty-nester, small family, or as a second home, this appealing Tudor adaptation holds a most livable floor plan. Besides the 31' gathering room/ dining room area and U-shaped kitchen with nearby washroom, there is a front study with large storage closet on the first floor. Three bedrooms on the second floor meet sleeping needs without a hitch. Notice the walk-in closets and the master-bedroom balcony.

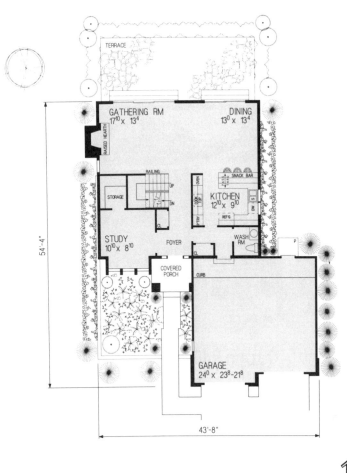

QUOTE ONE™
Cost to build? See page 336
to order complete cost estimate
to build this house in your area!

Design N4010

Main Level: 1,664 square feet
Lower Level: 1,136 square feet
Total: 2,800 square feet

● With the relaxed lifestyle of vacationers in mind, this design features plenty of living and leisure space. A large, wraparound deck accommodates sun worshippers. The carefully planned interior includes an open living room and dining room. The kitchen features a pass-through to the dining room to facilitate serving and clearing. Also on the main level are two bedrooms and a laundry room. The lower level boasts an enormous game room with fireplace and wet bar, a bunk room and a hobby room. Don't miss the patio.

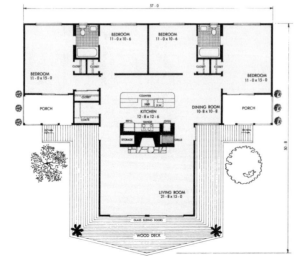

Design N4015

Square Footage: 1,420

● The perfect vacation home combines open, formal living spaces with lots of sleeping space. Study this plan carefully. The spacious living room has a warming fireplace and sliding glass doors onto the deck. Convenient to the dining room, the efficient kitchen is carefully placed so as not to interfere with the living room. Notice the four spacious bedrooms — there is plenty of room for accommodating guests. Two of the bedrooms boast private porches.

Design N4027
Square Footage: 1,232

● Good things come in small packages, too! The size and shape of this design will help hold down construction costs without sacrificing livability. The enormous great room is a multi-purpose living space with room for a dining area and several seating areas. Also notice the sloped ceilings. Sliding glass doors provide access to the wraparound deck and sweeping views of the outdoors. The well-equipped kitchen includes a pass-through and pantry. Two bedrooms, each with sloped ceiling and compartmented bath, round out the plan.

Optional Basement

Design N4012
Main Level: 1,216 square feet
Lower Level: 786 square feet
Total: 2,002 square feet

● This plan features the kind of indoor/outdoor relationship found in vacation homes. Sliding glass doors in the living room open onto a screened porch which, in turn, leads to a large deck. Note the built-in grille. The large living room with welcoming fireplace has enough space to accommodate an eating area. The sleeping quarters are split with two private bedrooms and baths on the entry level and a spacious dormitory with fireplace on the lower level. Just steps away is a covered patio.

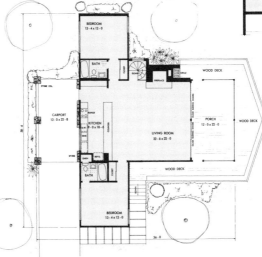

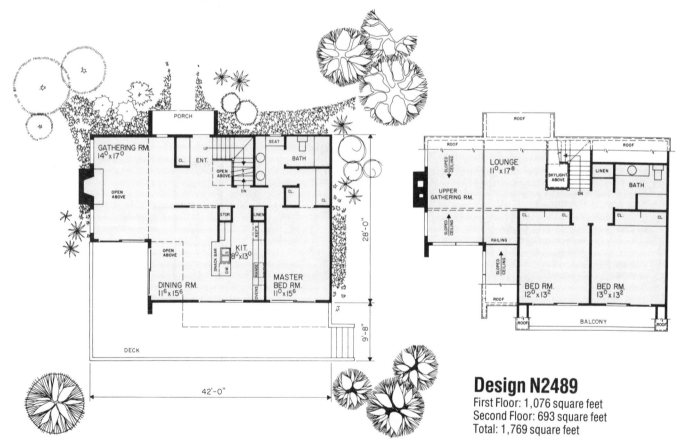

Design N2489

First Floor: 1,076 square feet
Second Floor: 693 square feet
Total: 1,769 square feet

● Outdoors-oriented families will appreciate the dramatic sliding glass doors and the sweeping decks that make this contemporary perfect. The plan of the first floor features a spacious two-story gathering room with sloping ceiling, a large fireplace and access to the large deck which runs the full length of the house. Also having direct access to the deck is the dining room which is half-open to the second floor above. A snack bar divides the dining room from the compact kitchen. The master bedroom is outstanding with its private bath, walk-in closet and sliding glass door. The second floor is brightened by a skylight and houses two bedrooms, lounge and full bath.

Design N2485 Main Level: 1,108 square feet
Lower Level: 983 square feet; Total: 2,091 square feet

● This hillside vacation home gives the appearance of being a one-story from the road. However, since it is built off the edge of a slope, the rear exterior is a full two-story structure. Notice the projecting deck and how it shelters the terrace. Each of the generous glass areas is protected from the summer sun by the overhangs and the extended walls. The clerestory windows of the front exterior provide natural light to the center of the plan.

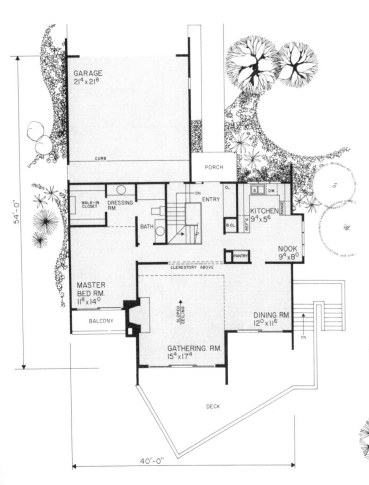

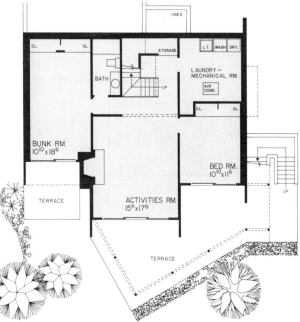

Design N1482

First Floor: 1,008 square feet
Second Floor: 637 square feet
Total: 1,645 square feet

● Here is a chalet right from the pages of travel folders. In addition to the big bedrooms on the first floor, there are three more upstairs. The large master bedroom has a balcony which overlooks the lower wood deck. There are two full baths. The first-floor bath is directly accessible from the outdoors. Note snack bar and pantry. A laundry area is adjacent to the side door.

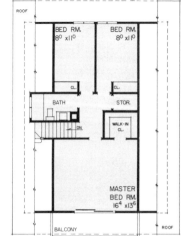

Design N2427

First Floor: 784 square feet
Second Floor: 504 square feet
Total: 1,288 square feet

● If ever a design had "vacation home" written all over it, this one does. The most carefree characteristic is the second-floor balcony which looks down onto the wood deck. Also on the second floor is the three-bunk dormitory. Panels through the knee walls give access to an abundant storage area. Downstairs there is yet another bedroom, a full bath and long living room.

Width 28'
Depth 44'

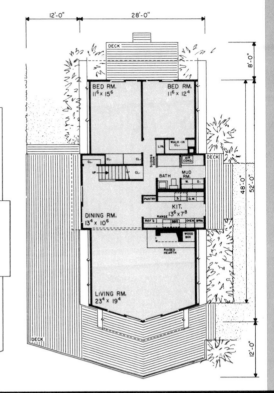

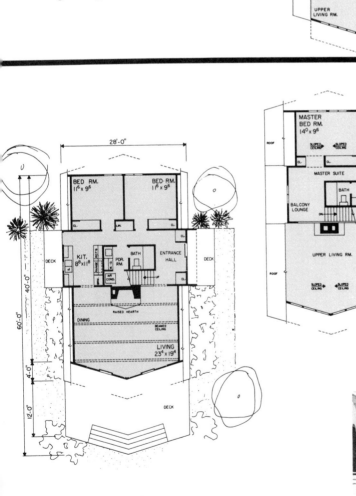

Design N2459

First Floor: 1,264 square feet
Second Floor: 556 square feet
Total: 1,820 square feet

● The look to this A-frame is dramatic. The soaring roof projections highlight the slanted glass gable end. The expanse of the roof is broken to provide access to the side deck from the dining room. Above is the balcony of the second-floor lounge. This room with its high sloping ceiling looks down into the spacious first-floor living room. The master bedroom also has an outdoor balcony. There are two large bedrooms, a kitchen, a big dining room and huge living room downstairs.

Design N2431

First Floor: 1,057 square feet
Second Floor: 406 square feet
Total: 1,463 square feet

● A favorite everywhere, the A-frame vacation home is easily recognizable. Inside, the beauty of architectural detailing is apparent. The living room sports a high ceiling which slopes and has exposed beams. The second-floor master suite has a private balcony, private bath and lounge. Don't miss the raised-hearth fireplace for cozy winter nights.

When You're Ready To Order . . .

Let Us Show You Our Home Blueprint Package.

Building a home? Planning a home? Our Blueprint Package contains nearly everything you need to get the job done right, whether you're working on your own or with help from an architect, designer, builder or subcontractors. Each Blueprint Package is the result of many hours of work by licensed architects or professional designers.

QUALITY

Hundreds of hours of painstaking effort have gone into the development of your blueprint set. Each home has been quality-checked by professionals to insure accuracy and buildability.

VALUE

Because we sell in volume, you can buy professional-quality blueprints at a fraction of their development cost. With our plans, your dream home design costs only a few hundred dollars, not the thousands of dollars that custom architects charge.

SERVICE

Once you've chosen your favorite home plan, you'll receive fast efficient service whether you choose to mail your order to us or call us toll free at 1-800-521-6797.

SATISFACTION

Our years of service to satisfied home plan buyers provide us the experience and knowledge that guarantee your satisfaction with our product and performance.

ORDER TOLL FREE 1-800-521-6797

After you've studied our Blueprint Package and Important Extras on the following pages, simply mail the accompanying order form on page 349 or call toll free on our Blueprint Hotline: 1-800-521-6797. We're ready and eager to serve you.

Each set of blueprints is an interrelated collection of floor plans, interior and exterior elevations, dimensions, cross-sections, diagrams and notations showing precisely how your house is to be constructed.

Among the sheets included may be:

Frontal Sheet
This artist's sketch of the exterior of the house, done in realistic perspective, gives you an idea of how the house will look when built and landscaped. Large ink-line floor plans show all levels of the house and provide a quick overview of your new home's livability, as well as a handy reference for studying furniture placement.

Foundation Plan
Drawn to 1/4-inch scale, this sheet shows the complete foundation layout including support

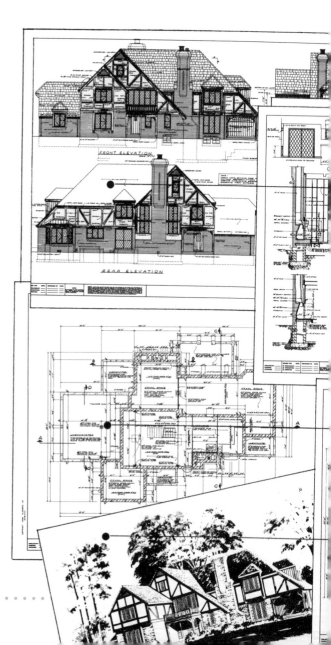

walls, excavated and unexcavated areas, if any, and foundation notes. If slab construction rather than basement, the plan shows footings and details for a monolithic slab. This page, or another in the set, also includes a sample plot plan for locating your house on a building site.

Detailed Floor Plans

Complete in 1/4-inch scale, these plans show the layout of each floor of the house. All rooms and interior spaces are carefully dimensioned and keys are provided for cross-section details given later in the plans. The positions of all electrical outlets and switches are clearly shown.

House Cross-Sections

Large-scale views, normally drawn at 3/8-inch equals 1 foot, show sections or cut-aways of the foundation, interior walls, exterior walls,

floors, stairways and roof details. Additional cross-sections are given to show important changes in floor, ceiling or roof heights or the relationship of one level to another. Extremely valuable for construction, these sections show exactly how the various parts of the house fit together.

Interior Elevations

These large-scale drawings show the design and placement of kitchen and bathroom cabinets, laundry areas, fireplaces, bookcases and other built-ins. Little "extras," such as mantelpiece and wainscoting drawings, plus moulding sections, provide details that give your home that custom touch.

Exterior Elevations

Drawings in 1/4-inch scale show the front, rear and sides of your house and give necessary notes on exterior materials and finishes. Particular attention is given to cornice detail, brick and stone accents or other finish items that make your home distinctive.

Sample Package

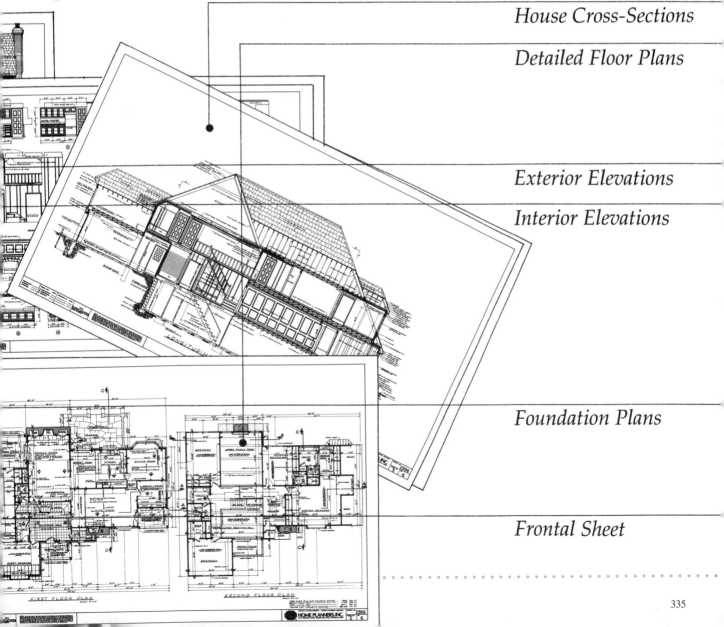

House Cross-Sections

Detailed Floor Plans

Exterior Elevations

Interior Elevations

Foundation Plans

Frontal Sheet

Important Extras To Do The Job Right!

Introducing eight important planning and construction aids developed by our professionals to help you succeed in your home-building project.

MATERIALS LIST & DETAILED COST ESTIMATE

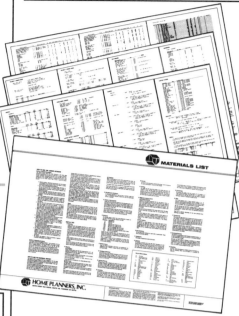

The **Materials List** outlines the quantity, type and size of materials needed to build your house. Included are framing lumber, windows and doors, kitchen and bath cabinetry, rough and finish hardware, and much more. This handy list helps you or your builder cost out materials and serves as a reference sheet when you're compiling bids.

The **Quote One™ Detailed Cost Estimate** matches line for line over 1,000 items in the Materials List (which is included when you purchase this estimating tool). It allows you to determine building costs for your specific area and for your specific home design. Space is allowed for additional estimates from contractors and subcontractors. (See **Quote One™** below for further information.)

Make informed decisions about your home-building project with a customized materials take-off and a Quote One™ Detailed Cost Estimate. These tools are invaluable in planning and estimating the cost of your new home.

The Materials List/Detailed Cost Estimate package can be ordered up to 6 months after a blueprint order. Because of the diversity of local building codes, the Materials List does not include mechanical materials. Detailed Cost Estimates are available for select Home Planners plans only. Consult a customer service representative for currently available designs.

SPECIFICATION OUTLINE

This valuable 16-page document is critical to building your house correctly. Designed to be filled in by you or your builder, this book lists 166 stages or items crucial to the building process. It provides a comprehensive review of the construction process and helps in making choices of materials. When combined with the blueprints, a signed contract, and a schedule, it becomes a legal document and record for the building of your home.

QUOTE ONE™

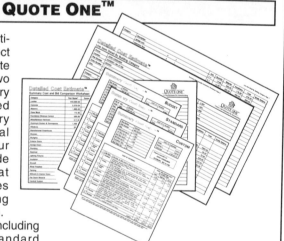

This new service helps you estimate the cost of building select Home Planners designs. Quote One™ system is available in two separate stages: The Summary Cost Report and the Detailed Cost Estimate. The Summary Cost Report shows the total cost per square foot for your chosen home in your zip-code area and then breaks that cost down into ten categories showing the costs for building materials, labor and installation. The total cost for the report (including three grades: Budget, Standard and Custom) is just $25 for one home; and additionals are only $15. These reports allow you to evaluate your building budget and compare the costs of building a variety of homes in your area.

The Detailed Cost Estimate furnishes an even more detailed report. The material and installation (labor + equipment) cost is shown for each of over 1,000 line items provided in the Standard grade. Space is allowed for additional estimates from contractors and subcontractors. This invaluable tool is available for a price of $110 ($120 for a Schedule E plan) which includes the price of a materials list which must be purchased at the same time.

To order these invaluable reports, use the order form on page 349 or call **1-800-521-6797**.

CONSTRUCTION INFORMATION

If you want to know more about techniques—and deal more confidently with subcontractors—we offer these useful sheets. Each set is an excellent tool that will add to your understanding of these technical subjects.

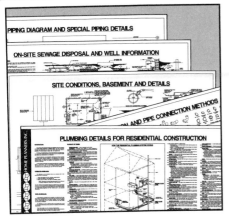

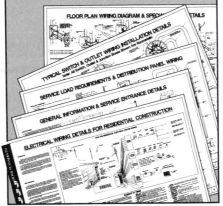

PLUMBING

The Blueprint Package includes locations for all the plumbing fixtures in your new house, including sinks, lavatories, tubs, showers, toilets, laundry trays and water heaters. However, if you want to know more about the complete plumbing system, these 24x36-inch detail sheets will prove very useful. Prepared to meet requirements of the National Plumbing Code, these six fact-filled sheets give general information on pipe schedules, fittings, sump-pump details, water-softener hookups, septic system details and much more. Color-coded sheets include a glossary of terms.

ELECTRICAL

The locations for every electrical switch, plug and outlet are shown in your Blueprint Package. However, these Electrical Details go further to take the mystery out of household electrical systems. Prepared to meet requirements of the National Electrical Code, these comprehensive 24x36-inch drawings come packed with helpful information, including wire sizing, switch-installation schematics, cable-routing details, appliance wattage, door-bell hookups, typical service panel circuitry and much more. Six sheets are bound together and color-coded for easy reference. A glossary of terms is also included.

CONSTRUCTION

The Blueprint Package contains everything an experienced builder needs to construct a particular house. However, it doesn't show all the ways that houses can be built, nor does it explain alternate construction methods. To help you understand how your house will be built—and offer additional techniques—this set of drawings depicts the materials and methods used to build foundations, fireplaces, walls, floors and roofs. Where appropriate, the drawings show acceptable alternatives. These six sheets will answer questions for the advanced do-it-yourselfer or home planner.

MECHANICAL

This package contains fundamental principles and useful data that will help you make informed decisions and communicate with subcontractors about heating and cooling systems. The 24x36-inch drawings contain instructions and samples that allow you to make simple load calculations and preliminary sizing and costing analysis. Covered are today's most commonly used systems from heat pumps to solar fuel systems. The package is packed full of illustrations and diagrams to help you visualize components and how they relate to one another.

Plan-A-Home®

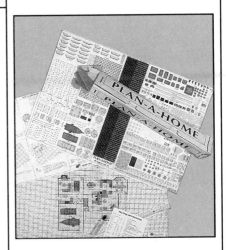

Plan-A-Home® is an easy-to-use tool that helps you design a new home, arrange furniture in a new or existing home, or plan a remodeling project. Each package contains:

- **More than 700 reusable peel-off planning symbols** on a self-stick vinyl sheet, including walls, windows, doors, all types of furniture, kitchen components, bath fixtures and many more.

- **A reusable, transparent, 1/4-inch scale planning grid** that matches the scale of actual working drawings (1/4-inch equals 1 foot). This grid provides the basis for house layouts of up to 140x92 feet.

- **Tracing paper** and a protective sheet for copying or transferring your completed plan.

- **A felt-tip pen,** with water-soluble ink that wipes away quickly.

Plan-A-Home® lets you lay out areas as large as a 7,500 square foot, six-bedroom, seven-bath house.

To Order, Call Toll Free 1-800-521-6797

To add these important extras to your Blueprint Package, simply indicate your choices on the order form on page 349 or call us Toll Free 1-800-521-6797 and we'll tell you more about these exciting products.

337

D *The Deck Blueprint Package*

Many of the homes in this book can be enhanced with a professionally designed Deck Plan. Those home plans highlighted with a D have a matching or corresponding deck plan available which includes a Deck Plan Frontal Sheet, Deck Framing and Floor Plans, Deck Elevations and a Deck Materials List. A Standard Deck Details Package, also available, provides all the how-to information necessary for building *any* deck. Our Complete Deck Building Package contains 1 set of Custom Deck Plans of your choice, plus 1 set of Standard Deck Building Details all for one low price. Our plans and details are carefully prepared in an easy-to-understand format that will guide you through every stage of your deck-building project. See these pages for 25 different Deck layouts to match your favorite house.

SPLIT–LEVEL SUN DECK
Deck Plan D100

BI–LEVEL DECK WITH COVERED DINING
Deck Plan D101

FRESH–AIR CORNER DECK
Deck Plan D102

BACK–YARD EXTENDER DECK
Deck Plan D103

WRAP–AROUND FAMILY DECK
Deck Plan D104

DRAMATIC DECK WITH BARBECUE
Deck Plan D105

SPLIT–PLAN COUNTRY DECK
Deck Plan D106

DECK FOR DINING AND VIEWS
Deck Plan D107

BOLD, ANGLED CORNER DECK
Deck Plan D108

SPECTACULAR "RESORT–STYLE" DECK
Deck Plan D109

TREND–SETTER DECK
Deck Plan D110

TURN–OF–THE–CENTURY DECK
Deck Plan D111

WEEKEND ENTERTAINER DECK
Deck Plan D112

STRIKING "DELTA" DECK
Deck Plan D113

CENTER–VIEW DECK
Deck Plan D114

KITCHEN–EXTENDER DECK
Deck Plan D115

BI–LEVEL RETREAT DECK
Deck Plan D116

SPLIT–LEVEL ACTIVITY DECK
Deck Plan D117

OUTDOOR LIFESTYLE DECK
Deck Plan D118

TRI–LEVEL DECK WITH GRILL
Deck Plan D119

CONTEMPORARY LEISURE DECK
Deck Plan D120

ANGULAR WINGED DECK
Deck Plan D121

DECK FOR A SPLIT–LEVEL HOME
Deck Plan D122

GRACIOUS GARDEN DECK
Deck Plan D123

TERRACED DECK FOR ENTERTAINING
Deck Plan D124

For Deck Plan prices and ordering
information, see pages 344-349.
Or call **Toll Free,**
1-800-521-6797.

⬛ The Landscape Blueprint Package

For the homes marked with an ⬛ in this book, Home Planners has created a front-yard landscape plan that matches or is complementary in design to the house plan. These comprehensive blueprint packages include a Frontal Sheet, Plan View, Regionalized Plant & Materials List, a sheet on Planting and Maintaining Your Landscape, Zone Maps and Plant Size and Description Guide. These plans will help you achieve professional results, adding value and enjoyment to your property for years to come. Each set of blueprints is a full 18" x 24" in size with clear, complete instructions and easy-to-read type. See the following pages for 40-different front-yard Landscape Plans to match your favorite house.

Regional Order Map

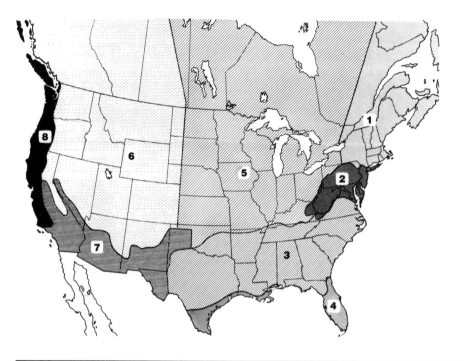

Most of the Landscape Plans shown on these pages are available with a Plant & Materials List adapted by horticultural experts to 8 different regions of the country. Please specify Geographic Region when ordering your plan. See pages 344-349 for prices, ordering information and regional availability.

Region	1	Northeast
Region	2	Mid-Atlantic
Region	3	Deep South
Region	4	Florida & Gulf Coast
Region	5	Midwest
Region	6	Rocky Mountains
Region	7	Southern California & Desert Southwest
Region	8	Northern California & Pacific Northwest

CAPE COD TRADITIONAL
Landscape Plan L200

WILLIAMSBURG CAPE
Landscape Plan L201

CAPE COD COTTAGE
Landscape Plan L202

GAMBREL–ROOF COLONIAL
Landscape Plan L203

CENTER–HALL COLONIAL
Landscape Plan L204

CLASSIC NEW ENGLAND COLONIAL
Landscape Plan L205

SOUTHERN COLONIAL
Landscape Plan L206

COUNTRY–STYLE FARMHOUSE
Landscape Plan L207

PENNSYLVANIA STONE FARMHOUSE
Landscape Plan L208

RAISED–PORCH FARMHOUSE
Landscape Plan L209

NEW ENGLAND BARN–STYLE HOUSE
Landscape Plan L210

NEW ENGLAND COUNTRY HOUSE
Landscape Plan L211

TRADITIONAL COUNTRY ESTATE
Landscape Plan L212

FRENCH PROVINCIAL ESTATE
Landscape Plan L213

GEORGIAN MANOR
Landscape Plan L214

GRAND–PORTICO GEORGIAN
Landscape Plan L215

BRICK FEDERAL
Landscape Plan L216

COUNTRY FRENCH RAMBLER
Landscape Plan L217

FRENCH MANOR HOUSE
Landscape Plan L218

ELIZABETHAN TUDOR
Landscape Plan L219

TUDOR ONE–STORY
Landscape Plan L220

ENGLISH–STYLE COTTAGE
Landscape Plan L221

MEDIEVAL GARRISON
Landscape Plan L222

QUEEN ANNE VICTORIAN
Landscape Plan L223

GOTHIC VICTORIAN
Landscape Plan L224

BASIC RANCH
Landscape Plan L225

L–SHAPED RANCH
Landscape Plan L226

SPRAWLING RANCH
Landscape Plan L227

TRADITIONAL SPLIT–LEVEL
Landscape Plan L228

SHED–ROOF CONTEMPORARY
Landscape Plan L229

WOOD–SIDED CONTEMPORARY
Landscape Plan L230

HILLSIDE CONTEMPORARY
Landscape Plan L231

FLORIDA RAMBLER
Landscape Plan L232

CALIFORNIA STUCCO
Landscape Plan L233

LOW–GABLE CONTEMPORARY
Landscape Plan L234

NORTHERN BRICK CHATEAU
Landscape Plan L235

MISSION–TILE RANCH
Landscape Plan L236

ADOBE–BLOCK HACIENDA
Landscape Plan L237

COURTYARD PATIO HOME
Landscape Plan L238

CENTER–COURT CONTEMPORARY
Landscape Plan L239

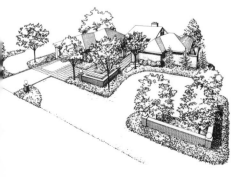

For Landscape Plan prices and ordering information, see pages 344-349.

 Or call **Toll Free,**
1-800-521-6797.

343

Price Schedule & Plans Index

House Blueprint Price Schedule
(Prices guaranteed through December 31, 1996)

	1-set Study Package	4-set Building Package	8-set Building Package	1-set Reproducible Sepias	Home Customizer® Package
Schedule A	$280	$325	$385	$485	$535
Schedule B	$320	$365	$425	$545	$595
Schedule C	$360	$405	$465	$605	$655
Schedule D	$400	$445	$505	$665	$715
Schedule E	$520	$565	$625	$725	$775

Additional Identical Blueprints in same order................$50 per set
Reverse Blueprints (mirror image).....................$50 per set
Specification Outlines ....$10 each
Materials Lists (not available for California Service):
    Schedule A-D $50
    Schedule E $60
Exchanges.......$50 exchange fee for the first set; $10 for each additional set
    $70 total exchange fee for 4 sets
    $100 total exchange fee for 8 sets

Deck Plans Price Schedule

CUSTOM DECK PLANS

Price Group	Q	R	S
1 Set Custom Plans	$25	$30	$35

  Additional identical sets:...$10 each
  Reverse sets (mirror image):...$10 each

STANDARD DECK DETAILS
1 Set Generic Construction Details...$14.95 each

COMPLETE DECK BUILDING PACKAGE

Price Group	Q	R	S
1 Set Custom Plans 1 Set Standard Deck Details	$35	$40	$45

Landscape Plans Price Schedule

Price Group	X	Y	Z
1 set	$35	$45	$55
3 sets	$50	$60	$70
6 sets	$65	$75	$85

Additional Identical Sets ....$10 each
Reverse Sets (mirror image) ....$10 each

These pages contain all the information you need to price your blueprints. In general the larger and more complicated the house, the more it costs to design and thus the higher the price we must charge for the blueprints. Remember, however, that these prices are far less than you would normally pay for the services of a licensed architect or professional designer.

Custom home designs and related architectural services often cost thousands of dollars, ranging from 5% to 15% of the cost of construction. By ordering our blueprints you are potentially saving enough money to afford a larger house, or to add those "extra" amenities such as a patio, deck, swimming pool or even an upgraded kitchen or luxurious master suite.

Index

To use the Index below, refer to the design number listed in numerical order (a helpful page reference is also given). Note the price index letter and refer to the House Blueprint Price Schedule above for the cost of one, four or eight sets of blueprints or the cost of a reproducible sepia. Additional prices are shown for identical and reverse blueprint sets, as well as a very useful Materials List for some of the plans. Also note in the Index below those plans that have matching or complementary Deck Plans or Landscape Plans. Refer to the schedules above for prices of these plans. All designs can be customized with our exclusive Home Customizer® Package. See page 349 for more information. Some plans are also part of our

Quote One™ estimating service, indicated by this symbol: 🏠. See page 336 for more information. For our customers in California, we now offer California Engineered Plans (CEP) and California Stock Plans (CSP) to help in meeting the strict California building codes. Check Plan Index for homes that are available through this new service or call 1-800-521-6797 for more information about the availability of the service and prices.

To Order: Fill in and send the order form on page 349—or call toll free 1-800-521-6797 or 520-297-8200. If you prefer, send it on our FAX line: 1-800-224-6699 or 1-520-544-3086.

DESIGN	PRICE	PAGE	CALIFORNIA PLANS	QUOTE ONE™	DECK	DECK PRICE	LANDSCAPE	LANDSCAPE PRICE	REGIONS
N1989	C	299			D100	Q	L220	Y	1-3,5,6,8
N1993	D	37					L213	Z	1-8
N2131	B	59			D117	S	L203	Y	1-3,5,6,8
N2133	D	24			D106	S			
N2135	C	268							
N2142	C	302			D106	S			
N2145	A	196		🏠			L209	Y	1-6,8
N2146	A	197			D114	R	L203	Y	1-3,5,6,8
N2170	B	213					L221	X	1-3,5,6,8
N2176	B	32			D112	R	L206	Z	1-6,8
N2181	C	275			D100	Q	L226	X	1-8
N2192	D	27			D117	S	L218	Z	1-6,8
N2206	B	216		🏠			L220	Y	1-3,5,6,8
N2211	B	42			D117	S	L201	Y	1-3,5,6,8
N2220	C	282			D114	R	L217	Y	1-8
N2256	C	276							
N2283	C	29			D114	R	L206	Z	1-6,8
N2318	B	298					L220	Y	1-3,5,6,8
N2356	D	79			D119	S	L219	Z	1-3,5,6,8
N2391	C	74							
N2396	B	60			D100	Q			
N2427	A	332							
N2431	A	333							
N2459	A	333							
N2485	B	331							
N2488	A	322	✓	🏠	D102	Q			
N2489	A	330							
N2490	A	103		🏠					
N2491	A	67		🏠					
N2505	A	227		🏠	D113	R	L226	X	1-8
N2511	B	314			D108	R	L229	Y	1-8
N2515	C	302			D101	R			
N2519	C	289							
N2520	B	4			D105	R	L201	Y	1-3,5,6,8
N2533	B	230							
N2534	D	276		🏠			L227	Z	1-8
N2538	B	45			D113	R	L201	Y	1-3,5,6,8
N2540	B	83			D113	R	L205	Y	1-3,5,6,8
N2543	D	35			D107	S	L218	Z	1-6,8
N2544	C	279			D124	S			
N2559	B	203			D112	R			
N2562	D	100			D122	S			
N2563	B	5		🏠	D114	R	L201	Y	1-3,5,6,8
N2565	B	221		🏠	D101	R	L225	X	1-3,5,6,8
N2569	A	198			D112	R	L200	X	1-3,5,6,8
N2570	A	212			D113	R	L225	X	1-3,5,6,8
N2573	C	296	✓		D114	R	L220	Y	1-3,5,6,8
N2594	C	281			D120	R			
N2596	B	197			D114	R	L201	Y	1-3,5,6,8
N2597	B	235		🏠	D114	R	L226	X	1-8
N2603	B	241		🏠	D106	S	L220	Y	1-3,5,6,8
N2606	A	216		🏠			L221	X	1-3,5,6,8
N2607	A	215					L220	Y	1-3,5,6,8
N2608	A	320		🏠	D112	R	L228	Y	1-8
N2610	C	38		🏠	D114	R	L204	Y	1-3,5,6,8
N2615	D	201			D106	S	L211	Y	1-8
N2622	A	45		🏠	D103	R	L200	X	1-3,5,6,8
N2628	A	320			D105	R	L234	Y	1-8
N2633	C	28							
N2640	B	39			D114	R	L205	Y	1-3,5,6,8
N2657	B	196		🏠			L200	X	1-3,5,6,8
N2659	B	41		🏠	D113	R	L205	Y	1-3,5,6,8
N2661	A	56	✓	🏠	D113	R	L202	X	1-3,5,6,8
N2662	C	31		🏠			L216	Y	1-3,5,6,8
N2665	D	51	✓	🏠					
N2667	B	49					L216	Y	1-3,5,6,8
N2668	B	48		🏠			L214	Z	1-3,5,6,8
N2670	D	261	✓	🏠			L236	Z	3,4,7
N2671	B	255		🏠	D114	R	L234	Y	1-8
N2672	B	234		🏠	D112	R	L226	X	1-8
N2675	C	275			D106	S			
N2678	B	215			D117	S	L220	Y	1-3,5,6,8
N2679	C	310							
N2680	C	56			D114	R	L224	Y	1-3,5,6,8
N2682	A	194		🏠	D115	Q	L200	X	1-3,5,6,8
N2683	D	3		🏠	D101	R	L214	Z	1-3,5,6,8
N2684	C	57			D114	R	L204	Y	1-3,5,6,8
N2693	D	285							
N2694	C	150	✓	🏠			L209	Y	1-6,8
N2699	C	200		🏠			L211	Y	1-8
N2707	A	223		🏠	D117	S	L226	X	1-8
N2711	B	108	✓	🏠	D105	R	L229	Y	1-8
N2716	C	314					L229	Y	1-8
N2728	B	214			D112	R	L221	X	1-3,5,6,8
N2729	B	109					L234	Y	1-8
N2731	B	42			D114	R	L205	Y	1-3,5,6,8
N2733	B	44		🏠	D100	Q	L205	Y	1-3,5,6,8
N2737	B	217					L220	Y	1-3,5,6,8
N2738	B	241							
N2739	D	288							
N2745	C	279							
N2756	C	274			D101	R	L234	Y	1-8
N2766	C	275			D101	R			
N2767	D	278			D106	S			
N2768	D	278							
N2769	C	319							
N2774	B	2	✓	🏠	D100	Q	L207	Z	1-6,8
N2776	B	158		🏠	D113	R	L207	Z	1-6,8
N2778	C	280			D120	R			
N2779	D	284		🏠	D100	Q	L217	Y	1-8
N2781	C	106		🏠	D121	S	L230	Z	1-8
N2783	D	288					L211	Y	1-8
N2784	C	281							
N2785	C	303			D100	Q	L220	Y	1-3,5,6,8
N2786	B	318							
N2787	B	318			D105	R	L228	Y	1-8
N2789	C	257			D117	S	L228	Y	1-8
N2791	D	265							
N2795	B	255							
N2800	B	69		🏠	D113	R	L220	Y	1-3,5,6,8
N2802	B	218		🏠	D118	R	L220	Y	1-3,5,6,8
N2803	B	218		🏠	D118	R	L225	X	1-3,5,6,8
N2804	B	218		🏠	D118	R	L232	Y	4,7
N2805	B	219		🏠	D113	R	L220	Y	1-3,5,6,8
N2806	B	219		🏠	D113	R	L220	Y	1-3,5,6,8
N2807	B	219		🏠	D113	R	L220	Y	1-3,5,6,8
N2810	B	238			D112	R	L204	Y	1-3,5,6,8
N2811	B	238			D112	R	L204	Y	1-3,5,6,8
N2812	B	239			D112	R	L204	Y	1-3,5,6,8
N2813	B	239			D112	R	L204	Y	1-3,5,6,8
N2814	B	238			D112	R	L204	Y	1-3,5,6,8
N2815	B	238			D112	R	L204	Y	1-3,5,6,8
N2816	B	239			D112	R	L204	Y	1-3,5,6,8
N2817	B	239			D112	R	L204	Y	1-3,5,6,8
N2818	B	256		🏠	D101	R	L234	Y	1-8
N2822	A	104	✓	🏠			L229	Y	1-8
N2823	B	315		🏠	D112	R	L229	Y	1-8
N2824	B	254							
N2826	B	92		🏠	D116	R			
N2828	B	317							
N2832	C	269			D113	R			
N2841	B	308					L208	Z	1,2,5,6,8
N2843	C	182					L228	Y	1-8
N2850	C	182			D122	S	L236	Z	3,4,7
N2851	C	283		🏠			L217	Y	1-8
N2854	B	69		🏠	D112	R	L220	Y	1-3,5,6,8
N2855	B	77			D103	R	L219	Z	1-3,5,6,8
N2857	D	267					L239	Z	1-8
N2858	C	266							
N2864	A	253	✓	🏠	D100	Q	L225	X	1-3,5,6,8
N2867	C	273					L220	Y	1-3,5,6,8
N2869	B	225							
N2871	B	254		🏠	D117	S			
N2875	B	185		🏠	D113	R	L236	Z	3,4,7

DESIGN	PRICE	PAGE	CALIFORNIA PLANS	QUOTE ONE™	DECK	DECK PRICE	LANDSCAPE	LANDSCAPE PRICE	REGIONS
N2877	C	297			D114	R	L220	Y	1-3,5,6,8
N2878	B	15	✔	🏠	D112	R	L200	X	1-3,5,6,8
N2879	D	277		🏠					
N2880	C	291		🏠	D114	R	L212	Z	1-8
N2883	C	205							
N2887	A	207							
N2888	D	290					L211	Y	1-8
N2889	D	17	✔	🏠	D107	S	L215	Z	1-6,8
N2894	C	7					L229	Y	1-8
N2901	C	312					L229	Y	1-8
N2902	B	252		🏠			L234	Y	1-8
N2905	B	100		🏠	D121	S	L229	Y	1-8
N2907	B	152					L224	Y	1-8
N2908	B	149	✔	🏠	D117	S	L205	Y	1-3,5,6,8
N2911	A	240							
N2912	B	191		🏠					
N2913	B	253			D124	S			
N2915	C	9	✔	🏠	D114	R	L212	Z	1-8
N2916	B	291					L221	X	1-3,5,6,8
N2917	B	252					L221	X	1-3,5,6,8
N2920	D	8	✔	🏠	D104	S	L212	Z	1-8
N2921	D	6	✔	🏠	D104	S	L212	Z	1-8
N2922	D	188	✔	🏠					
N2925	B	108							
N2926	D	305							
N2927	B	90	✔	🏠	D100	Q			
N2929	B	212							
N2931	B	225							
N2937	C	316		🏠			L229	Y	1-8
N2938	E	264					L221	X	1-3,5,6,8
N2940	E	118		🏠	D114	R	L230	Z	1-8
N2941	B	220		🏠	D112	R			
N2942	B	220		🏠	D112	R			
N2943	B	220		🏠	D112	R			
N2944	C	310							
N2945	B	151							
N2946	C	16		🏠	D114	R	L207	Z	1-6,8
N2947	B	14	✔	🏠	D112	R	L200	X	1-3,5,6,8
N2948	B	166	✔	🏠					
N2949	C	161	✔	🏠					
N2950	C	167	✔	🏠					
N2951	E	122							
N2952	E	116					L235	Z	1-3,5,6,8
N2953	E	115	✔	🏠	D111	S	L223	Z	1-3,5,6,8
N2954	E	114					L223	Z	1-3,5,6,8
N2955	E	123							
N2956	E	117							
N2957	D	73			D107	S	L218	Z	1-6,8
N2959	B	72		🏠					
N2961	D	297							
N2962	B	299		🏠					
N2963	D	30							
N2964	B	204		🏠					
N2966	D	304							
N2967	B	66					L217	Y	1-8
N2968	E	119		🏠			L227	Z	1-8
N2969	C	140			D110	R	L223	Z	1-3,5,6,8
N2970	D	141	✔	🏠			L223	Z	1-3,5,6,8
N2971	C	134					L223	Z	1-3,5,6,8
N2972	B	136					L223	Z	1-3,5,6,8
N2973	B	136	✔	🏠			L223	Z	1-3,5,6,8
N2974	A	133	✔	🏠			L223	Z	1-3,5,6,8
N2975	D	30							
N2977	D	25		🏠			L214	Z	1-3,5,6,8
N2979	C	49							
N2981	D	153					L224	Y	1-3,5,6,8
N2984	E	18					L214	Z	1-3,5,6,8
N2989	D	128		🏠			L215	Z	1-6,8
N2992	E	127	✔	🏠	D103	R	L203	Y	1-3,5,6,8
N2993	D	125		🏠	D115	Q	L214	Z	1-3,5,6,8
N2995	D	198	✔	🏠	D106	S	L217	Y	1-8
N3126	A	199			D114	R	L203	Y	1-3,5,6,8
N3300	E	120					L230	Z	1-8
N3301	E	124		🏠					

DESIGN	PRICE	PAGE	CALIFORNIA PLANS	QUOTE ONE™	DECK	DECK PRICE	LANDSCAPE	LANDSCAPE PRICE	REGIONS
N3302	A	68		🏠			L205	Y	1-3,5,6,8
N3303	D	19		🏠			L215	Z	1-6,8
N3304	E	144		🏠			L209	Y	1-6,8
N3305	E	121							
N3307	C	159		🏠	D111	S	L207	Z	1-6,8
N3308	E	145		🏠			L207	Z	1-6,8
N3309	B	137	✔	🏠			L209	Y	1-6,8
N3310	C	33		🏠	D111	S	L227	Z	1-8
N3311	D	306		🏠	D109	S	L220	Y	1-3,5,6,8
N3313	B	208		🏠			L200	X	1-3,5,6,8
N3314	B	12	✔	🏠			L200	X	1-3,5,6,8
N3315	D	13		🏠			L200	X	1-3,5,6,8
N3316	A	193		🏠			L202	X	1-3,5,6,8
N3318	B	202		🏠	D111	S	L202	X	1-3,5,6,8
N3319	C	294		🏠	D112	R	L217	Y	1-8
N3320	D	20		🏠			L215	Z	1-6,8
N3321	C	206		🏠	D116	R	L209	Y	1-6,8
N3322	C	169		🏠	D118	R	L234	Y	1-8
N3323	C	175		🏠			L223	Z	1-3,5,6,8
N3324	E	157			D114	R	L207	Z	1-6,8
N3325	C	152	✔	🏠	D100	Q	L238	Y	3,4,7,8
N3326	C	93		🏠			L220	Y	1-3,5,6,8
N3327	C	271		🏠	D110	R	L217	Y	1-8
N3328	D	154		🏠					
N3329	C	261		🏠			L233	Y	3,4,7
N3330	A	95		🏠					
N3331	A	67	✔	🏠			L203	Y	1-3,5,6,8
N3332	B	293	✔	🏠			L200	X	1-3,5,6,8
N3333	C	81		🏠			L204	Y	1-3,5,6,8
N3334	C	64		🏠			L207	Z	1-6,8
N3335	C	75		🏠			L201	X	1-3,5,6,8
N3336	B	270		🏠			L200	X	1-3,5,6,8
N3337	D	22		🏠			L214	Z	1-3,5,6,8
N3338	B	102		🏠			L204	Y	1-3,5,6,8
N3339	B	21		🏠			L215	Z	1-6,8
N3340	B	11		🏠			L224	Y	1-3,5,6,8
N3341	B	327		🏠			L234	Y	1-8
N3342	B	66		🏠			L217	Y	1-8
N3343	C	63		🏠			L202	X	1-3,5,6,8
N3344	D	184		🏠			L211	Y	1-8
N3345	B	209		🏠			L220	Y	1-3,5,6,8
N3346	B	300		🏠			L204	Y	1-3,5,6,8
N3347	D	102		🏠			L230	Z	1-8
N3348	C	292	✔	🏠			L200	X	1-3,5,6,8
N3349	E	26		🏠	D107	S	L216	Y	1-3,5,6,8
N3350	B	226		🏠	D115	Q	L205	Y	1-3,5,6,8
N3351	C	203		🏠	D115	Q	L209	Y	1-6,8
N3352	B	98		🏠	D108	R	L229	Y	1-8
N3353	C	204		🏠	D113	R	L206	Z	1-6,8
N3354	E	75		🏠	D104	S	L212	Z	1-8
N3355	A	10		🏠	D117	S	L220	Y	1-3,5,6,8
N3356	C	91		🏠	D103	R	L217	Y	1-8
N3357	D	262		🏠	D115	Q	L211	Y	1-8
N3360	D	308		🏠			L207	Z	1-6,8
N3361	D	307		🏠			L230	Z	1-8
N3362	D	311		🏠					
N3364	D	111		🏠			L204	Y	1-3,5,6,8
N3366	D	309		🏠			L220	Y	1-3,5,6,8
N3368	C	263		🏠	D104	S	L220	Y	1-3,5,6,8
N3369	E	74		🏠	D121	S	L206	Z	1-6,8
N3372	C	62		🏠	D102	Q	L200	X	1-3,5,6,8
N3373	A	224	✔	🏠	D110	R	L202	X	1-3,5,6,8
N3374	A	224		🏠	D110	R	L202	X	1-3,5,6,8
N3375	A	224		🏠	D110	R	L202	X	1-3,5,6,8
N3376	B	210		🏠	D114	R	L205	Y	1-3,5,6,8
N3380	E	23		🏠					
N3381	E	76		🏠	D106	S	L204	Y	1-3,5,6,8
N3382	C	129		🏠	D110	R	L202	X	1-3,5,6,8
N3383	C	131		🏠	D111	S	L205	Y	1-3,5,6,8
N3384	C	131		🏠	D115	Q	L207	Z	1-6,8
N3385	C	132		🏠	D100	Q	L207	Z	1-6,8
N3386	E	139		🏠	D111	S	L216	Y	1-3,5,6,8
N3389	C	135		🏠	D115	Q	L205	Y	1-3,5,6,8
N3390	C	132		🏠	D106	S	L207	Z	1-6,8

DESIGN	PRICE	PAGE	CALIFORNIA PLANS	QUOTE ONE™	DECK	DECK PRICE	LANDSCAPE	LANDSCAPE PRICE	REGIONS
N3392	D	142		🏠	D110	R	L223	Z	1-3,5,6,8
N3393	C	135		🏠	D115	Q	L207	Z	1-6,8
N3394	D	138		🏠	D111	S	L207	Z	1-6,8
N3395	E	113		🏠	D111	S	L223	Z	1-3,5,6,8
N3396	C	154		🏠	D111	S	L207	Z	1-6,8
N3397	D	156	✔		D110	R	L209	Y	1-6,8
N3398	C	155		🏠	D111	S	L224	Y	1-3,5,6,8
N3399	D	157		🏠	D110	R	L224	Y	1-3,5,6,8
N3400	C	260		🏠			L236	Z	3,4,7
N3403	C	192	✔	🏠			L237	Y	7
N3404	D	97		🏠			L230	Z	1-8
N3405	D	161	✔	🏠			L236	Z	3,4,7
N3407	D	183		🏠			L237	Y	7
N3409	D	101		🏠			L230	Z	1-8
N3411	C	258		🏠			L233	Y	3,4,7
N3412	B	173		🏠			L233	Y	3,4,7
N3413	C	165		🏠			L238	Y	3,4,7,8
N3414	C	176		🏠			L233	Y	3,4,7
N3415	C	258		🏠			L233	Y	3,4,7
N3416	A	325		🏠			L239	Z	1-8
N3417	A	47		🏠			L239	Z	1-8
N3419	B	168		🏠			L239	Z	1-8
N3420	B	178	✔	🏠			L233	Y	3,4,7
N3421	B	164		🏠			L238	Y	3,4,7,8
N3422	B	168		🏠			L239	Z	1-8
N3423	C	170		🏠					
N3424	B	174		🏠			L233	Y	3,4,7
N3425	C	176		🏠					
N3427	C	170		🏠			L239	Z	1-8
N3429	C	181		🏠			L233	Y	3,4,7
N3420	C	173		🏠			L233	Y	3,4,7
N3431	B	187	✔	🏠					
N3432	C	179		🏠			L233	Y	3,4,7
N3433	C	187		🏠			L213	Z	1-8
N3434	D	186		🏠			L233	Y	3,4,7
N3435	C	177		🏠			L227	Z	1-8
N3436	C	190	✔	🏠			L227	Z	1-8
N3437	C	177		🏠			L212	Z	1-8
N3438	C	112		🏠			L209	Y	1-6,8
N3439	C	107		🏠			L205	Y	1-3,5,6,8
N3440	C	172		🏠			L233	Y	3,4,7
N3441	C	180	✔	🏠			L239	Z	1-8
N3442	A	242		🏠	D115	Q	L200	X	1-3,5,6,8
N3443	B	146		🏠	D110	R	L220	Y	1-3,5,6,8
N3444	B	86		🏠	D105	R	L220	Y	1-3,5,6,8
N3445	B	89		🏠	D114	R	L205	Y	1-3,5,6,8
N3446	C	110		🏠	D115	Q	L220	Y	1-3,5,6,8
N3447	D	180		🏠	D120	R	L237	Y	7
N3449	C	175		🏠			L236	Z	3,4,7
N3450	C	65		🏠	D106	S	L229	Y	1-8
N3451	B	211		🏠			L220	Y	1-3,5,6,8
N3452	C	71		🏠			L220	Y	1-3,5,6,8
N3453	A	324		🏠			L238	Y	3,4,7,8
N3454	B	210		🏠	D110	R	L220	Y	1-3,5,6,8
N3455	B	55		🏠	D105	R	L238	Y	3,4,7,8
N3456	C	110		🏠			L238	Y	3,4,7,8
N3457	B	52		🏠			L217	Y	1-8
N3458	C	70		🏠	D105	R	L222	Y	1-3,5,6,8
N3459	C	53		🏠			L220	Y	1-3,5,6,8
N3460	A	233	✔	🏠			L200	X	1-3,5,6,8
N3461	B	147		🏠			L204	Y	1-3,5,6,8
N3462	B	146		🏠			L207	Z	1-6,8
N3463	C	54		🏠			L238	Y	3,4,7,8
N3464	C	54		🏠	D110	R	L233	Y	3,4,7
N3465	A	242		🏠			L205	Y	1-3,5,6,8
N3466	B	237		🏠	D110	R	L207	Z	1-6,8
N3467	B	148		🏠			L203	Y	1-3,5,6,8
N3468	B	160		🏠			L209	Y	1-6,8
N3469	B	148		🏠			L204	Y	1-3,5,6,8
N3470	C	34		🏠	D114	R	L211	Y	1-8
N3471	E	96		🏠			L236	Z	3,4,7
N3472	C	20		🏠					
N3473	C	107		🏠					
N3474	A	321		🏠			L202	X	1-3,5,6,8
N3475	D	260		🏠			L236	Z	3,4,7
N3476	B	94		🏠			L205	Y	1-3,5,6,8
N3477	C	32		🏠			L205	Y	1-3,5,6,8
N3478	B	324		🏠			L238	Y	3,4,7,8
N3479	B	88		🏠	D111	S	L200	X	1-3,5,6,8
N3480	B	189		🏠	D112	R	L238	Y	3,4,7,8
N3481	B	243		🏠			L200	X	1-3,5,6,8
N3482	C	34		🏠	D114	R	L211	Y	1-8
N3484	B	87		🏠	D105	R	L200	X	1-3,5,6,8
N3485	C	46		🏠			L238	Y	3,4,7,8
N3486	B	186		🏠					
N3487	B	232		🏠			L209	Y	1-3,5,6,8
N3488	B	214		🏠	D112	R	L220	Y	1-3,5,6,8
N3489	C	270		🏠	D112	R	L220	Y	1-3,5,6,8
N3490	B	232		🏠	D112	R	L220	Y	1-3,5,6,8
N3492	C	47		🏠			L236	Z	3,4,7
N3493	C	62		🏠			L220	Y	1-3,5,6,8
N3494	B	64		🏠			L200	X	1-3,5,6,8
N3495	C	89		🏠	D111	S	L200	X	1-3,5,6,8
N3497	B	207		🏠					
N3498	B	294		🏠					
N3502	E	72		🏠	D111	S	L224	Y	1-3,5,6,8
N3503	E	40		🏠	D108	R	L210	Y	1-3,5,6,8
N3508	C	80		🏠			L206	Z	1-6,8
N3511	B	202		🏠					
N3512	D	130		🏠	D110	R	L223	Z	1-3,5,6,8
N3513	D	126							
N3514	C	149							
N3558	C	78		🏠	D105	R	L203	Y	1-3,5,6,8
N3559	C	287	✔	🏠	D111	S	L217	Y	1-8
N3560	B	259	✔	🏠			L234	Y	1-8
N3562	B	105		🏠	D110	R	L238	Y	3,4,7,8
N3563	B	99		🏠	D115	Q	L233	Y	3,4,7
N3565	C	162		🏠	D110	R	L233	Y	3,4,7
N3568	D	90		🏠	D115	Q	L205	Y	1-3,5,6,8
N3569	B	163		🏠	D105	R	L238	Y	3,4,7,8
N3571	B	39		🏠	D115	Q	L202	X	1-3,5,6,8
N3572	D	91		🏠	D110	R	L227	Z	1-8
N3600	C	272		🏠			L200	X	1-3,5,6,8
N3601	C	272		🏠			L200	X	1-3,5,6,8
N3602	C	301		🏠			L220	Y	1-3,5,6,8
N3603	C	301		🏠			L220	Y	1-3,5,6,8
N3605	C	158		🏠	D111	S	L209	Y	1-6,8
N3606	C	155		🏠	D110	R	L224	Y	1-3,5,6,8
N3608	D	143		🏠			L223	Z	1-3,5,6,8
N3612	C	284		🏠			L206	Z	1-6,8
N3614	D	143		🏠	D111	S	L209	Y	1-6,8
N3615	B	138		🏠			L200	X	1-3,5,6,8
N3630	C	286		🏠			L209	Y	1-6,8
N3632	C	286		🏠			L237	Y	7
N3636	C	295		🏠			L238	Y	3,4,7,8
N3637	D	295		🏠			L235	Z	1-3,5,6,8
N3639	C	171		🏠			L217	Y	1-8
N3700	A	250							
N3701	A	251							
N3704	A	251							
N4010	C	328							
N4012	A	329							
N4015	A	328							
N4027	A	329							
N4061	A	323	✔	🏠	D115	Q			
N4115	B	313							
N4125	A	326							
N4153	A	325			D115	Q	L202	X	1-3,5,6,8
N4287	B	111			D111	S	L230	Z	1-8
N4308	C	313					L231	Z	1-8
N8888	C	250							
N8889	A	248							
N8890	B	249							
N8893	B	249							
N8895	A	248							
NG201	$85	295							

(Additional sets for G201 are $10 each)

Before You Order . . .

Before filling out the coupon at right or calling us on our Toll-Free Blueprint Hotline, you may want to learn more about our services and products. Here's some information you will find helpful.

Quick Turnaround
We process and ship every blueprint order from our office within 48 hours. Because of this quick turnaround, we won't send a formal notice acknowledging receipt of your order.

Our Exchange Policy
Since blueprints are printed in response to your order, we cannot honor requests for refunds. However, we will exchange your entire first order for an equal number of blueprints at a price of $50 for the first set and $10 for each additional set; $70 total exchange fee for 4 sets: $100 total exchange fee for 8 sets. . . *plus* the difference in cost if exchanging for a design in a higher price bracket or *less* the difference in cost if exchanging for a design in a lower price bracket. **(Sepias are not exchangeable. No exchanges can be made for the California Engineered Plans since they are tailored to your specific building site.)** All sets from the first order must be returned before the exchange can take place. Please add $10 for postage and handling via ground service; $20 via 2nd Day Air; $30 via Next Day Air.

About Reverse Blueprints
If you want to build in reverse of the plan as shown, we will include an extra set of reverse blueprints (mirror image) for an additional fee of $50. Although lettering and dimensions will appear backward, reverses will be a useful visual aid if you decide to flop the plan.

Modifying or Customizing Our Plans
With such a great selection of homes, you are bound to find the one that suits you. However, if you need to make alterations to one of our designs, you need only order our Home Customizer® Package or call 1-800-521-6797 for more information (see additional information on page 349).

Architectural and Engineering Seals
Some cities and states are now requiring that a licensed architect or engineer review and "seal" your blueprints prior to construction. This is often due to local or regional concerns over energy consumption, safety codes, seismic ratings, etc. For this reason, you may find it necessary to consult with a local professional to have your plans reviewed. This can normally be accomplished with minimum delays, for a nominal fee.

Compliance with Local Codes and Regulations
At the time of creation, our plans are drawn to specifications published by the Building Officials and Code Administrators (BOCA) International, Inc.; the Southern Building Code Congress (SBCCI) International, Inc.; the International Conference of Building Officials; or the Council of American Building Officials (CABO). Our plans are designed to meet or exceed national build-ing standards. Some states, counties and municipalities have their own codes, zoning requirements and building regulations. Before building, contact your local building authorities to make sure you comply with local ordinances and codes, including obtaining any necessary permits or inspections as building progresses. In some cases, minor modifications to your plans by your builder, architect or designer may be required to meet local conditions and requirements.

Foundation and Exterior Wall Changes
Most of our plans are drawn with either a full or partial basement foundation. Depending upon your specific climate or regional building practices, you may wish to convert this basement to a slab or crawlspace. Most professional contractors and builders can easily adapt your plans to alternate foundation types. Likewise, most can easily convert 2x4 wall construction to 2x6, or vice versa. If you need more guidance on these conversions, our handy Construction Detail sheets, shown on page 337, describe how such conversions can be made.

How Many Blueprints Do You Need?
A single set of blueprints is sufficient to study a home in greater detail. However, if you are planning to obtain cost estimates from a contractor or subcontractors—or if you are planning to build immediately—you will need more sets. Because additional sets are cheaper when ordered in quantity with the original order, make sure you order enough blueprints to satisfy all requirements. The following checklist will help you determine how many you need:

_____Owner

_____Builder (generally requires at least three sets; one as a legal document, one to use during inspections, and at least one to give to subcontractors)

_____Local Building Department (often requires two sets)

_____Mortgage Lender (usually one set for a conventional loan; three sets for FHA or VA loans)

_____TOTAL NUMBER OF SETS

The Home Customizer®

"This house is perfect...if only the family room were two feet wider." Sound familiar? In response to the numerous requests for this type of modification, Home Planners has developed **The Home Customizer® Package**. This exclusive package offers our top-of-the-line materials to make it easy for anyone, anywhere to customize any Home Planners design to fit their needs.

Some of the changes you can make to any of our plans include:

- exterior elevation changes
- kitchen and bath modifications
- roof, wall and foundation changes
- room additions and more!

The Home Customizer® Package includes everything you need to make the necessary changes to your favorite design. The package includes:

- instruction book with examples
- architectural scale and clear work film
- erasable red marker and removable correction tape
- ¼"-scale furniture cutouts
- 1 set reproducible, erasable Sepias
- 1 set study blueprints for communicating changes to your design professional
- a copyright release letter so you can make copies as you need them
- referral list of drafting, architectural and engineering professionals in your region who are trained in modifying Home Planners designs efficiently and inexpensively

The price of the **Home Customizer® Package** ranges from $535 to $775, depending on the price schedule of the design you have chosen. **The Home Customizer® Package** will not only save you 25% to 75% of the cost of drawing the plans from scratch with a custom architect or engineer, it will also give you the flexibility to have your changes and modifications made by our referral network or by the professional of your choice.

Now it's even easier and more affordable to have the custom home you've always wanted.

☎ **CALL TOLL-FREE 1-800-521-6797**

California Customers!!

For our customers in California, we now offer California Engineered Plans (CEP) and California Stock Plans (CSP) to help in meeting the strict California building codes. Check Plan Index for homes that are available through this new service or call 1-800-521-6797 for more information about the availability of the service and prices.

BLUEPRINTS ARE NOT RETURNABLE

ORDER FORM

HOME PLANNERS, INC., 3275 WEST INA ROAD
SUITE 110, TUCSON, ARIZONA 85741

THE BASIC BLUEPRINT PACKAGE
Rush me the following (please refer to the Plans Index and Price Schedule in this section):

_____	Set(s) of blueprints for plan number(s) _____.	$_____
_____	Set(s) of sepias for plan number(s) _____.	$_____
_____	Home Customizer® Package for plan number(s) _____.	$_____
_____	Additional identical blueprints in same order @ $50 per set.	$_____
_____	Reverse blueprints @ $50 per set.	$_____

IMPORTANT EXTRAS
Rush me the following:

_____	Materials List: @ $50 Schedule A-D; $60 Schedule E	$_____
_____	Specification Outlines @ $10 each.	$_____
_____	**Quote One™** Summary Cost Report @ $25 for 1, $15 for each additional, for plans _____.	$_____
	Building location: City _____ Zip Code _____	
_____	**Quote One™** Detailed Cost Estimate @ $110 Schedule A-D; $120 Schedule E for plan _____ (Must be purchased with Blueprints set; Materials List included)	$_____
	Building location: City _____ Zip Code _____	
_____	Detail Sets @ $14.95 each; any two for $22.95; any three for $29.95; all four for $39.95 (save $19.85). ❏ Plumbing ❏ Electrical ❏ Construction ❏ Mechanical (These helpful details provide general construction advice and are not specific to any single plan.)	$_____
_____	Plan-A-Home® @ $29.95 each.	$_____

DECK BLUEPRINTS

_____	Set(s) of Deck Plan _____.	$_____
_____	Additional identical blueprints in same order @ $10 per set.	$_____
_____	Reverse blueprints @ $10 per set.	$_____
_____	Set of Standard Deck Details @ $14.95 per set.	$_____
_____	Set of Complete Building Package (Best Buy!) Includes Custom Deck Plan _____. (See Index and Price Schedule) Plus Standard Deck Details	$_____

LANDSCAPE BLUEPRINTS

_____	Set(s) of Landscape Plan _____.	$_____
_____	Additional identical blueprints in same order @ $10 per set.	$_____
_____	Reverse blueprints @ $10 per set.	$_____

Please indicate the appropriate region of the country for Plant & Material List. (See Map on page 340): Region _____

POSTAGE AND HANDLING	1-3 sets	4+ sets
DELIVERY (Requires street address - No P.O. Boxes)		
•Regular Service (Allow 4-6 days delivery)	❏ $8.00	❏ $10.00
•2nd Day Air (Allow 2-3 days delivery)	❏ $12.00	❏ $20.00
•Next Day Air (Allow 1 day delivery)	❏ $22.00	❏ $30.00
CERTIFIED MAIL (Requires signature) If no street address available. (Allow 4-6 days delivery)	❏ $10.00	❏ $14.00
OVERSEAS DELIVERY	fax, phone or mail for quote.	

NOTE: ALL DELIVERY TIMES ARE FROM DATE BLUEPRINT PACKAGE IS SHIPPED.

POSTAGE (from box above)	$_____
SUBTOTAL	$_____
SALES TAX (Arizona residents add 5% sales tax; Michigan residents add 6% sales tax.)	$_____
TOTAL (Sub-total and tax)	$_____

YOUR ADDRESS (please print)

Name _____

Street _____

City _____ State _____ Zip _____

Daytime telephone number (_____) _____

FOR CREDIT CARD ORDERS ONLY

Please fill in the information below:

Credit card number _____

Exp. Date: Month/Year_____

Check one ❏ Visa ❏ MasterCard ❏ Discover Card

Signature _____

Please check appropriate box:
❏ Licensed Builder-Contractor
❏ Homeowner

Order Form Key

ORDER TOLL FREE
1-800-521-6797 or
520-297-8200

TB22BP

349

Helpful Books & Software

Home Planners wants your building experience to be as pleasant and trouble-free as possible. That's why we've expanded our library of Do-It-Yourself titles to help you along. In addition to our beautiful plans books, we've added books to guide you through specific projects as well as the construction process. In fact, these are titles that will be as useful after your dream home is built as they are right now.

COUNTRY	BUDGET-SMART	FAMILY HOMES	NARROW-LOT	REGIONAL BEST	EXPANDABLES	BEST SELLERS	NEW ENGLAND

1 200 country designs from classic to contemporary by 7 winning designers. 224 pages $8.95

2 200 efficient plans from 7 top designers, that you can really afford to build! 224 pages $8.95

3 200 stylish designs for today's growing families from 7 hot designers. 224 pages $8.95

4 200 unique homes less than 60' wide from 7 designers. Up to 3,000 square feet. 224 pages $8.95

5 200 beautiful homes from across America by 8 regional designers. 224 pages $8.95 NEW!

6 200 flexible plans that expand with your needs from 9 top designers. 224 pages $8.95 NEW!

7 NEW! Our 50th Anniversary book with 200 of our very best designs in full color! 224 page $12.95

8 260 of the best in Colonial home design. Special interior design sections, too. 384 pages $14.95

AFFORDABLE	LUXURY	ONE-STORY	TWO-STORY	VACATION	MULTI-LEVEL	OUTDOOR	DECKS

9 430 cost-saving plans specially selected for modest to medium building budgets. 320 pages $9.95

10 154 fine luxury plans—loaded with luscious amenities! 192 pages $14.95

11 470 designs for all lifestyles. 860 to 5,400 square feet. 384 pages $9.95

12 478 designs for one-and-a-half and two stories. 1,200 to 7,200 square feet. 416 pages $9.95

13 345 designs for recreation, retirement and leisure. 312 pages $8.95 NEW!

14 312 designs for split-levels, bi-levels, multi-levels and walkouts. 320 pages $6.95

15 42 unique outdoor projects. Gazebos, strombel-las, bridges, sheds, playsets and more! 96 pages $7.95 NEW!

16 25 outstanding single double- and multi-level decks you can build. 112 pages $7.95

ENCYCLOPEDIA	MODERN & CLASSIC	TRADITIONAL	VICTORIAN	SOUTHERN	WESTERN	EMPTY-NESTER	STARTER

17 500 exceptional plans for all styles and budgets—the best book of its kind! 352 pages $9.95

18 341 impressive homes featuring the latest in contemporary design. 304 pages $9.95

19 403 designs of classic beauty and elegance. 304 pages $9.95

20 160 striking Victorian and Farmhouse designs from three leading designers. 192 pages $12.95

21 207 homes rich in Southern styling and comfort. 240 pages $8.95 NEW!

22 215 designs that capture the spirit and diversity of the Western lifestyle. 208 pages $9.95

23 200 exciting plans for empty-nesters, retirees and childless couples. 224 pages $8.95

24 200 easy-to-build plans for starter and low-budget houses. 224 pages $8.95

Landscape Designs

FRONT & BACK	BACKYARDS	EASY CARE

25 The first book of do-it-yourself landscapes. 40 front, 15 backyards. 208 pages $12.95

26 40 designs focused solely on creating your own specially themed backyard oasis. 160 pages $12.95

27 NEW! 41 special landscapes designed for beauty and low maintenance. 160 pages $12.95

Design Software

BOOK & CD ROM	HOME ARCHITECT

28 NEW! Both the Home Planners Gold book and matching Windows™ CD ROM with 3D floor-plans. $24.95

29 The only complete home design kit for Windows™. Draw floor plans and landscape designs easily. Includes CD of 500 floor plans. $42.95

Interior Design

HOME DECORATING	BATHROOMS	KITCHENS

30 Special effects and creative ideas for all surfaces. Includes simple step-by-step diagrams. 96 pages $8.95

31 An innovative guide to organizing, remodeling and decorating your bathroom. 96 pages $8.95

32 An imaginative guide to designing the perfect kitchen. Chock full of bright ideas to make your job easier. 176 pages $12.95

...anning Books & Quick Guides

TRIM & MOLDING

34 Step-by-step ...ructions for installing ...boards, window ...d door casings and more. ...ages $6.95

PAINTING

34 Tips from the pros on everything from preparation to clean-up. 80 pages $6.95

ROOFING

35 Information on the latest tools, materials and techniques for roof installation or repair. 80 pages $6.95

WALLS & MORE

36 A clear and concise guide to repairing or remodeling walls and ceilings. 80 pages $6.95

FLOORS

37 All the information you need for repairing, replacing or installing floors in any home. 80 pages $6.95

PATIOS & WALKS

38 Clear step-by-step instructions take you from the basic design stages to the finished project. 80 pages $6.95

WINDOWS & DOORS

39 Installation techniques and tips that make your project easier and more professional looking. 80 pages $6.95

PLUMBING

40 Tackle any plumbing installation or repair as quickly and efficiently as a professional. 160 pages $9.95

ADDING SPACE

1 Convert attics, ...sements and bonus ...oms to useful living ...ace. ...0 pages $9.95

HOME REPAIR

42 An owner's manual for your home. Sound advice on home maintenance and improvements. 256 pages $9.95

TILE

43 Every kind of tile for every kind of application. Includes tips on use installation and repair. 176 pages $12.95

WALLPAPERING

44 Use the book the pros use. Covers tools and techniques for every type of wallcovering. 136 pages $12.95

BASIC WIRING

45 A straight forward guide to one of the most misunderstood systems in the home. 160 pages $12.95

HOUSE CONTRACTING

46 Everything you need to know to act as your own general contractor...and save up to 25% off building costs. 134 pages $12.95

VISUAL HANDBOOK

47 A plain-talk guide to the construction process; financing to final walk-through, this book covers it all. 498 pages $19.95

CONTRACTING GUIDE

48 Loaded with information to make you more confident in dealing with contractors and subcontractors. 287 pages $18.95

FRAMING

49 For those who want ...take a more-hands on ...pproach to their dream. ...9 pages $19.95

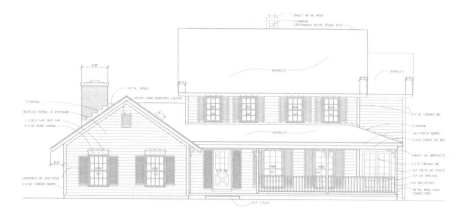

OVER 3 MILLION BLUEPRINTS SOLD

"We instructed our builder to follow the plans including all of the many details which make this house so elegant... Our home is a fine example of the results one can achieve by purchasing and following the plans which you offer... Everyone who has seen it has assured us that it belongs in 'a picture book.' I truly mean it when I say that my home 'is a DREAM HOUSE.'"

S.P.
Anderson, SC

"We have had a steady stream of visitors, many of whom tell us this is the most beautiful home they've seen. Everyone is amazed at the layout and remark on how unique it is. Our real estate attorney, who is a Chicago dweller and who deals with highly valued properties, told me this is the only suburban home he has seen that he would want to live in."

W. & P.S.
Flossmoor, IL

"Home Planners' blueprints saved us a great deal of money. I acted as the general contractor and we did a lot of the work ourselves. We probably built it for half the cost! We are thinking about more plans for another home. I purchased a competitor's book but my husband only wants your plans!"

K.M.
Grovetown, GA

"We are very happy with the product of our efforts. The neighbors and passersby appreciate what we have created. We have had many people stop by to discuss our house and kindly praise it as being the nicest house in our area of new construction. We have even had one person stop and make us an unsolicited offer to buy the house for much more than we have invested in it."

K. & L.S.
Bolingbrook, IL

"The traffic going past our house is unbelievable. On several occasions, we have heard that it is the 'prettiest house in Batavia.' Also, when meeting someone new and mentioning what street we live on, quite often we're told, 'Oh, you're the one in the yellow house with the wrap-around porch! I love it!'"

A.W.
Batavia, NY

"I have been involved in the building trades my entire life... Since building our home we have built two other homes for other families. Their plans from local professional architects were not nearly as good as yours. For that reason we are ordering additional plan books from you."

T.F.
Kingston, WA

"The blueprints we received from Home Planners were of excellent quality and provided us with exactly what we needed to get our successful home-building project underway. We appreciate Home Planners invaluable role in our home-building effort."

T.A.
Concord, TN